Language Rights and Language Survival

Sociolinguistic and Sociocultural Perspectives

Edited by

Jane Freeland & Donna Patrick

St. Jerome Publishing
Manchester, UK & Northampton MA

First published 2004 by St. Jerome Publishing
2 Maple Road West, Brooklands
Manchester, M23 9HH, United Kingdom
Telephone +44 (0)161 973 9856] Fax +44 (0)161 905 3498
stjerome@compuserve.com / http://www.stjerome.co.uk

ISBN 1-900650-74-6 pbk)
ISSN 1471-0277 (*Encounters*)

Printed and bound in Great Britain by
T. J. International Ltd., Cornwall, UK

Typeset by Delta Typesetters, Cairo, Egypt
Email: hilali1945@hotmail.com

British Library Cataloguing in Publication Data
A catalogue record of this book is available from the British Library

Library of Congress Cataloguing in Publication Data
Language rights and language survival / edited by Jane Freeland and Donna Patrick.
p. cm. -- (Encounters, ISSN 1471-0277; v. 4)
Chiefly papers presented at a colloquium "Language rights and wrongs" organized at the Sociolinguistics Symposium held in Ghent in 2002.
Includes bibliographical references and index.
ISBN 1-900650-74-6 (alk. paper)
1. Sociolinguistics--Congresses. 2. Language maintenance--Congresses. 3. Human rights--Congresses. 4. Language planning--Congresses. I. Freeland, Jane. II. Patrick, Donna, 1959- III. Sociolinguistics Symposium (2002:Ghent, Belgium) IV. Series: Encounters (St. Jerome Publishing) ; v. 4.
P40.5.L32L36 2004
306. 44--dc22

2003021095

Encounters

A new series on language and diversity
Edited by Jan Blommaert, Marco Jacquemet and Ben Rampton

Diversity has come to be recognized as one of the central concerns in our thinking about society, culture and politics. At the same time, it has proved one of the most difficult issues to deal with on the basis of established theories and methods, particularly in the social sciences. Studying diversity not only challenges widespread views of who we are and what we do in social life; it also challenges the theories, models and methods by means of which we proceed in studying diversity. Diversity exposes the boundaries and limitations of our theoretical models, in the same way it exposes our social and political organizations.

Encounters sets out to explore diversity *in* language, diversity *through* language and diversity *about* language. Diversity *in* language covers topics such as intercultural, gender, class or age-based variations in language and linguistic behaviour. Diversity *through* language refers to the way in which language and linguistic behaviour can contribute to the construction or negotiation of such sociocultural and political differences. And diversity *about* language has to do with the various ways in which language and diversity are being perceived, conceptualized and treated, in professional as well as in lay knowledge - thus including the reflexive and critical study of scientific approaches alongside the study of language politics and language ideologies. In all this, mixedness, creolization, crossover phenomena and heterogeneity are privileged areas of study. The series title, *Encounters*, is intended to encourage a relatively neutral but interested stance towards diversity, moving away from the all too obvious 'cultures-collide' perspective that is dominant within the social sciences. The target public of *Encounters* includes scholars and advanced students of linguistics, communication studies, anthropology, cultural studies, sociology, as well as students and scholars in neighbouring disciplines such as translation studies, gender studies, gay and lesbian studies, postcolonial studies.

Jan Blommaert is former Research Director of the IPrA Research Centre of the University of Antwerp and currently Professor of African linguistics at the University of Ghent. He is author of *Discourse* (Cambridge University Press, forthcoming), co-author of *Debating Diversity: Analysing the Discourse of Tolerance* (Routledge 1998), editor of *Language Ideological Debates* (Mouton de Gruyter 1999), and co-editor of the *Handbook of*

Pragmatics (John Benjamins 1995-2003) and *The Pragmatics of Intercultural and International Communication* (John Benjamins 1991).

Marco Jacquemet is Assistant Professor of Communication Studies at the University of San Francisco. His work focuses on the complex interaction of different languages and communicative practices in a globalized world. His current research seeks to assess the communicative mutations resulting from the intersection in the Mediterranean area between mobile people (migrants, local and international aid workers, missionaries, businessmen, etc.) and electronic texts (content distributed by satellites, local television stations, Internet connectivity, cellular telephony). As part of this research, in the early 1990s he studied the communicative practices of criminal networks in Southern Italy and the emerging Italian cyberculture. In 1994 he conducted fieldwork in Morocco and Italy on migratory patterns between the two countries. Since 1998, he has been involved in multi-site ethnographic fieldwork in Albania and Italy, investigating the linguistic and socio-cultural consequences of Albania's entry into the global system of late-modern capitalism. Marco Jacquemet is author of *Credibility in Court: Communicative Practices in the Camorra Trials* (Cambridge University Press 1996).

Ben Rampton is Professor of Applied and Sociolinguistics at King's College London. His work involves ethnographic and interactional discourse analysis, frequently also drawing on anthropology, sociology and cultural studies. His publications cover urban multilingualism; language, youth, ethnicities and class; language education; second language learning; and research methodology. Ben Rampton is author of *Interaction in an Urban School: Late Modern Language & Society* (Cambridge University Press, forthcoming), co-author of *Researching Language: Issues of Power & Method* (Routledge 1992), and co-editor of *The Language, Ethnicity & Race Reader* (Routledge 2003).

Acknowledgements

We would like to express our thanks to all of the contributors to this volume for their dedication in tailoring their chapters to the themes of this book and for their active participation during the editing process. Special thanks are also due to the *Encounters* series editors Jan Blommaert and Chris Bulcaen for their editing expertise and consistent support and to Ken and Mona Baker of St. Jerome Press for their support during the production of the book. We are also indebted to the conference organizers and participants of the *Sociolinguistics Symposium 14* held in Ghent, Belgium in April 2002 which brought together most of the contributors in this volume and allowed us to initiate the project. Finally, we would like to thank Ben Shaer and Alan Freeland for their patience and support during all the stages of this work.

Jane Freeland and Donna Patrick

Contents

1. Language Rights and Language Survival
Sociolinguistic and Sociocultural Perspectives

JANE FREELAND AND DONNA PATRICK

1. Introduction

In recent decades, the twin issues of language rights and language survival have gained importance among activists and academics concerned with indigenous and other minority languages. This comes in part from an increased understanding of the academic disadvantages that children face when they are educated in an imposed language (see e.g. Cummins 1993, 1996) – an awareness that has arguably been the major force behind the drive to make education in vernacular languages a universal right. It also arises from a concern, voiced in particular by linguists, over the rapid decrease in the number of languages throughout the world as they are pushed aside by state education policies or by the wider processes of globalization. This concern has been voiced most recently in ecological terms, as a plea for the preservation of the 'stability and resiliency' of the world's cultures by maintaining language diversity (Terralingua 2002, cited in Harvey 2003: 249).

These two currents of thought have recently come together in both popular and academic appeals for the universal support of language rights and the preservation and revitalization of the languages to which such rights are most relevant (Fishman 1991, 2001; Crystal 2000; Nettle and Romaine 2000; Skutnabb-Kangas 2000; Hinton and Hale 2001). These appeals attracted the attention of those who work in a range of disciplines, including linguistics, anthropology, sociology, legal studies, and language education. They have also been a source of support for minority group leaders, educators, and activists in their local, national, and international struggles to gain recognition for their languages and cultures, often as a means for wider group recognition.

Whilst both 'language rights' and 'language survival' discourses are able, at least in principle, to empower and emancipate minority communities, they are nevertheless fraught with complications and contradictions, related particularly to the terms on which language rights are granted and the way that these can interact with sociolinguistic realities 'on the ground' – with sometimes counterproductive effects. This volume sets out to explore these complications and contradictions as they arise in a number of contexts, in Africa, Asia, Europe, and Central and North America.

Most of the chapters of this volume were originally presented as papers at a colloquium on 'Language rights and wrongs' that we organized at the Sociolinguistics Symposium held in Ghent in 2002, the aim of which was to critically examine language rights and language survival discourses from a sociolinguistic perspective. This we saw as part of a larger project to provide a "forum in which theoretical explorations of rights, citizenship and related concepts can engage with empirical, contextual studies of rights processes" (Cowan *et al.*. 2001). We continue to believe this to be important at a time when developments in sociolinguistics and its companion disciplines of linguistic anthropology, ethnography, and cultural studies have been developing new frameworks for analysing language in context which, in fact, seemed to undermine the clarity of the case for language rights and language survival. More specifically, work on language ideologies has 'denaturalized' dominant assumptions about language and nationhood (Silverstein 1979, 1998; Blommaert 1996, 1999; Woolard and Schieffelin 1994; Woolard 1998); the social theory underpinning sociolinguistics has been subject to critique (Williams 1992; Cameron 1990; Pennycook 1990, 2001); and the postcolonialist movement has challenged the universalist claims of modernist thought on the grounds of its Eurocentricity (Said 1978; Spivak 1988). Being committed to the moral principles behind the linguistic human rights paradigm, we wish to examine in the light of these critiques how best to attain its goals.

The contexts that are the focus of these studies are ones in which discourses of language rights and language survival have become prominent and now interact with local practices, assumptions, and language ideologies. They include (1) contexts in which speakers of 'small' or minority languages have mobilized around both of these discourses to gain recognition and material and symbolic support within nation-states for their languages and by extension for the group itself; (2) transnational contexts, in which language rights are implicated in wider political and economic arrangements; and (3) contexts in which a local language (however 'language' is locally defined) might be thought of as 'dead' according to some criteria, yet in local perceptions 'survives' and is valued.

In all of these contexts, historical and political processes have shaped language form and function and created multiple shifting relationships between language, identity, power, and sociocultural meanings. The different chapters explore the historical contingency of these relationships and the consequent fluidity of the social categories in which they are based – not least the category of 'language' itself, which language rights discourse defines and objectifies in particular ways.

The volume as a whole raises a number of issues relating to the conceptual and empirical dimensions of language rights and language 'survival' discourse. In what follows, we will take up two themes that figure prominently throughout the volume. These are

1. the particular strengths and weaknesses of the language rights discourse as a special 'chapter' in a larger universalizing discourse of human rights;
2. the similar strengths and weaknesses of the developing 'ecological' discourse on language protection and survival, by analogy with the discourse on the preservation of biodiversity.

These two main themes are addressed in different chapters in terms of such sub-themes as:

- the essentialization of the link between linguistic and ethnic identities in rights discourse as contrasted with views of identity as situated practice, leading to insights into the fragmentation and multiplicity of identities;
- the strategic use of language rights and language survival discourses in political movements to gain increased autonomy within dominant power structures;
- the institutionalization of language rights in ways – particularly those related to formal education – that reproduce the modernist project of nation-building, and the social inequities associated with this. This process may push minorities into the contradictory position of mobilizing to gain rights around one language variety and turning this into a new form of dominant language, often at the expense of other local varieties and registers;
- the dominance of particular approaches to language that tend to focus on formal properties of language varieties, and the consequences of imposing these approaches in particular social contexts and on speakers' own definitions of what languages they speak;
- the larger issue of globalization and the impact of new economies on speakers and their languages. This includes issues of mobility and the changing local and global values that speakers place on different language varieties;
- finally, the moral question that language 'experts' and scholars examining the social processes of language movements must address: where they position themselves in the political struggle associated with these movements.

In the rest of this introduction, we will address some of these issues before summarizing the different chapters.

2. Language Rights Discourse

The volume's first major theme, as we have just noted, is the particular strengths and weaknesses associated with treating 'language rights' as a special 'chapter' in a wider, universalizing discourse on human rights. Upholding the principle that all people are created equal, this critique places discrimination on the basis of a person's language – which Skutnabb-Kangas (e.g. 1988) has termed *linguicism* – in the same category as other forms of morally unacceptable discrimination, including discrimination on the basis of ethnic or national origin, religion, sex, and sexual orientation. This linkage with other universal rights enables discriminated groups to legitimately demand that a language variety associated with the group – and by extension the group itself – receive protection against symbolic domination within larger state or supra-state structures. For all of these reasons, the importance of work that has sought to conceptualize and defend language rights (e.g. Capotorti 1979; Thornberry 1991; de Varennes 1996; Kymlicka 1995; Phillipson and Skutnabb-Kangas 1994; Phillipson 1998; Skutnabb-Kangas 2000) has grown considerably over the past few decades.

Yet it is important to remember that this 'universal' discourse originated at a particular time and place – namely, those of the European Enlightenment – and that the liberal ideal of individual liberty that it asserts was conceived in resistance to particular forms of injustice, such as slavery, lack of legal or political representation, and so forth. Moreover, as this discourse has framed political struggles for liberal ideals extending from wars of independence in the Americas to more recent processes of decolonization, it has become a hegemonic paradigm for pursuing these goals. This, too, is part of its power: it is couched in terms that can exert a moral appeal to nation-states that espouse similar liberal principles. Yet, especially as it travels across temporal, territorial and cultural boundaries, it also becomes the source of the kinds of contradiction we are highlighting.

Central to the development of nation-states is the notion of an 'imagined community' (Anderson 1993), uniting people within the state's borders across often profound social differences into a transcendental identity, through a common, homogeneous, language. Yet, as Irvine and Gal (2000: 76) observe: "Missing from [this] perspective (…) is the insight that homogenous language is as much imagined as is community (…) [It is] as if linguistic homogeneity were a real-world precondition rather than a construction concurrent with, or consequent to, print capitalism". Thus, the ideology of linguistic homogeneity is part and parcel of nation-building.

In the construction of the state, one variety, usually associated with dominant groups, becomes 'the national language' whilst others are deemed to be 'dialects' – a political rather than a linguistic designation in most cases – and ignored, erased, or suppressed with varying degrees of coercion.

In the French tradition of civic nationhood, the unifying language is bestowed and acquired as a privileged mark of citizenship both at home and in the colonies. In the German tradition of ethnic nationhood, the 'mother tongue' or 'genetic fingerprint' is deemed to be inherent in the people as it is passed down from generation to generation.[1] Either way, language becomes inseparably associated with a territorially bounded identity in a relationship that takes language, territory, and identity to be isomorphic. One implication of this is that ideally, the nation should be monolingual, with adherence to another language often (mis)read as a lack of loyalty to the national identity. As noted in a number of chapters in this book, including those by Wright, Heugh and Stroud, Blommaert, Martín Rojo, May, Whaley, and Patrick, it is the nation-state that creates linguistic minorities.

Nation-state ideology creates one of the central paradoxes of claiming minority language rights in a discourse based on equality, individual liberties, and national unity. At present, the concept of language rights is embedded in a legal discourse that starts from a politics of the state. Claims are made upon states and granted by states (as in most of the cases described in this volume). Indeed, even the international legal instruments by which rights are recognized depend on agreement among states,[2] and therefore only embody what states are prepared to concede. They are therefore inevitably couched in the same 'nationist' terms on which states themselves are based. Claims to minority language rights effectively challenge the founding concepts of these states, or even their integrity, and can succeed only insofar as states are willing to or able to

---

[1] Indeed, in the original struggle to develop a separate German nation, philosophers such as Fichte contended that a shared language indicated that a separate nation existed which should by rights become a separate state. Irvine and Gal (2001) show how colonial administrators then used this notion to identify 'peoples' (later tribes or races), producing either unconsciously or strategically biased mappings of languages onto groups and territories which often bore little relationship to the sociolinguistic realities.

[2] This agreement is not easily arrived at – see e.g. Banton (1996) on the Latin American blocking of the UN Convention on the Elimination of Racial Discrimination, and Skutnabb-Kangas (2002) on the difficulties of bringing the draft Declaration on Language Rights to UN convention status.

reconceptualize themselves.[3] As Jaffe points out, in her comments on Martín Rojo's chapter (p 13), even when a state such as Spain rhetorically espouses novel multilingual and multicultural principles, it does so only so far as its own interests permit. Yet given the hegemony and apparent universality of this discourse, this is the mould into which minorities must fit their claims.

This same universalism again becomes a weakness of the discourse once it becomes time to frame and implement language rights that have already been recognized. Indeed, Coulmas (1998: 72) goes so far as to say that "[w]hile general proclamations of linguistic human rights may not do much harm, it is doubtful that they can be translated into law". We would argue that such translation is not necessarily impossible, but that like any other translation, its success depends on recognizing that terms, concepts, and ideological assumptions need to be negotiated within and between contexts – in other words, that they are not universal.

It is in this arena that the discourse of language rights meets, and often conflicts with, local understandings about language, or language ideologies, that have their source in everyday practices. In these circumstances of unequal power, the 'universal' discourse becomes hegemonic. Here local language ideologies are often dismissed as mere 'folk linguistics' as governments call upon various kinds of linguistic experts to supplement their own limited knowledge of conditions 'on the ground'.[4] Sometimes, problems arise because modern states construct the ethnic groups within their borders as homogeneous, nation-like blocs and treat them as such (Blommaert 1999: 428-429, commenting on Bokhorst-Heng 1999).

An extreme example of the contradictions that can follow such treatments is described in the chapter by Whaley on the Oroqen. Whaley recounts how the People's Republic of China adopted Stalin's solution to 'the national question', recognizing ethnic minorities within China's borders as 'nations', where a nation is "a historically formed stable community arising on the basis of a common language, common territory, common economic life and a typical cast of mind manifested in a common culture"

---

[3] This is especially the case when we recall that most states are in fact 'state-nations' (Fishman 1972): states incorporating more than one ethnicity whose national identities are created after their foundation, and often only tenuously held together, especially in the case of the 'weak' post-colonial states of Africa and Latin America.

[4] Yet, as recent studies have shown, 'folk linguistics' is an important expression of the linguistic ideology of groups who become the object of language planning (e.g. Cameron 1995; Niedzielski and Preston 1999), and may even be an identifying trait of "local language communities" (Silverstein 1998: 401).

(Whaley, p. #). Whaley shows how both the Oroqen 'nation' and its 'language' were in reality artifacts of this discourse, the concepts of which were superimposed on the network of hunting clans and on their mutually intelligible but clan-marked dialects. The imposed language category bore little resemblance to the Oroqen's own self-understanding and ways of performing their identity. A less extreme case is recounted in Stephen and Petrus Atin's chapter on Malaysian pluralist policies where debates over what constitutes distinct languages in multilingual regions construct complex dialect configurations. The treatment of the Rungus people as part of a larger ethnolinguistic grouping has engendered a need to be recognized as a separate group, a need that conflicts with their awareness of having multiple identities. In both instances, unequal encounters between different ways of conceiving and valuing languages have led local communities and minority language speakers into contradictory stances.

In these encounters, not only do different conceptions of the relationship between language and identity come into play, but also two broadly different senses of language itself. The one informing the linguistic human rights and language survival paradigms is rooted both in a tradition of 'professionalized' and 'scientific' linguistic enquiry, and in the universalizing discourse of the European Enlightenment (see Bauman and Briggs 2000). From the unreliable and often emotionally charged variations of daily language use it abstracts the 'etic' features of 'languages': those structural and denotational properties available to external observation and systematization. This is the approach that underpins a great deal of field linguistics (as noted in Silverstein 1998; Kroskrity 2000b; and Darnell, this volume) and the historical and comparative linguistics work that establishes relationships between languages on the basis of their formal similarities and differences (Michalove *et al.* 1998). On this basis rests the very notion of what constitutes language 'loss', 'shift' and 'endangerment', and many of the methods prescribed for the revitalization of languages which involve their isolation in particular domains of use (e.g. Fishman 1991; Mühlhäusler 1996).

Most of the chapters in this volume offer critiques of this approach, on the grounds that it sets aside factors that empirical research shows to be important for language survival and revitalization: speakers' own linguistic understanding, based in contextualized practice informed by local language ideologies. In this way, they add to current critiques of the social theoretical foundations of sociolinguistics (e.g. Williams 1992; Cameron 1990; Pennycook 2001) and the structuralist foundations of linguistics. So Darnell, 'socialized' as she puts it, into the field linguistics tradition, criticizes its tendency to reveal 'only absences' (Darnell p. #), and the purism associated with its methodology of recovering what is lost from earlier 'authentic' texts. Freeland's chapter focuses centrally on the limitations of the approach in dealing with hybridized, creolized languages, which may be completely discounted as languages and dismissed as 'mere dialects', to the extent that they have no clear formal boundaries. This point is further illustrated in Darnell's and Laakso and Östman's chapters (see also Silverstein 1998; Urciuoli 1995 on the variability of linguistic boundaries once speaker perceptions are taken into account).

To deal with these issues, many of the chapters in this book favour an 'emic' approach that focuses on speaker practices more than on objectified languages, on the indexical, context-related role of language in the performance of identities, and on the 'folk' interpretations or language ideologies that the 'scientific' tradition discounts. Importantly, too – especially for some of the multilingual contexts featured in this collection – such an approach treats language users, according to Silverstein's useful distinction (1998: 404-407), not only as members of bounded 'linguistic communities' displaying various degrees of allegiance to the 'grammar' (in its broad sense) of a language, but also of wider 'speech communities', which may be plurilingual and share pragmatic understandings of what it means to use and even mix different language varieties in practice. Indeed, Silverstein suggests that "the speech community is the context of emergence, sustenance, and transformation of distinct local language communities" (*ibid.*: 407).

Our point here is not to weigh the merits of these two approaches. Like any account of processual phenomena, each sharply reveals certain aspects of language and underplays others, and indeed the 'emic' approach recognizes its need for the 'etic'. The issue, then, is to be aware of the radically different properties of the two approaches and to problematize the claims to universality of the 'autonomous linguistics' approach, particularly as the basis for what are inherently social and political processes and calls to political action that revolve around language.

The approach adopted in this volume, then, blurs the boundaries between languages, and makes it less easy to arrive at simple mappings of language onto ethnic group or territory. Yet the dominant, 'scientific' conception of discrete, 'hard-edged' languages has considerable symbolic power as part of the dominant discourse, and is strategically useful to minorities in their struggle for language rights (as noted in the chapters by May and Patrick). As Jaffe's commentary highlights, it is difficult to rally around multiple identities and blurred linguistic boundaries (p. #). Schieffelin (2000) and Kroskrity (2000b) both also point out that local language ideologies, like languages themselves, are not stable but alter through contact; groups will adopt linguistic essentialism not only to appeal to nation-states, but also to reinforce existing aspects of their local language ideology. This means that it is not a simple matter to design language policy according to the wishes of minority groups. Often, too, groups will exploit the similarities and differences between languages established by historical and comparative linguistics to bolster claims to ethno-nationalist boundaries and to historical continuity (see e.g. Gal and Woolard 2001: 4; Gal 2001). This conceptualization of language will continue to hold power as long as the struggle is for 'linguistic rights', notionally mapped onto notional peoples, rather than for the wider goal of "social, political and economic equality for linguistic minorities" advocated by Stroud and Heugh (page 191, [n. 2]) and others in this volume.

3. The 'Ecological' Discourse of Language Survival

The second major theme of this volume – the nature of language survival discourse and the links it establishes with the preservation of biodiversity – is covered either explicitly or implicitly in a number of chapters in this book, including Blommaert, May, Darnell, Laasko and Östman, Patrick, and Whaley. When we think about the preservation of minority languages and cultures, the idea that languages survive or die seems completely natural. But this is only because the metaphor that likens 'languages' to 'species', endangered languages to endangered species and linguistic diversity to biological diversity, has become completely naturalized, largely due to the dominant ideology that languages can be viewed as discrete objects. The discourse that likens language preservation to biological preservation carries a great deal of rhetorical power, evident in the prominent use of this metaphor in national and international campaigns for resources to be committed to the promotion and revitalization of languages undergoing shift. Yet if the parallel between languages and species is to be understood as more than simply a powerful metaphor – that is, if it is to be taken as a real reason for preserving languages and as a basis for developing policy – then its identification of linguistic elements as kinds of biological elements must be made more plausible.

Linguistic investigation has revealed only one clear sense in which language is part of biology: this is that every human being has the same biological endowment with respect to language learning. What this means is that languages themselves are not biologically inherited (England 2002: 142); and that differences between languages cannot be traced to biological differences between speakers (on colonial beliefs that they could, see Irvine 2001; Gal 2001). What this also means is that the death of a given language does not reduce actual biological diversity in the way that the death of a species can. This is because the speakers of a 'dead' language – unless they are actually killed off – live to see another day and continue to speak using some new form of language. To use a rather obvious example: the 'death' of Latin neither arose from nor resulted in the death of speakers; instead, speakers of Latin gradually came to be (recognized as) speakers of, for example, French, Italian, Portuguese, and Romanian. This is why, as May points out in his chapter, the ecological metaphor can all too easily be turned against those who seek to advocate language survival: if languages are species and species die 'naturally', then so will languages.

This is another reason for adopting an approach to language study that shifts the focus from languages as 'species' or objects in the world to language speakers themselves – the living beings who use language in multiple ways – and to the complex social, political, and cultural practices for which they use them. This point is highlighted in the chapters by Darnell, Freeland, Heugh and Stroud, Jaffe, and Patrick.

It is worth noting that despite the problematic nature of equating languages with species, there are some useful links to be made between linguistic diversity and biological diversity. Mülhäusler (1996, 2003) discusses the ways in which biological diversity maintains the ecological balance in a habitat, and relates this to the way that social and economic conditions shape the language choices that people make. However, Mühlhäusler (1996) then goes on to imply that we should seek to conserve these habitats in order to protect the species inhabiting them. Yet to do so would seem to assume that conditions should not change, and that once a habitat has been 'invaded' by an 'alien' language-as-species, there is no new balance to be struck. In some circumstances, if a collectivity so desires – and if it is faced with the right conditions, including a political space to fight for resources to promote and legitimize their language variety – it might indeed be possible to protect the conditions favouring its continued use. This is brought out particularly strongly in Patrick's study (this volume and 2003) of how the Inuktitut language survives in the context of traditional practices and in new domains, and how the persistence of 'tradition' has been enabled by the Inuit's status as a First Nation with specific territorial and other rights.

In other circumstances, as suggested in the chapters by May and Blommaert in this volume and in other work (May 2001; Blommaert 2003), such a conservationist approach to language planning can seem to advocate tying speakers to the specific localities or 'niches' where their languages are valid and unacceptably preclude their moving, either physically to other places or figuratively to different kinds of work and social, cultural, and political activities.

Nor need such movement necessarily result in 'disequilibrium'. Economic shifts, national and transnational movements of peoples, and globalized telecommunication networks, commodities and cultural forms will inevitably alter the patterns of living languages and create new forms of usage as people form new social networks and allegiances. Whilst we might note that human behaviour has hastened these social processes, it is also true that speakers' linguistic practices continue to be constituted in cultural practices, conveying particular cultural meanings and ideologies that do not 'die', although they may change. It is these cultural continuities, and their expression in new forms of language, to which we should attend.

If the metaphorical link between biological diversity and linguistic diversity is to work at all, then it might indeed be better to think less of preserving 'species' *per se*, and more of understanding and protecting the 'habitats' of language users – that is the whole environment that supports a speech or language community, including the social and economic conditions under which language varieties are valued and their interrelations with other languages and language varieties in a given social and political space. As sociolinguists, we need to make use of more sophisticated ways of relating language to context. This means attending not just to languages but to registers and genres and to the way that these may be distributed among several languages, and finding ways to describe and understand the links between this distribution and the local and global forces at play in sociocultural, historical, and economic environments. Such an approach would give a new cast to the problem of language survival as currently formulated by proponents of the ecological argument, for whom what is lost is diversity in the ways of 'doing language' (Hale 1992; Hinton and Hale 2001), or particular world views associated with the denotative structure of languages according to the Whorfian hypothesis (on this see Silverstein's 2000 critique of the way this relationship between language and world view has been oversimplified). As Darnell shows in her chapter, world views remain, change, and are cast in new linguistic forms.

4. Ethnography, Language Markets, and 'Habitus'

It follows from all that we have said so far that what is crucial for understanding the dynamics of multilingual situations is detailed ethnographic research – as shown in the chapters by Freeland, Stroud and Heugh,

Patrick, and Martín Rojo. This must include a close examination of the relationships between language use and context; that is, between changing economic and social conditions and the expression of multiple, shifting identity positions under specific historical, cultural, political, and economic conditions. Through ethnographic accounts, too, we stand a better chance of seeing how certain language forms and cultural meanings develop across generations, in a combination of continuity and transformation.

Many of the studies in this volume find a useful approach to the linkage between language varieties and political, social and economic contexts in the work of Bourdieu (1977, 1982). Patrick and Freeland both use Bourdieu's concept of the language economy, which encompasses notions of linguistic and cultural capital and the values attached to particular language varieties in the 'linguistic marketplace'. This metaphor illuminates the ways in which linguistic norms associated with government, legal, and educational spheres constitute valued linguistic capital, whilst different norms of use have currency in other community settings, especially in the further distinction between 'dominant' and 'alternative' linguistic markets (see the use of this distinction in e.g. Woolard 1985; Heller 1994; Jaffe 1999; Patrick 2003). This is a useful concept through which to examine how minority language forms are ascribed value through their links to cultural and economic practices outside institutionally legitimated domains – for instance in activities that range from poetry, music, and buying and selling in local markets to harvesting local food and forming bonds through informal social networks. Ethnographic research can help us to understand how these markets operate, how they are kept apart, and also how they might become related to each other in ways other than direct confrontation.

Also from Bourdieu (1982, 1992) is the notion of 'habitus' that May's chapter draws upon to overcome the classic impasse between essentialist and instrumentalist positions on the relationship between language and identity, language and culture. For Bourdieu, 'habitus' is a set of embodied dispositions acquired through socialization into particular groups and milieux. Although they do not determine behaviour, they do predispose us to respond in particular ways to both new and familiar situations. One of the most important classes of these dispositions is linguistic habitus, which encompasses not only the structural forms of language – indeed these may be the easiest to change – but the pragmatics of linguistic interaction. The concept releases people from the more absolute associations between language and culture proposed by the crude Whorfianism that Silverstein (2000) criticizes, and explains why people can be both attached to and able to move beyond certain ways of behaving. The notion of 'habitus' also helps explain how the Solfians studied by Laakso and Östman and the Nicaraguan Creoles studied by Freeland are both proud of their 'language' and relaxed about its changing, and why the Algonquin and Iroquois of Darnell's study can perform certain aspects of their culture in a form of English informed by their indigenous pragmatic habitus, but feel the need to perform others in the original language.

Together, these theoretical and methodological tools can provide a deeper understanding of how certain minority language varieties persist in the face of their speakers' experiences of symbolic, material, and political domination.

As we noted above, it is important to understand the relationship between 'dominant' and 'alternative' markets if we are not to fall into the trap of advocating that languages be kept in their 'alterative' niches. Minority language movements often seek a role in the dominant market, not least because a central plank of the linguistic rights discourse is the right for children to be educated in a familiar language. This is often seen as indispensable, not only to guard against educational disadvantage, but also to give children the positive cognitive advantages of bilingualism, as repeatedly demonstrated in psycholinguistic research. The use of a minority language in dominant domains, such as schools, also confers prestige, although not necessarily power, as Patrick's chapter demonstrates. However, this way of institutionalizing minority languages is also fraught with complications and contradictions.

One source of such contradictions, as demonstrated in the chapters by Freeland, Stroud and Heugh, Patrick, Stephen and Petrus Atin, and Wright, is that, if it is not handled carefully, institutionalization can reproduce the same inequitable discursive structures that are characteristic of modernist projects of nation-building. For example, the processes of standardization usually associated with making languages the medium of formal education tend to favour certain language varieties over others, or to force speakers who claim more than one 'mother tongue' to choose between these for their own or their children's education.[5]

Another source of problems is that a given minority language variety may not have sufficient speakers to merit institutionalization, or – as

---

[5] These choices, we should also recognize, are situated in a global politics of language, which means that in certain cases, speakers might not even choose one of their mother tongues as the language of their education. For example, in contexts where mother tongue education might not provide the greatest access to social mobility, they might prefer to learn a dominant language (see e.g. Brutt-Griffler 2002a, 2002b).

described in the chapter by Stephen and Petrus Atin – might, for historical or political reasons, be treated as part of a larger language group. Still another complication, highlighted in the chapter by Freeland, is that the decision about which language variety gains status in schools might, and in the case of creole languages usually does, give rise to ideological battles. Even in relatively homogeneous minority language communities, certain language forms are more highly valued than others in educational institutions, and the standardized variety almost always constitutes highly valued capital for success in the school system and associated employment. Thus, non-standard varieties of the minority language – and the speakers who use them – can easily become marginalized in institutions where gate-keeping mechanisms are in operation. This is particularly the case in schools, where standard language forms earn higher marks and produce greater career opportunities.

Of course, standardization becomes a significant issue only when language varieties are promoted primarily through formal, state-supported education. Yet many minorities perceive this to be a key site for legitimizing and hence ensuring the 'survival' of the language. Indeed, as described in the chapter by Freeland, it may be the case that the use of a language variety in formal education is the *only* source of legitimacy supported by the state. Yet, this kind of institutionalization may actually run counter to language 'survival', forcing the development of the language indirections that may be at odds with the ideologies associated with its everyday use and value to local speakers. The case described in the chapter by Patrick shows that the use of Inuktitut in formal education has managed to avoid such negative results precisely because the language is already supported and 'lives' in the everyday social life of speakers, outside of formal domains. Even so, as Patrick points out, this prestigious extension of the language is still fraught with contradictions. And, as noted by, for instance Fishman (1991), Mülhäusler (1996), and Le Page and Tabouret-Keller (1985), minority language varieties can 'survive' without legitimization and standardization in schools. In fact, it is not even clear how important institutionalized language use is in language maintenance efforts, if the language is not valued in economic and cultural activities beyond the school or in practices associated with an 'alternative' language market.

Education itself is a contested field, where state structures are reproduced through ideologies of monolingual norms of language teaching (Heller 1999). Innovative and effective teaching practices are not guaranteed simply by applying these norms to other languages – although it must be recognized that many minority language programmes, when properly resourced, do remarkably well. This success stems largely from the allocation of resources for language and curriculum development, textbooks and materials, and pre- and in- service teaching training. Thus, procuring language rights in institutional domains is a meaningless pursuit if the necessary power and resources are not available to actively promote and use the language in teaching and learning.

Given the contested nature of minority language use and valorization in modern, often politicized contexts, we have to position ourselves carefully, along with other sociolinguists and researchers working in the field, in relation to the minority language struggles taking place in the particular sociopolitical context in which we work. Perhaps this is best summed up in Heller's afterword to this volume and the chapter by Stroud and Heugh. Both address the need to reflect on the effect one inevitably has upon the situation in which one is working, upon the influence one may have on decisions about "what is the right thing to do" (Heller p 283) and upon one's political and moral commitment. Working with minority language groups and their struggles, first to gain recognition and resources for their languages, and then to realize in practice the language rights they may be granted, means that researchers must also deal with the everyday social inequities and marginalization that minority groups face. In taking a critical stance in relation to the language rights and language survival discourses, we are aware that we could seem to undermine the claims such minorities seek to make upon the states where they live. Equally, we are aware that once these claims are granted, their chance of success is considerably improved when implementation is founded in clear analysis of the sociolinguistic, political, and economic context.

In an important footnote, Stroud and Heugh (p 191 [n.2]) voice a personal commitment to the egalitarian principles underlying the linguistic human rights discourse. At the same time, they declare firmly that, based on their experiences, they "do not believe that LHR (the linguistic human rights paradigm) is the best means to attain goals of social, political, and economic equity for linguistic minorities". Similar commitments and reservations, arising from different but comparable experiences, underpin all the chapters in this volume.

As language 'experts' and scholars examining the social processes of language movements, we all need to address these issues seriously and to be open to new ways of imagining the social order and the place that the recognition of language varieties and the needs of speakers can play in a broader political economic landscape. The chapters in this book offer some new directions for such imaginings. They not only raise important issues and questions concerning minority languages in the social world; they provide a number of examples, based on real-life contexts and dilemmas, that can steer sociolinguistic research into new areas of inquiry and investigation and towards a better understanding of our role in minority language movements.

In the following section, we summarize the chapters in this book, highlighting the main arguments of each chapter, linking them to each other and to the basic themes in this introduction.

5. Chapter Summaries

The chapter by Stephen May, 'Rethinking Linguistic Human Rights: Answering Questions of Identity, Essentialism, and Mobility' opens up a theme underlying most of this book's chapters; that whilst the moral principles of the language rights and language ecology movements are incontestable, their theoretical foundations need strengthening through critical re-assessment in the light of recent theoretical and empirical research. May tackles first the case made for linguistic diversity by analogy with biological/ecological diversity, showing how it also encourages resignation or apathy to language loss, or even belligerent opposition to defending diversity, by suggesting that such loss is natural, a consequence of irresistible evolutionary cycles. Moreover, he argues that treating languages as the 'species' in the ecology and their decline as a linguistic process arising from competition and contact overlooks the speakers of languages, and especially the political power relations within which their languages interact.

May's chief concern, however, is with the notion of ethnic identity that underlies language rights advocacy, and its assumption that language is a principle indicator of that identity. This notion easily falls prey to postmodern arguments (and indeed empirical evidence) that ethnicity is a largely constructed identity that is defined not by essential cultural traits, but by the way these are deployed to establish ethnic boundaries in particular political and economic circumstances. Hence, the saliency and even the character of ethnic attributes will change over time, according to their instrumental usefulness to the group. Indeed a group may even express its identity in another language and survive. May illustrates how politicians wield crudely simplified versions of these findings to argue for the spread of more 'instrumentally useful' (i.e. dominant) languages and against 'ghettoizing' communities within less useful ones.

Nevertheless, whilst language is demonstrably a *contingent* factor of identity, this does not mean that it is neither significant nor constitutive of identity. May suggests a way out of the false dichotomy between essentialist and anti-essentialist views of identity, and of over-rigid views of language rights, through Bourdieu's notion of 'habitus', which in recognizing how cultural influences are embodied in people, acknowledges both "the continuing purchase *and* malleability of ethnicity, and the particular languages associated with it, at any given time and place".

The chapter by Jan Blommaert, 'Rights in Places: Comments on Linguistic Rights and Wrongs' teases out further the dichotomy May highlights, between supposed 'ghettoization' within the confines of a marginalized language and the social mobility offered by dominant languages. Framing his discussion as an extension of recent anthropological work on the semiotics of space/place in the conceptualization of identity and its expression in languages, he demonstrates the recurrence in the discourse on linguistic rights of an association between minority languages and locality. Rights are granted by territorially bounded states, to minorities "within their respective territories",[6] according to distinctions along the "classic Herderian triad of territory-culture-language". This is even truer of the 'ecological' discourse on linguistic diversity: languages are like species because they encode in their semantic and grammatical relations particular interpretations of their local environment, or serve highly localized social functions; they become vulnerable when their 'territory' is invaded by imperialistic, international, deterritorialized languages, or they become dysfunctional as they move away from that territory and its cultural practices.

It is, Blommaert argues, this implicit localism and territoriality that makes the ecological discourse particularly vulnerable to the mobility vs. ghettoization argument. Speakers of marginalized languages themselves perceive dominant languages as vehicles of escape from marginalized localities to more prosperous centers, which explains their ambivalence towards bilingual programmes based in their vernaculars. This leaves language planners with Mufwene's 'wicked problem' (2002: 377): whether to help speakers escape their economic predicament or to save their language.

Although there is no easy way out of Mufwene's dilemma, Blommaert points us towards World-Systems Analysis and the fact that 'centers' and 'peripheries' or margins are not always absolute, but relative to the scale on which one looks at things. Although on a global economic scale the

---

[6] This issue has in fact generated a whole literature on whether language rights, like others, should be individual rather than territorial, a particular issue in contexts such as Wales or Catalunya, whose languages have recognizable territorial centers where they have the potential to become majority languages, but are spoken in other territories where they do not.

relation between them seems quite stable and appears to condemn many groups to absolute marginalization, at other levels centrality and peripherality are significantly linked through opportunities for people to acquire, develop and use different languages, or more importantly, varieties of languages, for different ranges of activity. This, however, is rarely taken into account in the linguistic rights discourse, nor in policies devised to realize its goals. Several of the ensuing case studies illustrate this in various ways (e.g. Darnell, Stroud and Heugh, Whaley, and Patrick).

The chapter by Ville Laakso and Jan-Ola Östman, 'Minority, but Non-Confrontational: Balancing the Double-edged Sword of Hegemony and Ambivalence' reinforces aspects of both May's and Blommaert's contributions. Through the particular case of Solv, they further explore questions of marginality and the implications for language rights when ethnic identities not only remain strong despite language shift, but successfully exploit the ambivalence afforded by such shift. They also provide a link to a dominant theme of the book by problematizing some of the approaches to linguistic investigation, including linguistic classification, categorization, and 'musealizing' (p 74) that underpin current language rights discourse.

Solv is a language variety spoken in Solf, one of about 80 comparable village communities in Finland. Traditionally classified as a dialect of Finland-Swedish, Solv enables its speakers to locate themselves on 'a multiple margin' of language varieties and identities, distinguishing themselves not only from speakers of Swedish in Sweden and Finnish in Finland, but also of the class-based variety of 'Finland-Swedish' that identifies the "Swedish-speaking community in Finland". This multiple marginality is revealed in an apparent paradox. According to a 2003 attitudes study, Solf people perceive Solv to be their mother tongue and speak it with pride. Yet in the language many of them produce it is not possible to find formal traces of Solv according to the categories of classic descriptive linguistics.

This, the authors argue, is a paradox only in terms of the linguistics paradigm that generated these categories. In fact, Solv is a variety largely articulated through discourse-performative contrasts with surrounding varieties; its social meaning is pragmatically constituted as speakers 'focus' (in Le Page and Tabouret-Keller's sense, 1985) their language towards or away from the identities associated with them. As Finland has changed, offering Solf people new identity positions and making old ones less relevant, both their Solvness and the language indexing it have remained fluid, open to variation and change; both perdure precisely because their boundaries and interrelationships are not fixed, allowing a necessary degree of ambivalence in the performance of identity.

However, as Laakso and Östman suggest, the conception of language inherent in the current language rights discourse leads in a completely different direction from such flexible durability. Eschewing context and pragmatic meaning, this conception focuses on discrete 'languages' defined by the formal traits that Solv now 'lacks', which it then associates with discrete, clearly bounded identities according to principles of linguistic nationism rooted in European models of nation-building. Yet as cultural globalization increases the identity positions available to people, even to the most marginalized, such fluidity and ambivalence are likely to become more important than stark either/identity choices.

It might be objected that the non-confrontational character of the Solv case, although it raises interesting questions in the abstract, is not generalisable beyond its relatively prosperous Finnish context, where language does not materially limit life chances. However, the chapter by Regna Darnell, 'Revitalization and Retention of First Nations Languages in Southwestern Ontario' also makes a powerful case for a shift towards pragmatics in the linguistic paradigm of language rights discourse, in relation to the highly politicized aspirations for language revitalization among First Nations in Canada. Indeed, she argues (with Deleuze and Guattari 1987) that the focus of pragmatics on "variables of expression or of enunciation" make it effectively 'a politics of language', not 'extralinguistic' but internal to language and thus a vital key to understanding and foregrounding speakers' own agency in the processes of cultural maintenance and transmission, in a world whose effects on traditional cultures and languages will increase.

In this chapter, the need for such an approach is articulated in relation to languages that according to the traditional paradigm have apparently become 'extinct' or highly 'endangered'. This paradigm finds 'adulterated' remains of languages impossible to revive, left behind as former speakers shifted to the languages of power and mobility, first under the pressure of historic assimilationist policies and now through increasing globalization. However, when the focus shifts from 'languages' to the performance of First Nation identity, it emerges that traditional cultures do persist and are indeed being revitalized through a wide variety of community strategies that challenge established sociolinguistic expectations. The eclecticism of these strategies contrasts dramatically with the purist ideologies which Darnell finds inherent in the field linguistics tradition into which she was professionally socialized, whose preferred targets are "immobilized, idealized precontact languages" (p 96) preserved in written texts that sever them from their roots in performance and incorporate them into a scholarly tradition far removed from the personalized transmission of information of their originating societies.

Most strikingly, Darnell shows how the pejoratively named 'Indian English' spoken by the Iroquians and Algonquians she works with is not a negative sign of assimilation but takes its place among a rich array of codes. Ranging between symbolic uses of traditional languages to fluent formal English, this array permits not only the performance of multiple identities, but even the maintenance and transmission of traditional culture. By performing traditional ceremonies in English, for instance, elders include those less fluent in the appropriate languages; oral histories are published in English to the same end. These mixed forms increase people's knowledge and commitment and motivate them to assume roles associated with particular ritual and specialist practices or the responsibilities of elders, and thence to learn their 'lost' languages.

Here is another call for a linguistic paradigm shift. In the two approaches to linguistic revitalization that Darnell explores there reside dramatically different assumptions about the relationship of indigenous peoples not only to the societies where they live but also to the linguists who offer them help. One constructs identities for them, from languages belonging to an idealized past; the other engages with their own agendas and processes of 'linguistic becoming'.

This tension between different approaches to language rights and language revitalization is echoed in the chapter by Jane Freeland, 'Linguistic Rights and Language Survival in a Creole Space: Dilemmas of Nicaragua's Caribbean Coast Creoles'. Her discussion centres on the complex links between language, identity, and schooling in the multilingual region of Nicaragua's Caribbean Coast, which have emerged since the granting of language rights to the Caribbean Coast Region under Nicaragua's 1987 Law of Autonomy. Freeland's chapter, like many others in this volume, challenges the essentialist assumption that language and identity have fixed boundaries and that there is a necessary connection between them. The paper further problematizes the notion of 'mother tongue', presenting an ethnographic examination of the language varieties into which Creole speakers are socialized and the cultural and social meanings and values that they place on these languages.

Drawing on Hall's and Gilroy's work on Black diaspora cultures and identities, she highlights some of the dilemmas surrounding Creole cultures and the implementation of language policies based on universal notions of 'linguistic rights'. Freeland shows how notions of 'authentic', clearly bounded, homogeneous cultures have been pitted against transnational, syncretized cultural realities in the Creole diaspora. Focusing on the 'space between' artificially rigid cultural borders, Freeland documents how different subject positions were constructed and articulated among the Creole speakers of Bluefields at the time that language rights were granted and 'mother tongue' education was promoted by the Nicaraguan state.

Freeland documents the arguments and counter-arguments given for choosing one or another language variety for the state-sponsored 'mother-tongue' literacy and bilingual programmes instituted for Nicaraguan Creoles. Central to these arguments has been the issue of using Creole itself as a medium of instruction in schools. This idea is problematic for some, given that the fluidity of the language runs counter to commonly held assumptions both about what constitutes a language and about which language varieties are suitable for education. Freeland shows how the dominant discursive framework of language rights imposed by the Nicaraguan state, with its monolithic conception of language, cannot accommodate the multivocality of Creole positions on language use in literacy and bilingual education. Thus, the language rights discourse, despite its well-intentioned emancipatory rhetoric, paradoxically constrains efforts to promote Creole language use, whilst its 'ethnic absolutist' terms restrict local identity positions.

An extreme case of a people condemned to "developing a self-identity on someone else's terms" (p 148) is that of the Oroqen of northern China discussed by Lindsay Whaley in his chapter 'Can a Language that Never Existed be Saved? Coming to Terms with Oroqen Language Revitalization'. Whaley unravels the historical processes leading to this group's modern predicament as "a people that in one sense never existed working to promote a language that never really existed in a context that discourages them from forging the necessary sense of group distinctiveness" (ibid.). This paradox, however, was brought about not through repression, but by ethnic rights policies with progressive intentions, but based on abstract notions of peoplehood and language. The Oroqen case illustrates well some of the problems inherent in applying such rights in practice, especially where languages have lost the significance they once derived from their local roots.

Up to the formation of the People's Republic of China (PRC) in 1949, the people now known as the Oroqen lived as a loose cluster of clans related by a complex, fluid web of kinship and mutually intelligible Tungusic language varieties that indexed clan membership and were richly expressive of their reindeer-hunting activities. Group identity derived from these smaller units, and clan membership was pragmatically negotiated and open to endogamy. There was no need, then, to imagine an overarching identity beyond the clans, nor to evolve a unifying language to express it.

The PRC approached the ethnic pluralism of the new nation by defining the minorities within its borders as 'nationalities' with rights to legal recognition. 'Nationalities' were defined according to Stalin's Marxist analysis of 'the national question', as groups sharing a history, language, territory, economic life and culture; that is, in terms of the classic European paradigm. Nationalities so construed were to enjoy rights of the kind promoted by the language rights movement: support for their languages and cultures; a degree of self-rule to accomplish this; and measures to improve their standard of living. Yet the very terms of these rights contributed to undermine Oroqen identity and hasten their assimilation into mainstream Chinese culture.

Whaley details how the combined effects of centrally planned efforts to improve minority living standards gradually moved the Oroqen clans away from all that had contributed to their self-understanding as a group and left them scattered among other groups in small, numerically insignificant groups, across two provinces. In recent years, whilst the privileges of their minority status have disposed them positively towards the Chinese state, awareness of their assimilation has motivated some Oroqen, especially older, fluent speakers of the Oroqen language varieties, to try revitalize at least their language. Yet this goal can now only be conceived and executed in terms of a distinct, unified Oroqen language commensurate with their national minority identity, both external constructs incongruent with their own self-understanding. Moreover, it is difficult to establish a standard variety of Oroqen independent of clan identities, or indeed to differentiate clearly between Oroqen varieties and other Tungusic varieties spoken by close neighbours in what is a complex dialect continuum. Attempts to base language revitalization in local varieties have also failed because they are too local to be sustainable. In this instance, improving the life conditions of the Oroqen has gradually removed them from the 'habitats' that sustained their traditional culture and language use, and made it difficult for them to create new ones. The case illustrates well Mufwene's 'wicked problem' (2002: 377) to which Blommaert refers, and raises questions we have yet to resolve as to how these often conflicting goals can be reconciled.

Whaley's approach to understanding the application of language rights to indigenous language contexts is similar to that taken by Jeannet Stephen and Veronica Petrus Atin in their chapter, 'Language and Intergroup Perception in Sabah: A Case Study of the Rungus Ethnic Community' in multilingual Malaysia. The interest of this approach derives from its ability to bring together issues that are often seen as unrelated in either nationist-essentialist or ecological, localist conceptions of language rights. These issues include the danger of imposing monolithic constructs of identity and language that are incongruent with the self-perception of groups and the difficulties of conceiving rights in terms of discrete languages in dialect continua which themselves often signal complex continua of group identity.

Stephen and Petrus Atin describe a situation where categorization of language varieties into discrete languages and monolithic notions of ethnic 'group' identity in language rights discourse runs counter to lived experiences and the ideas about language held by indigenous speakers. The writers situate their study in the multiethnic and multilingual region of Sabah, Malaysia, where the indigenous language, Rungus, has been classified under a larger umbrella category, Kadazandusun. The crux of this chapter is its exploration of how historical, political, and social factors have come into play in creating different notions of what constitutes a 'language' or a 'dialect', according to state bodies, linguists, and local speakers. It also addresses the question of which language varieties are granted rights to educational resources and for what reasons.

Through data based on historical accounts and interviews with community leaders, language teachers and local Rungus-identified villagers, Stephen and Petrus Atin highlight some of the problems associated with linguistic nomenclature and categorization dating from the late nineteenth century. Tracing colonial and more recent encounters between indigenous groups in Sabah (formerly North Borneo) and the Malaysian state, the authors enter into a dialogue with Rungus speakers who have recently had access to indigenous-language schooling through the Kadazandusun standard. Education in this language, however, has recently been stopped in Rungus villages, and Stephen and Petrus Atin (who themselves are Kadazandusun) set out to discover why.

Stephen and Petrus Atin found that despite the structural impediments to successful language teaching – including the facts that teachers lacked technical resources and curricular support and that classes were taught after regular school hours and without state examinations at the end of the course – there were other issues to investigate. These concerned the attitudes that local speakers hold towards the Kadazundusun language and towards their designation as a member of this larger ethnic group, which makes them eligible for rights and benefits associated with this designation.

Both the attachment of Rungus speakers to their language and their attitudes towards the (politically motivated) categorization of their language as a dialect of Kadazandusun are complex. Bolstered by myths of the origin of the Kadazandusun people, the Rungus leadership justify their association with the larger Kadazandusun ethnic group politically, socially, economically, and ideologically. Yet, despite these historical ties between Rungus and other Kadazandusun language varieties, Rungus is, to all intents and purposes, a distinct language, and its speakers consider themselves a distinct group. The ambivalence and fluid identities indicated by leaders and community members alike suggest intricate links between language and identity in the sociopolitical relationships between indigenous groups in this region. In this context, local, regional, and national political concerns come into play in language policy and practice, as do historical, local, and strategic maneuverings and positionings of speakers as they try to reconcile local concerns with the sociopolitical realities of everyday life.

The chapter by Donna Patrick, 'The Politics of Language Rights in the Eastern Canadian Arctic' further explores this reconciliation between local, regional, national and global concerns about indigenous rights and the links between language and politics in everyday life. On the face of it, her study is a success story in terms of both the language rights and the biological/ecological discourses on language survival. The Inuktitut language is officially supported in formal education, appears stable and vital, and takes its place among a range of varieties of different languages that facilitate Inuit mobility. Yet, as Patrick shows, success here is an effect not so much of granting language rights as of a complex interaction between the terms on which they were granted and a very particular historico-social context: the deep history of the Inuit's political, social and economic relations with the Canadian state, which illustrates the power of ethnic identities and the way they can be used instrumentally in the defence of wider interests.

Key constituents of this process were the coincidence of Inuit claims to land and language with the Quebec nationalist movement of the 1960s and 1970s, which enabled the Inuit to take political advantage of parallels between Francophone claims and their own; the indirect effects of Canadian-US politico-military relations during the Cold War that assisted Inuit land claims; the East Arctic Inuit's relatively late sedentarization compared with other Canadian 'First Nations'; the persistence of traditional knowledge and harvesting activities, such as whaling, and their viability in terms of the wider economy. Interacting over time, these processes ensured that Inuktitut language varieties maintained clear social functions associated with these traditional activities as well as acquiring new social meanings in interactions with dominant groups. The right to use Inuktitut in education therefore became part of this context, and has not been the language's sole source of legitimacy and value.

Using Bourdieu's concepts of economies of language or linguistic markets, Patrick suggests that the vitality of Inuktitut today stems from its dual value, both in the dominant linguistic market, where it is subject to language rights legislation in institutional spheres, and in the 'alternative market' where 'traditional' practices are valued.

In schools, a standardized and modernized Inuktitut provides new symbolic capital for accessing education-related job markets. Yet this alone would not guarantee its survival, since in this market it also competes on unequal terms with the region's two dominant (European) languages, which offer greater symbolic capital: access to higher education and higher paid jobs. It is the complementarity of these linguistic markets, which enables Inuit people to use different varieties of Inuktitut, as well as other languages, to project and perform multiple identities in different social spheres. This in turn has avoided some of the problems associated with standardizing a minority language, in particular the creation of inequalities between standard speakers and speakers of more traditional, non-standard varieties. Instead, Inuktitut becomes part of an extended range of varieties, each with clear social functions carrying their own positive values.

This case shows, then, how the granting of language rights is a necessary, but not a sufficient condition for language survival. It also reveals some of the inherent dangers of a too facile use of ecological metaphors as a blueprint for language survival. The 'species' in the ecology are not 'languages', Patrick points out, but people who use different language varieties to live changing lives in shifting relationships of power, and it is these relationships that constitute the species 'habitat'. Hence, following this analogy, language survival cannot be guaranteed by protecting this habitat, as one might protect a nature reserve by keeping out predators. Rather, it depends on understanding in detail how people interact with, even appropriate, 'predatory' elements to their own purposes, and then tailoring language policy to this understanding.

The chapter by Christopher Stroud and Kathleen Heugh, 'Language Rights and Linguistic Citizenship' draws on data from Southern Africa to critique the narrow focus of linguistic human rights (LHR) discourse and to offer a post-liberal understanding of citizenship. Stroud and Heugh argue that LHR is a liberal discourse that is rendered ineffective in many post-colonial contexts, since many languages are excluded from legal and political policy-making. When legal and political provisions have been made for minority language varieties, they have often been accompanied by ineffective or inappropriate institutionalization (as also noted in the chapters by Freeland, Stephen and Petrus Atin, and Martín Rojo). Language rights discourse, as used in the South African context, has thus inadvertently reproduced colonial practices of language domination and further marginalized some minority communities. In these contexts, Stroud and Heugh suggest, LHR has paradoxically served to diminish the world's languages, since not all languages have been given rights, and those that have do not necessarily benefit from institutionalization.

Echoing other chapters in this volume (most notably those by Blommaert, May, Freeland, Laasko and Östman, and Wright), Stroud and Heugh critique the essentialist notions of identity that LHR discourse relies on, and offer in their place a concept of 'linguistic citizenship' that whose goal is to enable real participation in governance for all citizens, in a way not guaranteed by the more abstract legal rights conferred by the liberal LHR paradigm. In this framework, all of a speaker's linguistic resources are valued and become key elements in their political and social participation. Linguistic citizenship, as outlined in the chapter, emphasizes language as (i) a *symbolic resource*, which is linked to its role in *actorhood*; (ii) a *material resource*, which is linked to political and economic arrangements; (iii) a *global resource*, whereby global and regional concerns are enacted locally; and (iv) an *intimate resource*, whereby diversity and multivocal identities are acknowledged and respected.

Stroud and Heugh conclude that notions of linguistic citizenship can open possibilities for reducing conflict in local, national, and transnational encounters, building solidarity and promoting action and commonality across national borders. The chapter illustrates how the seeds for realizing these aims are already evident in current practices of 'horizontal' migration between African countries, and in the spread of indigenous skills and resources that comes with this mobility, contrasting them with the tendency to create and maintain frontiers and boundaries that is associated with essentialized notions of ethnicity, language and identity.

The chapter by Sue Wright, 'Language Rights, Democracy, and the European Union' echoes aspects of Stroud and Heugh's critique of the limitations for democracy of the language rights discourse and of liberal conceptions of citizenship. Her study of the 'democratic deficit' inherent in the European Union's communication policies and practices convincingly demonstrates why a reconceptualization of citizenship needs to be extended also to supranational political structures. Wright focuses on the multilingual reality of the European Union, where the issues of language rights and democratic process unite in complex ideological ways. She explores how the European Union is 'imagined', constructed, and unified as a democratic, supranational entity and how plurilingualism (involving 11 languages) is managed in this context.

As Wright notes, Western notions of democracy are intimately bound up with language. By means of a detailed account of the language policies and practices of the European Parliament, Commission, and Council,

Wright explores the democratic reality and 'deficit' in the EU and calls for a 'community of communication'. Drawing on Habermas, she shows how the expectations of the populace, based on Western liberal democratic ideologies, are not met in the day-to-day language practices of the EU – how problems arise when the experiences and expectations of nation-state processes are transferred to supra-state structures. Here the ideologies of nation-building, which include notions of representative democracy, come into conflict with Europe's larger supranational power structures, and the social inequities associated with the nation-state are reproduced at the supra-state level. Minority languages within nations are often denied legitimization when they are seen as threatening or too expensive to uphold – as in the case of the English-Only movement in the USA and the denial of minority language rights in France.

As Wright demonstrates, multilingualism in the EU is becoming unmanageable. The plurilingual policies on which the political structure was founded have broken down in practice as the number of member state languages has grown, so that it is now increasingly impractical to provide the translation and interpretation to and from all the languages that would enable their speakers to operate on an equal institutional footing. Thus while in principle the languages of all member-states are recognized as working languages, English increasingly operates as the de facto lingua franca, without being recognized as such.

Wright's paper poses some interesting questions. Can pluralism be realized in the European context through educational and other institutional policies? Is there a way to create a 'community of communication' under current socio-political conditions? Do we need a new model for managing multilingual democracies? Can the pragmatic realities of English as a lingua franca be formally recognized and accepted in the contemporary plurilingual European context? Can English ever be accepted as such a lingua franca, given the political and ideological baggage associated with its current global dominance? Wright offers insightful discussion and opens the debate on these and other issues that arise when liberal language rights discourse intersects with ideologies of nation and democracy. Her chapter is of particular interest because it demonstrates how the contradictions of this discourse, explored in other chapters in the more familiar context of minority claims within single nation-states, are replicated at the suprastate level.

The chapter by Luisa Martín Rojo, 'Ideological Dilemmas in Language and Cultural Policies in Madrid schools' examines minority language rights in the context of educational practices in the autonomous region of Madrid. As she points out, Spain has been a leading country in the granting of autonomous rights, including control over language policy, to its so-called 'peripheral' nationalities (the Catalans, Basques, Galicians, etc.), and now has seventeen autonomously administered regions.

Drawing on critical discourse analysis and ethnographic data, Martín Rojo examines the contrast between an official Spanish discourse of plurality and respect for diversity and the discourse of teachers and administrators involved in the education of immigrant minority groups, a discourse which draws on older, more deeply ingrained nationalist ideologies promoting 'equality' for such minorities by assimilation into a 'stable' culturally homogeneous nation-state. Martín Rojo shows how these two discourses mix into what she labels a 'double discourse', especially in the Madrid region, until recently the monolingual centre of a centralized Spanish state. She goes on to illustrate how, in classroom practice, this 'double discourse' defeats pluralist aims and produces segregation and marginalization of immigrant groups rather than their integration.

Martín Rojo, who sees schools as potentially a key site in the transformation of the Madrid region from a monolingual society into a linguistically and culturally diverse one, offers an analysis of linguistic and cultural policies in primary and secondary schools in Madrid. She shows that, whilst a few schools are moving towards pluralist goals, using methods that value pupils' home languages, this is the exception rather than the norm. In most schools, variants of the assimilationist model prevail, forcing pupils into 'either/or' choices of language and identity. In general, she concludes, linguistic policy in this region remains fundamentally unclear as a consequence of the 'double discourse' and the slippage it allows between approaches to diversity. In light of her analysis, Martín Rojo suggests that the only real solution to the dilemma lies in the construction and circulation of new discourses that both value the dominant language of power and validate minority varieties. Echoing the conclusions of Stroud and Heugh, and also of Wright, she acknowledges that this involves nothing less than a redefinition of notions of 'nationhood' and 'citizenship'.

The chapter by Alexandra Jaffe, 'Language Rights and Wrongs: a Commentary' links some of the themes discussed in this introduction with others that emerge in the various chapters, suggesting new directions for sociolinguistic inquiry. Jaffe first highlights how many chapters focus on the multiple, often ambivalent acts of identification that emerge in language practices in social contexts, in contrast to traditional notions of fixed, essentialized identities. In the social practice of everyday life, she suggests, dominant cultural forms often overlap with local cultural practices so that 'pure' cultural or linguistic categories no longer remain. These relational and often ambivalent links between language and culture, on the one hand, and identity, on the other, are best accounted for through research practices that respect speakers' own claims and divergent stances regarding their identities.

Nevertheless, Jaffe also points to the difficulties associated with 'radical resistance', that is, a resistance based in an alternative discourse to that of linguistic essentialism, and also to the inequities often hidden behind inclusive discourses about language rights and diversity. As Jaffe notes, 'diversity' is still something that needs to be promoted within institutions, communities, nations, and supranational structures such as the EU.

Struggles for language rights, survival, and revitalization are never just about language, but are a part of broader political, economic, and cultural struggles over who receives official recognition, in what ways, and with what material and ideological effects. Our research, as Jaffe notes, needs to focus on "the social processes of identification and distinction and the variable role language plays in these processes, both as a practice and as an object of discourse" (p 280). Many of the chapters in this volume work with this contingent relationship between linguistic variation and its implications for ideas of acknowledging, 'saving', 'losing', or revitalizing a minority language.

The afterword by Monica Heller, 'Analysis and Stance Regarding Language and Social Justice' draws out another aspect of the research reflected in this volume: its moral and reflexive dimension. Heller points out that as researchers we must distance ourselves from an "uncritical acceptance of the categories of language and collective identity" (p 285) that figure in the struggles we engage in. Yet, on the other hand, we also need to take a clear political stance in relation to these struggles. In certain circumstances, this may even require us to make use of 'strategic simplification' in order to support groups in their struggles; in other circumstances, we may have to maintain our distance from them even if this brings criticism from community members who may not be happy with our position. As Heller reminds us, it is our responsibility as researchers to be aware that we are part of the situations we study, and to decide on this basis when to say what – based on our own grounded understanding of a situation – whether legal, academic, or community-based.

Together, the chapters in this volume present a cross-section of sociolinguistic research that takes seriously the complexities associated with minority language struggles and seeks to understand how these are embedded in local, regional, national, and transnational contexts. The contexts in question are those in which issues of language rights and language 'survival' have become bound up with particular localized conceptions of language, culture, and identity. These localized constructions are not considered in isolation, but in relation to the broader social and political forces of globalization, nation-building, and minority struggles. This volume can thus be seen as an invitation to look beyond the local, to problematize everyday assumptions, and to imagine new ways of understanding and acting in our social world.

References

Anderson, Benedict (1991) [1993] *Imagined Communities: Reflections on the Origin and Spread of Nationalism*, 2nd ed, London: Verso.

Banton, Michael (1996) 'International Norms and Latin American States' Policies on Indigenous Peoples', *Nations and Nationalism* 2(1): 89-103.

Bauman, Richard, and Charles L. Briggs (2000) 'Language Philosophy as Language Ideology: John Locke and Gottfried Herder', in Paul Kroskrity (ed) *Regimes of Language*, Sante Fe: School of American Research Press, 139-204.

Blommaert, Jan (1996) 'Language Planning as a Discourse on Language and Society: The Linguistic Ideology of a Scholarly Tradition', *Language Problems and Language Planning* 20(3): 199-222.

------ (ed) (1999) *Language Ideological Debates*, Berlin/New York: Mouton de Gruyter.

------ (2003) 'A Sociolinguistics of Globalization', in N. Coupland (ed) Special Issue on Sociolinguistics and Globalization, *Journal of Sociolinguistics* 7(4):607-623.

Bokhorst-Heng, Wendy (1999) 'Singapore's *Speak Mandarin Campaign*: Language Ideological Debates in the Imagining of a Nation', in Jan Blommaert (ed) *Language Ideological Debates*, Berlin/New York: Mouton de Gruyter, 235-266.

Bourdieu, Pierre (1992) *Language and Symbolic Power*, London: Polity Press.

------ (1982) *Outline of a Theory of Practice*, Cambridge: Cambridge University Press.

------ (1977) 'The Economics of Linguistic Exchanges', *Social Science Information* 16(6): 645–68.

Brutt-Griffler, Jarina (2002a) *World English: A Study of Its Development*, Clevedon: Multilingual Matters.

------ (2002b) 'Class, Ethnicity, and Language Rights: An Analysis of British Colonial Policy in Lesotho and Sri Lanka and Some Implications for Language Policy', *Journal of Language, Identity, and Education* 1(3): 207-234.

Cameron, Deborah (1990) 'Demythologizing Sociolinguistics: Why Language Does not Reflect Society', in John E. Joseph and Talbot J. Taylor (eds) *Ideologies of Language*, London: Routledge, 79-93.

------ (1995) *Verbal Hygiene*, London/New York: Routledge.

Capotorti, Francesco (1979) *Study on the Rights of Persons Belonging to Ethnic, Religious and Linguistic Minorities*, New York: United Nations.

Coulmas, Florian (1998) 'Language Rights – Interests of State, Language Groups and the Individual', *Language Sciences* 20: 60-72.

Cowan, J., M-B. Dembour and R. A. Wilson (eds) (2001) *Culture and Rights: Anthropological Perspectives*, Cambridge: Cambridge University Press.

Crystal, David (2000) *Language Death*, Cambridge: Cambridge University Press.

Cummins, Jim (1993) 'Bilingualism and Second Language Learning', *Annual Review of Applied Linguistics* 13: 51-70.

------ (1996) *Negotiating Identities: Education for Empowerment in a Diverse Society*, Toronto: California Association for Bilingual Education.

Deleuze, Gilles and Félix Guattari (1987) *A Thousand Plateaus: Capitalism and Schizophrenia*, Minneapolis: University of Minnesota Press.

de Varennes, F. (1996) *Language, Minorities and Human Rights*, The Hague: Martinus Nijhoff Publishers.

England, Nora (2002) 'Commentary: Further Rhetorical Concerns', *Journal of Linguistic Anthropology* 12(2): 141-143.

Fishman, Joshua (1989 [1972]) 'Language and Nationalism: Two Integrative Essays', In J. Fishman (ed) *Language and Ethnicity in Minority Sociolinguistic Perspective.* Cleveland: Multilingual Matters.

------ (1991) *Reversing Language Shift*, Clevedon, Avon: Multilingual Matters.

------ (2001) *Can Threatened Languages Be Saved? Reversing Language Shift Revisited: A 21st Century Perspective*, Clevedon, Avon: Multilingual Matters.

Gal, Susan (2001) 'Linguistic Theories and National Images in Nineteenth-century Hungary', in Susan Gal and Kathryn Woolard (eds) *Languages and Publics*, Manchester: St. Jerome Press, 30-45.

------ and Kathryn Woolard (2001) *Languages and Publics: The Making of Authority*, Manchester: St. Jerome.

Hale, Kenneth (1992) 'On Endangered Languages and the Safeguarding of Diversity', *Language* 68(1): 1-10.

Harvey, Sharon (2003) 'Critical Perspsectives on Language(s), *Journal of Sociolinguistics* 7(2): 246-259.

Heller, Monica (1994) *Crosswords: Language, Education and Ethnicity in French Ontario*, Berlin/New York: Mouton de Gruyter.

------ (1999) *Linguistic Minorities and Modernity: A Sociolinguistic Ethnography*, London/new York: Longman.

Hinton, Leanne and Ken Hale (2001) *The Green Book on Language Revitalization in Practice*, San Diego: Academic Press.

Irvine, Judith (2001) 'The Family Romance of Colonial Linguistics: Gender and Family in Nineteenth-century Representations of African Languages', in Susan Gal and Kathryn Woolard (eds) *Languages and Publics: The Making of Authority*, Manchester: St. Jerome Publishing.

------ and Susan Gal (2000) 'Language Ideology and Linguistic Differentiation', in Paul Kroskrity (ed) *Regimes of Language,* Santa Fe: School of American Research Press, 35-84.

Jaffe, Alexandra (1999) *Ideologies in Action: Language Politics on Corsica*, Berlin/New York: Mouton de Gruyter.

Kroskrity, Paul V (ed) (2000a) *Regimes of Language: Ideologies, Polities, and Identities*, Santa Fe: School of American Research Press.

------ (2000b) 'Regimenting Languages: Language Ideological Perspectives', in Paul Kroskrity (ed) *Regimes of Language*, Santa Fe: School of American Research Press, 1-34.

Kymlicka, Will (1995) *Multicultural Citizenship*, Oxford: Clarendon Press.

Le Page, Robert (1993) 'Conflicts of Metaphor in the Discussion of Language and Race', in Ernst Håkon Jahr (ed) *Language Conflict and Language Planning*, Berlin/New York: Mouton de Gruyter, 143-164.

------ and Andrée Tabouret-Keller (1985) *Acts of Identity: Creole-based Approaches to Language and Ethnicity*, Cambridge: Cambridge University Press.

May, Stephen (2001) *Language and Minority Rights: Ethnicity, Nationalism and the Politics of Language*, Harlow: Longman/Pearson Education.

Michalove, Peter A, Stefan Georg and Alexis Manaster Ramer (1998) 'Current Issues in Linguistic Taxonomy', *Annual Review of Anthropology* 27: 451-72.

Mufwene, Salikoko (2002) 'Colonisation, Globalisation, and the Future of Languages in the Twenty-first Century'. *MOST Journal of Multicultural Societies* 4/2: 1-48. http://www.unesco.org/most

Mühlhäusler, Peter (2003) 'Language Endangerment and Language Revival', *Journal of Sociolinguistics* 7(2): 232-245.

------ (1996) *Linguistic Ecology: Language Change and Linguistic Imperialism in the Pacific Region*, London: Routledge.

Nettle, Daniel and Suzanne Romaine (2000) *Vanishing Voices: The Extinction of the World's Languages*, Oxford: Oxford University Press.

Niedzielski, Nancy A and Dennis Preston (1999) *Folk Linguistics*, Berlin/New York: Mouton de Gruyter.

Patrick, Donna (2003) *Language, Politics, and Social Interaction in an Inuit Community*, Berlin/NewYork: Mouton de Gruyter.

Pennycook, Alastair (1990) 'Towards a Critical Applied Linguistics for the '90s', *Issues in Applied Linguistics* 1: 8-28.

------ (2001) *Critical Applied Linguistics: A Critical Introduction*, Mahwah, NJ: Lawrence Erlbaum Associates.

Phillipson, Robert (1998) *Linguistic Imperialism*, Oxford: Oxford University Press.

O'Riagáin, P. and N.Nic Shuibine (1998) 'Minority Language Rights', *Annual Review of Applied Linguistics* 17: 11-29.

Said, Edward (1978) *Orientalism*, London: Routledge & Kegan Paul.

Schieffelin, Bambi (2000) 'Introducing Kaluli Literacy: A Chronology of Influences', in Paul Kroskrity (ed) *Regimes of Language*, Santa Fe: School of American Research Press, 293-328.

Silverstein, Michael (1979) 'Language Structure and Linguistic Ideology', in Paul Clyne, William Hanks and Carol Hofbauer (eds) *The Elements: A Parasession on Linguistic Units and Levels*, Chicago: Chicago Linguistics Society, 193-248.

------ (2000) 'Whorfianism and the Linguistic Imagination of Nationality', in P. Kroskrity (ed) *Regimes of Language*, Sante Fe: School of American Research Press, 85-138.

------ (1998) 'Contemporary Transformations of Local Linguistic Communities', *Annual Review of Applied Anthropology* 27: 401-26.

Skutnabb-Kangas, Tove (2002) 'Marvellous Human Rights Rhetoric and Grim Realities: Language Rights in Education'. *Journal of Language, Identity and Education* 1(3): 179-206.

------ (2000) *Linguistic Genocide in Education – or Worldwide Diversity and Human Rights?*, Mahwah, NJ: Lawrence Erlbaum.

------ (1988) 'Multilingualism and the Education of Minority Children', in Tove Skutnabb-Kangas and Jim Cummins (eds) *Minority Education: From Shame to Struggle*, Clevedon, Avon: Multilingual Matters, 9-44.

------ and Robert Phillipson (eds) (1994) *Linguistic Human Rights – Overcoming Linguistic Discrimination*, Berlin: Mouton de Gruyter.

Spivak, Gayatri Chakravorty (1988) 'Can the Subaltern Speak?', In C. Nelson and L. Grossberg (eds) *Marxism and the Interpretation of Culture*, London: Macmillan, 271-313.

Thornberry, P. (1991) *International Law and the Rights of Minorities*, Oxford: Claredon Press.

Urciuoli, Bonnie (1995) 'Language and Borders', *Annual Review of Anthropology* 24: 524-546.

Weinstein, B. (1990) *Language Policy and Political Development*, Norwood, NJ: Ablex.

Williams, Glyn (1992) *Sociolinguistics: A Sociological Critique*, London: Routledge.

Woolard, Kathryn (1985) 'Language Variation and Cultural Hegemony: Toward an Integration of Sociolinguistic and Social Theory', *American Ethnologist* 12: 738-748.

------ (1998) 'Introduction: Language Ideology as a Field of Inquiry', in Bambi Schieffelin, Kathryn Woolard and Paul Kroskrity (eds) *Language Ideologies: Practice and Theory*, New York: Oxford University Press, 3-47.

------ and Bambi Schieffelin (1994) 'Language Ideology', *Annual Review of Anthropology* 23: 55-82.

2. Rethinking Linguistic Human Rights

Answering Questions of Identity, Essentialism and Mobility[1]

STEPHEN MAY

1. Introduction

The language ecology movement, and the linguistic human rights movement with which it is closely associated, have come under increasing criticism in recent years – both from within and without – for a number of key limitations (see, for example, Blommaert 2001; Brutt-Griffler 2002). The first is a tendency to present a 'preservationist' and 'romanticist' account of minority languages[2] and their loss. A second is to assume – in their less sophisticated manifestations, explicitly, and even in their most sophisticated forms, at least implicitly – an almost ineluctable connection between language and (ethnic) identity. In response, critics of language and ecology and linguistic human rights present two counter-claims. The first is what might best be described as 'resigned language realism' – that as much as we might not like the process of language shift and loss, there is little, if anything, we can do about it. Edwards (1984, 1985, 1994) perhaps best exemplifies this position. The second is a constructivist/postmodernist rejection of any intrinsic link, even any *significant* link, between language and identity; a position that, as we shall see, continues to be widely held within the sociology and anthropology of ethnicity and nationalism, as well as among a growing number of sociolinguists, linguistic anthropologists, and critical applied linguists (Rampton 1995; Silverstein 1998; Heller 1999; Norton 2000; Pennycook 2001).

---

[1] An earlier version of this paper was presented at the colloquium on 'Linguistic Rights and Wrongs' at the Sociolinguistic Symposium 14, Ghent, April 2002. My thanks to Donna Patrick and Jane Freeland for inviting me to contribute to such an important colloquium, and to Jan Blommaert and Monica Heller for our various lively and illuminating discussions around these issues.

[2] In what follows, I employ the usual distinction between so-called 'minority' and 'majority' languages in the linguistic human rights literature; a distinction that is based not on numerical size, but on clearly observable differences among language varieties in relation to power, status and entitlement. That said, such a distinction needs to be treated with some caution since the dichotomy inevitably understates the complex *situatedness* of particular language varieties with respect to power relations (Phillipson 1998; Pennycook 1998).

These two broad critiques of linguistic human rights are clearly compelling – the first, materially and politically (see also Blommaert this volume), and the second, intellectually. While I have also made these criticisms myself (May 2000), it is nonetheless my contention here that one can still mount a defence of minority language rights that addresses and remedies these concerns. To do so, however, requires a sociohistorical/sociopolitical rather than a biological/ecological analysis of language rights. Similarly, one has to account for the clear contingency of language and identity, while at the same time highlighting how and why language is nonetheless often a central factor in many ethnic/national conflicts in the world today. From this, one can also provide, in turn, a critique of the positions adopted by many language rights 'sceptics' themselves, particularly those that defend majoritarian forms of linguistic essentialism and those that sever the instrumental/identity aspects of language. But before we can even begin to mount such a defence, we need first to tackle directly the identified limitations inherent in the language ecology and linguistic human rights literature to date.

2. Language Ecology and Linguistic Human Rights

The language ecology and linguistic human rights movements have emerged primarily as a response to the exponential loss of the world's languages (for a useful overview, see Skutnabb-Kangas 2000). Language ecologists (see, for example, Harmon 1995; Mühlhäusler 1996; Maffi 2000; Nettle and Romaine 2000) argue that the loss or extinction of a language equates with the extinction of animal and plant species. In other words, issues of biodiversity are broadly comparable to issues of linguistic diversity. Consequently, as with ecological loss, the loss of a language is seen as diminishing the world in which we live in both the short and longer term.

In the short term, language loss results – clearly and simply – in a diminution of the linguistic gene pool. In the longer term, just as ecological destruction – such as deforestation of the Amazon – may not only affect those in the immediate vicinity, but have wider implications for all of us as a result of global climate change, so too might the current exponential loss of many of the world's languages actually be a prelude to wider linguistic catastrophe.

The parallels that are drawn by language ecologists between linguistic- and biodiversity have their merits, particularly in the clear resonances between the two processes. Thus, Steven Pinker observes that "the wide-scale extinction of languages [currently underway] is reminiscent of the current (though less severe) wide-scale extinction of plant or animal species" (1995: 259). Likewise, James Crawford argues that each "fall[s] victim to predators, changing environments, or more successful competitors", each is encroached upon by "modern cultures abetted by new technologies" and each is threatened by "destruction of lands and livelihoods; the spread of consumerism and other Western values…" (1994: 5).

But despite the usefulness of these parallels, there are significant limitations to language ecology arguments, not least because such arguments actually reinforce, albeit unwittingly, the inevitability of the evolutionary change that they are protesting about. This is because while biological/ecological metaphors are useful in highlighting the scale and seriousness of the potential loss of languages to the world, they also contribute, ironically, to the equanimity with which potential language loss on such a scale is usually greeted. In effect, such metaphors reinforce, by implication, a widely held view that language loss is an inevitable part of the cycle of social and linguistic *evolution*. Thus, one could view the loss or death of a language as simply a failure on its part, or that of its speakers, to compete adequately in the modern world where, of course, only the fittest languages can (and should) survive (Ladefoged 1992). Certainly, we do not need to look far to find this form of linguistic social Darwinism being propounded in support of these changes. It is widely articulated by majority language speakers – conveniently secure in their own linguistic and cultural heritage – but it is by no means limited to them. Many minority language speakers likewise see their social, cultural and economic advancement, or evolution, in the guise of a majority language.

As a result, what tends to be lost from sight are the wider political power relations which underlie language loss – or linguistic genocide, as Skutnabb-Kangas (2000) would have it – and the wider processes of social, cultural and political displacement of which it inevitably forms a part. Language loss is not only, perhaps not even primarily, a linguistic issue – it has much more to do with power, prejudice, (unequal) competition and, in many cases, overt discrimination and subordination. As Noam Chomsky asserts: "Questions of language are basically questions of power" (1979: 191). Thus, it should come as no surprise that the vast majority of today's threatened languages are spoken by socially and politically marginalized and/or subordinated groups. These groups have been variously estimated at between 5000 and 8000 (Stavenhagen 1992) and include within them the 250–300 million members of the world's indigenous peoples (Tully 1995; Davis 1999), perhaps the most marginalized of all people groups.

But even here, we could draw a further parallel between bio- and linguistic diversity, since those who are immediately affected by the destruction of biodiversity – for example, the various indigenous peoples of the Amazon area – are often the most socially, economically and politically marginalized of groups, and are thus the least able to defend themselves against such encroachment. So too with the destruction of linguistic diversity since, as Crawford (1994) notes, language death seldom occurs in communities of wealth and privilege, but rather to the dispossessed and disempowered. Moreover, linguistic dislocation for a particular community of speakers seldom, if ever, occurs in isolation from sociocultural and socioeconomic dislocation as well (Fishman 1995). The loss of a minority language almost always forms part of a wider process of social, cultural and political displacement. It is this further recognition of the power relations underlying language loss that is the principal feature of the linguistic human rights movement.

In response to ongoing patterns of language loss, linguistic human rights advocates argue that minority languages, and their speakers, should be accorded at least some of the protections and institutional support that majority languages already enjoy (see, for example, Kontra, *et al.* 1999; Skutnabb-Kangas and Phillipson 1995; Skutnabb-Kangas 1998, 2000, 2002). These arguments are also echoed in much of the academic legal discourse that has developed in recent years with respect to minority group rights (see Capotorti 1979; Thornberry 1991a, b; de Varennes 1996a, b). However, linguistic human rights arguments, at least as they have been constructed up until now, also have some serious limitations. One I have already addressed, albeit only by implication – is that the linguistic human rights movement tends towards too symbiotic a relationship with the language ecology movement. Since I have already canvassed my concerns with the language ecology movement, I will not pursue this point further here. What I do want to examine are two other key and recurring limitations of linguistic human rights arguments, along with potential responses to them:

1. Advocates of linguistic human rights tend still to assume unproblematically that language can be regarded as a principal indicator of group identity. This is a highly contentious (and contested) assumption, not only within sociolinguistics, but also particularly within the sociology and anthropology of ethnicity, where more constructivist and postmodernist accounts of identity hold sway.
2. In focusing so prominently on the link between language and identity, linguistic human rights advocates are often trumped by arguments about the greater utility/mobility offered by other languages. Yes, re-

taining one's original linguistic identity may be important, but when this is widely perceived to hold little or no instrumental value, advocating such a position seems not only naïve and futile, but actively counterproductive.

Issue 1: Language and identity

The first problem that needs to be addressed by advocates of linguistic human rights is the widespread consensus in social and political theory, and in some areas of sociolinguistics, that language is at most only a contingent factor of one's identity. In other words, language does not define us, and may not be an important feature, or indeed even a necessary one, in the construction of our identities, whether at the individual or collective levels. This view has been put forward in sociolinguistics by, among others, John Edwards (1985, 1994, 2001) and Carol Eastman (1984) who have argued that language is often only a secondary or surface characteristic of ethnicity (see also, Coulmas 1992; Bentahila and Davies 1993). The consequence of such a view is obvious – if language use is merely a surface feature of ethnic identity, adopting another language would only affect the language use aspect of our ethnic identity, not the identity itself. Thus, the loss of a particular language is not the 'end of the world' for a particular ethnic identity – the latter simply adapts to the new language. As Eastman asserts, "there is no need to worry about preserving ethnic identity, so long as the only change being made is in what language we use" (1984: 275).

These arguments are even more trenchantly promoted within the sociology of ethnicity and nationalism where the prevailing consensus over the last 30 years has been that ethnicity is a largely constructed identity. In other words, 'primordial' accounts of ethnicity which argue that ethnicity is determined by particular objective cultural characteristics such as language, ancestry and history – what Barth (1969) has described as the 'cultural stuff' of ethnicity – is rejected out of hand as reified and essentialist. In its place is posited a 'situational' view of ethnicity, which is defined not by the specific characteristics of a particular identity itself, but by the way those characteristics are employed to distinguish one identity from another. On this view, ethnicity is about social relationships rather than specific cultural properties since "we can assume no simple one-to-one relationship between ethnic units and cultural similarities or differences" (Barth 1969: 14). Cultural attributes – such as a particular language, for example – are not significant in themselves since any one of a range of cultural properties could be used to fill the 'organisational vessel' of a particular ethnicity (ibid.; see also Eriksen 1993).

Instead, it is the *perceived* usefulness of these cultural attributes in maintaining ethnic boundaries which is central. Cultural attributes only become significant as markers of ethnic identity when a group deems them to be *necessary*, or socially effective, for such purposes. Thus, particular cultural attributes may vary in salience, may be constructed or reconstructed, and may even be discarded by an ethnic group, depending on the particular sociohistorical circumstances of their interactions with other groups, and the need to maintain effectively the boundaries between them. It is these ethnic boundaries which determine in the end who is and who is not a member of a particular ethnic group, as well as designating which ethnic categories are available for individual identification at any given time and place (Nagel 1994). In short, shared culture in this model is best understood as generated in and by the processes of ethnic boundary maintenance rather than the other way around (Jenkins 1997).

This position also helps to explain why the particular attributes associated with an identity can change over time – as soon as the attribute in question is no longer seen as important in distinguishing the group from others, it may be changed or dropped. Language clearly falls within this category. Thus, Irish identity, while once distinguished by Irish Gaelic, is now distinguished primarily by a dialectal version of English (Edwards 1994; May 2001). Identity, in this conception, is dynamic and changing and, in the process, particular languages may come and go, depending on what is deemed necessary to maintain the wider identity in changing circumstances, and in relation to other groups.

In short, situational accounts of identity suggest there is nothing *intrinsic* to one's ethnic identity and thus specifically reject any significant or even any particular link between ethnicity and language. Of course, this position on ethnicity also accords broadly with the wider postmodernist rejection of *any* kind of monolithic identity – rather, all forms of identity are multiple, shifting, contingent, and invariably hybrid. On both counts, holding onto the idea of a link between a particular language and identity – as linguistic human rights advocates appear to do – seems not only irremediably passé, but unrealistic, since multiple identities, including multiple linguistic identities, are now the order of the day.

Issue 2: Language and mobility

And then there is a further issue that linguistic human rights advocates have to address or answer – the question of utility and/or mobility. Even if one were to argue successfully for the importance of the retention of a particular language on the grounds of its significance to one's identity, if the language is no longer regarded as 'useful' or even 'helpful', there seems little point in pursuing what looks inevitably like an already lost, and perhaps even actively counter-productive, linguistic cause.

Many critics of linguistic human rights repeatedly return to this point. Minority language advocates are criticized for consigning, or ghettoizing, minority language communities within the confines of a language that does not have a wider use, thus constraining their social mobility (see, for example, Schlesinger 1992; Barry 2000). Little wonder, they observe, that many within the linguistic minority itself choose to ignore the pleas of minority language activists and instead 'exit' the linguistic group by learning another (invariably, more dominant) language. It is one thing, after all, to proclaim the merits of retaining a particular language for identity purposes, quite another to have to live a life delimited by it – foreclosing the opportunity for mobility in the process.

We can broadly summarize the logic of this argument as follows:

- Majority languages are lauded for their 'instrumental' value, while minority languages are accorded 'sentimental' value, but are broadly constructed as obstacles to social mobility and progress
- Learning a majority language will thus provide individuals with greater economic and social mobility
- Learning a minority language, while (possibly) important for reasons of cultural continuity, delimits an individual's mobility; in its strongest terms, this might amount to actual 'ghettoization'
- If minority language speakers are 'sensible' they will opt for mobility and modernity via the majority language
- Whatever decision is made, the choice between opting for a majority or minority language is constructed as oppositional, even mutually exclusive

Whether we like it or not, it seems that majority languages are those (and only those) that are the most *instrumentally* useful. Simply put, we can accomplish a lot more in and by a majority language. This is a difficult argument to refute and may well explain why the social justice arguments underlying linguistic human rights, which are hard to fault, at least in my view, seem to be simply ignored in the Realpolitik of language shift and loss. After all, democratic and justice sentiments are all very well, but they are not necessarily going to increase one's standard of living, or provide a useful, upwardly mobile education for one's children. Indeed, opponents of minority language rights have gone so far as to argue that to opt for an education in a minority language in the face of this critique is a sign of irresponsible parenthood, even a form of 'child abuse'. This is perhaps best exemplified in a 1995 court case in Amarillo, Texas where a judge ordered a mother not to speak Spanish to her child at home on these very grounds:

> If she starts [school] with the other children and cannot even speak the language that the teachers and others speak, and she's a full-blooded American citizen, you're abusing that child ... Now get this straight: you start speaking English to that child, because if she doesn't do good in school, then I can remove her because it's not in her best interests to be ignorant. (cited in de Varennes 1996a: 165-166)

However much one might disagree with these sentiments – and certainly, the only ignorance demonstrated here appears to be the judge's – such views remain widely held. The US English Only Movement, for example, likewise argues that English is essential for social mobility in US society, or rather, a lack of English is seen to *consign* one inevitably to the social and economic margins. As Linda Chávez, a former President of US English, has argued: "Hispanics who learn English will be able to avail themselves of opportunities. Those who do not will be relegated to second class citizenship" (cited in Crawford 1992: 172). Guy Wright, a prominent media supporter of English Only policies, takes a similar line in a 1983 editorial in the *San Francisco Examiner*, asserting that "the individual who fails to learn English is condemned to semi-citizenship, condemned to low pay, condemned to remain in the ghetto" (cited in Secada and Lightfoot 1993: 47). A more recent example can be found in US English advertising in 1998: "Deprive a child of an education. Handicap a young life outside the classroom. Restrict social mobility. If it came at the hand of a parent it would be called child abuse. At the hand of our schools … it's called 'bilingual education'" (see Dicker 2000: 53).

This position is also broadly endorsed by significant academic commentators. Thus, Thomas Pogge, a prominent US political theorist, could argue recently that minority parents who opted for an education for their children in a minority language may be "perpetuating a cultural community irrespective of whether this benefits the children concerned…" (Pogge 2003: 118). In other words, it is illiberal and injurious for parents to 'consign' their children to a minority language education. Two other political theorists, David Laitin and Rob Reich, have also argued that "individuals have no influence over the language of their parents, yet their parents' language if it is a minority one … constrains social mobility". As a result, "those who speak a minority (or dominated) language are more likely to stand *permanently* on the lower-rungs of the socio-economic ladder" (Laitin and Reich 2003: 92; my emphasis). Indeed, they proceed to observe that if minority individuals are foolish enough to perpetuate the speaking of a minority language, then they can simply be regarded as 'happy slaves', having no one else to blame but themselves for their subsequent limited social mobility.

In the light of these trenchant (not to mention, paternalistic) attitudes, in both political and academic commentary, it is perhaps not surprising that arguments for linguistic human rights appear to be making so little headway. Certainly, both of these two key challenges, just outlined, are considerable and continue to delimit and undermine the effectiveness of linguistic human rights. How might one respond to each of these challenges – indeed, given the apparent strengths of these critiques, should we even bother? I think we should, for the following reasons.

Response 1: Identity and essentialism

With respect to the charges of essentialism levelled against linguistic human rights, one first needs to acknowledge that situational accounts of ethnicity are broadly right. Language clearly *is* a contingent marker of ethnic identity and adopting any other position involves, inevitably, an essentialized and reified view of the language-identity link (see May 2001 for an extended discussion here). Where one might beg to differ, however, is in refusing to take the next step that is often then taken by constructivists. That is, to assume that if language is merely a contingent factor of identity it cannot therefore (ever) be a *significant* or *constitutive* factor of identity. In other words, contingency is elided with unimportance or peripheralism – an additional move that is neither necessary nor warranted.

Indeed, this position is extremely problematic, not least because it simply does not reflect adequately, let alone explain, the heightened saliency of language issues in many historical and contemporary political conflicts, particularly at the intrastate level (see Weinstein 1983, 1990; Blommaert 1996, 1999; May 2001). In these conflicts, particular languages clearly *are* for many people an important and constitutive factor of their individual, and at times, collective identities. In theory then, language may well be just one of many markers of identity. In practice, it is often much more than that. Indeed, this should not surprise us since the link between language and identity encompasses both significant cultural and political dimensions.

The cultural dimension is demonstrated by the fact that one's individual and social identities, and their complex interconnections, are inevitably mediated in and through particular languages. The political dimension is significant to the extent that those languages come to be formally (and informally) associated with particular ethnic and national identities. These interconnections also help to explain why, as Fishman (1997) argues, a 'detached' scientific view of the link between language and identity may fail to capture the degree to which language is *experienced* as vital by those who speak it. It may also significantly understate the role that language plays in social organization and mobilization. The "shibboleth of language", as Toynbee (1953) coined it, still holds much sway.

Another way to explain these apparent contradictions is actually to rethink the whole primordial/situational dichotomy of ethnicity, discussed above. There is an increasing consensus among writers on ethnicity that this dichotomy is in the end unhelpful and unnecessary and that one can, and should, combine elements of the two (see May 2001 for an extended discussion; see also Jenkins 1997; Fenton 1999). Adopting this more dynamic, dialectical position on ethnicity helps to explain, on the one hand, why the cultural and linguistic characteristics of ethnic groups may not (indeed, almost certainly do not) define or delimit such groups, and yet on the other hand they also often continue to hold considerable purchase for their members. Bourdieu's notion of 'habitus' perhaps best captures this dual emphasis since 'habitus' refers to a set of embodied meanings that do not determine how individuals and groups might act, but nonetheless constitutes a powerful frame of reference, which influences and shapes, at least to some degree, how we see the world (see Bourdieu 1984, 1990a, 1990b; Bourdieu and Passeron 1990; Bourdieu and Wacquant 1992). In particular, the four key dimensions of habitus highlighted in Bourdieu's work – embodiment, agency, the interplay between past and present, and the interrelationship between collective and individual trajectories – provide us with a useful means of examining both the continuing purchase *and* malleability of ethnicity, and the particular languages associated with them, at any given time and place. I discuss these four dimensions extensively elsewhere (see May 1999a, 2001) but let me, by way of example, briefly elaborate here on the first – embodiment.

For Bourdieu, habitus is not simply about ideology, attitude or perception, it is a set of *embodied* dispositions – or ways of viewing, and living in the world. This set of dispositions – what Bourdieu would call 'bodily hexis' – operates most often at the level of the unconscious and the mundane and, in the case of ethnicity, often involves language use. Indeed, linguistic habitus, in Bourdieu's (1991) terms, is a sub-set of the dispositions which comprise the habitus: it is that set of dispositions acquired in the course of learning to speak in particular social and cultural contexts.

The key point for Bourdieu is that ethnic attitudes and practices, including language use, are usually lived out implicitly as a result of historical and customary practice. As such, they may provide the parameters of social action for many. However, they are also never limited to those parameters, and may change over time, both internally, as a result of their ongoing use, and externally in relation to wider economic, social and political influences. This helps to explain why languages that have been traditionally associated with a particular ethnicity can continue to hold such importance for particular ethnic identities. However, it can also explain why such languages can equally come to be replaced over time with other languages. Bourdieu's construction of habitus here – along with his allied discussions of linguistic markets – also usefully allows one to explore the wider social and cultural forces that invariably underpin these processes of language maintenance and/or language shift (see May, 2001: chapter 4 for an extended discussion).

Adopting this approach also allows us to critique the closed, static position so often advocated by opponents of minority rights towards the position(ing) of majority languages within nation-states, along with their interactions with other languages. This is most clearly seen in arguments for, on the one hand, the supposedly greater linguistic – and, by extension, social and political – efficacy of majority languages, and, on the other hand, their supposed vulnerability to the encroachment of minority languages (see, for example, Schlesinger 1992; Barry 2000). What we see here, in effect, is exactly the thinking that minority language rights' advocates are supposedly being criticized for – a conception of language (in this case, the majoritarian language of the state) as pre-given, closed, unchanging – unable to deal with interaction and engagement with other languages in an ongoing, dialogic manner. Why shouldn't the public language of the state not be open to change in the same way as all languages? Or, to put it another way, why should cultural and linguistic change and adaptation always be unidirectional – *from* a minority language/culture *to* a majority one? The short answer is it needn't and, for reasons that will soon become apparent, to suggest otherwise is both inconsistent and unjust.

Response 2: Language, mobility and multiplicity

And this brings me to the second response – addressing and answering the question of language and mobility. What I want to suggest here is that the presumptions and assumptions that equate linguistic mobility *solely* with majority languages are themselves extremely problematic.

For a start, this position separates the instrumental and identity aspects of language. On this view, minority languages may be important for identity but have no instrumental value, while majority languages are construed as primarily instrumental with little or no identity value. We see this in the allied notions of majority languages as 'vehicles' of modernity, and minority languages as (merely) 'carriers' of identity. Or so the story goes. This is simply wrong (and wrongheaded) since it is clear that *all* language(s) embody and accomplish both identity and instrumental functions for those who speak them. Where particular languages – especially majority/minority languages – differ is in the *degree* to which they can accomplish each of these functions, and this in turn is dependent on the social and political (not linguistic) constraints within which they operate (Carens 2000). Thus, in the case of minority languages, their instrumental value is often constrained by wider social and political processes that have resulted in the privileging of other language varieties in the public realm. Meanwhile, for majority languages, the identity characteristics of the language *are* clearly important for their speakers, but often become subsumed within and normalized by the instrumental functions that these languages fulfil. This is particularly apparent with respect to monolingual speakers of English, given the position of English as the current world language.

On this basis, we can argue that the limited instrumentality of particular minority languages at any given time need not always remain so. Indeed, if the minority position of a language is the specific product of wider historical and contemporary social and political relationships, changing these wider relationships positively with respect to a minority language should bring about both enhanced instrumentality for the language in question, and increased mobility for its speakers. We can see this occurring in Wales and Catalunya, with the emergence of these formerly subjugated languages into the public domain (May 2000, 2002).

In the case of Wales, for example, the (1993) *Welsh Language Act* (*Mesur yr Iaith Gymraeg*) treated Welsh for the first time as having 'a basis of equality' with English within Wales, although it qualifies this equality as being that which is appropriate within the circumstances and 'reasonably practicable'. To this end, the Act provides for the right to use Welsh in courts, given suitable notice, and also states that public documents in Welsh should carry the same legal weight as those in English. However, perhaps its most significant feature is the *statutory* recognition provided to *Bwrdd yr Iaith Gymraeg* (the Welsh Language Board). Under the Act's aegis, the *Bwrdd yr Iaith* is authorized not only to promote and facilitate the use of the Welsh language but also to ensure its adoption within the public sector. The latter is to be achieved via formal language schemes provided by public organizations to the Board. These schemes are to specify the measures each organization aims to take in order to provide *effective* bilingual public services in Wales. Again, there is the caveat invoked that such bilingual services will be provided "so far as is both appropriate in the circumstances and reasonably practical". However, as the subsequent Draft Guidelines for implementation of the Act outline, it is *Bwrdd yr Iaith*, crucially, not the organizations, which determines the parameters of reasonableness and practicality: "It will not be acceptable for those preparing schemes to adopt a highly subjective and restricted view of what is appropriate in their circumstances or reasonably practicable" (Welsh Language Board 1995: 6). Likewise, the Draft Guidelines stipulate that organizations should not rely on the *current* demand for services in Welsh as a basis for their schemes, on the premise that once more effective bilingual services become available so too will demand increase:

> It is acknowledged that, in the past, many Welsh speakers turned to English in dealing with public organizations because they were not certain what services were available in Welsh. Some were also concerned that using Welsh could lead to delay or a lower standard of service. Therefore, *whatever their experience to date*, organizations should plan for an increase in demand and respond accordingly. (1995: 5; my emphasis)

The end result envisaged for each organization is that public service provision through Welsh should be a natural, integral part of the planning and delivery of that service – that is, that Welsh can be as *instrumentally* useful for accessing all public services in Wales, as English.

Providing Welsh-speakers with the choice of using Welsh as a public as well as private language also usefully highlights for majority language speakers (English speakers in the Welsh context) the combined identity/instrumental dimensions of *all* languages. If majority language speakers are made to realise that their own languages fulfil important identity functions for them, both as individuals and as a group, they may in turn be slightly more reluctant to require minority language speakers to dispense with theirs. Or to put it another way, if majority languages do provide their speakers with particular and often significant individual and collective forms of linguistic identity, as they clearly do, it seems unjust to deny these same benefits, out of court, to minority language speakers.

In adopting this broad position, one can also address another issue often raised as a critique of linguistic human rights – the formal acknowledgement of multiple linguistic identities – that is, that it is somehow problematic and/or burdensome to operate publicly (and even privately) in more than one language. Dismantling the identity-instrumental opposition between minority and majority languages, which is clearly a major feature of the critique of the retention of minority languages, immediately brings into question the idea of incommensurate linguistic identities on which it is based. In other words, the distinctions often made by opponents of linguistic human rights with respect to majority and minority languages are themselves predicated on a singular, exclusive and oppositional notion of linguistic identity – we must have one linguistic identity *or* the other, we cannot have both.

In contrast, one can and should argue for the ongoing opportunity or potential for holding multiple, *complementary* cultural and linguistic identities at both individual and collective levels. On this view, maintaining one's minority ethnically affiliated language – or one's national majority language, for that matter – avoids 'freezing' the development of particular languages in the roles that they have historically, or perhaps still currently, occupy.[3] Equally importantly, it questions and discards the requirement of a singular and/or replacement approach to the issue of other linguistic identities.

Linguistic identities – and social and cultural identities more broadly – need not be constructed as irredeemably oppositional. Narrower linguistic identities do not necessarily need to be traded in for broader ones – one can clearly remain both Spanish-speaking and American, Catalan-speaking and Spanish, or Welsh-speaking and British. The same process applies to national and international language identities, where these differ. To insist otherwise betrays both a reductionist and an essentialist approach to language and identity – something, ironically, which critics of linguistic human rights are supposedly so centrally concerned to repudiate.

4. Conclusion

To conclude, I want to suggest that linguistic human rights still has some merit and mileage in it. Certainly, there is no reason why linguistic human rights cannot develop a position that effectively acknowledges and addresses the concerns raised by its many opponents. That said, the real challenge for linguistic human rights is the same as it has always been – to

---

[3] For example, Welsh was historically regarded as the language of 'the chapel' – indeed, this is primarily what kept the language alive over time – but this is diminishing rapidly now, as a result of the church's own diminishing influence in Wales. Likewise, while Welsh was excluded for over four centuries as a language of the state and government, it is clearly in the process now of being reinstantiated in the public domain, as my earlier discussion makes clear.

influence, and if possible change the wider social, cultural and political processes that have seen the construction of, and distinction between, so called minority and majority languages in the first place.

This clearly remains a formidable task – and it must be acknowledged that it may indeed be an impossible one. After all, the social and political forces arraigned against minority languages, and in favour of the ongoing process of linguistic social Darwinism, remain both firmly in place and considerable.

But if one can hold onto the fact that the linguistic human rights movement has so usefully highlighted – that processes of linguistic change are often, if not always, the result of wider social and political processes – then this provides a useful basis from which to mount an effective political challenge. From this, one can also question and critique the apparently ineluctable link between majority languages, mobility and 'progress', and in turn look to ways in which minority languages may be reconstituted not simply as 'carriers' of identity but also as instrumentally useful.[4]

If linguistic human rights can accomplish this, there just might be a chance, however slim, of changing the current parlous circumstances of at least some minority languages, along with those of their speakers, for the better. For all the complexities and difficulties attendant upon such a task, this still seems like a goal worth fighting for.

---

[4] Establishing this increased instrumentality for minority languages does not necessarily require their full re-integration into the public domain, as in the case of Wales (or Catalunya, or Quebec), There is clearly a continua of use here, depending on the status and reach of particular minority languages, along with the number of speakers. Education is one alternative – or, more accurately, allied – arena where the linguistic instrumentality of minority languages can be re-established. Many community-based indigenous language education initiatives, for example, often involve small-scale, local community-based initiatives (see McCarty and Zepeda 1995; May 1999; May and Aikman 2003). Even here though, there can be considerable differences of scale and influence, depending on the wider political context. In Aotearoa/New Zealand, Finnmark in Norway, and Nunavut in Canada, for example, there are significant indigenous education initiatives that have been recognized at national or regional level (see May 2001: Ch. 8, and Patrick, this volume).

References

Barry, B. (2000) *Culture and Equality: An Egalitarian Critique of Multiculturalism*, Cambridge MA: Harvard University Press.

Barth, F. (1969) 'Introduction', *Ethnic Groups and Boundaries: The Social Organization of Culture Difference*, Boston, MA: Little Brown & Co, 9-38.

Bentahila, A. and E. Davies (1993) 'Language Revival: Restoration or Transformation?', *Journal of Multilingual and Multicultural Development* 14: 355-374.

Blommaert, Jan (1996) 'Language and Nationalism: Comparing Flanders and Tanzania', *Nations and Nationalism* 2: 235-256.

------ (ed) (1999) *Language Ideological Debates*, Berlin/New York: Mouton de Gruyter.

------ (2001) 'The Asmara Declaration as a Sociolinguistic Problem: Notes in Scholarship and Linguistic Rights', *Journal of Sociolinguistics* 5(1): 131-142.

Bourdieu, Pierre (1984) *Distinction: A Social Critique of the Judgement of Taste*, Cambridge, MA: Harvard University Press.

------ (1990a) *In Other Words: Essays towards a Reflexive Sociology*, Cambridge: Polity Press.

------ (1990b) *The Logic of Practice*, Cambridge: Polity Press.

------ (1991) *Language and Symbolic Power*, Cambridge: Polity Press.

------ and J-C. Passeron (1990) *Reproduction in Education, Society and Culture*, (2nd ed.), London: Sage.

Bourdieu, Pierre and L. Wacquant (1992) *An Invitation to Reflexive Sociology*, Chicago, IL: Chicago University Press.

Brutt-Griffler, J. (2002) 'Class, Ethnicity and Language Rights: An Analysis of British Colonial Policy in Lesotho and Sri Lanka and Some Implications for Language Policy', *Journal of Language, Identity and Education* 1(3): 207-234.

Capotorti, F. (1979) *Study on the Rights of Persons Belonging to Ethnic, Religious and Linguistic Minorities*, New York: United Nations.

Carens, J. (2000) *Culture, Citizenship and Community: A Contextual Exploration of Justice as Evenhandedness*, Oxford: Oxford University Press.

Chomsky, Noam (1979) *Language and Responsibility*, London: Harvester.

Coulmas, Florian (1992) *Language and Economy*, Oxford: Blackwell.

Crawford, J. (ed) (1992) *Language Loyalties: A Source Book on the Official English Controversy*, Chicago, IL: University of Chicago Press.

------ (1994) 'Endangered Native American Languages: What Is To Be Done and Why?', *Journal of Navajo Education* 11(3): 3-11.

Davis, W. (1999) 'Vanishing Cultures', *National Geographic* (August 1999), 62-89.

de Varennes, Ferdinand (1996a) *Language, Minorities and Human Rights*, The Hague: Kluwer Law International.

------ (1996b) 'Minority Aspirations and the Revival of Indigenous Peoples', *International Review of Education* 42: 309-325.

Dicker, S. (2000) 'Official English and Bilingual Education: The Controversy over Language Pluralism in U.S. Society', in J. Kelly Hall and W. Eggington (eds) *The Sociopolitics of English Language Teaching*, Clevedon, England: Multilingual Matters, 45-66.

Eastman, Carol (1984) 'Language, Ethnic Identity and Change', in John Edwards (ed) *Linguistic Minorities, Policies and Pluralism*, London: Academic Press, 259-276.

Edwards, John (1984) 'Language, Diversity and Identity', in J. J. Edwards (ed) *Linguistic Minorities, Policies and Pluralism*, London: Academic Press, 277-310.

------ (1985) *Language, Society and Identity*, Oxford: Basil Blackwell.

------ (1994) *Multilingualism*, London: Routledge.

------ (2001) 'The Ecology of Language Revival', *Current Issues in Language Planning* 2: 231-241.

Eriksen, T. (1993) *Ethnicity and Nationalism: Anthropological Perspectives*, London: Pluto Press.

Fenton, S. (1999) *Ethnicity: Racism, Class and Culture*, London: Macmillan.

Fishman, J. (1995) 'Good Conferences in a Wicked World: On Some Worrisome Problems in the Study of Language Maintenance and Language Shift', in W. Fase, K. Jaspaert, and S. Kroon (eds) *The State of Minority Languages: International Perspectives on Survival and Decline*, Lisse, Netherlands: Swets & Zeitlinger.

------ (1997) 'Language and Ethnicity: The View from Within', in F. Coulmas (ed) *The Handbook of Sociolinguistics*, London: Blackwell, 327-343.

Harmon, D. (1995) 'The Status of the World's Languages as Reported in the *Ethnologue*', *Southwest Journal of Linguistics* 14: 1-28.

Heller, M. (1999) *Linguistic Minorities and Modernity: A Sociolinguistic Ethnography*, London: Longman.

Jenkins, R. (1997) *Rethinking Ethnicity: Arguments and Explorations*, London: Sage.

Kontra, M., T. Skutnabb-Kangas, R. Phillipson and T. Várady (eds) (1999) *Language: A Right and a Resource. Approaches to Linguistic Human Rights*, Budapest: Central European University Press.

Ladefoged, P. (1992) 'Another View of Endangered Languages', *Language* 68: 809-811.

Laitin, D. and R. Reich (2003) 'A Liberal Democratic Approach to Language Justice', in W. Kymlicka and A. Patten (eds) *Language Rights and Political Theory*, Oxford: Oxford University Press.

Maffi, L. (ed) (2000) *Language, Knowledge and the Environment: The Interdependence of Biological and Cultural Diversity*, Washington D.C.: Smithsonian Institute Press.

May, Stephen (1999a) 'Critical Multiculturalism and Cultural Difference: Avoiding Essentialism', in S. May (ed) *Critical Multiculturalism: Rethinking Multi-cultural and Antiracist Education*, London & New York: Routledge Falmer, 11-41.

------ (ed) (1999b) *Indigenous Community-based Education*, Clevedon, England: Multilingual Matters.

------ (2000) 'Uncommon Languages: The Challenges and Possibilities of Minority Language Rights', *Journal of Multilingual and Multicultural Development* 21(5): 366-385.

------ (2001) *Language and Minority Rights: Ethnicity, Nationalism and the Politics of Language*, London: Longman.

------ (2002) 'Developing Greater Ethnolinguistic Democracy in Europe: Minority Language Policies, Nation-states, and the Question of Tolerability', *Sociolinguistica* 16: 1-13.

------ (2003) 'Misconceiving Minority Language Rights: Implications for Liberal Political Theory', in W. Kymlicka and A Patten (eds) *Language Rights and Political Theory*, Oxford: Oxford University Press, 123-152.

------ and S. Aikman (2003) 'Indigenous Education: New Possibilities, Ongoing Restraints', Special Issue, *Comparative Education* 39: 2.

McCarty, T. and O. Zepeda (eds) (1995) Special Issue: Indigenous Language Education and Literacy, *Bilingual Research Journal* 19 (1).

Mühlhäusler, P. (1996) *Linguistic Ecology: Language Change and Linguistic Imperialism in the Pacific Region*, London: Routledge.

Nagel, J. (1994) 'Constructing Ethnicity: Creating and Recreating Ethnic Identity and Culture', *Social Problems* 41: 152-176.

Nettle, D. and S. Romaine (2000) *Vanishing Voices: The Extinction of the World's Languages*, Oxford: Oxford University Press.

Norton, B. (2000) *Identity and Language Learning: Gender, Ethnicity and Educational Change*, London: Longman.

Pennycook, Alistair (1998) 'The Right to Language: Towards a Situated Ethics of Language Possibilities', *Language Sciences* 20: 73-87.

------ (2001) *Critical Applied Linguistics*, Mahwah, NJ: Lawrence Erlbaum.

Phillipson, Robert (1998) 'Globalizing English: Are Linguistic Human Rights an Alternative to Linguistic Imperialism?', *Language Sciences* 20: 101-112.

Pinker, Stephen (1995) *The Language Instinct*, London: Penguin.

Pogge, T. (2003) 'Accommodation Rights for Hispanics in the US', in W. Kymlicka and A. Patten (eds) *Language Rights and Political Theory*, Oxford: Oxford University Press.

Rampton, Ben (1995) *Crossing: Language and Ethnicity among Adolescents*, London: Longman.

Secada, W. and T. Lightfoot (1993) 'Symbols and the Political Context of Bilingual Education in the United States', in M. Arias and U. Casanova (eds) *Bilingual Education: Politics, Practice, and Research*, Chicago: The National Society for the Study of Education/University of Chicago Press, 36-64.

Schlesinger, A. (1992) *The Disuniting of America: Reflections on a Multicultural Society*, New York: W.W. Norton & Co.

Silverstein, Michael (1998) 'Contemporary Transformations of Local Linguistic Communities', *Annual Review of Anthropology* 27: 401-426.

Skutnabb-Kangas, Tove (1998) 'Human Rights and Language Wrongs – A Future for Diversity?', *Language Sciences* 20: 5-27.

------ (2000) *Linguistic Genocide in Education – or Worldwide Diversity and Human Rights?*, Mahwah, NJ: Lawrence Erlbaum.

------ (2002) 'Marvellous Human Rights Rhetoric and Grim Realities: Language Rights in Education', *Journal of Language, Identity and Education* 1(3): 179-206.

------ and Robert Phillipson (1995) 'Linguistic Human Rights, Past and Present', in Tove Skutnabb-Kangas and R. Phillipson (eds) *Linguistic Human Rights: Overcoming Linguistic Discrimination*, Berlin: Mouton de Gruyter, 71-110.

Stavenhagen, R. (1992) 'Universal Human Rights and the Cultures of Indigenous Peoples and Other Ethnic Groups: The Critical Frontier of the 1990s', in A. Eide and B. Hagtvet (eds) *Human Rights in Perspective*, Oxford: Blackwell, 135-151.

Thornberry, P. (1991a) *International Law and the Rights of Minorities*, Oxford: Clarendon Press.

------ (1991b) *Minorities and Human Rights Law*. London: Minority Rights Group.

Toynbee, A. (1953) *A Study of History* (Vols. VII-IX), London: Oxford University Press.

Tully, J. (1995) *Strange Multiplicity: Constitutionalism in an Age of Diversity*, Cambridge: Cambridge University Press.

Weinstein, B. (1983) *The Civic Tongue: Political Consequences of Language Choices*, New York: Longman.

------ (1990) *Language Policy and Political Development*, Norwood, NJ: Ablex.

Welsh Language Board (1995) *Draft Guidelines as to the Form and Content of Schemes*, Cardiff: Welsh Language Board.

3. Rights in Places

Comments on Linguistic Rights and Wrongs

JAN BLOMMAERT

Introduction

Commenting on issues such as linguistic rights involves one in rather classic moral dilemmas, dilemmas that often characterize the work of socially committed scientists: we believe we know what is right, but what is right does not work in practice, either because it is just not the way in which reality works, or because the people don't believe it is right.[1] In the case of linguistic rights we face a situation in which on the one hand, there are hardly any arguments *against* linguistic human rights, except for the brutal fact that a practical approach based on this rights paradigm either does not work or even backfires. The world does not fit the linguistic rights paradigm. And now we can do two things: either insist on the correctness of our thesis, or try to understand the reasons why it does not work. I opt for the second tactic.

What I want to do in these comments is to dwell at some length on a motif which is very often only implicitly articulated in some discourses on minorities and linguistic rights: space/place. This motif has recently drawn the attention of some linguistic anthropologists, either in a more or less established sense of investigating the cultural and linguistic expressions of spatial relations through deixis and gestures (Hanks 1990; Haviland 1998; De Leon 1998; Kataoka 1998; Bickel 2001), a more recent concern of the semiotization of space as 'place' in identity and history narratives (Johnstone 1990, 1999; Collins 1998; Feld and Basso 1996) or even more recent as symbolic domains in which globalization processes and concerns can be identified, often in contexts of research that have a pedigree in Ulf Hannerz's urban anthropology (Hannerz 1996; Low 2001). Central to the arguments offered in much of this recent work is the observation that the production and reception of meaningful semiotic behaviour is

---

[1]I had the opportunity to discuss this paper during the colloquium on Linguistic rights and wrongs at the Sociolinguistics Symposium 14, Ghent, April 2002. I am grateful to the audience and the other panelists for comments and suggestions. A particular debt is due to the convenors Jane Freeland and Donna Patrick, as well as to Stephen May, Ben Rampton, Salikoko Mufwene and Alastair Pennycook, with whom I was able to discuss central issues from this paper at length.

deeply anchored in spatial relations and processes that serve both as a source of meaning or as a target of meaning.[2] To quote Barbara Johnstone (1999: 517): "people continue to ground aspects of their identities, in a variety of ways, in actual places".

I intend to argue that there are good reasons to stretch the field a bit so as to include popular linguistic ideologies and specific metadiscourses on language such as linguistic and sociolinguistic discourse (cf. Blommaert 1996; see also Silverstein 1998). There is, on the one hand, a lot of evidence pointing to ways in which people associate languages with places – think about language-as-property metaphors, dialect accents and so forth (Johnstone 1999) – as well as to ways in which language as an index of geographical origin structures social categorization, discrimination and so forth (Gumperz's work offers numerous examples of this, e.g. Gumperz and Roberts 1991). Similarly, Silverstein (1998: 403-4) argues that local linguistic communities produce (and *need* to produce) a sense of boundedness and an orientation to a centre, what one could call an ideology of *chez nous*. In what follows I will argue that this idea of boundedness and centring is also a feature of sociolinguistic discourse, in particular of the linguistic rights paradigm.

***

One of the striking features of the literature on linguistic rights is the way in which authors appear to assume the spatial 'fixedness' of people, languages and places. The discourse of minority rights is in general a discourse of locality, and the first lines of the UN Declaration on the Rights of Persons Belonging to National or Ethnic, Religious and Linguistic Minorities read: "States shall protect the existence and the national or ethnic, cultural, religious and linguistic minorities *within their respective territories*, and shall encourage conditions for the promotion of that identity" (quoted in Skutnabb-Kangas and Phillipson 1999). This Declaration is an agreement between states, which are here presented as territorially bounded entities in the space of which a particular regime can and should be developed with respect to 'minorities', defined in the same move as minorities within that particular ('state') territory. The rights granted by this Declaration are territorially bounded and organized rights, and distinctions

[2] The notion of 'cultural geography' developed by Denis Cosgrove (Cosgrove 1984; Cosgrove and Daniels 1988) offers interesting similarities. Landscapes are seen as symbolically meaningful forms in their own right – a symbolic, historical resource for communities which can be rendered meaningful in a wide variety of practices, including discursive ones.

between groups evolve along the classic Herderian triad of territory-culture-language (Blommaert and Verschueren 1992, 1998).[3]

This discourse of locality is usually couched in environmental-ecological metaphors: a particular place is characterized by specific features ranging from climate through biodiversity to people, cultures and languages. The relationship between these different components is seen as a form of synergy: it is through human variability that diversity in the environment is sustained, for the languages and cultures of local people provide unique views on this environment and help sustain it. See, for example, the point of view articulated by one of the most vocal advocates of linguistic rights, *Terralingua* (1999, from their website):

> We know that a diversity of species lends stability and resilience to the world's ecosystems. Terralingua thinks that a diversity of languages does the same for the world's cultures – and that these manifestations of the diversity of life are interrelated.

This diversity is invariably seen as something that needs to be preserved, consequently. It literally needs to be 'kept in place'. To go by the words of Skutnabb-Kangas and Phillipson (1995: 84): "[t]he perpetuation of linguistic diversity can (...) be seen as a recognition that all individuals and groups have basic human rights, and as a necessity for the survival of the planet, in a similar way to biodiversity" (see also Skutnabb-Kangas and Phillipson 1999; Nettle and Romaine 2000; see Mufwene 2002 and Blommaert 2001 for a critique).

There is a linguistic-ideological dimension to this, in which it is assumed that language functions in a community because it provides *local* meanings: meanings that provide frames for understanding the local environment, to categorize and analyse the (strictly) local world. References to the unique worldviews enshrined in these languages often revolve around local functionality as well: the worldviews are expressed in terms and

---

[3] This territorial boundedness is often overlooked in discussions of Herderianism, as it is in definitions of minorities. Yet, the labels given to minorities often contain crucial spatial qualifiers, raising and indexing their problematic relation in and towards a majority-controlled space. Think, for example, of *Aboriginal* or *indigenous* peoples, *Native* Americans, migrants or even *proto-nations*, i.e. ethnonational groups who do not control a territory of their own: 'nations without states' (Guibernau 1999). Note how in the same move the state is reduced to a controlled territory separate from others. May (2001) and Heller (1999) provide useful discussions on these topics. Jaffe (1999) is an excellent example of the problems of control over geographical, symbolic, and discursive-linguistic spaces.

grammatical relations that address or articulate local decodings of the world. Let us return to Skutnabb-Kangas and Phillipson 1995: 89):

> Linguistic diversity at local levels is a necessary counterweight to the hegemony of a few 'international' languages. The 'World Languages' should, just as roads and bridges, be seen as tools for communication of ideas and matter, but the creation of authentic ideas and products (instead of mass-products) is in most cases necessarily best done locally.

The worldviews are invariably local worldviews, or to use a more fashionable term, territorialized worldviews, that are linked to particular regional surroundings. A people's language localizes these people, it sets them within a particular, spatially demarcated ecology.[4]

It is this view of local functionality that underpins the strong claims, cited above, that the survival of minority languages is crucial for the survival of the planet, for with every language that disappears a uniquely functional local set of meanings about the environment is lost. Languages are seen as local repositories of knowledge, and such local knowledges are essential for understanding the (local) world. Consequently, when people are moved into a different environment, the language may lose (part of) its functions (see e.g. Whaley, this volume). Conversely, when another language is introduced into a particular environment, it may as well be dysfunctional for it does not articulate the particular local meanings required for the sustenance of this environment. This idea in turn underpins the idea of linguistic imperialism, invariably conceived as a non-local language (usually the ex-colonial language, and usually English) penetrating or invading local spaces and disturbing the ecological balance that existed between people, their language and culture, and their environment (Skutnabb-Kangas 2000; Skutnabb-Kangas and Phillipson 1995, 1999 and Heugh 1999 provide examples).

In sum, what we see here is how language functions are territorialized, tied to particular local environments. Language apparently works excellently in its own, original place, and it loses functions as soon as the stable, original, 'autochthonous' (or 'native', 'aboriginal') link between language

---

[4] Silverstein (2000) provides an insightful discussion of the particular versions of Whorfianism that underpin ethnolinguistic nationalisms. Silverstein's work testifies both to the resurgence of linguistic relativity in recent years (e.g. Gumperz and Levinson 1996) as well as to the enormous distance between mature and sophisticated readings of Whorf's work and vulgarized versions of it, the latter often serving as rhetorical or conceptual strategies in ethnolinguistic nationalisms.

and place is broken. Consequently, a programme aimed at stimulating or promoting these local languages (invariably mother tongues of apparently inherently monolingual and monocultural people) ties the speakers of these languages to a place and reinforces the presumed fixed connection between people and their environment.

***

All of this sounds more or less acceptable, at least when some aspects of reality are conveniently overlooked. A rather disturbing aspect of reality, and one that has attracted the attention of quite a good number of scholars in relation to globalization (see the references above as well as e.g. Appadurai 1990 and Castells 1996) is *mobility*. In contemporary social structures, people tend to move around, both in real geographical space and in symbolic, social space. And all of these processes of mobility appear to display complex connections with language (Rampton 1995, 1999). In order to demonstrate this, I will have to shift the focus a bit into the more concrete domains of language attitudes and language planning, and I will start with a general empirical observation.

Language as a social thing, i.e. something in which people have made investments and to which they have attributed values, seems to have awkward relations to space, the main axes of which are those of territorialization and deterritorialization. Territorialization stands for the perception and attribution of values to language as a local phenomenon, something which ties people to local communities and spaces. Customarily, people's mother tongue (L1) is perceived as 'territorialized language', alongside orality and the use of dialects. All of these forms of language emanate locality. Conversely, deterritorialization stands for the perception and attribution of values to language as something which does not belong to one locality but which organizes translocal trajectories and wider spaces. Second or other languages (L2) as well as linguae francae, standardized varieties and literacy are seen as 'deterritorialized language', language that does not exclusively belong to one place (Jacquemet 2000, Maryns and Blommaert 2001).

Language variation allows, defines and organizes spatial trajectories. Literacy, on the other hand, allows a text to be moved, both really, across spaces in the world, as well as symbolically, across social spheres. A standard variety of a language allows moving to adjacent places where people speak similar dialects, as well as across social spaces, into the elite. International languages such as French or English allow insertion in large transnational spaces and networks as well as access to the elites. All of these patterns of mobility are real, they revolve often around life-chances and opportunities, and consequently people often articulate relations between language or code choice and spaces. The choice for English/French rather than indigenous languages in education is at the grassroots level often motivated by means of discourses of 'getting out of here' and towards particular centres – metropolitan areas – where upward social mobility at least looks possible.

Moving through the various levels of education often involves moving through layered regimes of language, each time seen as allowing deterritorialization and hence social as well as geographical mobility. Senses of belonging to a particular community conversely often go hand in hand with the creation (or re-creation) of particular varieties that tie people to that community while at the same time indexing displacement and deterritorialization. 'Gangsta' English, for instance, is now widespread in African urban centres as a language of the townships and the slums, where particular (often imaginarily violent) youth cultures develop. Such linguistic ideologies connecting language varieties to dynamics of locality and mobility, active both at the folk level and at institutional levels, often motivate resistance by target groups against the promotion of indigenous, minority languages – a point often reported by fieldworkers, but rarely written down in publications.[5]

Though one might deplore this, the reasons are usually sound enough. Symbolic marginalization is often just one correlate of real, material marginalization (Stroud 2001, also Fraser 1995); L1 promotion is a form of symbolic upgrading of marginalized resources, and resistance against it is often based on an acute awareness of the persistence of real marginalization. L1 promotion, if performed within a monoglot strategy (i.e. a strategy aimed at constructing 'full monolingualism' and rejecting bilingualism as a road to language attrition or language death) is thus seen as an instrument *preventing* a way out of real marginalization and amounting to keeping people in their marginalized places. Imagine a family in the very marginalized and poor North-Eastern parts of South Africa, speaking Venda. Education in Venda is likely to be perceived as keeping people in the marginalized region, as long as good, white-collar jobs and higher education are in effect concentrated in places like Johannesburg – and require access to English and/or Afrikaans. If the family wants to offer its children upward social mobility, then, it needs to offer them geographical

[5] There are some exceptions: see Heath (1972) on Mexico, Hornberger (1988) on Peru and Freeland (1995) on Nicaragua. I am grateful to Jane Freeland for calling my attention to these studies.

mobility and consequently linguistic mobility as well. Language shift, under such conditions, is a strategy for survival. In the eyes of the speakers, the upgrading of marginalized symbolic goods may still be seen as less empowering than the creation of access to the real prestige goods. Mufwene (2002: 377) captures the core of this 'wicked problem' well: "[i]t sometimes boils down to a choice between saving speakers from their economic predicament and saving a language".

World-Systems Analysis has taught us that although centres and peripheries may depend on the scale on which one looks at things (a town marketplace may be a 'centre' for adjacent villages), as soon as one starts looking at larger systems, centres and peripheries are rather stable. Large urban centres in the third world will remain 'centres' of economic activity, money, politics, intellectual life, education and outward contacts for a long time to come. People seem to be very accurately aware of their location in centres or peripheries, and this is something that cannot be changed at a symbolic level alone.[6] Some serious, real changes are needed to tip the balance.

***

We can now summarize the dilemma facing language planners working from a linguistic rights paradigm. Such an approach in which indigenous languages are promoted as instruments for education and public life (in all situations, according to authors such as Skutnabb-Kangas and Phillipson) is caught in a web of conflicting factors:

- It is largely symbolic, at least in the short and medium term, pending local elite creation and serious economic development;
- It is thus at odds with people's understanding of what they want and need in the short and medium term;
- It also runs counter to the existing trajectories of upward social mobility, often involving 'moving out' to some other place;
- It is therefore often understood by the target groups as preventing them from achieving upward social mobility by tying them to locality.

---

[6] In a recent paper (Blommaert and Van der Donkt 2002) we found such imaginings of people's location in centers and peripheries in a Tanzanian novel. Sociocultural geography was used as a central motif in the construction of the plot and the identification of characters in the novel, and center-periphery models were developed at various levels (the city, the country, the world). Thus even in a very 'local' semiotic product, closely tied to Tanzanian realities, we could see real processes of flow as well as images of globalization at work.

In conclusion, two things can be suggested on the basis of my comments here. First, linguistic rights can be a *durée* perspective, a target formulated in the long term but unachievable as long as nothing is done to undo the real dimensions of marginalization characterizing the target groups. Politically, it is a sound perspective and the arguments about democracy given by its advocates are compelling. But sociolinguistically, it needs to be approached as something that could cause more harm than good if advocated and implemented with immediate effect. The predicament of a 7-year old who is denied an education in a language he/she understands is a terrible one, and the problems in that field are enormous, crucial to the life chances of millions, and in their present state endangering these same life chances. The greater is the need to provide the right answers and to mobilize the best possible science in order to arrive at them. Criticizing the linguistic rights paradigm is not a rejection of linguistic rights, nor a denial of the problems motivating the idea. It is what it is: a critique of scholarly practices.[7]

Second, perhaps we should revise our view on language as something tied to locality, and start viewing it as an instrument for mobility. The locality trope dominates much sociolinguistic discourse, but it seems to be at odds with the investments people make in their languages, repertoires and registers. It fits into (and adds to) the linguistic-ideological complex of locality described by Silverstein (1998: 404): "groups of people are increasingly challenged to have newly active, positive cultural processes emanating from centring institutions, so that what we have here termed the relative and seemingly residual fact of locality gets semiotically turned into a positive attribute of their identity". The linguistic rights paradigm may be such a 'centring institution' *creating* locality.

Maybe people's rights consist in using languages to move around, and perhaps a sociolinguistics of mobility could find new ways to address these old questions.

---

[7] I am reiterating here points made and argued at greater length in Blommaert (2001). One of the arguments made there was that the kinds of interventions into language – standardization, the creation of orthographic norms, its use in formal education and the construction of a complex of language laws – advocated by linguistic rights activists would precisely remove the perceived and cherished 'naturalness' of the languages that invites biodiversity comparisons. If one would carry the metaphor a bit further, in fact, it would be a gross violation of the ecosystem.

References

Appadurai, Arjun (1990) 'Disjuncture and Difference in the Global Cultural Economy', *Theory, Culture and Society* 7: 295-310.

Bickel, Balthasar (2001) 'Deictic Transposition and Referential Practice in Belhare', *Journal of Linguistic Anthropology* 10(2): 224-247.

Blommaert, Jan (1996) 'Language Planning as a Discourse on Language and Society: The Linguistic Ideology of a Scholarly Tradition', *Language Problems and Language Planning* 20(3): 199-222.

------ (2001) 'The Asmara Declaration as a Sociolinguistic Problem: Notes in Scholarship and Linguistic Rights', *Journal of Sociolinguistics* 5(1): 131-142.

------ and Lieselotte Van der Donckt (2002) 'African Literature and Globalization: Semiotizing Space in a Tanzanian Novel', *Journal of African Cultural Studies* 15(2):137-148.

------ and Jef Verschueren (1992) 'The Role of Language in European Nationalist Ideologies', *Pragmatics* 2(3): 355-375. Reprinted in Bambi Schieffelin, Kathryn Woolard and Paul Kroskrity (eds) *Language Ideologies: Practice and Theory*, New York: Oxford University Press, 189-210.

------- and Jef Verschueren (1998) *Debating Diversity: Analysing the Rhetoric of Tolerance*, London: Routledge.

Castells, Manuel (1996) *The Rise of the Network Society*, London: Blackwell.

Collins, James (1998) *Understanding Tolowa Histories: Western Hegemonies and Native American Responses*, New York: Routledge.

Cosgrove, Denis E. (1984) *Social Formation and Symbolic Landscape*, London: Croom Helm.

------ and Stephen Daniels (eds) (1988) *The Iconography of Landscape: Essays on the Symbolic Representation, Design and Use of Past Environments*, Cambridge: Cambridge University Press.

De Leon, Lourdes (1998) 'The Emergent Participant: Interactive Patterns in the Socialization of Tzotzil (Mayan) Infants', *Journal of Linguistic Anthropology* 8(2): 131-161.

Feld, Steven and Keith Basso (eds) (1996) *Senses of Place*, Santa Fe: SAR publications.

Fraser, Nancy (1995) 'From Redistribution to Recognition: Dilemmas of Justice in a 'Post-socialist Age', *New Left Review* 212: 68-93.

Freeland, Jane (1995) 'Why Go to School to Learn Miskitu?', Changing Constructs of Bilingualism, Education and Literacy among the Miskitu of Nicaragua's Atlantic Coast, *International Journal of Educational Development* 15(3): 245-262.

Guibernau, Montserrat (1999) *Nations without States*, Cambridge: Polity.

Gumperz, John and Celia Roberts (1991) 'Understanding in Intercultural

Encounters', in Jan Blommaert and Jef Verschueren (eds) *The Pragmatics of Intercultural and International Communication*, Amsterdam: John Benjamins, 51-90.

------ and Stephen Levinson (eds) (1996) *Rethinking Linguistic Relativity*, Cambridge: Cambridge University Press.

Hanks, William (1990) *Referential Practice: Language and Lived Space among the Maya*, Chicago: University of Chicago Press.

Hannerz, Ulf (1996) *Transnational Connections*, London: Routledge.

Haviland, John (1998) 'Early Pointing Gestures in Zinacantan', *Journal of Linguistic Anthropology* 8(2): 162-196.

Heath, Shirley Brice (1972) *Telling Tongues: Language Policy in Mexico, Colony to Nation*, New York: Teachers College Press.

Heller, Monica (1999) *Linguistic Minorities and Modernity: A Sociolinguistic Ethnography*, London: Longman.

Heugh, Kathleen (1999) 'Languages, Development and Reconstructing Education in South Africa', *International Journal of Educational Development* 19: 301-313.

Hornberger, Nancy (1988) *Bilingual Education and Language Maintenance*, Dordrecht, Holland/Providence R.I., USA: Foris Publications.

Jacquemet, Marco (2000) 'Beyond the Speech Community', paper presented at the 7th International Pragmatics Conference, Budapest, July 2000.

Jaffe, Alexandra (1999) *Ideologies in Action: Language Politics on Corsica*, Berlin: Mouton de Gruyter.

Johnstone, Barbara (1990) *Stories, Community and Place: Narratives from Middle America*, Bloomington: Indiana University Press.

------ (1999) 'Uses of Southern-sounding Speech by Contemporary Texas Women', *Journal of Sociolinguistics* 3(4): 505-522.

Kataoka, Kuniyoshi (1998) 'Gravity or Levity: Vertical Space in Japanese Rock Climbing Instructions', *Journal of Linguistic Anthropology* 8(2): 222-248.

Low, Setha (ed) (2001) *Remapping the City: Place, Order and Ideology*, Special issue of *American Anthropologist*, 103(1): 5-111.

Maryns, Katrijn and Jan Blommaert (2001) 'Stylistic and Thematic Shifting as Narrative Resources: Assessing Asylum Seekers' Repertoires', *Multilingua* 20: 61-84.

May, Stephen (2001) *Language and Minority Rights: Ethnicity, Nationalism and the Politics of Language*, London: Longman.

Mufwene, Salikoko (2002) 'Colonization, Globalization and the Plight of "Weak" Languages', *Journal of Linguistics* 38: 375-395.

Nettle, Daniel and Suzanne Romaine (2000) *Vanishing Voices: The Extinction of the World's Languages*, Oxford: Oxford University Press.

Rampton, Ben (1995) *Crossing: Language and Ethnicity among Adolescents*, London: Longman.

------ (1999) '"Deutsch" in Inner London and the Animation of an Instructed Foreign Language', *Journal of Sociolinguistics* 3(4): 480-504.

Silverstein, Michael (1998) 'Contemporary Transformations of Local Linguistic Communities', *Annual Review of Anthropology* 27: 401-426.

------ (2000) 'Whorfianism and the Linguistic Imagination of Nationality', in P. Kroskrity (ed) *Regimes of language*, Santa Fe: SAR Press, 85-138.

Skutnabb-Kangas, Tove (2000) *Linguistic Genocide in Education – or Worldwide Diversity and Human Rights?*, Mahwah NJ: Lawrence Erlbaum.

------ and Robert Phillipson (1995) 'Linguicide and Linguicism', *Rolig Papir 53*, Roskilde Universitetscenter, Denmark, 83-91.

------ and Robert Phillipson (1999) 'Language Ecology', in Jef Verschueren *et al.* (eds) *Handbook of Pragmatics, 1999 Instalment*, Amsterdam: John Benjamins.

Stroud, Christopher (2001) 'African Mother-tongue Programmes and the Politics of Language: Linguistic Citizenship versus Linguistic Human Rights', *Journal of Multilingual and Multicultural Development* 22(4): 339-355.

4. Minority, but Non-confrontational

Balancing on the Double-edged Sword of Hegemony and Ambivalence

VILLE LAAKSO AND JAN-OLA ÖSTMAN

1. The Scene

In an influential statement more than a decade ago, Deborah Cameron (1990) 'demythologizes' sociolinguistics, arguing that non-circular explanations for sociolinguistic correlations need to be sociologically rather than 'linguistically' based. In this study we try to apply and extend Cameron's insights by exploring a very fluid, local-level language/identity situation, and by demanding a recourse to transdisciplinary conceptualizations in order to be able to interpret and understand what is going on. In a sense, the situation we are dealing with in this study, and the sociohistorical processes involved, come very close to what is discussed by Tabouret-Keller (1992: 193) in relation to what she calls 'focusing': membership identification to a community through language, paralleled with the consequences of agencies that support social integration processes which the people themselves may not wish.[1]

In an attempt to partly respond to Tabouret-Keller's (ibid.: 193) question "why it is so essential for people to be able to assert unity in their social identities", we have chosen to approach the setting from a slightly different angle, combining the theme of "asserting unity in social identities" with the theme of what Urciuoli (1995: 538) and Butler (1997: 11) see as embodied borders in the performative construction of identities. Continuing from Cameron's (1990: 81) remarks to the effect that quantitative sociolinguistics is built on a naïve and simplistic social theory, we seek to address the demand for analytical perspectives on concepts like 'norm' and 'identity'. One of the main issues in our argumentation is to confront the possible conceptual gap between the demands for situated knowledge that can help understand **localized** processes of normativity (cf. Butler 1997) and identification, and the epistemological uniformity presupposed by academia as the collective consumer of knowledge.

In discussions of linguistic rights, discourses on non-confrontational

---

[1] We are greatly indebted to the volume and series editors for extremely useful suggestions on earlier versions, as well as to the SS14 participants in Gent and the PIC crowd in Helsinki, especially Maija Urponen, for lengthy discussions.

situations are rare. One obvious, and understandable reason why non-confrontational situations do not come up in such contexts is that linguistic rights discourse – and rightly so – takes the position of the underdog, demanding changes for the better. Whatever distress there may exist in non-confrontational, majority-minority situations is typically not easy to articulate: the people and languages constitute 'the ordinary', where it is not at all clear, even to the minority itself, how to draw the borders around – and consequently, how to be able to express in positive terms – its collective identity. As our case study shows, traditional ways of making sense of the situation by relying on ethnicity or nationism (cf. Le Page and Tabouret-Keller 1985: 235) may sometimes be completely out of place. In fact, non-confrontational situations might not be articulated as minority situations at all – the self-identification of the people is likely to be thoroughly constructed through the normativity of the surrounding majority.[2] We want to argue that such cases are excellent examples of how "imagined communities" (Anderson 1991) work in what Maffesoli (1988) calls our **neo-tribal** world, which is so obsessed with a continuous search for community. (For a pertinent discussion, see Bauman 1991: 248-251.)

Our discussion will center around one village in Finland, its people, the language spoken in the village, and the perceived identities of the members of the village community. The particular village, Solf, is one of more than 80 clearly identifiable similar communities in the Swedish-speaking part of Finland (see note 4). We know the village and its people well, both as linguists and from the inside, i.e., from an ethnographic point of view: the second author is a native of Solf, with Solv as his mother-tongue.

2. Solf / Solv: Identity and Language on the Margins

The village of Solf is situated on the west-coast of Finland, some 400 kms north-northwest of Helsinki. The language spoken in the village is Solv.[3] Traditionally, Solv is classified as a dialect of Swedish in Finland, as a dialect of what is known as Finland-Swedish (Sw. *finlandssvenska*).[4]

---

[2] In this sense, any local identity – and, for that matter, the terminologies of 'minorities' and 'majorities' in general – would always be dependent on some determining *point de vue* (see below). We find the issues raised by this notion of *points de vue* very central to both the position of the subjects as well as to the position of the outside observers.

[3] The pronunciation of both the village and the language is [sɔɭv].

[4] What is today Finland was part of Sweden until 1809, when it became a Grand Duchy of Russia. Throughout the Swedish and Russian periods, Finnish and

In terms of both language and identity, Solv is located on a multiple margin. First, to the extent that Europe is a cultural construct with a core, the recognition of being on the margin of European-ness is an integral and constitutive aspect of Finnishness in general. Secondly, the whole Swedish-speaking community is a small minority in Finland (cf. footnote 4). Its marginality works two ways, requiring a distinction from both Swedish in Sweden and from Finnish in Finland. Thirdly, the term "Swedish-speaking community in Finland", paradoxically, covers a wide spectrum of local village-level communities which tend to identify themselves with a clear differentiation from the core position suggested by the term. The historical reason for this is that the urban upper-class variety of Finland-Swedish dominates the politicized identity of the "Swedish-speaking community in Finland", and, at the same time, historically symbolizes the language of the ruling class. This means that the contradistinctive identification that takes place in the local communities also induces marginality inside the Swedish-speaking community. Solv is thus situated through at least a four-way marginalization, but, consequently, also includes the potential to simulate the respective core positions of these overlapping differentiations.

In this sense, Solvness is very much a fluid identity. The directions of identification drastically depend on the context, although narrations of origin and tradition would typically refer to (Finland) Swedishness, whereas narrations of duty and organization would regularly utilize Finnishness. Two main sources of normativity and social coherence in the Solv community have been the (local, Lutheran) church, and agriculture,[5] but as

---

Swedish were used in parallel (although as part of the nationalistic spirit, a great number of especially urban Swedish speakers changed their names to Finnish names, and went over to speaking Finnish as early as towards the end of the nineteenth century). When Finland declared itself independent in 1917, Finnish and Swedish were made to be the two national languages of the country. In 1995 three further linguistic minorities were given mother-tongue rights: the Sámi, the Roma, and the Deaf. At present about 6 per cent of the population of Finland indicate that they have Swedish as their mother tongue.

Swedish speakers in the major towns are typically bilingual, but many (especially older) people living in the countryside in the southern and western parts of Finland are monolingual 'dialect' speakers with reading knowledge of standard Swedish. Linguistically, the Swedish-speaking area is divided into some 80 rural-dialect areas on the basis of the traditional provinces; Solf is one of these areas. Many of the 'dialects' (especially those close to urban areas) are going through a steady process of levelling at the moment, but as our recent field trips have shown, many of the languages spoken in the villages present great difficulties of understanding for speakers of standard Finland-Swedish.

[5] Church and agriculture are here referred to as institutions of every-day praxis, as

times (and Finland) have changed, these two have gradually lost their totalizing grip of the social. Solvness has now become even more fluid as it is in the process of distancing itself from these formerly so important determinants.

Solv has never had any stable shape as a written language or as a language of education. Thus, no unifying continuity can be derived from this aspect either. However, as a differentiated (language) identity Solv has always been articulated through strong discourse-performative contrasts (cf. Butler 1997; Urciuoli 1995, Darnell this volume) against neighbouring languages as well as against Finnish and Swedish (literary) standards.

Some twenty years ago Wiik and Östman (1983) devised and presented a writing system for Solv and the languages in neighboring villages. The writing system was in line with the half-century-long tradition of writing and publishing dialect writings in the area; in this sense, the enterprise can be seen as an explication of what had become a tradition. In addition, it was systematic, and based on functional and identity-related principles as much as on linguistic principles.[6] Both authors were members of the local communities, and saw dialect writing as a natural manifestation of their and other villagers' need to express themselves.

At the time of devising the writing system, written products in the dialects in the area had become partly obscure to the prototypical reader. Thus, it is not unfair to say that the writing system was also – albeit maybe implicitly – partly devised by two concerned citizens (members of the

---

the very concrete religious and productional duties which have been the most important manifestations of organization and self-control within the community, and which have to a large extent shaped the life in Solv.

[6] Wiik and Östman (1983) suggest three general principles for devising a writing system for an hitherto unwritten language – the *linguistic principles* are basically structural-linguistic in orientation, taking into account the phoneme inventory of the language in question and general phonotactic and morphophonological processes; the *functional principle* basically states that a writing system is made for a particular purpose, and thus a language may need several writing systems, e.g., one to be used as an aid in school, and another for writing poetry. The *identity principle* takes an ethnographic perspective and says that the people who speak the language as their native tongue and live in the community have the right to decide what their writing system should look like. This also means that if, for whatever aesthetic, political, foreign-looking reasons, a community does not like a symbol or a combination of symbols, their word has to be the rule. It further means that if they want to have a writing system that looks very different from that of the neighboring village, in order for it to be their own (i.e. as an identity marker), then so be it. The linguist has to let him/herself be appropriated (cf. further the discussion in the last section of this paper).

communities), as what they felt was one necessary step in vitalizing and maybe even revitalizing the language, and thereby the village culture.[7]

Towards the end of the 1980s, the writing system, and thus the language, were frequently used in funny short stories written by Saandis Oola and published in the local newspaper *Vasabladet*; in addition, Östman and Kuningas (forthcoming) have translated parts of the Bible into Solv using this writing system. However, it seems that in every-day writing Solfians mostly use standard Swedish orthography with some unsystematic modifications. These are usually interpretable as efforts to represent someone's actual speaking of Solv. (For further discussion, see Laakso forthcoming). Without the context of local identification, everyday writing in Solv would appear as an 'erroneous' or 'abnormal' application of the written Swedish standard (cf. Freeland in this volume).

Despite a lack of articulated institutionalized means of distinction for their language, Solfians have a very strong sense of identity as speakers of Solv. In a recent study of the attitudes of people living in Solf who consider themselves as having Solv as their mother tongue, Puranen (forthcoming) found that Solv is indeed very important for the identity of these speakers, to the extent that people who do not speak Solv are looked down upon. Members of the older generations have a stable sociolinguistic network of people who use Solv in their every-day interactions; especially men in Solf saw no negative aspects of using Solv in any situational context.

Members of the younger generations were also positively inclined towards Solv. On a field trip to the community, we found that even youngsters between the ages of ten and twenty were generally very proud of their language, and they felt that they themselves spoke Solv. However, as linguists, we could hardly find any trace of Solv in the language they produced. That is, the linguistic identity of this sub-group of members of the Solf community seems virtually non-connected to language.

We need to reflect more generally on this situation, both from the point of view of the villagers and from the point of view of our position as linguists. The issue that needs to be raised and scrutinized – both theoretically and ethnographically – is clearly the relationship between language and identity: What does it really mean when ethnolinguistic minority identities remain strong, but the languages themselves are subject to language shift?

---

[7] The writing system was not specifically devised for Solv, but more generally, the principles for devising writing systems for the area were established, and Solv and the Vassor dialect – as the native languages of the two authors – were used as the primary examples to illustrate these principles.

Minimally, the situation in Solf puts into question the typical approach by many descriptive linguists, where language is seen as the most important characteristic of what it means to belong to a group. What we find is that being a Solfian seemingly has become rather similar to belonging to a stamp-collecting association. Solfness provides one aspect of one's identity, but only one, and one's position with respect to this aspect does not seem to show any consistency or congruity with one's position with respect to other aspects of identity. Although language has in the past been the most important part of being a Solfian, it is not so any more (or, rather, this importance has changed its nature), since its potential for material differentiation has faded in the language of the younger generations. With no other traditional grounds for differentiation available, being a Solfian comes very close to what Bauman (1991: 248ff.) discusses under the heading of **neo-tribalism** – a style, a habitus, something more obviously imagined and less obviously factual than what a traditional conception of an ethnic identity would be.

The people in Solf have never expressed any particular claims for political recognition; no voices have been raised to make Solf an independent, sovereign, or somehow acknowledged national-political unit – in fact, what used to be the municipality of Solf was divided, with the natives' consent, into two parts in the early 1970s: the Solf and Munsmo villages became part of the municipality of Korsholm, and the Sundom villages became part of the near-by town Vasa.[8] Admittedly, views blossom up sporadically on the possibility of making the whole of Swedish-language Ostrobothnia semi-autonomous, along the lines of the status that the Åland Islands (between Finland and Sweden) have today.[9] Though no voice has suggested any official or political recognition for the Solf people, Solf

---

[8] We use the Swedish forms of place-names, despite the national recommendations that Finnish forms should be used in English texts. Thus, Solf/Solv is Sulva in Finnish and Sålv in Solv; Vasa is Vaasa in Finnish, Korsholm is Mustasaari in Finnish, etc.

[9] When Finland became independent, the Åland Islands expressed a forceful interest to be reunited with Sweden; this was not acceptable to the Finnish parliament, which in 1920 passed an autonomy act. This was not enough for the Ålanders, who took the question to the League of Nations, which in 1921 decided that Finland should have sovereignty over the islands. But Finland guaranteed the inhabitants of the Åland Islands their Swedish language, culture and customs; and the Islands furthermore constitute a demilitarized zone. Although the Islands are under Finnish rule, they have their own parliament, and thus a semi-autonomous status, and celebrate their own Autonomy day. There are also strict stipulations of who has the right to acquire land on the Åland Islands.

natives specifically point out that they speak Solv, not Ostrobothnian Swedish.

Ethnographic evidence thus suggests that discourses of local identification, whether in terms of ethnicity or **nationism**,[10] if ever mentioned, are *de facto* brought into, or upon, the community by linguists, sociologists and other experts in order for them to be able to make sense of what is going on in the village. A linguistic or traditional sociolinguistic approach simply does not have the means to deal with such fluid identities, because in the end these approaches rely on the kind of material stability of differentiation that can become observable only with reference to communities on a somewhat larger scale. Therefore, when analyzing the use of Solv by community members, a linguistic analysis cannot but imply that the linguistic act of speaking Solv means that the speakers of Solv are – and should be – constructing a contained identity for themselves as a potential nation (however small-scale). This academic perspective, however, bluntly ignores the ways identification takes place in multiple margins. It also ignores the possibility that at least some degree of nonconformity can exist in the presupposed world of 'homogeneous nation-state' identities.

3. Toward Non-essentialist Linguistics

When confronted with something which in terms of localized identities stands out as a language, but which seems too ambiguous to meet the unitary criteria of being a language in the framework of modernist[11] linguistics, then rather than coming to the conclusion that the language, in this case Solv, is experiencing a crisis, we need to bring up for discussion the extent to which *linguistics is in crisis*: the foundations of linguistic inquiry have to be scrutinized once we bring polyvalent narratives of identity to bear on our analyses.

Typically, 'lesser used' languages are treated in two ways as objects of

---

[10] It should be stressed here that we use nationism in the sense of Anderson (1991). In an Andersonian perspective nationism (which we are using instead of the more ideologically-loaded term, nationalism) is understood as the process of imagining a community, and thus of sustaining the imagined community.

[11] The term refers to the historical background of present-day linguistics as the 'science of language', the goal of which was to reveal and formulate the 'laws of nature' behind all observable linguistic behaviour. The tacit assumption shared by modernist approaches is the transcendental conception of social identities – be it in terms of 'ethnicities', 'norms', or 'volitional agencies'. (Cf. also Cameron 1990: 91-92.)

linguistics: on the one hand, linguistics, and often more specifically, linguistic typology, is interested in recording what is possible in languages or what is the range of variation in languages, and therefore is acutely concerned that a relevant description of a language is recorded before the language develops beyond the reach of accepted methods of empiricism, i.e. before it 'dies'. This can be described as the **musealizing** approach inherent in modernist linguistics. On the other hand, linguistically interesting languages, i.e. languages that are exotic and radically different from European languages, offer a specific field of expertise to linguistics and to linguists, an expertise which needs to be reported to the global academia to reify the importance and constant progress of linguistics as an independent domain of knowledge. This is the built-in **expertization** of linguistics. And we would maintain that both of these – the musealization and the expertization – are necessary by-products of an epistemological stance rather than simply avoidable extensions of a linguistic praxis. When we reflect on the social conditions for linguistic knowledge, the institutional-epistemological constraints will be the same in all research on social identities and on language, however empowering that research sets itself out to be (cf. also Cameron *et al.* 1992: 22-6).

Much of what we know as 'the linguistic tradition' has been moulded by experts in a Eurocentrist[12] fashion. The institutional criteria for linguistic knowledge – that is, the criteria for its alleged objectivity, universality and political neutrality – have for the most part been given solely within the European context. The motives to produce knowledge and the ways to consume knowledge are dependent on the European order of things. Regardless of the question whether such contingency could possibly have been differently organized or not, there is a crucial and immediate need for critical self-reflection. In particular, it is necessary to ponder why the position musealization constructs for its linguistic Others is the position of conserved samples, and why the position expertization constructs is the position of the possibility to 'become (or simulate) European'. Why is a certain transcendental European-ness – in relation to which everything out-bordered gets its function – taken as a foundation for these approaches without question? And what is it then that a linguist is an expert on? A discussion of this presumed foundation of linguistic inquiry requires and presupposes a discussion of the inherent form of epistemological essentialism in linguistics (i.e., the idea that language is an essence), which is

[12] With 'Eurocentrism' we do not mean a focus on Europe geographically, or in the sense of empiria; rather, the term refers to the shared tendency – or need – to commensurize in order to meet the terms of Western consumerism.

most manifest in a uniform standard within a homogeneous nation-state.

One further problem with musealization is the geographical positioning of languages that is typically concomitant with the approach (cf. also Blommaert in this volume). For instance, areal features were geographically areal when geography was a means through which people were in contact with other people; today, areality is pragmatically induced – Raukko and Östman (1994) talk about pragmareal linguistics. And once we bring in pragmatics, we also have to rethink the whole question of what is our object of study. If – pragmatically, and culturally speaking – we cannot separate discourse from its culture, then the morpho-syntactic aspects of language and discourse may turn out to be extremely peripheral characteristics. In fact, Östman (2000) even suggests that – pragmatically speaking – farmers in Europe may be seen to have a common contact-language despite the fact that they would not know any morpho-syntactically defined word in any other European language. And if that is the case, what aspect of a language could arguably then be placed in a museum while other aspects are deemed secondary?

In contradistinction to the musealization and expertization approaches, we see clear benefits in taking a non-essentialist perspective on both language and identity.[13] Such a perspective will force us to think about language as something that *is* ('esse') discursively, not as something that *exists* ('ens') as such. Both the linguist as expert and the linguist as collector (of languages) construe languages as the given of their *point de vue*, but tend to neglect perspectivity *per se*, and thus end up naturalizing their epistemological construct into an ontological given. But despite the strong claims such a shift makes possible, neither has access to language as an entity beyond the very narration of 'being a language'. We see the recognition of such inaccessibility as the necessary starting point for any effort towards a non-essentialist understanding.

An analysis of the kind we suggest would also steer us away from issues of 'ethnicity' and 'nationism' *per se* – not because these are by definition uninteresting, but because the very use of such notions presuppose a particular, essentialist way of relating linguistic aspects to pre-given categories and/or to pre-established tacit ideologies.

---

[13] In the case of language, non-essentialism would more accurately be related to meaning. Further, no non-essentialist approach to identity can do without some non-essentialist conception of meaning, and *vice versa*, since they are necessarily interconnected through the social and the construction of subjectivity in the social. Fixing or stabilizing one of them would immediately provide a transcendental basis for the other, too.

4. Hegemony and Ambivalence

The situation in Solf becomes more understandable when looked at through the eye-glasses of hegemony and ambivalence. Our most crucial question in this study has been the following: "How can one cope with, and deal with one's minority situation and everything that this situation brings with it, when there is no confrontation at stake, and when the eyes of the world are not turned towards you as a suffering minority?"

This is where the act of balancing comes in. The hegemonic establishment of any normativity requires that the actants – in this case, the people in Solf – 'know their place' and behave accordingly. But at the same time, being situated on the periphery of normativity leaves room for ambivalence. This ambivalence, *per se*, embodies variability and a favorable view of and openness towards change: ambivalence demands non-conformity and rebelry, and makes the peripheral Solfian identification possible. In order to survive in a changing world and retain one's identity (however defined), a Solfian has to carry out a tricky balancing act – and in fact, in so doing, attempt to reconcile both (what are traditionally construed as) the hegemonic and the ambivalent positions.

For instance, there is no sense in persuading people in Solf to give up any possibility they might have of becoming millionaires, in order to satisfy some Other's view that the community, the people, and their language are moderately unique and need to be saved for posterity. Revitalization has to have a purpose beyond mere revitalization.

The heavy genealogical burden of essentialism in the prototypical linguist's conception of meaning itself requires that we question the very presence of such essentialism. What would a concept of meaning look like that does away with essentialism? Is this at all feasible or even possible? We want to argue that this can be done by understanding meaningfulness as an aspect and a product of the continuous formation and maintenance of identities. This relation of co-construction between meaningfulness and identification is possible if the two analytical concepts *hegemony* and *ambivalence* are seen as necessary correlates of making sense.

Hegemony, in this sense, describes the materiality of a subject's/subjects' understanding of meaning.[14] The non-essentialist perspective would

---

[14]The materiality of 'meaning' for a speaking subject is always hegemonic in the sense that a meaning *in absentia* appears to the subject to be true and stable. Hegemony is materialized in the meaningfulness of a language as well as in the meaningfulness of any social institution. It is important to stress that in this sense the concept of hegemony cannot be reduced to relations of domination between

then mainly require a theoretization of identity and 'subjection', and could in that follow the argumentation presented by, for instance, Butler (1997) and Pulkkinen (1996), who suggest that any identity could be conceived of as performative and "as deconstructable into its construction in power" (Pulkkinen 249), and can thus be accounted for genealogically – without any notion of core essence.

Understood in the Gramscian sense of the term, hegemony conceptualizes the processes of consensual organization within the social. Hegemony is about social institutionalization, about making some differences converge so that they unite. Seen in a non-essentialist perspective, hegemony works on two levels, which can be described in terms corresponding to the respective parallelism of meaning and identity.

On the level of constructing meaning, hegemony works as a cohesive impetus to form a 'grid of intelligibility' (cf. '*grille d'intelligibilité*'; Foucault 1976: 122), which at the same time serves as a regulative foundation for subjecthood. Hegemony describes the process of organization, in which the constant limitation that keeps up the constitutive relation between meaningfulness and its subjects produces sites of normality. In the same process of limitation, the very normality is articulated as the positive origin of meaning. The subject positions close to this origin appear as invested with power, as having control over the 'true meaning'.

But this kind of hegemonic normativity requires of the respective community a certain critical mass, without which it cannot retain its assumed unity and become the source of lived true meanings for the members of the community. In Solf, we think, there is no longer enough of a social mass for the younger generations to have hegemony working this way – earlier this was the case, and traces of that past hegemony are still alive in the 'authentic Solvian' meaningfulness that the older generations' Solv provides (usually, of course, with a sense of nostalgia).

On the level of identity, hegemony is more about constructing a self as the foundation of subjectivity. With such a foundation subjectivity is supplied with an origin – the nature of the self, the self as (a given) nature. This construction is the crossing point for desires, values, motivations, intentions, feelings, and other kinds of conceivability. Through this construction it is possible for a subject to take the self as the true origin and

---

pre-given subjects – it is rather a concept that tries to convey the very production of subjectivity and the formative consensus that allows the 'subject-to-power' itself be the executionary agent of the same power. The 'hegemony as *consensual organization*' should then – in this context – be understood as a continuously contingent process of being a social *organ* and making *sense*. (Cf. Laclau 2000: 49.)

commanding agent of aspirations that are rather an executive manifestation of social formations. An illustrative example of how this works would be internalized consumerism: a consumer might honestly feel that the desire for a certain commodity is a uniquely original and true expression of the nature of his/her self, although in a social perspective, the desire might rather seem like something that is successfully imposed on homologised masses of consumers by commercials, fashion, lifestyle ideologies, social conformity, consumerist cultures, lived capitalism, etc. Despite this, there is no point in denying that the particular experienced desire is indeed true and original for the consumer; there is no alternative way to subjectivity, no 'real' subject behind the construction.

The identity aspect of hegemony is also connected to social (and civil) institutions, such as religion, media, profession (trade unionism), family, education, temperance movements, sports clubs, fan cults, and (folk-)linguistic ideologies. It is questionable if Solv/Solfianism has ever had means to establish this kind of hegemony for itself locally. Rather, the institutions which have had hegemonic effects of this kind in Solf, have always had some broader social framework and have partly constituted the Solv identity as consciously marginal; at the same time Solfians are very proud of the identificatory space they have been able to maintain almost within the borders – being self-consciously marginal, but not abjected. Because of the lack of self-determination of Solv(ness) in relation to the hegemonies that govern social normativity, we see Solv(ness) as especially vulnerable to the new hegemonic effects of globalization and to the rapidly increasing economization of cultures, i.e., in terms of becoming dependent on and measured by the discourses of economics.

For this reason, it seems that in the case of Solv, there would not even be any possibility for identity/language politics of what Jaffe (1999: 20-29) calls 'resistance of reversal' or 'resistance of separation'.[15] With some kind of what Jaffe terms 'radical resistance' conception of identity/language politics, Solv might struggle on: that is, the speakers would have to become aware of the constructedness of both notions – identity and language – and of the fact that there is no such thing as 'a neutral linguistic position' which would overcome the ambivalence of their situated contexts. In this way, Solv speakers could actively begin to realize the plurality

---

[15] Resistance of reversal refers to the strategy of replacement, where efforts are made for the 'minority' language to take over and replace the dominant language in its social and institutional functions; resistance of separation refers to the strategy of autonomy, where efforts are made to construct a separate social sphere from which the dominant language is actively kept away.

of their identity/language as reflected in their lived ambivalence. But it is unlikely that any of the natives would be at all interested in anything that suggests radicalism and which furthermore would probably involve challenging the ideological foundations of their conventional forms of life.

Bhabha (1990: 3-4) uses the notion of ambivalence to analyze the manifold effects of different modes of discursivity on the genealogically formative processes of identification, and how these modes work differently – though simultaneously – in limiting the spaces of meaning for particular identities. He points out that in this respect meanings are never whole, but constantly in the process of being made; the ambivalence of this openness is the source of productivity for the narrations that (by definition) try to conceal this very ambivalence.

In addition to the identity-related way in which Bhabha (ibid.) uses ambivalence, we also feel that an additional, linguistic aspect of ambivalence needs to be taken into account, since not only is the relation between language and identity characterized by ambivalence, but language itself, discourse, is by its very nature ambivalent. In relation to our view of developing a non-essentialist approach to linguistics, we thus use the notion of ambivalence not only in the sense that some matters, or some situations, or some manifestations of language are ambiguous, but that ambivalence is definitional of human communication and interaction.

Ultimately this means that the starting point for any attempt at understanding linguistic interaction must be a metatheoretical acceptance of 'understanding-differently' as the default (cf.Toolan 1996: 254). Even further, we have to seriously question the role of intention in discourse: ambivalence is the term we use for discourse production, where the language producer – or, typically, language producers in interaction – themselves do not necessarily and intuitively know what they are trying to get across to someone else. In fact, a strategic use of ambivalence by minority-language speakers can be a forceful countermove against any dominant hegemony (in line with Jaffe's (1999) different types of 'resistance'), and therefore, learning to understand the workings of ambivalence should be given top priority both by minority speakers, and by sociolinguists.

Braidotti (1994) talks about 'the polyglot as a linguistic nomad'. Her use of the term **polyglot** here refers to any linguistic multi-positionality involving crossing the boundaries of locally totalizing normativities of intelligibility. Basically, this multi-positionality will be an almost inevitable consequence of cultural globalization: only the most (globally) dominant subject positions can – as the effect of meeting the exclusivity of globally communicated normativities – escape the transfiguration of one's local normative contexts. This means that any local normativity tends to lose its potentiality and force to naturalize meanings as its subjects may now have the means to contrast this potentiality with similar potentialities in different normative contexts. The totality of narration is no longer achieved when the subjects have access to multiple narrations of identity. Linguistic nomadism, in turn, implies the awareness of "the treacherous nature of language that is never standing still", the understanding that there are no 'first languages' of stability and truth, "no mother tongues, just linguistic sites one takes her/his starting point from" (cf. ibid.: 13).

So far, linguists have stressed the importance of raising the consciousness of 'ordinary folk' with respect to what, for instance, politicians and advertisers are trying to do to us consciously. But we also need to raise our own and others' consciousness with respect to the force of ambivalence. We need to become proactive, rather than defensive or simply active interpreters. In fact, being aware of the ambivalent nature of (much) discourse is in itself good evidence of the force of ambivalence. Being (conscious about being) ambivalent is almost the same as being proactively negative, e.g as regards breaking the linguistic rules of a society. Not only do speakers of a particular language need to become more tolerant towards ambivalence and non-normity in their language, but in particular, linguists need to cultivate tolerance in this respect. And further, linguists need to learn how to deal with ambivalence 'critically', how to deal with variation when there is no standard (as there is no standard within the community in Solf), when the community under investigation does not invite us to think in terms of clear-cut normativity.

5. Identity Regained

What we experience in Solf is sustained *neo*-tribalization. The local institutions get more influence and power, the overall Finnish, or Finland-Swedish 'culture' is integrated and gradually – but implicitly – canonized. What is important is exactly *being a Solfian*. But what this means changes from one generation to the next, from one decade to the next, maybe even from one hour to the next. Adolescents find new manifestations and realizations of what it means to be a Solfian – yesterday it might have been an agricultural, church-centred society, today maybe snowboarding. What stays in the minds of members of the community is Solfness itself. And members within the group will see and construe in principle anything they do as being a realization of their Solfness, including the language they speak – irrespective of whether an Other sees or hears an 'objective' difference between their language and the language of the people in the nearby town.

The members of the community also typically belong to other communities, vegans, yuppies, IT-nerds, chicken-farmers, etc. 'Solfness' might not be all that different from 'vegetarianism'. But as linguists we have to ask ourselves: Should it really be seen as very different?

It is indeed possible to present the development through time of the hegemonic and ambivalent strands that have taken place in the Solf community and in relation to Solv, the language. This development can be abstracted into four consecutive stages:

Stage 1: 'the good old days'
Solf is hegemonic: the Solf culture is appreciated generally;
Solv is a language of its own, spoken by close to everyone in Solf;
education is given in Solf, and in Solv.

Stage 2
Solf is non-hegemonic: anti-movements against the hegemonic arise;
ambivalence is being made use of the Solf culture is appreciated generally;
Solv is seen as a dialect in relation to some standard of Otherness;
the standard is appreciated and used in education.

Stage 3
Solf is non-hegemonic: ambivalence increases in importance;
the Solf culture is appreciated generally;
Solv looks on the surface very close to the standard.

Stage 4
The standard is hegemonic: both culturally and with respect to the language; ambivalence is not acceptable, since even the 'view from inside' is that Solf 'caught up with' the standard (culture and language), not that the standard influenced or forced Solfians to change.

At present we are very close to being in the situation specified as 'Stage 4'. But even if we can for descriptive purposes present Solfness and the change in the Solv language over time as depicted above, such an objectified description is by its very nature essentialistic.

Our purpose in this study has been to criticize and problematize aspects of the hegemonic discourse on minority language 'maintenance', 'survival', and 'revitalization' and to show that the view that language is a core value in all perceptions of ethnic identity at least has to be seriously qualified. Thus, in a situation like the one presented as four stages above, we also have to ask: 'Who really influenced whom?' The Solf identity has taken on characteristics of consumerism; the individual identity, that everyone is entitled to, has taken over: every one feels they are unique, but they are all unique in the same way. Identification locally has become an abstract way of being; to be a Solfian is akin to being a postcard collector. Language as the carrier of identity has been reduced to a pin: 'I am me'.

Thus, if it is really true, as we say, that in many cases linguists can barely detect any features of the dialect in the speech of some members of the community who nevertheless themselves feel that they speak Solv and are an integral part of the community, then the issue of how and whether these features really 'exist' becomes a nonce question. The crucial object of study is then *the view of the native speaker* that distinctiveness exists, irrespective of whether such distinctiveness can be experienced by an outsider.

Even seemingly straightforward questions like why it is important for the people in Solf to maintain a distinct identity, we see as nonce questions, since such questions arise out of the scientist's/linguist's essentialist presupposition that there should be good representatives of categories.

Solv is a parasite on Swedish, and Solf is a parasite on Finnishness. Parasite here is not a negative characteristic *per se*, but a recognition of the fact that Solf and Solv are by definition explicable and understandable only in relation to the social and socio-political environment and context of which they are a part. Swedish and Finnishness provide the model; Solv and Solf do not qualify one hundred per cent – the elements of Swedish and Finnishness are there, but they do not exhaustively define Solv/Solf. Still, a parasite has to learn to live with, and from, its host: it is thus in the interest of the parasite that the 'parasitee' also feels good.

The final question then is this: If the available instruments (like questionnaires and interviews on the one hand, and observation and meticulous linguistic measurements on the other hand) are not enough, and even distort what we want to study, then how *could* these issues be investigated at all?

Our response to this question is a very pragmatic and practical one: We need to educate natives, not inside established towers of education, but in such a way as to maintain and retain the Self (which is typically seen as an Other by the majority), and accept *the minority's* gradual act of appropriating the majority manners of arguing and doing – in order to change the views of the majority, and to use 'them' for one's own cause. This is in direct contrast to what is most often happening at the moment, when representatives of the minority are *de facto* used as agents for the majority – for purposes of what we above called musealization. For instance, the purpose of devising a writing system was to get away from other hegemonies, but this could have become problematic, since we also at the same time did not want to impose yet another way of moving away from ambivalence. But the population in Solf reacted to the writing system the way they should: 'Interesting, but so what? I'll go on living my life as I want. Maybe I'll do something with the writing system, maybe not.' It is because we knew of the community members' suspicious attitudes towards inventions and introductions from outside[16] the community that even the thought of devising a writing system was felt to be feasible and an acceptable act in the first place – despite the risk of overdue intervention.

Our conclusion is that we need to approach minority situations and questions of linguistic rights and language survival in a non-essentialist manner: the very balancing on the edge of ambivalence and hegemony requires ethnographic standpoints, standpoints that are negotiated among the sociolinguist and the villager, the human being – also, and maybe especially, in cases where these two converge in one person. And the very first step on this road to a deeper understanding of the interaction between language and culture/society is to not overlook the ordinary, the non-confrontational, everyday situations that the people themselves so very often live (in).[17]

---

[16] After all, irrespective of how much you yourself as a linguist may feel that you are still part of the community, by staying away for longer periods of time at the university, you have to take seriously the community members' categorization of yourself – even if that categorization may be that you are 'an outsider'.

[17] In this sense we also see the work within perceptual dialectology (cf. e.g., Preston 1999) as an invaluable approach to the linguistic study of folk concepts, language beliefs, and the attitudes of the speaker-as-community-member.

References

Anderson, Benedict (1991) *Imagined Communities* [revised edition], London: Verso.

Bauman, Zygmunt (1991) *Modernity and Ambivalence*, London: Polity Press.

Bhabha, Homi K. (1990) 'Introduction: Narrating the Nation', in H. K. Bhabha (ed) *Nation and Narration*, London and New York: Routledge, 1-7.

Braidotti, Rosi (1994) *Nomadic Subjects*, New York: Columbia University Press.

Butler, Judith (1997) *The Psychic life of Power*, Stanford, CA: Stanford University Press.

Cameron, Deborah (1990) 'Demythologizing Sociolinguistics: Why Language Does not Reflect Society', in John E. Joseph and Talbot J. Taylor (eds) *Ideologies of Language*, London and New York: Routledge, 79-93.

------, Elizabeth Frazer, Penelope Harvey, M.B.H. Rampton and Kay Richardson (1992) *Researching Language. Issues of Power and Method*, London and New York: Routledge.

Foucault, Michel (1976) *Histoire de la sexualité 1. La volonté de savoir,* Paris: Gallimard.

Jaffe, Alexandra (1999) *Ideologies in Action. Language Politics on Corsica,* Berlin and New York: Mouton de Gruyter.

Laakso, Ville (forthcoming) 'Kirjoittaa sulvaa' [Writing Solv]', to appear in Jan-Ola Östman and Ville Laakso (eds) *Åm såłvsprååtje*.

Laclau, Ernesto (2000) Identity and Hegemony: The Role of Universality in the Constitution of Political Logics. In Judith Butler, Ernesto Laclau & Slavoj Zizek, (eds) *Contingency, Hegemony, Universality: Contemporary Dialogues on the Left*. London: Verso, pp. 44-89.

Le Page, Robert B. and Andrée Tabouret-Keller (1985) *Acts of Identity. Creaole-based Approaches to Language and Ethnicity*, Cambridge: Cambridge University Press.

Maffesoli, Michel (1988) 'Jeux de masques', *Design Issues* 4(1 and 2): 141ff.

Östman, Jan-Ola (2000) 'Ethics and Appropriation – with Special Reference to Hwalbáy', in Frances Karttunen and Jan-Ola Östman (eds) *Issues of Minority Peoples*, University of Helsinki: Department of General Linguistics. Publications 31, 37-60.

------ and Johanna Kuningas (forthcoming) 'On Translating the Holy Bible into Solv', in Jan-Ola Östman and Ville Laakso (eds) *Åm såłvsprååtje*.

Preston, Dennis R. (ed) (1999) *Handbook of Perceptual Dialectology, vol. 1*, Amsterdam and Philadelphia, PA: John Benjamins.

Pulkkinen, Tuija (1996) *The Postmodern and Political Agency*, Department of Philosophy, University of Helsinki.

Puranen, Pasi (forthcoming) 'Kielelliset asenteet Sulvalla' [Language Attitudes in Solf], in Jan-Ola Östman and Ville Laakso (eds) *Åm såłvspråątje*.

Raukko, Jarno and Jan-Ola Östman (1994) *Pragmaattinen näkökulma Itämeren kielialueeseen* [A Pragmatic Perspective on the Areal Linguistics of Baltic Europe], University of Helsinki, Department of General Linguistics Publications 25.

Tabouret-Keller, Andrée (1992) 'Language Contact in Focused Situations', in Ernst Håkon Jahr (ed) *Language Contact. Theoretical and Empirical Studies* [Trends in Linguistics. Studies and Monographs 60], Berlin and New York: Mouton de Gruyter, 179-194.

Toolan, Michael (1996) *Total Speech. An Integrational Linguistic Approach to Language*, London: Duke University Press.

Urciuoli, Bonnie (1995) 'Language and Borders', *Annual Review of Anthropology* 24: 525-546.

Wiik, Barbro and Jan-Ola Östman (1983) 'Skriftspråk och identitet' [Written Language and Identity], in Erik Andersson, Mirja Saari and Peter Slotte (eds) *Struktur och variation*, Turku: Publications of the Research Institute of the Åbo Akademi Foundation 85, 181-216.

5. Revitalization and Retention of First Nations Languages in Southwestern Ontario[1]

REGNA DARNELL

1. Introduction

Aboriginal language maintenance and revitalization in southwestern Ontario highlights many issues found across Canada, but is unique in at least two respects: Iroquoian and Algonquian linguistic and cultural traditions intermingle across the area, making the category of 'Aboriginal' remarkably heterogeneous; and fluent speakers of traditional languages, primarily Ojibwe and Mohawk, are rare and almost always elderly (although these languages have fluent speakers in other areas of Canada and the U.S.). This paper begins by locating the southwestern Ontario situation within Canadian linguistic diversity as a prelude to exploring the local conditions and community aspirations surrounding Indigenous languages in the region.

What may seem to outsiders to be dying languages arouse considerable passions for renewal in many communities. In other communities, however, there has been less interest in language as a key to maintaining Aboriginal identity under intensive pressure to assimilation, past and present. This paper will summarize a long-term research project on the Englishes spoken by Aboriginal peoples in southwestern Ontario. Here, English has been adapted in a sophisticated and effective fashion to the communicative needs of its speakers, who retain many pragmatic and semantic features of traditional languages they no longer speak. The paper concludes with some observations on the challenge that these local initiatives provide to conventional notions of language survival, language change and language purity. Linguists must change their way of thinking about the relationship between languages and their speakers if our work is to remain relevant and useful to Native communities. Collaborative projects with control in the local communities must become our norm.

---

[1] This paper is revised and expanded from a version presented to the International Pragmatics Association in Budapest in 2000 (Darnell 2001).

2. The National Context

Canada is a nation founded on bilingualism, but restricts language rights in the public domain to the 'official' languages of the French and English colonial founding nations. To be bilingual in Canada is to speak French and English, although protections exist for the practice of cultural traditions outside the mainstream; these traditions, of course, may include the speaking of a traditional language in non-official contexts. 'Multiculturalism' policy and legislation in Canada, however, target ethnic groups who have arrived in Canada after the French and English founders and take their places within a complex 'mosaic' of coexisting traditions. Aboriginal languages and cultures are virtually ignored in this formulation. Administratively, they fall under the purview of the Federal Department of Indian Affairs and Northern Development, not Citizenship and Immigration, which includes Heritage Canada. Despite this artificial separation from other linguistic and cultural maintenance situations in Canada, however, parallels with First Nations language retention and revitalization initiatives are drawn widely in the sociolinguistic literature. In an international context, minority ethnic groups formed through transnational migration and immigration and indigenous groups share many of the same problems. The uniqueness of the latter resides primarily in the absence of a homeland elsewhere which might preserve languages otherwise lost in contexts of immigration.

Incorporation of Aboriginal language issues into Canadian policy and public awareness is rendered more complex by the diversity among Canadian Aboriginal languages themselves. The Indian Act recognizes more than six hundred official bands, representing eleven linguistic families. These range from broadly-distributed, internally diverse and historically complex conglomerates of closely related languages (e.g. Algonquian, Athabaskan and Eskimo-Aleut) to Iroquoian (with six closely related languages spoken in Canada, of which Mohawk is the largest and most viable) to isolates from what were presumably once more extensive linguistic families (e.g. Kootenay, Tlingit and Haida).

Unsurprisingly, the number of speakers is correlated closely with the size and geographical distribution of the linguistic family. The 1991 census recognizes only three languages, two of them Algonquian, as viable speech communities in the foreseeable future. Almost half of Canada's 365,000 Algonquian people speak their traditional languages (94,000 Crees and 30,000 Ojibwes) (McMillan 1995: 124). Most of the remaining speakers are found in the Maritime provinces where Mi'kmaq (formerly Micmac) is most widespread . Language use is decreasing rapidly even among these relatively viable languages in the country's largest Aboriginal language family. In the context of this variability, however, no single model of Aboriginal language retention and revitalization can be postulated. Even within each language, local communities differ widely in their present circumstances and future aspirations.

This variability of language, culture, and local adaptation to contact with mainstream Canadian society has long been masked by a history of assimilationist policy administered through missionary-run residential schools that separated children from traditional socialization in their families of origin and punished them for speaking Aboriginal languages. Almost everywhere, the language of everyday communication is English or French (in Quebec), even where traditional languages are still spoken by people of all ages. Policies of internal colonialism persist despite three decades of systematic activism seeking self-government and Native control of Native education.

The urbanization of Canada's Aboriginal population further privileges the use of English, which becomes the lingua franca by default in areas where peoples of different Aboriginal descent and linguistic heritage live in close proximity. Over half of Canada's Aboriginal people now live off-reserve, mostly in urban areas. A network of friendship centres across the country provides a semblance of community network for many of these people. Many of them also move back and forth regularly between city and Reserve.

3. The Variable Local Context

The overview of Aboriginal language retention and revitalization in Canada is dire in the extreme. Many linguists have become demoralized by the number of languages that are already extinct or highly endangered. They are content to document remnant knowledge obtained from elderly, preferably monolingual, speakers before this generation disappears entirely. Reports of the last living speaker of various languages have, however, been highly exaggerated, beginning almost with contact.

At least under some local circumstances, it is possible to be more optimistic. Moreover, such optimism is appropriate in situations of language endangerment as well as in areas of strong linguistic continuity. To give up in advance on the possibility of language revitalization is to deny the effective agency of contemporary people, whether speakers of their traditional languages or not, as well as to reify the languages as they existed in some pristine past purity. Viable languages are used and may be expected to change, especially under conditions of intensive contact with other languages. This is a natural process, well documented in comparative linguistic studies around the globe.

My own experience has involved twenty-one years of fieldwork in Plains Cree communities of northern Alberta (1969-90). The Plains Cree moved from James Bay to the Rocky Mountains as middlemen in the Fur Trade, meeting new peoples, Aboriginal as well as European, and adapting their language and culture as they moved. Today, most Plains Cree live in (or at least come from) moderately isolated Reserve communities that retain considerable capacity for language retention and revitalization. Almost everywhere, language teachers fluent in the local dialect of Cree are available from within the community. Language programs, therefore, have developed relatively independently in each community since the early 1970's. During these years, I was consulted extensively on the preparation of curriculum materials adapted to local needs to enhance oral fluency and introduce literacy (with some communities choosing syllabic and others Roman orthography).[2] Although communities frequently duplicated efforts, each program received local support because the teaching materials were locally derived. A cohort of Cree language teachers developed across northern Alberta, forming the expert base for the Cree language and culture course that I taught at the University of Alberta with various of these Cree speakers and language teachers between 1970 and 1985. With the founding of the School of Native Studies in 1985, the Cree language teaching program moved entirely to Native control. There were good reasons to be optimistic about the future of Cree as a language of everyday communication in at least some communities. These communities served as political models and sources of linguistic expertise for neighbouring Plains Cree communities.

In 1990, I moved to London, Ontario (in local parlance, 'southwestern Ontario') about two hours drive south of Toronto. At first glance, the Aboriginal language situation was dramatically different. The area includes three distinct Aboriginal populations (Algonquian, Iroquoian, and urban/off-Reserve), each with a population of approximately 10,000.

The cultural traditions of the Algonquian and Iroquoian communities are as different as their linguistic affiliations. At the time of European contact, the Iroquoians were matrilineal horticulturalists, growing corn, bean and squash, and united within an already complex confederation of

---

[2] The syllabic writing system, which represents orthographically the morphological structures of Algonquian languages, was devised by nineteenth century Wesleyan missionary, James Evans, who worked with the Cree in what is now northern Manitoba.

linguistically and culturally related tribes. In contrast, the Algonquians (largely Ojibwe, Delaware and Potawatomi who moved into what is now Canada in the displacement following the War of 1812) were nomadic hunters and gatherers with bilateral social organization (lacking a clan structure comparable to that of the Iroquoians). Band leadership was fluid, informal, and situationally invoked.

Although the traditional subsistence patterns of horticulture and hunting have long since given way before the intensive settlement of south-western Ontario, the Iroquoian and Algonquian cultural traditions and communicative economies remain irrevocably distinct, in line with their precontact traditions. Despite relatively similar historical experience and contemporary political agendas, southwestern Ontario Aboriginal communities do not speak with a single voice. Particular communities, moreover, differ considerably in their linguistic profiles and aspirations.

A series of about two dozen small Algonquian Reserves are located south and west of London, Ontario, toward Detroit and the St. Clair River. They refer to themselves as distinct First Nations (e.g. Walpole Island First Nation, Chippewa-of-the-Thames First Nation, Moraviantown First Nation, etc.) rather than by the larger designations of Ojibwe, Delaware or Potawatomi. These tribes of the Three Fires Confederacy, formed in historic times, are distributed across many local Reserves, making identity a question of place more than of ethnicity (although all of these groups are closely related, both linguistically and culturally).

The Six Nations of the Grand River are located at Brantford, Ontario, northeast of London. Iroquoian allies of the British fled to this area after the American Revolution, accompanied by their Algonquian-speaking allies, the Missassauga and Delaware. Six Nations is the largest Indian Reserve in Canada. Other Iroquoians live at Oneida First Nation on the outskirts of the city of London.

London's 10,000 Native people, both Algonquians and Iroquoians, are virtually invisible in a total population of 320,000. The challenge posed by urban residence to Aboriginal language retention and maintenance is considerable, however passionately individuals may feel about the importance of speaking Ojibwe or Mohawk. Almost no one speaks a traditional language in the city. Because most of London's Native population lives close to home and retains ties to their Reserve, however, urban dwellers are not solely dependent on linguistic resources within the city (although some schools, in neighbourhoods with large Native population, offer Aboriginal language classes, and the N'Amerind Friendship Centre frequently offers adult language classes).

The greater problem is that the local Reserves do not have enough fluent language speakers to back up the urban desire for formal teaching and learning of traditional languages. On southwestern Ontario Reserves, most fluent speakers (of both Mohawk and Ojibwe) are over sixty years of age and speak English on an everyday basis. Language programs necessarily depend on the expertise that is available. For example, a Potawatomi-Ojibwe woman in her fifties with a passive command of the language from childhood teaches Ojibwe in a London high school with many Native students and consults her mother, one of the few locally acknowledged expert speakers, in preparing her lesson plans. Some area Ojibwe communities have resorted to hiring language teachers from northern Ontario whose Ojibwe is fluent but is a different dialect from that historically spoken by the Ojibwe of south-western Ontario, who are recent immigrants from further south.

4. Documenting Local Communicative Competence

In 1990, my colleague Lisa Valentine and I began to develop a long-term research project geared to conditions of language retention and revitalization in south-western Ontario. Lisa's previous work, summarized in her *Making it their own: Severn Ojibwe Communicative Practices* (1995), was carried out among the small, isolated Ojibwe-speaking communities of northern Ontario. Initially, both of us saw mostly absences, but we suspected that we were missing something creative and fascinating. So we resolved to study what the literature euphemistically and somewhat pejoratively labels 'Indian English', as spoken in southwestern Ontario. Our three successive grants from the Social Sciences and Humanities Research Council of Canada have enabled fieldwork of more than a dozen graduate students in a variety of southwestern Ontario communities over a decade beginning in 1991.[3]

---

[3] Principal investigators Regna Darnell and Lisa Valentine were later joined by political scientist Allan McDougall. Student researchers included: Lindy-Lou Flynn (discourses about healing from residential school abuse), Kathleen Buddle-Crow (First Nations media), Theresa McCarthy (influence of Native Studies courses on the construction of identity for high school students in schools near their home Reserve), Tim Bisha (consensus and factionalism in defining 'acts of agreement), Robert Wishart (hunting narratives in a wetlands ecology), Susanne Miskimmin (narratives about the C-31 revisions to the Indian Act that restored Indian status and band membership to women who had married out of their home communities and to their children), Molly Turnbull (kinship and identity), Bruce Lawrence (religious syncretism), Craig Proulx (Aboriginal justice initiatives), Karen Pennesi (white and Native standpoints toward environmental degradation), Elizabeth

The first stage of the project (1991-94) envisioned an inventory of communities and linguistic competencies by generation, following the methodology developed by William Labov for New York City and Gillian Sankoff and Henrietta Cedergren for Montreal, Quebec. This perspective did not prove particularly illuminating given the absence of a monolingual elder generation in virtually all communities. Most speakers, regardless of age, whether Algonquian or Iroquoian, spoke an English which was quite distinct from the mainstream English of southwestern Ontario. This difference, however, was not stratified by age.

The second stage of the project (1994-97) focused not so much on the indigenous languages as on performing First Nations identity in English, in an effort to demonstrate the pervasiveness of traditional culture even when expressed in English. We found that English was creatively adapted to traditional purposes (although most speakers were minimally aware of this process). Cross-cultural mis-communication resulted, moreover, from the mainstream assumption that Native people who spoke English must be assimilated. English itself was seen to be monolithic by Native and non-Native respondents alike. A focus on discourse enabled us to identify consistent differences between Iroquoian and Algonquian Englishes as well as communication gaps to the mainstream. For example, it is more important who speaks than what is said. Therefore, narratives begin with biographical material, which establishes the authenticity of the speaker whose experience will be reflected in what follows. Pause structures, leaving time for listeners to consider what has been told to them, are much longer than in mainstream English. In addition, indirectness is highly valued. Algonquian and Iroquoian groups identify the same traits in each other but each values their own way of doing things; Algonquians find Iroquoians verbally aggressive, while Iroquoians complain that Algonquians can never come to a decision.

The third phase of the project (1997-2001) turned to the larger context of ethnicity, power and identity. Mainstream Canada has failed to incorporate the richness and sophistication of First Nations cultures, especially as expressed in English, into the national imaginary. Exceptions and exhortations are found in John Ralston Saul (1997) and Darnell (2000). For Canada, as for the First Nations, language remains at the core of a troubled search for a national identity that can be embraced by all constituent communities.

Guerrier (maritime fishing rights), Barry Milliken (storied life history), Paul Hogan (First Nations curriculum), Marcia Simon (community identity in political crisis). Local communities studied included: Toronto, London, Walpole Island, Stony and Kettle Point, Sarnia, Oneida, and Six Nations.

5. Rethinking Language Revitalization Agendas

The innovative adaptation of English in southwestern Ontario (and doubtless elsewhere as well) has produced an ideology and practice of traditional language maintenance that differs considerably from established sociolinguistic expectations.

Native political organizations established in the 1960s and 1970s have shifted dramatically from the economic emphasis of their early years. The intervening decades have brought recognition that many contemporary social problems must be traced back to the isolation imposed on multiple generations of residential school students separated from their communities and therefore from traditional oral forms of knowledge transmission. Widespread recognition of the 'residential school syndrome' has engendered a powerful political rhetoric framing individual and community experience of language loss alongside the loss of land in the ideological construction of First Nations oppression since European contact. Economic progress has been considerable, although problems certainly remain; symbolic grounds for individual and community identity now hold at least equal weight. A new generation of well-educated fluent speakers of English privileges traditional language maintenance as an idealized expression of contemporary political aspirations. Language forms a critical pillar of reconstituted cultural authenticity and pride, although very few of those who habitually employ this rhetoric are themselves fluent speakers of a traditional language. These young leaders are often too busy for systematic language study. They tend to drop out of language classes and settle for symbolic use of the languages lost to them as a result of the colonial experience of their immediate forbears. Language loss, moreover, functions politically as a moral justification for continued special status for Aboriginal peoples within Canadian Confederation (a contention disputed by many Canadians who lump Native people with immigrants).

Outsider linguists have tended to dismiss such non-fluent use of traditional languages as merely symbolic. This approach, however, masks the vibrant commitment of local communities to retain their Aboriginal identity without becoming paralyzed by the ever-receding image of a pristine idealized past. Crucially, this ideology of linguistic revitalization as a recovery from colonial oppression is not found in isolated communities like the ones in which Lisa Valentine and I did our initial field research. As long as traditional language use and cultural identity can be taken for granted, people do not need to talk about them. An increasing rate of urbanization (with over half of Canada's Aboriginal people now living off-Reserve) portends the increasing dissolution of isolated community boundaries. Escalating processes of globalization suggest that the experience of the present generation that must revitalize rather than maintain their traditional languages will become typical in the future, if it is not already. The processes of rapid social change within traditional communities must be understood in order to preserve the linguistic (and cultural) expertise existing today, so that new forms of transmission can be devised for new circumstances.

Despite cross-community variability and apparently accelerating 'loss' of linguistic fluency, there is cause for optimism. This is especially the case if, as linguists working in the field, we can abandon the purist ideologies associated with our work. Globalization produces resistance as well as accommodation. The emerging English-speaking Aboriginal elites of southwestern Ontario proudly define themselves as Mohawk, Ojibwe, etc. They have at their disposal linguistic resources beyond the immediate demographics of progressive language loss. In some communities, elsewhere, children are still learning languages that are endangered locally. For example, an Ojibwe language teacher from northern Ontario may speak an unfamiliar dialect but still offer insights that come from a culturally conservative socialization to traditional subsistence patterns (today, this means a trapline and continued nomadic existence for the family, at least seasonally). In literal historical terms, the Chippewa who moved across the U.S. border to south-western Ontario were Woodland peoples, not buffalo hunters or sub-Arctic trappers. Nonetheless, many of them have adopted the non-local symbols of the northern fur trade to mediate between partially shared and overlapping cultural histories. Cultural and linguistic authenticity is unassailable in local eyes in southwestern Ontario, even though the classroom format is an innovation. Moreover, local elders visit school classrooms to transmit their traditional knowledge in English. Because the context of traditionalism has already been established in the classroom, the community accepts this transmission process matter-of-factly as 'traditional'. That is, it has continuity with the past and enables further continuity. Despite a rhetoric of loss that functions to exhort active efforts toward revitalization, continuity is recognized and valued. Outsiders often take the rhetoric at face value and assume that elders have given up.

Similarly, the immersion program in Mohawk language at Six Nations can turn to linguistically fluent traditionalists for support. At least some parents are learning the language alongside their children. Even when fluency is far from attainment, pride in increased ability to use the traditional language gives cause for optimism. Breakdown in the isolation of Reserve communities from the Canadian mainstream certainly proceeds apace. But it is no longer automatically accompanied by rejection of traditional languages in favour of English. And this phenomenon crosses both generations and linguistic fluencies. There is a powerful political will to maintain and revitalize these languages in communities which still retain substantial resources of linguistic fluency and traditional knowledge.

Maintenance of traditional ceremonial practices provides an additional resource for language revitalization. Iroquoian longhouse ritualists still perform the seasonal cycle, including the reading of the Great Law of the Hodenosaunee (the League of the Iroquois) in Cayuga, Onondanga and Mohawk. Among the Algonquian communities, the successive esoteric grades of the Midewewin medicine society are being transmitted and practiced. Such continuing traditionalism directly motivates revitalization of languages in which these ceremonies were devised and are still felt to be ideally transmitted. Even though initial access is often in English today, practitioners often turn to traditional language as their knowledge and commitment increase and as they move into the statuses of elder, grandparent, and traditional teacher.

Language policies and aspirations vary considerably from community to community within southwestern Ontario. Some pursue cultural authenticity aggressively and use language as a tool in a self-conscious political agenda. Others deploy bilingual competencies across a wide spectrum of Native and non-Native performance contexts; decisions about situationally appropriate language and register are arrived at pragmatically rather than ideologically. Most Native people accept this range of behaviours and strategies as legitimate individual choices.

Such eclectic strategies, however, pose a more serious challenge to linguistics, at least as traditionally practiced. Many of the linguistic innovations and neologisms contradict our inherited traditions of what Aboriginal languages ought to sound like (at levels ranging from phonology to discourse to communicative style). Our own professional socialization has made us linguistic purists in a way that speakers of a language rarely are. Although we acknowledge in principle that languages change, partly in response to their contact with other languages, in practice we have immobilized idealized precontact languages as the preferred targets of our investigation. Increasingly over the past century, linguists have been collaborating with Aboriginal individuals and communities to record texts, prepare dictionaries and grammars, and train linguists from the community (see Valentine and Darnell eds 1999 for discussion of the ethical implications).

Much of this work, of course, is invaluable. For example, H.C. Wolfart of the University of Manitoba, in collaboration with Plains Cree elder and linguist Freda Ahenakew, has produced a series of philologically sophisticated texts recorded in the 'high Cree' of fluent monolingual speakers. However, the project assumes that bilingualism produces distortion, regardless of the degree of traditional language fluency. Similarly, Canadian poet Robert Bringhurst's new English translation of the Haida texts collected by Boasian linguist John Swanton at the turn of the century (Bringhurst 1999) explicitly restricts itself to the 'classic Haida' of individual poets. This language is quite different from the everyday language now spoken on the Haida Gwaii homeland in the Queen Charlotte Islands of British Columbia.

Neither of these ongoing projects intends to denigrate the linguistic competence of contemporary bilingual speakers or the widely spread efforts to revitalize traditional Aboriginal languages through classroom teaching. Indeed, both provide curriculum resources for such language revitalization. Nonetheless, the textual approach privileged by most linguists reflects an embedded and often subconscious purism that is received with ambivalence by many Native individuals and communities who consider themselves, and their contemporary usage, to be the appropriate standard for the viability of their traditional languages. There is widespread acknowledgement that the texts constitute a powerful resource when they are placed in Native hands. On the other hand, the texts were stolen from their original speakers, in a way directly comparable to the theft of traditional languages by the residential school system. Texts are reified caricatures of the legitimate intellectual property of ritualists and storytellers within a vibrant oral tradition. Writing them down rigidifies and reifies such speakings because they are cut off from their roots in authentic cultural performance. As a final insult, linguists' texts are conventionally published under the authorship of the outsider linguist. Moreover, Canadian copyright law gives sole rights to the recorder in the writing down of oral performance. Under these conditions, written texts remove control of traditional knowledge transmission from the producers of that knowledge.

In southwestern Ontario, efforts at linguistic and cultural revitalization have used whatever is available, whether in traditional languages or in English. Despite the practical advantages of linguistic standardization and pooling of resources across communities, logistics have held less priority than ideology. Programs are developed at the local level, in fits and starts, in response to the skills and commitments of particular individuals (usually supported by band councils, community cultural centres and school committees). The core participants in such local programs have grown up in an oral tradition. They take for granted that significant information is highly personalized and ideally transmitted through face-to-face communication with known and respected persons, usually elderly. Ownership, defined as the capacity for internalization of traditional knowledge, crucially depends on the maintenance of this traditional communicative economy.

This set of assumptions, shared by many outsider linguists, conflicts dramatically with the underlying assumptions of the western educational system on which the success of linguistic revitalization programs increasingly depends. If Native language classrooms are unable to operate within local communicative conventions, it is highly unlikely that classroom knowledge can be transferred effectively to attain either linguistic fluency or community goals. Although they rarely formulate the challenge in these terms, language planners and teachers from within local communities are systematically devising new pedagogical forms to recreate the underlying strategies of traditional socialization. Outside technology is adopted where appropriate to these goals.

Recent efforts of the Centre for Research and Teaching of Canadian Native Languages at the University of Western Ontario, of which I serve as Director, illustrate the range of relevance. On the traditional language front, Rand Valentine (1998) retranslated the texts given to Leonard Bloomfield at Walpole Island,[4] with pedagogical addenda directed toward contemporary local use at Walpole Island and nearby Ojibwe communities. The Centre's Associate Director, Tyendinega Mohawk linguist David Kanatawahkan Maracle teaches Mohawk at Western and several other Ontario universities and has developed a CD-ROM version of his classroom materials.

Seemingly at the other end of the spectrum, writer and artist Barry Milliken, a member of the Stony and Kettle Point band, recorded and transcribed in English life stories narrated by the late Annie Rachel Shawkence, also of the Stony and Kettle Point band (1997). A fluent bilingual, aged eighty-seven at the time of recording, Mrs. Shawkence spoke in English because the younger members of her community no longer understand Ojibwe. Although these young people were her primary intended audience, she also hoped that mainstream Canadians could learn to comprehend the plight of her beleaguered community. Members of the former Stoney Point band had been forcibly amalgamated with the Kettle Point band in 1942 under a War Measures Act appropriation of their Reserve. In protest at failure to return their land more than half a century after the end of the war, Stoney Point claimants and their descendants

[4] Texts are 'given' to learners within the culture as well as to outsider linguists and anthropologists. Such a 'gift' entails an obligation to use it to the benefit of the community as well as in one's individual life.

occupied Crown land at Ipperwash Provincial Park. The standoff, rendered intractable when in 1996 provincial police shot dead the unarmed band member Dudley George, has been characterized by hostility, ill-will, and mis-communication on all sides. Mrs. Shawkence's stories are designed, in part, to defuse this hostility. Her stories are domestic, not overtly political. They are personal. She makes few explicit judgments, but her experiences lead the reader to feel deeply both the injustice done to her community and the richness of her authentic cultural tradition. Her expressive style is fundamentally alien to that of mainstream Canadian society, despite the 'English' surface form. Barry Milliken has now completed a volume of veterans' stories from the same band, representing different wars and different generations of Ojibwe warriors (Milliken 2003).

The death of Mrs. Shawkence not long after the appearance of the volume (the first in a Centre series entitled 'Voices from the Communities') ensures that her words remain available to her grandchildren and beyond (as do Cruikshank's (1990) life histories of three southern Yukon women, elders who also speak in English for the sake of monolingual descendants). Although writing is not a traditional medium, such stories have the potential to supplement oral tradition, both within the community of their origin and in other Native and non-Native communities. Annie Rachel Shawkence is a known person in the memory of her community. The new technology of writing functions positively to extend the reach of memory, to offset the effects of rapid and destructive culture change.

New technologies do not necessarily break down the boundaries of traditional community identities, as long as the changes remain under local control. This logic of adapting what is useful to traditional purposes has allowed Aboriginal communities across Canada to establish closer ties among themselves through exchange of audio and visual materials, satellite communication, and the Internet. Globalization coexists with and operates in relation to local diversity. New communities facilitate the imagining of communities beyond the range of face-to-face communication (cf. Anderson 1983). Increasingly, the elders of contemporary locales may be from other places and even other times. Adaptation to local purposes, however, makes them 'local'.

Turning to an Iroquoian example of using new technologies in English in the service of traditional language revitalization, the late Cayuga traditional chief Jake Thomas performed the Great Law in four languages in the 1990s: Cayuga (the language of the traditional keepers of the central fire of the Hodenosaunee), Onondaga, Mohawk, and English. Although the inclusion of the latter within his repertoire was certainly controversial at Six Nations, Jake's logic was that the young people would be eager to attend ceremonies performed in English. Being there would cause them to realize that English was an alien and imperfect medium for authentic cultural knowledge belonging to them as their rightful inheritance. He also taught Cayuga language at Six Nations and at Trent University, considering the linguistic and cultural knowledge to be inseparable. Audio and video recordings of his English performances of the Great Law are available for continuing community use.

The existence of a Mohawk immersion program at Six Nations reflects the numerical preponderance of this Nation on the Reserve and demonstrates that the community shares Jake's commitment to language revitalization. Which Iroquoian language or languages are to be revitalized is less important at this stage of commitment, I believe, than the engagement of young people with a renewed traditionalism that establishes continuity with the past. Parents who are latent bilinguals support their children and rapidly reactivate their own passive knowledge of the language. Under such conditions, linguists have too often assumed that languages or ceremonies are moribund and found instead that new performers step forward when their skills are called upon by their communities.

6. Conclusion

Linguists are not accustomed to thinking this way. Rather we expect, and perhaps create by our own expectation, constants of *langue*, of competence, which serve to mask, obscure or distort the realities of actual communicative behaviour. This rapid overview demonstrates that multiple resources available to southwestern Ontario Iroquoian and Algonquian communities are consistent with traditional practice. These resources are being adapted to ongoing use, despite demographic signals of their limited potential for successful revitalization. If, however, pragmatics is internal to language, and context is not what used to be called 'extralinguistic', then it follows that pragmatics "brings to light variables of expression or of enunciation" (Deleuze and Guattari 1987: 82). Deleuze and Guattari insist that pragmatics must be defined as 'a politics of language'. If people care enough, what they create by collective action will become a language, will colonize, as it were, the language it adapts.

From this perspective, English in south-western Ontario cannot remain the same language, because new variants are being added; similarly, Mohawk and Ojibwe are becoming new languages. I find this result intellectually as well as politically palatable, although it would have startled me greatly at the beginning of my career. I want to understand the process by which such linguistic becoming occurs. Linguistics, like the minority 'traditional' languages that linguists wish to isolate and study, is becoming something different under conditions of rapid social and cultural change. Ideologies of linguistic revitalization, both those of language speakers and of linguists, reside at the very core of such changes.

The codeswitching capacities of the new generation of Native Canadian communities and their political and intellectual leaders break new ground whether the Aboriginal language they command is enshrined by linguists or spoken before Columbus 'discovered' America. Students participating in language revitalization programs today are rapidly becoming spokespersons for renewed traditionalism in a contemporary political agenda. What is at stake is no less than a long-overdue reconfiguration of the political spectrum of Native-white relations in Canada.

References

Ahenakew, Freda and H.C. Wolfart (1992) *Our Grandmothers' Lives as Told in Their Own Words*, Saskatoon: Fifth House.

Anderson, Benedict (1983) *Imagined Communities: Reflections on the Origin and Spread of Nationalism*, London: Verso.

Bringhurst, Robert (1999) *A Story as Sharp as a Knife: The Classical Haida Mythtellers and their World*, Vancouver and Toronto: Douglas and McIntyre.

Cruikshank, Julie (1990) *Life Lived Like a Story*, Lincoln: University of Nebraska Press.

Darnell, Regna (2000) 'The Invisible Alternative: First Nations and Canada's Self-Image at the Millennium', *Anthropologica* 42: 165-174.

------ (2001) 'Pragmatic Constraints on Revitalization of First Nations Language Education in Southwestern Ontario, Canada', in Eniko T. Nemeth (ed) *Pragmatics in 2000: Selected Papers from the 7th International Pragmatics Conference, vol. 2*, Antwerp, Belgium: International Pragmatics Association, 146-155.

Deleuze, Gilles and Felix Guattari (1987) *A Thousand Plateaus: Capitalism and Schizophrenia*, Minneapolis: University of Minnesota Press.

McMillan, Allan D. (1995) *Native Peoples and Cultures of Canada: An Anthropological Overview*, Vancouver and Toronto: Douglas and McIntyre.

Milliken, Barry (ed) (1997) *Stories of Annie Rachel Shawkence*, London, Ontario: Centre for Research and Teaching of Canadian Native Languages, University of Western Ontario.

------ (ed) (2003) *Veterans' Stories from Stony and Kettle Point*, London, Ontario: Centre for Research and Teaching of Canadian Native Languages, University of Western Ontario.

Saul, John Ralston (1997) *Reflections of a Siamese Twin: Canada at the End of the Twentieth Century*, Toronto: Viking.

Valentine, Lisa (1995) *Making it their Own: Severn Ojibwe Communicative Practices*, Toronto: University of Toronto Press.

------ and Regna Darnell (eds) (1999) *Theorizing the Americanist Tradition*, Toronto: University of Toronto Press.

Valentine, J. Randolph (1998) *The Andrew Medlar Ojibwe Texts from Walpole Island, Ontario*, London, Ontario: Centre for Research and Teaching of Canadian Native Languages, University of Western Ontario.

Wolfart, H.C. and Freda Ahenakew (1991) *The Cree Language is Our Identity: The Lac La Ronge Lectures of Sarah Whitecalf*, Winnipeg: University of Manitoba Press.

------ (1993) *Their Example Showed Me the Way: A Cree Woman's Life Shaped by Two Cultures*, Edmonton: University of Alberta Press.

6. Linguistic Rights and Language Survival in a Creole Space

Dilemmas for Nicaragua's Caribbean Coast Creoles[1]

JANE FREELAND

1. Introduction

This chapter examines some dilemmas faced by the Creoles of Nicaragua's Caribbean Coast in claiming and implementing the linguistic rights granted them under Nicaragua's Law of Autonomy for the Caribbean Coast Regions (1987). It argues that 'diaspora' groups like these (Hall 1990 [1993], 1996; Gilroy 1993) are particularly ill-served by the unitary notions of peoplehood, identity and language that underpin Western state language policies and minority challenges to them (Woolard 1998: 17). *Creole* has, after all, become the technical term for the opposite of these notions: for transnational, hybridized languages usually analyzed as continua or bridges between African and European languages; and by extension for the transnational, syncretized cultural identities with which these languages are associated (Pieterse 1994).

The problems highlighted by this case are not peculiar to Nicaragua's Creoles, nor indeed to Black diaspora cultures; they merely write large issues affecting all minoritized groups who seek to assert the legitimacy

---

[1]This chapter draws on field work in Nicaragua since 1989 including teaching courses on Sociolinguistics and on Language Policy and Planning for the Licenciatura (BA) in Intercultural Bilingual Education at the University of the Autonomous Regions of the Caribbean Coast of Nicaragua (URACCAN). Students of the predominantly Creole group in 2001, all experienced teachers in the Programa de Educación Intercultural-Bilingüe [Intercultural-Bilingual Education Programme] (PEIB) requested that we focus on the question of writing Creole. Our discussions were the main stimulus for this paper, which is greatly enriched by the students' insights and their permission to cite some of their course work. I am indebted to the NGO consortium 'Sahwang' and to the Instituto para la Promoción e Investigación de Lenguas y Culturas [Institute for Research and Promotion of Languages and Cultures] (IPILC) at URACCAN and its director Guillermo McLean, for their financial and moral support for this teaching. An earlier version of the paper was presented to the colloquium 'Linguistic rights and wrongs' at Sociolinguistics Symposium 14, held in Ghent in April 2002, and has benefited from the discussion there, and from those of Donna Patrick and Mark Sebba on the written version.

of their languages and cultures within prevailing discourses around cultural difference. The work of writers such as Hall and Gilroy has not only served to illuminate the dilemmas of Creole cultures; it is part of a more general critique of identity politics, and by extension language politics (see also May, this volume). I use the Nicaraguan Creole case in a similar way, to suggest that the discourse of linguistic rights is not as universal as it appears and needs critical re-examination if it is truly to assist language survival.

The first section briefly examines the ideological roots of the Sandinistas' discourse on minority rights for the Caribbean Coast region, highlighting key features which made it particularly inappropriate to the Creoles and relating it to the international discourse on language rights. The second section describes the complexities of the Nicaraguan Creoles' multi-faceted diaspora identity, and the third section their correspondingly complex use of and attitudes to their Creole language. A fourth section examines the problems these complexities have brought to the articulation and implementation of Nicaraguan Creoles' linguistic rights, especially in education. The final section discusses a recently proposed solution to these problems: that writing is a necessary route to legitimacy for the Creole language. It argues that this proposal is not so much a solution to the problem as one of its most concrete expressions.

2. Revolution, Ethnicity and Language

Since Spain first colonized Central America's Pacific Coast in the sixteenth century, and England, ignoring Spanish claims to the whole isthmus, occupied the Caribbean Coast from the seventeenth century, the histories of these two regions have followed opposed but interacting courses (Vilas 1989; Hale 1994; Gordon 1998). By the time of the Sandinista revolution of 1979, this dual history had produced contrasting social formations.

The western, Pacific Region was the centre of a Nicaraguan state constructed on an ideology of *mestizaje* (economic, racial, cultural and linguistic assimilation) which had contributed to the near demise of indigenous communities and identities. By contrast, the Caribbean Coast was a multilingual, 'interethnic region' (Díaz Polanco 1985: 100), where five indigenous/ethnic groups had coexisted, interacted and indeed intermarried for centuries. Early British colonialism by indirect rule through the Miskitu Indians and their king, followed by a century of North American enclave capitalism, plus the failure of attempts by successive national governments to incorporate the region effectively into the Nicaraguan state, had all contributed to an illusion of autonomy in the region.

This history had left *Costeños* (Coast people), especially the Miskitu and Creoles, with strong 'Anglo affiliations' (Hale 1994), a distrust of Mestizo interventions, and ambitions to regain their autonomy. So when revolutionary cadres arrived to bring the revolution to the Coast, they spoke a different language than Costeños in many senses. Although Costeños and Sandinistas ostensibly shared the goal of ending racial and ethnic discrimination in the region, their ideologies gave widely divergent values to key concepts like 'self-determination' and, especially, 'culture'.

Sandinismo approached the Coast's diversity through a reinterpretation of *indigenismo* [indigenism], "the hallmark of progressive thinking [for] liberal and revolutionary [Latin American] governments until well into the second half of the [twentieth] century" (Adams 1991: 202-203, n. 190). *Indigenismo* envisaged national unity as a benign form of *mestizaje* that would blend the best of indigenous and European cultures into a unique Latin American culture. However, it rested on idealized notions of the indigenous past and little understanding of its present-day continuation (Hale 1994: 89-94, 207-211).

These notions were, anyway, inapplicable to the Coast, which under English and American rule had remained marginal to the Hispanic colonial process. Their ambivalence about the contribution of peoples of African descent to the racial and cultural make-up of the nation and its distrust of their 'Anglo' culture made it particularly inapplicable to the Creoles (Romero Vargas 1992; Gordon 1998: 121).

The Sandinista discourse displayed two further tendencies of old-style *indigenismo*: a static, reified conception of culture, and a tendency to separate material and non-material cultural practices. The Sandinistas gave this separation a Marxian twist, such that they could plan simultaneously to 'develop' the Coast's economic base, and to foster its 'superstructural' symbolic cultures (Vilas 1989: 71). In line with the anthropological tradition that supported *indigenismo*, language was the aspect of these cultures singled out for particular consideration. Indeed, in early Sandinista texts, 'language' appears so frequently as a near-synonym of culture that the two become conflated (Freeland 1999). Moreover, this past-oriented, essentialist and purist view of culture could not distinguish cultural change from loss of authenticity: it envisioned the revitalization of languages (and so cultures) as their *rescate* (rescue) in terms reminiscent of marine archaeology, as if like sunken ships they could be dredged up from the depths of time and their missing elements inferred and restored from what had survived.

This equation of language with culture was also, of course, embedded in classic European ideologies of language and nation, in Hispanic mode.[2] Early Latin American nation-builders had seen Spanish both as the language of equal citizenship and a gift of access to 'civilized' values for 'primitive' peoples. What more logical than to recognize other peoples through their languages?

3. Nicaragua's Creoles – A 'Disparate Diaspora' in a 'Creole Space'

Nicaragua's Creoles (as they designate themselves) number about 50,000. They are the third largest of the Coast's six ethnic groups (including the Spanish-speaking *Mestizos*), constituting 19.5% of the population of the Coast and 1.1% of the national population (URACCAN 1998). In Gordon's apt phrase, they are a 'disparate diaspora', which does not fit "standard historical narratives of the African Diaspora and disrupts facile assumptions about black resistance to racial terror and ideologies" (Gordon 1998: 30-31). Their group identity "emerged, not from a specific biological admixture but as a consequence of (...) often contradictory tactical maneuverings within and against specific relations of power" (ibid.: 32). Its content, "the salient 'racial' and cultural features of its members (...) changed over time as socio-political conditions changed and as racially and culturally different peoples interacted with or were incorporated into the group" (ibid). This is equally true of the Creoles' language, on which Gordon touches only briefly, and of their 'linguistic ideology' or 'linguistic culture': "that set of behaviours, assumptions, cultural forms, prejudices, folk belief systems, attitudes, stereotypes, ways of thinking about language, and religio-historical circumstances associated with a particular language" (Schiffman 1996: 5). I shall first discuss the complexities of Creole identity formation and production, then link these to their linguistic culture.

In Gordon's words:

> Creoles [have] historically inhabited three transnational identities simultaneously, with the popularity and salience of each varying historically. These three can be identified by the names that Creoles have called themselves. (...) Creole black Caribbean diasporic identity is signified by their calling themselves blacks (*negros*), (...) Creole

---

[2] In Freeland (1998) I explore more fully the particular significance of a unifying language for Hispanic nation builders. On the influence of various popularized versions of Whorfianism in nationalism, see Silverstein 2000.

> Anglo diasporic identity (...) by their calling themselves Creole (...) [and] Creole indigenous identity (...) by their calling themselves Costeños (Coast people). (1998: 192-193)

Each identity marks a different boundary from, and allows different alliances with other Coast groups. All mark distinctions from the Mestizos, who are "the Coast ethnic group (...) most different from, and most threatening to, the Creoles' position" (ibid: 194-195), and are perceived as usurpers of their rightful place as leaders of the Coast region, especially since its forcible annexation (in Anglo accounts) or 'reincorporation' (in Hispanic ones) into the Nicaraguan state in 1894.

In the last decade or so, British Creole writers such as Stuart Hall and Paul Gilroy have explored some of the special difficulties faced by Creole diaspora groups around the world in asserting the validity of such multifaceted, transnational, syncretised cultural identities, against a prevailing, 'ethnic absolutist' discourse that assumes 'authentic' cultures to be clearly bounded, coterminous with national or ethnic boundaries, homogenous, and historically continuous (Gilroy 1993: 2-5). From this viewpoint, creolization, *métissage*, hybridity, all "rather unsatisfactory ways of naming the processes of cultural mutation and restless (dis)continuity", smack of pollution and impurity (op.cit.: 5). The colour-coding of this discourse places different facets of these identities on either side of an apparently immutable divide and forces impossible choices between them.

Nor are these problems solved by a post-modern, anti-essentialist discourse that views identities as contingent, instrumental constructs:

> Black identity is not simply a social and political category to be used or abandoned according to the extent to which the rhetoric that supports and legitimizes it is persuasive or institutionally powerful (...). [I]t is lived as a coherent (if not always stable) experiential sense of self. Though it is often felt to be natural and spontaneous, it remains the outcome of practical activity: language, gesture, bodily significations, desires. (ibid.: 100)[3]

Both Hall and Gilroy focus instead on the way these cultures are constantly *produced* in the 'space between' these artificially rigid borders.[4]

---

[3] See also May (this volume) who highlights the same false antithesis in discussions of ethnic identity in general, and relates the way it is lived in the body to Bourdieu's concept of 'habitus'.

[4] The idea has much in common with Östman and Laakso's treatment (this volume) of identity production on multiple margins.

Hall borrows from Aimé Césaire and Léopold Senghor the idea of an *Espace Créole* to help him "rethink the positioning and repositioning of Caribbean cultural identities" between three "presences": "*Présence Africaine, Présence Européenne,* and (...) *Présence Américaine*" (Hall 1990 [1993]: 397-398).[5] In the same spirit, Gilroy offers a more open-ended metaphor, that of the "Black Atlantic" that borders Africa, Europe, America and the Caribbean countries, constantly traversed by ships, "the living means by which the points within that Atlantic were joined (…), mobile elements that stood for the shifting spaces between the fixed places that they connected" (1993: 16). These images focus attention on "the circulation of ideas and activists as well as the movement of key cultural and political artefacts" (ibid).

The space these writers identify is not empty, nor static. It is, rather, a kind of forcefield "composed of intersections of mobile elements. It is in a sense articulated by the ensemble of movements deployed within it" (Certeau 1984: 117, quoted by Gilroy 1993: note 33, p. 227). This emphasis on movement is important; the elements or forces moving in this space manifest differently in different historical contexts. In the Nicaraguan Creole space, for instance, there are two European presences, the English and the Spanish, which exert competing powers of attraction and repulsion. If relationships with even one 'European presence' can become "the site of a profound splitting and doubling" (Hall, op.cit.: 400), when there are two, these splittings become multiple, polyvalent.

It is within just such a space that Nicaraguan Creoles have not only historically exercised their political common sense, as Gordon puts it (1998), after Gramsci, but have responded more recently to the opportunity offered by the Sandinista recognition of ethnic rights to assert their particular cultural identity.

When Creoles call themselves 'Black', they draw closest to the 'African presence', identifying with the wider Black identity politics of the Caribbean and the US. This 'Black' identification is relatively recent, coming to Nicaragua via Jamaica and the intense but short-lived influence of Garveyism (Wünderich 1986), through the Rastafarianism encountered when young Creoles 'shipped out' on Caribbean cruise ships,

---

[5] The 'American presence' is the New World, the juncture point of many cultural tributaries: "the place of many, continuous displacements (...). It stands for the endless ways in which Caribbean people have been destined to 'migrate' (…) the signifier of migration itself (...) of the Antillean as the prototype of the modern or postmodern New World nomad, continually moving between centre and periphery" (Hall, op.cit 401).

and through Protestant versions of culturally sensitive liberation theology training in Costa Rica (Savery 1986: 43).[6] Immediately prior to the Sandinista revolution, this aspect of Creole identity had begun to find expression through two social and cultural movements: the United Committee for Community Development (UCCOD) and its successor the Southern Indigenous and Creole Council (SICC), which organized activities to foster pride in Creole Afro-culture, including poetry written in Creole, and the collection and diffusion of Creole oral history (Gordon 1998: 75-76, 182-188). As the Somoza regime began to crumble, aspects of this identification were linked with the anti-imperialism of the revolution by a group of young Black Sandinistas (op.cit: 205-225).

When they call themselves 'Creole', Creoles assert an identity rooted in their "appropriation of and identification with metropolitan English and Anglo mission-Protestantism and the Anglo roots of their culture" (op. cit.: 193, 32-35, 137). Creoles trace their ancestry back to a small elite of 'free people of colour', the favoured children of black slave women and European (mainly British) masters who, during a forced hiatus in the British presence (1787-1821) prospered and acquired considerable power, forming independent communities which, augmented by other 'free coloureds' and escapees, became the main Creole centres of today (op.cit.: 32-35, 137). When the British returned, the Creoles consolidated this position, though now only as the auxiliaries of first British colonial and then U.S. economic power (op.cit.: 43).

Central to this process was the Moravian Mission which from 1845 began evangelizing and founding schools in the region.[7] Converting to Moravianism meant exchanging 'heathen' African religious practices and lifeways for Protestant culture and its intellectual traditions. Mission education fitted Creoles to become teachers, church pastors, middle managers in the US enclaves, or entrepreneurs in their own right. Accepting this exchange, though, placed them in an ambivalent middle position in the

---

[6] Hall points out that conscious identification with this African aspect of Creole identities became 'historically available' in Jamaica only in the 1970s, mediated 'through the impact on popular life of the post-colonial revolution, the civil rights struggles, Rastafarianism and reggae' (1990 [1993]: 400). Gordon (1998: 96-100) shows that conscious identification with Africa varies considerably among Nicaraguan Creoles.

[7] Originally from Bohemia, the Moravians first evangelized among the Creoles and subsequently among the indigenous peoples, initially in English. Their policy was to build a school beside every church. See Holm 1978, Freeland 1995, and their references, for fuller accounts of the mission's impact on the politics and languages of the region.

racial pecking order: 'more civilized' than the indigenous peoples, yet as 'black and brown' people always socially inferior to whites (op. cit.: 45-47). Consequently, although "Creoles identified with and emulated the Anglos, they also developed an identity and culture that were different and oppositional" (op.cit: 48). In Nicaragua, this Anglo Creole identity, deriving from one of the European presences on the Coast, became the platform upon which Creoles built their opposition to the other, the Hispanic presence.

Initially, the designation 'Creole' distinguished a lighter-skinned, older-established group from 'Negroes' – escaped and freed slaves, immigrant labourers – and marked a clear class-ethnic divide. Over time, 'Negroes' assimilated 'upwards', until the designation 'Creole', came to denote the whole group, although some still distinguish a 'blacker' group and a so-called 'Creole aristocracy'. Today, orientations towards Anglo culture, education, and respectability and towards a more resistant popular, mundane, even "sinful" culture (Savery 1986: 41) coexist within the group, and appear with different degrees of saliency, not only at particular historical moments, but in social, and especially linguistic interaction within the group. The two are observable in one of the Creoles' most distinctive cultural events, the Maypole dances celebrating the start of the rainy season on the Coast in early May. There is a "Puritan-Conservative Version – danced ceremoniously with carefully placed steps and rhythms, without smiling or expressing emotions, like well-lubricated pieces in a machine" – and a "Liberal-Erotic Version – danced with constant rhythmic improvisations of both the music and the movements, and violent erotic contortions of the body in different positions: both vertical and horizontal. Emotions are undisguised" (Sujo Wilson 1988b; see also Savery 1986 on this duality in Creole music). Not only has the 'liberal' version appropriated elements from the 'conservative' one, but each exists in creative opposition to other, so that neither is complete on its own.

When Creoles call themselves '*Costeños*' (Coast people) they make common cause as an oppressed minority with the Coast's indigenous groups – some even trace blood relationships – and with the spirit behind the international indigenous movements through which these groups organize their resistance (Gordon 1998: 192-193). Here, they remember particularly their own resistance to Hispanic colonialism since the Coast's 1894 annexation into the Nicaraguan state. This facet of their identity, the expression in this context of the 'American presence' in the Creole space, is represented in the title of SICC (Southern Indigenous and Creole Council), and exists in tension with the 'Anglo Creole' identity which claims Creole superiority over the other minorities. The 'Costeño' identity became more salient in the early days of the revolution, asserted against a Sandinista discourse that, out of distrust for the Creoles' Anglo affiliations, attempted initially to distinguish them unfavourably from the 'autochthonous' Miskitu, Sumu and Rama.

These mutual misinterpretations illustrate the tensions or 'splittings' inherent in Creoles' assertion of their ethnicity and cultural distinctiveness. Against Hispanic tendencies to treat all the Coast's minority cultures as inferior, they cleave to their Anglo, European identity. Yet to do so is to connive in devaluing their 'Black' identity. Yet inasmuch as the 'Anglo identity' gives Creoles a sense of superiority to other groups, it creates tensions with their 'Costeño identity'. These tensions become particularly evident in relation to language.

4. Language and Identity(ies)

The Creole 'linguistic culture' is produced in this same dynamic space. Creoles speak 'Mosquito Coast Creole' (MCC) (Holm 1978, 1983, 1989)[8] or 'Nicaraguan English' (Shopen 1987; O'Neil and Honda 1987), an English-lexicon Creole which, like that of Belize, has admixtures from Miskitu and more recently from Spanish. It is a key group identity marker for 'Costeño', 'Black', or 'Anglo' Creoles, though it is differently constructed from each identity position.

Before 1894 there existed on the Coast an observable post-Creole continuum. English-medium mission schooling supported the lexifier language, and there was a significant community of native acrolect speakers, North American and British, in the mission churches and schools, and in the company enclaves. These were also the contexts where Standard English (SE) was required, and through which it acquired its high prestige and association with formal registers. At school, children's Creole, termed 'broken English', was harshly proscribed, the equivalent in speech of overcoming the old Afro ways.

> There used to be some old gentlemen and ladies, that (...) even though they were black they behaved like English gentlemen, they spoke like English gentlemen, they dressed like English gentlemen (...) I am speaking about men that those that are alive they have around eighty years (...) While the other Creoles that age that didn't go to school

[8]Holm 1978 is a masterly sociolinguistic history of the development of MCC and its relations to other Coast languages and Caribbean Creoles; it is epitomized in Holm 1983 and 1989.

> they spoke the real old Creole. (HSW, Director of CIDCA Bluefields, interview 1989)[9]

Developments following the 1894 annexation brought a gradual loss of contact with the acrolect. Initially, Spanish replaced English in all schools, though English was later re-admitted as a useful curriculum subject. Models of SE and contexts for its use became scarcer with the shrinking of consistent institutional support, the withdrawal of the enclave companies (from the 1960s), and the migration of Creole SE speakers to the external language markets of Managua, 'shipping out', or to the US. By the 1980s, SE was spoken with ease mainly by a dwindling, older minority (Yih and Slate 1985: 26), almost by definition prosperous, urbanized, middle-class, or aspiring to be so.

Whilst this group handles appropriately Standard English, Spanish and at least some Creole, the majority of Creole-speakers "focus" their speech along the middle or lower range of the continuum in complex 'acts of identity' (Le Page and Tabouret-Keller (1985), some commanding a larger spectrum of styles than others.[10] Among educated younger Creoles, the linguistic repertoire described by this informant is more typical:

> I identify myself as a Creole but I talk Spanish (…) which is not the language that I talk at home – the language that I talk at home is Creole – but I would practically have to say that my first language is Spanish because that's the language I feel most comfortable in (…) I can say more things… if it's something very serious that I got to talk

---

[9]To clarify the provenance of my data, I identify informants by their initials and by indicating aspects of their public or private identity relevant to the issues treated here. For a full list of informants see the appendix. All of them knew me as a researcher interested in the issue of Creole in education, or as a teacher on their EIB course, and as a non-Creole-speaking, British Standard English speaker, to whom they considerately converged their speech. Quotations are given in the language of the interaction, unless otherwise stated. My transcriptions of Nicaraguan Caribbean English (NCE) speech beg all the questions considered later in this chapter; they use Standard English orthography, but remain true to speakers' syntax and lexis.

[10] "Focusing" involves (largely) unconscious convergence towards the speech of groups with which one wishes to identify and which accept the identification. It can contribute to the evolution of both non-standard and standard varieties, without intervention from linguists. Freeland (2003) discusses the importance of this concept for understanding the intercultural communicative practices of all language groups of the Coast.

> to – about – I choose Spanish – sure if I come to a place and there is some Costeños there – I go to talk Creole.
> (JH, 'Black' Sandinista leader, interview 1989)

Indeed, for many such speakers, Spanish has replaced English as the language of formal contexts and registers and for interaction with non-Creoles, so much so that many preferred to use it with me. So Creole now stands in a diglossic relationship at least as much with Spanish as with SE. SE has become a tenuous, almost mythified presence, which has no clear referent and is maintained with increasing difficulty by private Protestant schools, notably the Moravian School, generally held to be the producer of the best SE speakers, and the ultimate authority on SE teaching:

> If we're gonna talk about the good English or the best English, or the Standard English we don't know which is the best, if it's from England, from the United States or from wherever. But each one should have their value and I think that we haven't learned to love our own selves as Black people with our own language.
> (NT, Cultura Pro-Autonomía [Culture for Autonomy] activist, interview, 1991)[11]

Even so, most Creoles (unless they are language activists or are being asked to reflect on language) still call their language 'English', opposing their Anglo-allegiances to 'Spanish'.

In practice and perception, then, SE is a vague 'not Creole' at which it is difficult to aim. This is an extreme example of that "structural disparity between *knowledge* of the legitimate language and (...) *recognition* of this language (...), between aspirations and the means of satisfying them" described by Bourdieu as the source of linguistic insecurity, "tension and pretension" (1982 [1992], author's emphasis):

> I (...) learned my English at the Moravian School, but it also created a complex in me, because when I'm going to say something, I have to stop and think "Must I say so-and-so, or must I say so-and-so?" I'm not free to just come out and say – and that depend on who I'm talking to. If I'm talking to [one of her former teachers], I have to make sure

[11]Speakers' uncertainty about the actual referent of the term 'Standard English', explicitly referred to here, was confirmed in countless interviews. My suggestion that it could refer to a Nicaraguan Standard English prompted reactions ranging from amusement through incredulity to rejection.

> I place my verbs and I place everything in the right place.
> (AB, former leader of the PEIB technical team, interview, 1991)

> Creoles trying to speak SE, that's what's happening, you could hear that every single day (…) and they believe they are speaking SE, at least some of them (…) but surely they aren't there to speak Creole, they are there in their own conviction (…) speaking English. You know you would hear some very (…) strange things.
> (HSW, then director of the Centre for Research and Documentation of the Atlantic Coast (CIDCA), interview 1991)

If Standard English is the stressfully 'other' form of speech, Creole is familiar and free; a feeling expressed from all identity positions. Nevertheless, expressions of delight in this freedom often draw upon and so feed into assumptions that anything goes because it is 'not a proper language'.

> Although it's *only an oral language* with no written form *even so* it's a language with which the Black ethnic group identifies fully and *as a Black woman* I feel very relaxed when I'm expressing myself in Creole because it's *the lack of spelling and linguistic rules* makes Creole such a special language – because I dare to think it's *the only one with that sweet taste like honey*. You feel so good when you pronounce your Creole words and *you don't have to wonder if I pronounced it right …the essence of Creole is that every word you say any how is correct*.
> (GG, PEIB teacher, written work for Sociolinguists, URACCAN 2000, my emphasis, my translation from Spanish)

5. Claiming and Using Language Rights

During the first year of the revolution (1979-80), all the Coast's minorities made broad claims for recognition of their cultures, led by MISURASATA, a predominantly Miskitu organization recognized in 1979 as the official mass organization of all the Coast's indigenous people and the vanguard of ethnic claims.[12] Claims focused initially on education, an early Sandinista priority, and thence on language. They were couched in terms reminiscent of such international instruments as the UNESCO Declarations on Vernacular Languages in Education (1953), which supported *mother tongue* education, both for its cognitive advantages and to strengthen children's ethnic identity:

---

[12]The Miskitu acronym means "Miskitu, Sumu and Rama in unity with the Sandinistas".

> Our education should provide our children with a knowledge of their own culture, so that they can be proud of it and in this way strengthen *their ethnic identity*, and in addition develop a broad knowledge of our country. For this, teaching at the community level must begin in the ethnic group's mother tongue during the first five years and then pass over to a bilingual system.
> (MISURASATA 1980: 54, my emphasis, translated from Spanish in Ohland and Schneider 1983).[13]

These claims chimed easily with the Sandinista discourse on language and cultural identity and brought a rapid response: extensions to the 1980 Literacy Crusade in three Coast languages (English, Miskitu and Sumu/Mayangna) and a Law on Education in Indigenous Languages on the Atlantic Coast (1980), which "recognised that teaching in *the mother tongue* constitutes a *fundamental factor in giving a sense of identity to individuals as well as peoples* and a determining factor in the process of integration and for the consolidation of National Unity" (JGRN 1980: 81, my emphasis, translated from Spanish in Ohland and Schneider 1983).

Further developments were blocked, however, when the Coast became a major theatre of the counter-revolutionary war into which wider indigenous grievances were co-opted. In the ensuing peace negotiations (1983-1987), language again became a leading issue. Two and a half years of consultation culminated in a Law on Autonomy for the Atlantic Coast (1987) which accorded extensive political, material and cultural rights to all the Costeño minorities. It broadened the terms of the 1980 law, making all Coast languages, whether in use or not, official within the region. It provided for all groups:

> To promote and develop their languages, religions and cultures (…).
> To be educated in their own languages, through programmes that take into account their historical heritage, their traditions and the characteristics of their environment, *all within the framework of the national education system.*
> (Law on Autonomy 1987: Article 12, clauses 2 and 4, official translation from Spanish, my emphasis)

In 1984, pilot 'bilingual-bicultural' education programmes were initiated, first in Miskitu and the next year in English and Sumu/Mayangna, each with Spanish. In 1993, a new Languages Law further specified language

---

[13]Aikman (1996: 153-155) traces the spread of this discourse through international, national and indigenous networks.

rights in relation to the media, public documents, announcements and signs. In principle it turns the Programa de Educación Intercultural-Bilingüe [Intercultural-Bilingual Education Programme] (PEIB) into a maintenance programme, extending it to the end of primary school and providing for teaching "the official languages of the Coast" (a change of terminology from the 'mother tongue' of 1980) as subjects in intermediate and adult education and on teacher training courses in the region (Law 162, Art. 3). Many of these amplifications have yet to be realized. Indeed, subsequent governments have reverted to an ideology more closely resembling early *indigenismo* and have observed only the linguistic rights provided for by the Autonomy Law. The PEIB has thus acquired great symbolic value as the only tangible realization of autonomy rights (González Pérez 1997: 193; McLean 2001: 121).

Within this process, Creole claims encountered particular problems. Initially, Creoles had adopted their 'indigenous', 'Costeño' identity position, following MISURASATA's lead in claiming a Literacy Crusade and then school programmes in 'English' as their 'mother tongue'.[14] The Sandinistas, however, from their essentialist conception of cultural identity and the anti-imperialist ideology of the revolution, interpreted this as a claim for programmes in *Creole* and Spanish:

> One of the persons that had some say [in the Ministry of Education, MED] at the beginning (...) who had been connected with the Coast (...) he kept insisting that [the literacy manuals] should be in Creole – "we don't want no American English". We didn't know at that point, remember, and we went and did consultation with the *bases* [grassroots] (...) and people didn't want [Creole] – "If you goin' teach us *teach us good*". But the mentality of the people at the MED, the Frente [Sandinista] people, was that it was not really English, it was Creole, because they took it for granted that these Creoles should *go back to* their Creole.
> (GMcL, Costeño Mestizo leader of the Literacy Technical Team, interview 1994, my emphasis)

Given that this was an issue of language in education, the consultation

---

[14] According to Tove Skutnabb-Kangas's useful unpacking of the term 'mother tongue' (1981: 12-34), this claim conflates two of its possible four senses: those of first language and language of ethnic identification. See also critiques of 'ethnic absolutist', quasi-racist uses of the term in Rampton (1995: 340-343) and Le Page (1993: 144).

result was unsurprising. For Adult Literacy, SE was a practical choice: the Language of Wider Communication in which there was plenty to read, from the Bible onwards.[15] Moreover, education in SE was historically associated with the production of the 'Anglo Creole' facet of the Creole identity. Hence, Creoles naturally associated language rights with the restoration of the SE-medium education they had long been denied. However, this also meant insisting that Creole be constructed as a 'dialect of English', actively denying that it was 'a language'. On the other hand, a Creole-based literacy campaign would over-privilege the 'Costeño' aspects of Creole identity, taking them 'back to' a position on a par with other indigenous groups with unwritten languages, denying the superiority acquired by their Anglo associations. These different understandings of the notion 'mother tongue' epitomized wider misunderstandings between Sandinistas and Creoles. To the Sandinistas, Creole allegiance to SE, the language of their imperialist enemy (and to the Anglo ways that went with it) seemed a suspect denial of their 'true' ethnic identity; Creoles for their part interpreted Sandinista essentialism as an attack on their historic ethnic rights.

When the question of developing more permanent bilingual education arose again, in the context of the autonomy negotiations, Creoles based their proposals more firmly in the 'Anglo Creole' identity position, stressing pedagogical and economic arguments and underplaying those from 'ethnic identity'. The 'Creole *dialect*' would be used "in order to realise education in the mother tongue" (Hamilton, Walsh and Brooks, n.d: 88, my emphasis) but literacy would be exclusively in SE. Some early proposals did consider creating reading primers to start where SE and Creole were most similar and gradually differentiate them (Brooks 1984: 81), but the final programme was bilingual in 'English' and Spanish, where 'English' was effectively SE.

Counter-arguments promoting the use of Creole emerged from the 'Black' Creole identity perspective: "to teach standard English would be to impose an alien *language and culture* on the students, as is happening now with Spanish" and "would be a surrender to cultural domination by historical oppressors. Included in both views [for and against Creole] is the concern that *the Creole language and culture* would be implicitly devalued" (Yih and Slate 1985: 56, my emphasis). However, these voices, mainly from a younger generation, carried little authority. Not only did they violate the rules of the 'Anglo' dominated power field of education;

[15]Indeed, even the Miskitu of the bilingual villages around Pearl Lagoon opted for 'English' literacy on these grounds.

they also seemed to strengthen Sandinista arguments in favour of Creole. In the article where they are quoted – from the multilingual journal of the recently-founded, politically independent Centre for Research and Information on the Atlantic Coast (Centro de Investigación y Divulgación de la Costa Atlántica, CIDCA), they are authoritatively overridden by commonsense arguments for Standard English: "if you tried to conduct classes in Creole you'd have political uproar on your hands"; "It's *beautiful* to speak Creole, but it's *intelligent* to know standard English" (ibid. , quoting Ray Hooker, a much-respected Creole educational leader and then Sandinista delegate to the National Assembly).[16]

The terms of the argument made it difficult to develop a clear role for Creole in the new bilingual programmes (Hurtubise 1990; Freeland 1993), since they forced politicized either/or choices between what were in daily practice two aspects of the same identity. By 1994, an uncomfortable compromise had been reached. In classes I visited, teachers and pupils freely used in Creole personal interaction, but showed clear signs of strain when reaching for SE. Literacy in either SE or Spanish progressed too slowly, linguistic insecurities were reinforced and the PEIB floundered. The result was a kind of voicelessness:

> I have been in classrooms where they have their moment for oral expression, OK, and bein' I'm sitting there, the teacher feel like she must use her best English. And the kids are conscious that I'm there, so they do not want to use their – even though I – my Creole I use it when I – they do not want to use their Creole. And do you know what happen? They do not participate (...). But if teachers and students know that this moment they are free to make use of their Creole to express what they feel and what they think, it would be much easier for us to link this with the reading-writing process.
> (AB, former leader of the PEIB technical team in Bluefields, interview 1991)

These failures, which also had financial and logistical causes, seemed to prove to many parents the validity of opposition to Creole in the classroom. At the grassroots level, Bluefields parents removed their children to monolingual Spanish schools, where English is taught as a foreign language, or to the Moravian College if they could afford it. There are now

---

[16]This juxtaposition of the 'beautiful' and the 'intelligent' speaks to the classic association highlighted by May (this volume) of ethnic languages with sentiment and dominant languages with instrumentality.

only two schools in the city that run the PEIB, though the programme does well in rural Creole communities with less choice.[17]

Foreign linguists and educators, politically committed to the success of the programme, tried to demonstrate the pedagogical advantages of using Creole in various approximations to a trilingual programme (Shopen 1987; Hurtubise 1990). But their efforts, premised on the understanding that Creoles are languages in their own right, met with indifference or hostility, and the Creole materials they prepared in teacher workshops remained unused.

This rejection was not at all straightforward. To appreciate its complexity it is worth looking in some detail at the following text, the core of an article in *Sunrise,* the local bilingual weekly newspaper. At first glance, it seems to be a classic 'Anglo' rejection of Creole, and in the polarizing circumstances of the times that is how it was interpreted by many. In fact, it is an example of the kind of 'heterogeneous' discourse (Fairclough 1992: 34-35) that emerges from and addresses just the kind of conflict we have been describing, particularly at moments of ideological change. In this particular text, all three language-identity positions come into play with different degrees of saliency, illustrating how intricately inter-connected they are:

> A strange tendency (…) has emerged, *whose true origins and purposes cannot be defined* (…) trying with slight pressure to *impose upon* or *to force* the vast majority of Creoles to accept and to speak *a level or variety of Creole* English *which has now been surpassed*. It is dedicated to reviving and promoting a *very archaic form of Creole* English and is trying to declare it a 'native language' and – *if it were possible* – an 'official language' [a promotion that is] counterproductive, *unnatural* and illogical (…).
>
> [But] I want to state very plainly that no conscientious Creole is renouncing *his own* Creole speech. For he knows and sees *with pride* that the Creole language *which he uses at home, in the street, with his friends*, is a *rich and powerful means of expressing* the beautiful as well as the ugly, the decent as well as the obscene. It's a pleasure to speak *one's own* Creole. That without doubt is not the 'wada huda' of past generations that *due to foreign influences* has recently been promoted in *cleverly written and outdated* pieces.

---

[17] These grassroots reactions raise interesting research questions about the efficacy of different approaches to bilingual education, which it is beyond the scope of this paper to address. Some of these are discussed in Freeland 2003.

> In their realism and pragmatism, the Creoles of the Atlantic Coast of Nicaragua neither want nor ask for the services of *linguistic engineers to construct* the *rich, powerful and vital form of language they speak today*, which is at the *height of its evolution.*
> (Sujo Wilson 1988a, my emphasis)[18]

The text's rejection of attempts by "foreign influences" with unknown purposes to "force" on Costeños an "outdated" and "surpassed" form of language expresses at one level a broad 'Costeño' resistance especially to the over-emphasis on the 'Black', Creole *mother tongue* identity still attributed to Sandinista cadres on the Coast. The fact that some of the 'cleverly written pieces' came from the Anglo world, normally a trusted ally, may account for the hostility of tone. Much of the text's argument, though, seems to epitomize the 'Anglo Creole' opposition to using Creole in the classroom: its emphasis on the "evolution" (progress towards modernity?) of Creole from "archaic forms", "the 'wada huda' of past generations"; its corollary assumption that "naturally", "logically", Creole *cannot* be an official language; its complicity with Creole's diglossic subordination to SE and relegation to private domains, away from the sources of power. All these support classic 'Anglo' arguments against using Creole in education.

At the same time, the writer's insistence that Creole is a "rich and powerful (…) language" with which Creoles should identify proudly voices 'Black' resistant, pro-Creole attitudes. Hence, he simultaneously defends Creole and advocates an education policy that will shift its speakers towards Standard English, a shift Hugo Sujo confirmed in an interview with me not long after the publication of his article:

> As far back as I can remember, from a kid (…) the Creoles that are studying (…) are abandoning more and more the Creole. What they are speaking is something, maybe we could call it the same Creole, but it's evolving towards the Standard English (…) and so therefore a good amount of the *genuine Creole* terms you know, Creole vocabulary that *we used to hear from the old folks* are out of use among the younger people.
> (HSW, interview 1991, my emphasis)[19]

---

[18]Hugo Sujo Wilson was then the Director of CIDCA in Bluefields, a respected educator who took a position of critical sympathy to the Sandinista enterprise, standing as a FSLN candidate in the 1990 elections to the Autonomy Council. He was also a founder member of an Association of Black Nicaraguans formed in the 1980s.

[19]Beckford Wassink finds a similar combination of active resistance to the use

The heterogeneity of Sujo's text, then, voices the 'splitting' referred to in the quotations from Hall earlier in this chapter, that comes from trying to be both 'Black' and European, to straddle ideologies that associate the second with modernity and devalue the first as archaic and primitive. This splitting is exacerbated here because the whole argument is centred on education, designated under the Autonomy Law as a key domain for legitimizing languages, and the very domain where SE had been defended against the encroachment of Hispanization during the long years of proscription of English. It is also, of course, the domain in which the 'European presence' and its particular construction of identity through language are strongest. To the extent that Sandinista policy made the formal education system a central locus for legitimating languages and cultures, it forced Creoles, more than other groups, into either/or choices between aspects of their identity in tension.

Among the various voices expressed in the text, one at least hints at the possibility of occupying a 'space between' these poles. This contests 'foreign' notions of linguistic/cultural *rescate* (rescue), with their static, purist assumptions about language and their one-to-one associations between language and identity, from a position of relaxed acceptance of linguistic change, rooted in an understanding that Creole has drawn on multiple sources and contacts, and continues to do so freely within the *espace créole* of the Coast, as part of the multilingual repertoire Creoles use to perform their complex 'acts of identity' (Le Page and Tabouret-Keller 1985). Looked at in this way, it seems entirely reasonable to object to having 'one's own' language 'constructed' by 'linguistic engineers' from outside the speech community, with reference to some archaic identity associated with a bygone age, especially if one of its most valued features is, as we saw it to be, its freedom and idiosyncracy. Here, the writer's emphasis on the scope Creole gives to 'one's own' personal, idiosyncratic expression is important, and suggests an unwillingness to have it constrained and fixed. It speaks to a sense of Creole as part of a 'Black' oppositional culture, a sense potentially separable from its construction as

---

of Creole in education, acceptance of decreolization and a desire for children to identify with Creole's 'rich cultural heritage' among older Creoles in Jamaica (1999: 70). See also Morgan's (1994) overview of attitudes to African American English in the US, and e.g. Collins's (1999) account of the Ebonics debate there. Niedelski and Preston (2003: 213-17) find a similar relaxed bidialectalism to Sujo's among US speakers of Black Vernacular English, and an assumption that school is for learning Standard English (239-240).

a dialect in the sense of 'not a proper language'. For of course, bringing Creole into school, especially as a 'language' defined in Eurocentric terms, could potentially deprive it of its associations with a culture of resistance.

During the Sandinista years, moreover, cultural institutions fostered by the Ministry of Culture with support from international solidarity provided alternative sites where Creole language and other cultural expressions could be developed and legitimated. The last of these, Cultura Pro-Autonomía [Cultural Action for Autonomy] (CPA), had fostered in its heyday an oral history project, Afro-Caribbean music, painting and sculpture, and a poetry group which both performed and published regularly in *Sunrise*, freely using Creole, Spanish and SE (interviews with Sidney Francis, CPA project documents). Such projects, with their particular emphasis on popular culture, enabled 'Black' Creole cultural and linguistic expressions to develop free from the formalities of school and SE.[20] Given that, in different degrees, both Creole and SE needed revitalization and maintenance, some such parallel development is vital. The project persisted after the Sandinista electoral defeat, and for a while became an important element in the realization of autonomy on the Coast.[21]

In sum, this text illustrates that the question of how Creole culture can both survive and change is not fully answerable within the prevailing discursive framework. Read within this framework, indeed, the text appears to be an 'Anglo Creole' argument against using Creole in formal education that pays mere lip-service to Creole. Rather, I argue, it is a multivocal text, in which all three 'voices' of the Creole identity struggle to be heard but cannot be integrated.

6. Writing for Legitimacy?

Another, more recent, manifestation of the impasse we are examining was discussed with me by students on my 2001 URACCAN course on Language Policy and Planning, all experienced teachers in the PEIB. They had concluded that the way to have Creole accepted in the PEIB is to

---

[20] Searle's (1984) discussion of language policy during the Grenadian revolution (1979-1983) describes the parallel development of SE and Creole, through official support for calypso artists, on the one hand, and school work that recognized a quasi-bilingual situation on the other. See also Davidson's (1986) criticisms of the transitional use of Creole.

[21] Its function has been taken over, to a considerable extent, by the Instituto para la Promoción e Investigación de Lenguas y Culturas (IPILC, Institute for Promotion and Research of Languages and Cultures) of the URACCAN. Like all Nicaraguan universities, this one is severely underfunded, and dependent on short-term project funding of various kinds.

develop it as a written language and so prove its credentials as a 'proper language'. Several separate, but interacting factors appear to have led to this conviction. The first, and most constant, is their sense that the PEIB is still failing because it is not firmly grounded in Creole children's first language, and that this leaves many Creole children educationally disadvantaged. The second factor relates, I would contend, to unforeseen effects of the growing emphasis on cultural authenticity in the teaching materials of the PEIB, a very welcome emphasis in principle, provided it is based in a sophisticated sense of such authenticity. In Nicaragua, however, it is still conceived in terms of one-to-one links between mother-tongues and associated 'mother cultures', so to speak. This linkage leaves 'Black' Creoles with the sense that their Creole culture is being suppressed, along with the Creole language.

These perceptions are to some extent confirmed by a third factor, the gradual withdrawal of support for Creole and Creole culture outside the education system, of the kind provided under Sandinista cultural policy. This has left the PEIB as the only legitimating site for Creole 'language-and-culture'. As a consequence, Creole appears inferior to the Coast's other 'ethnic languages' which, as the medium of formal education, are being codified in orthographies, dictionaries and grammars, and their oral tradition transcribed and collected into books and school texts. Creole, in contrast, does not enjoy such attention.

This conjunction of pedagogical experience and identity politics has persuaded Creole teachers that the PEIB's failings cannot be remedied as long as 'Anglo' Creole resistance blocks serious consideration of bringing Creole into the classroom. Opinions vary as to what position it should occupy in relation to SE. It is probably easiest to argue for using Creole as a transitional language towards SE, but many worry that this would encourage the very language shift they seek to counter. They therefore favour a language maintenance approach to Creole that is much more difficult to argue.

Writing the language, these teachers conclude, will counter the central assumption of 'Anglo' discourse: that Creole is 'not a proper language' and is unworthy to be taught in schools. This assumption, as we saw, is present in both grassroots and intellectual discourses. Writing, moreover, will give the Creole culture the concreteness and visibility that seem to confer authority on other cultures:

> In (...) Nicaragua, where Creole lives in the shadow of Standard English and [where] the dominant language is Spanish, Fishman's point [that dominant languages pull others towards them] is even more possible. We have been able to observe, *or rather to hear* that Creole has

> been losing its richness, getting increasingly close to Standard English and with increasing *borrowing* from Spanish, *which we do not condemn, but we do consider it necessary to avoid* this situation advancing to the point where Creole is overwhelmed.
> (DAO and JS, senior teachers in the English PEIB, Sociolinguistics essay for URACCAN, 2000, my emphasis, my translation from Spanish)

> The Creole *ethnia* also wanted to have *its* language (...) *like the other peoples or nations* (English, French, Spanish) codified and written; one of the *significant traces* of the language of any group is writing, without doubt the chief one (…) because there have been strong cultures in history which have disappeared, but have left writing and culture as a symbol (…) But if we run back through the history of the Creole *ethnia*, there are no *visible, recorded traces of its culture.*
> (WW, senior teacher in the English PEIB, Sociolinguistics essay for URACCAN, 2000, my emphasis, my translation from Spanish)

> That's a serious problem, the *search for our identity*, the *need for us to be able to tie ourselves to something*, and it comes around the same thing, that we don't know much about ourselves, because *we have not collected anything*. Over the years, *nothing has really been left that we can go back* and say well these are some of the artefacts, these are some of the writings. (…) So we get the feeling that our ancestors *didn't do anything, because they didn't leave anything*, and pretty soon we get the feeling that we don't worth a damn anyway.
> (FD, Moravian priest, former Director of the Moravian College, interview 1994, my emphasis)

To propose writing on these terms, however, is effectively to capitulate to the position the project seeks to contest. It means conceding that cultures are constituted by static assemblages of visible objects or traces, rather than by process and practice, that written languages are somehow more real than oral ones, accepting the need for unification around a standard that formal writing entails. Here, I emphatically do not mean that there is no case for writing Creole; my aim is to highlight problems in making the case this way, in trying to "gain entry into an existing (…) symbolic market place, and not to construct an alternative one" (Jaffe 1999: 119).

As we have seen, a key characteristic of 'Black' Creole culture (not only in Nicaragua) is that it formed historically outside the cultural mainstream, "displaced from the logocentric world – where the direct mastery of cultural modes meant the mastery of writing" (Hall 1992 [1996]: 470).

From this position of resistance Creole diasporas have developed other modes of expression: a "rich, deep, and various attention to speech, (…) its inflections towards the vernacular (…), its rich production of counter-narratives" (ibid.).[22] The full realization of Creole cultural rights therefore entails addressing "deep questions of cultural transmission and inheritance, and of the complex relations between African origins and the irreversible scatterings of the diaspora" (Hall 1996: 470-471), through an appropriate "diaspora aesthetic" (ibid.) and, I would add, a matching (socio)linguistics.

Besides, writing Creole means developing an appropriate orthography, which is never a neutral matter. The very value and authority that writing is expected to confer on the Creole language in this context will turn it into a symbol of authenticity, raising matters of choice far exceeding the already complex technical issue of representing spoken language graphically. As Hornberger (1995) shows in relation to the writing of Quechua, particular graphical choices become identified with particular identity positions and bring them into conflict. When the language is a Creole, whose boundaries by definition are exceptionally fluid, the problems become particularly challenging (see e.g. Schieffelin and Doucet 1998; Sebba 1998, 2000; Jaffe 2000; Miethaner 2000). Deciding how to write this one, especially for the particular purposes envisaged, will thus *require*, not produce, a resolution of the 'dialect or language' question, and could intensify rather than calm the struggles we have considered by further hardening the opposition between different aspects of the Nicaraguan Creole identity from all the above, the following framework of debate is predictable. If this Creole is a 'dialect', as the 'Anglo Creole' discourse holds, and is to be used to ease the transition to SE literacy, there are arguments for writing it using a modified form of SE orthography (Coulmas 1989: 233, cited Sebba 2000: 937). This would also satisfy the 'Costeño Creole' need for it to be distinct from Spanish, and hence not too phonemic (Morren 2001).[23] Yet such a choice has the potential to accelerate the

---

[22]The dangers of capitulating to this kind of logocentrism beset all the oral cultures and languages of the Coast (see Freeland 2003); the Creole dilemma is a more complicated version of a more general problem, recently addressed for Latin America in a collection of papers that explores from many angles the complexities of 'translating' oral cultures into writing (López and Jung 1998).

[23]Morren (2001) describes the development of an orthography for *trilingual* programmes in Creole ('Island English'), SE and Spanish for the Colombian islands of San Andrés, Providencia and Santa Catalina. The early colonial history of these islands was similar to that of the Coast – indeed they are still the object of territorial dispute between Nicaragua and Colombia – although the very different

already perceived shift of Creole towards Standard English (Sebba 1998; Davidson 1986). Moreover, to the extent that such orthographies resemble 'incorrect' English (Hellinger 1986, quoted by Sebba 1998: 5), this choice would reinforce perceptions of Creole's inferior 'dialect' status and so undermine the whole symbolic project. If the objective is to establish Creole as a separate language, according to 'Black Creole' ideals, then the more distant its orthography from SE the better (Sebba 1998; Shopen 1987). Yet this might move it towards the phonemic appearance of Spanish. On these terms, then, writing does not *per se* provide a way out of the deadlock, but perhaps its most concrete illustration.

Starting in 2002, a project was initiated that attempts to cut this Gordian knot. Sponsored jointly by the URACCAN and the Finnish government's FOREIBCA programme (Fortalecimiento de la Educación Intercultural-Bilingüe de la Costa Atlántica/ Strengthening Intercultural Bilingual Education for the Atlantic Coast), it starts from teachers' perceptions and end of year findings that Creole children are failing academically by comparison with those of other groups, and concludes that this is because they lack a good foundation in their first language. Its strategy is to introduce Creole into the schools and demonstrate its advantages, under the aegis of the Sistema de Educación Autónomo Regional (SEAR: Autonomous Regional Education system) instituted in 2002, to implement the provision under the Autonomy Law of 1987 that the Coast should manage its own education system (SEAR 2002, Consejo Regional Autónomo Atlántico Norte *et al.* 2003).

The chosen level of intervention is to be the Normal School that trains teachers for the EIB, to produce a cadre of teachers able to use both 'Kriol' and Standard English with the confidence and appropriacy teachers have so far lacked.

To these ends, direct links were developed with the Belizean Creole Council, and between 2002 and 2003 four workshops were held on the linguistics of Creole and on the best way of writing it. I attended the last of these, held in Bluefields in August 2003 and led by Silvana Woods, a co-founder of the Belizean Creole Council.[24] By then, the decision had

---

political construction of the three languages in the islands has made it easier to use Island English for early literacy. The orthography adopted, taking account of similar symbolic considerations, is adapted from a 'Rule-based Phonemic Model' of orthography developed in Belize. This appears to accommodate some variation of spelling, but has been made more phonemic in light of practical experience.

[24] The Belizean Creole Council is a voluntary body which has been working over

been taken to follow the Belizean example, and to develop a distinctively 'Kriol' orthography to distance Creole from SE.

Conducted entirely in Creole, itself a new experience for most of the forty or so Nicaraguan Creole participants, the workshop produced an adaptation to the demands of Nicaraguan Creole of the latest version of the Belizean orthographic system, and a test draft of a transitional primer, *YOU can read and write Kriol* (FOREIBCA-IPILC 2003), also adapted from a Belizean model. The primer comprises a chart of all the orthographic symbols, with their sound equivalents in the IPA, Creole words to illustrate the use of the symbols, translations of these words into Standard English, practice spelling games, and a series of stories in Kriol written and illustrated by the workshop participants. It is designed to be used with trainee teachers in the Normal Schools of the region, as well as for sale to parents and anyone with an interest in the project.[25] There are more stories in the pipeline to be worked up into separate story books for use both at home and in school.

This final workshop rapidly became transformed from a technical exercise to a celebration and strengthening of the 'Black' Creole aspect of Creole identity, and a lesson in how to promote it. Here, the link beyond Nicaragua to Belize was important in creating a sense of community and

---

the last ten years or so to promote Creole writing and its use in schools. It is just beginning to have its work accepted, at least nominally, by the Belizean Ministry of Education.

[25] The Normal School is part of secondary education in Nicaragua; students enter at eleven and complete their secondary education with a teacher training component, which only recently has been reformed to include bilingual education. The Belizean primer was designed with the assistance of the Summer Institute of Linguistics for teacher training and also to help other literate Creole-speakers to read and write Creole. It therefore starts from the assumption that people have already learned to read Belizean Standard English. The same approach was adopted for the Nicaraguan primer, although it was recognized that explanations might also need to be given in Spanish in this Spanish-dominated context. Whilst this is not the place to go into the technical details of the orthography, it is worth noting that whereas Belizean Kriol (BK) favours symbolizations related to Standard English, Nicaraguan Kriol (NK) uses representations closer to Spanish conventions: e.g. in BK, the long /o:/ is represented as 'oo' and the long /i:/ as 'ee'; in NK, these sounds are symbolized respectively as 'uu' and 'ii'. There were also interesting tendencies among the participants to represent Kriol / English aspirate /h/ with 'j', presumably derived from the velar aspirated Spanish /x/ or 'jota'. Here, potential ideological objections to getting too close to Spanish gave way to practical considerations of what would help young readers.

shared culture among diaspora peoples. The level of enthusiasm and confidence the workshop generated was palpable, as was the delight in telling and writing the stories and in turning into 'proper Creole' poems which some participants had written earlier using spontaneous spellings, to make them accessible to all. To this participant observer, these activities were especially interesting for the way they stimulated group creativity in the reworking of popular oral tradition.

In the workshop's final session, a 'Kriol Kamishan' [Creole Commission] was formed from leading participants, with a Central Committee, area representatives to cover the various Creole-speaking communities scattered up and down the Coast and around Pearl Lagoon, and a campaign plan to raise the profile of Kriol and of the primer, especially at the forthcoming celebrations of the centenary of the city of Bluefields. Wider promotion of the project was also initiated, when a group of participants led by Woods appeared on three local phone-in radio programmes to publicize the workshop and its goals.

However, it is in the responses to these initiatives that some of the problems of the project's next stage are foreshadowed. As one Normal School teacher pointed out, initial parental reactions to her experimental use of Creale in her Normal School classes were quite negative; students came back reporting that their parents thought Kriol was 'bad English', a 'bastard language'. Since the students themselves find the new regime enjoyable and empowering, they are now trying to resolve some of this conflict between their homes and their schooling, a first stage of their role as promoters of the new system.

The radio phone-in responses were also mixed, though in a proportion of three to two in favour of the project.[26] Those against wielded the standard 'Anglo-Creole' arguments, especially emphasizing the economic wisdom of 'getting good English', enabling the participants to begin the argument that this was not an either/or choice: using Kriol would not prevent children from learning SE, but might even help. It was also notable

---

[26] This may have had something to do with the radio stations themselves, and the time of transmission. The three stations were Reijo Ridm (Radio Rhythm) a distinctly 'Black' oriented music station strong on the latest Caribbean music, where the broadcast went out in the morning; La Costeñísima (literally 'the most Costeño'), another popular station, where the broadcast went out in the early afternoon, and Radio Zinica, a station which broadcasts news and discussion programmes as well as a similar diet of music, in two slots, one during the day, and a second which gave space for a more prolonged discussion as a feature in Zinica's Sunday morning magazine programme. Unfortunately, I was not able to hear this last broadcast, nor reactions to it.

how many of the phone-in advocates of SE imagined that they were speaking what they advocated, when in fact, as Woods pointed out, they were speaking "riil priti Kriol". Clearly, the next stage of this process, spreading and gaining acceptance for this bold corpus planning initiative, will not be easy in view of all our analysis, especially since its chosen ground is the highly conflicted domain of education.

Many of the difficulties looming ahead were explored with the Director of Zinica in a rich preliminary discussion to his programme held at the workshop. Clearly, the authority of the sponsoring university, URACCAN, will be an important counterweight to the older educational establishment, especially in view of its collaboration with the Educational Commission of the Regional Council, and the key role it is playing in developing the SEAR. Even so, key posts within the Ministry of Education on the Coast still tend to be political appointments, and are currently held by people with little sympathy for this aspect of the 'Black Creole' discourse, or for a project emanating from a university that many people still think of as a Sandinista initiative, despite the context of profound political change which has shaped it and its efforts to remain politically neutral.

There may also be hidden reefs still to negotiate with regard to the symbolization of Kriol. Even within the workshop there were differences of view as to the validity of some of the chosen representations, which I interpret as stemming from two related sources. One is the tendency to want the Kriol orthography to be phonetic rather than phonemic, to reflect individual or regional variations people consider important. Although by the end of the workshop most people understood the principle of the phoneme, and particularly that this way of writing would not require them to change their style of speech to fit the orthography, it may be less easy to persuade the general public of this.

The other has to do with which part of the current array of Creole social styles properly represents 'real' Creole, a question that has some bearing on the particular graphical representations chosen. As Woods noted on several occasions during the workshop, the Kriol of most of its participants is markedly more de-Creolized than that of comparably educated Belizeans. Yet paradoxically, it falls to these teachers, who have been incompletely educated out of their Creole, to lay the foundations of a new orthography to be used with children many of whom may speak a much 'deeper' Kriol than they. This kind of issue will become more prominent as the orthography is tried out among a wider range of speakers, and could provoke the kind of controversy that attended the writing of Haitian Kreyòl (Schieffelin and Doucet 1998). As Woods constantly emphasized, experimentation and flexibility must characterize these early stages.

Conclusion

Writing Kriol, then, has given the 'Black Creole' aspect of Nicaraguan Creole identity a great fillip, and has moved the conflict between this and other facets of Creole identity onto another plane. However, it has not of itself resolved that conflict, nor can it be expected to do so, as some of the proponents of writing quoted earlier had supposed. The struggle to have this language and its writing accepted in schools is still to be waged, and will again become be the ground upon which 'ethnic absolutist' notions of what are really different aspects of the one Creole identity are pitched in opposition to each other. In the relaxed spirit of the workshops, participants could and did move easily between passionate 'Black' Creole advocacy of the value and beauty of Kriol, common sense assumptions that Standard English is an indispensable part of the Creole heritage, and celebration of the Costeño identity 'in Kriol'; that is, between the three reference points of the true Creole identity.[27] I heard no participant suggest that these aspects could be mutually exclusive. It was as though the workshop took to a more reflective level the daily communicative practice that performs Creole identity. If this could be further explored and sustained, the project could help counter essentialist rigidity and purism, and begin to argue for either/or choices to be replaced "with the potentiality or the possibility of an 'and'" (Hall 1996: 472).

Nevertheless, this confidence will have to be maintained against the dominant discourse which, as we have seen, assumes discrete identities and languages, polarizes identity facets and sets them against each other. As Gilroy points out (1993: 191), the solution does not lie in simply adding opposed Creole identity positions together, as Stuart Hall's 'and' seems to imply. Rather, the tension between them, their 'antagonistic indebtedness' (Gilroy 1993: 191), is also an intrinsic part of Creole identity, and can become the springboard for a new critical awareness of what it means to live in the space between.

---

[27] The Costeño identity was prominent throughout the workshop. Indeed, one of the tasks it undertook with relish was the translation into Kriol of the Coast anthem to autonomy, originally written in Spanish and already translated into the other Coast languages in use. The anthem was then sung in chorus, recorded, and broadcast on two of the radio programmes. The translation process itself was an interesting illustration of the decreolization of NK, and of the potential in writing it of revaluing and revitalizing it. Initially, the instinct was to translate into English, with NK spelling. Then, under the guidance of Woods, groups began to suggest 'proper Creole ways' of rendering certain ideas.

Part of the problem, as we have seen, is that the principal site for this battle is still education, historically the powerhouse of only one facet of the Creole identity, and is currently governed by policies rooted, at both nation-state and regional levels, in the discourse that Creoles need to contest. As we saw, the 'Black' in Creole culture needs also to draw its legitimacy from outside the mainstream of education if it is to retain its oppositional, resistant edge. A too close identification of this element with formal education and its assumptions about what constitutes a language, therefore carries potential risks.

For instance, I mentioned earlier the development of Creole poetry. Relaxed, confident Creole speech ranges with grace and wit between all the linguistic reference points of their *Espace Créole* as Creoles use language to perform their identities. In the same way, Creole poets avail themselves of different voices: Creole, Standard English and Spanish, sometimes in different poems, sometimes within one. Carlos Rigby, for example, has developed a poetic language that amalgamates all three (see Rigby 1990), selectively excluding or mocking speakers of only one.[28] In these poems, Creole has hitherto been spelt freely, though not always arbitrarily; spellings also add meaning (for examples and some discussion see Hurtubise 1995; see also Sebba 1998 on the significance of "rebel" spellings among British Creole-speakers). Given appropriate outlets and support, such practices produce novel, innovative written forms of incontestable modernity, impossible to achieve from within any one of the Creole identities alone (see e.g. Gilroy's discussion of the novels of Toni Morrison and other Black American writers, 1993: 217-222). Whilst there is clearly much to be gained from writing 'in proper Kriol', especially if it enables children to share in and contribute to this creativity, it would be a pity if these expressive variants, the written equivalents of codeswitching, were to be frowned upon and 'standardized'. Here it will be important not to become lured into the notion of languages as fixed, discrete objects associated with written form.

It will also be important not to overemphasize the written to the detriment of children's oral skills, to abandon the oral culture in order to espouse

---

[28]Such cross-linguistic mockery is also part of a Nicaraguan Mestizo tradition that goes back to the popular seventeenth-century drama known as *El Güegüense*, one of the earliest expressions of its kind in Latin America. Ostensibly written in Spanish, it features canny peasants whose apparent servility to their conquerors is undercut with double-entendres that only Spanish-Nahuatl bilinguals can fully grasp. Given that Nahuatl is no longer spoken among Pacific Coast indigenous people, much of its impact is lost today.

the 'logocentrism' on the margins of which Creole cultures have gained their strength and originality (Hall 1992 [1996]: 470-71). The workshop itself, with its telling and writing of stories and poems, in fact provided a potential model for the relationship between the two: the writing triggered off the story-telling and then enriched it. Neither should either Kriol writing or children's spontaneous Kriol speech be viewed merely as bridges to Standard English, although some bridge does have to be built. This argument is clearly necessary in the early stages of contesting fears that Kriol will replace English, as the radio broadcasts showed, but it must be a tactical move only.

The same project, and the curriculum development it will give rise to, could work deliberately to foster children's oral skills. Initially, this could be done through creative oral work for which "meaningful reward" is given (Roberts 1994), so as to promote a sense of Kriol as "a separate and alternative instrument" to SE (and in this context also to Spanish), with its own functions and strengths (ibid). With the addition of a Kriol writing system, this perception could be strengthened by encouraging pupils, as Roberts also suggests (ibid.), to read both local poetry and wider West Indian Creole literature, when they are firmly enough rooted in their own orthographic system to cope with the regional orthographic variations that currently exist. A Kriol orthography would also make it possible to allow children to write spontaneously, currently not the practice anywhere in the PEIB system.

Clearly, this project is still in its infancy. To carry it off successfully will require not only enthusiasm, but also intelligent, patient argument backed by clear demonstrations of what is gained. Certainly, its development will be an intriguing process to follow in the coming years; a litmus paper of how Creoles take to a new stage the maintenance of their rich, hybrid identity against the false polarities and choices posed by 'ethnic absolutism'.

References

Adams, Richard N. (1991) 'Strategies of Ethnic Survival in Central America', in Greg Urban and Joel S. Sherzer (eds) *Nation States and Indians in Latin America*, Austin: University of Texas Press, 181-206.

Aikman, Sheila (1996) 'The Globalisation of Intercultural Education and an Indigenous Venezuelan Response', *Compare* 26(2): 153-165.

Beckford Wassink, Alicia (1999) 'Historic Low Prestige and Seeds of Change: Attitudes towards Jamaican Creole', *Language and Society* 28(5): 57-92.

Bourdieu, Pierre (1982 [1992]) *Language and Symbolic Power*, Cambridge: Polity Press.

Brooks, Ronald (1984) 'El problema lingüístico en Zelaya Sur: Alternativas [The Linguistic Problem in Zelaya Sur: Some Options], in Hurtbise (1990) Appendix 4, 79-84.

Collins, James (1999) 'The Ebonics Controversy in Context: Literacies, Subjectivities, and Language Ideologies in the United States', in Jan Blommaert (ed) *Language Ideological Debates*, Berlin/New York: Mouton de Gruyter, 201-234.

Consejo Regional Autónomo Atlántico Norte / Consejo Regional Autónomo Atlántico Sur/ Comisiones de Educación CRA RAAN y RAAS (2003) *A contar el cuento del SEAR!!! Memoria taller Autonomía y Educación: Avanzando hacia la implementación del SEAR [Telling the SEAR Story: A Report of the Workshop on Autonomy and Education: Advancing towards Implementing the SEAR]*, Bilwi, Puerto Cabezas, RAAN, internal document.

Coulmas, Florian (1989) *The Writing Systems of the World*, Oxford: Blackwell.

Davidson, Hubert (1986) *Language and Liberation: Creole Language Politics in the Caribbean*, London: Karia Press.

Díaz-Polanco, Héctor (1985) *La cuestión étnico-nacional* [The Ethno-national Question], Mexico: Editorial Línea.

Fairclough, Norman (1992) *Discourse and Social Change,* Cambridge: Polity Press.

Freeland, Jane (1993) '"I Am a Creole, So I Speak English", Cultural Ambiguity and the "English"/Spanish Bilingual-bicultural Programme of Nicaragua's Atlantic Coast', in David L. Graddol, Louise Thompson, and Mike Byram (eds) *Language and Culture*, Clevedon: BAAL / Multilingual Matters, 71-83.

------ (1995) 'Nicaragua', in Minority Rights Group (eds) *No Longer Invisible: Afro-Latin Americans Today*, London: Minority Rights Group, 181-210.

------ (1998) 'An Interesting Absence: The Gendered Study of Language and Linguistic Diversity in Latin America', *International Journal of Educational Development* 18(3): 161-179.

------ (1999) 'Can the Grass Roots Speak? The Literacy Campaign in English on Nicaragua's Atlantic Coast', *International Journal of Bilingual Education and Bilingualism* 2(3): 214-232.

------ (2003) 'Intercultural-bilingual Education for an Interethnic-plurilingual Society? The Case of Nicaragua's Caribbean Coast', *Comparative Education*, Special Issue on Indigenous Education, 39(2): 239-260.

FOREIBCA-IPILC (2003) *YOU Can Read and Write Kriol*, Bluefields, Nicaragua: FOREIBCA-IPILC.

Gilroy, Paul (1993) *The Black Atlantic: Modernity and Double Consciousness*, London/New York: Verso.

González Pérez, Miguel (1997) *Gobiernos pluriétnicos: La constitución de regiones autónomas en Nicaragua* [Pluriethnic Governments: The Constitution of Autonomous Regions in Nicaragua], Managua: Universidad de las Regiones Autónomas de la Costa Caribe Nicaragüense (URACCAN) / Mexico: Plaza y Valdés Editores.

Gordon, Edmund T. (1998) *Disparate Diaspora: Identity and Politics in an African-Nicaraguan Community*, Austin: University of Texas Press.

Hale, Charles R. (1994) *Resistance and Contradiction: Miskitu Indians and the Nicaraguan State, 1894-1987*, Stanford: Stanford University Press.

Hall, Stuart (1990 [1993]) 'Cultural Identity and Diaspora', in Patrick Williams and Laura Christian (eds) *Colonial Discourse and Post-Colonial Theory: A Reader*, London: Harvester Wheatsheaf, 392-403.

------ (1996) 'What is This "Black" in Black Popular Culture?', in David Morley and Kuan-Hsing Chen (eds) *Stuart Hall: Critical Dialogues in Cultural Studies*, London/New York: Routledge, 465-475.

Hamilton, Donald, Robert Walsh and Ronald Brooks (n.d.) 'Proyecto de Educación Bilingüe/Bicultural: Justificación [Bilingual/Bicultural Education Project, a Justification]', in Hurtubise (1990), Appendix 5, 85-90.

Hellinger, Marlis (1986) 'On Writing English-related Creoles in the Caribbean', in Gorlach, Manfred and John Holm (eds) *Focus on the Caribbean*. Amsterdam: John Benjamins.

Holm, John (1978) *The Creole English of Nicaragua's Miskito Coast: Its Sociolinguistic History and a Comparative Study of Its Lexicon and Syntax*, unpublished Ph.D dissertation, University College London.

------ (1983) 'Nicaragua's Miskito Coast Creole English', in John Holm (ed) *Central American English*, Varieties of English around the World, T2, Heidelberg: Julius Groos Verlag, 95-130.

------ (1989) *Pidgins and Creoles, Vols. I and II*, Cambridge/New York/Melbourne: Cambridge University Press.

Hornberger, Nancy (1995) 'Five Vowels or Three? Linguistics and Politics in Quechua Language Planning in Peru', in James W. Tollefson (ed) *Power and Inequality in Language Education*, New York: Cambridge University Press, 187-205.

Hurtubise, Josef (1990) *Bilingual Education in Nicaragua: Teaching Standard English to Creole Speakers*, unpublished dissertation for the Diploma in Education, University of Aukland, New Zealand.

------ (1995) 'Poesía en inglés criollo nicaragüense' [Poetry in Nicaraguan Creole English], *Wani* 16: 43-56.

Jaffe, Alexandra (1999) *Ideologies in Action: Language Politics on Corsica*, Berlin, Mouton de Gruyter.

------ (2000) 'Non-standard Orthography and Non-standard Speech', in Alexandra Jaffe (ed) *Non-standard Orthography and Non-standard Speech*, Themed issue of *Journal of Sociolinguistics,* 4/4: 497-513

JGRN (Junta de Gobierno de Reconstrucción Nacional/Government for National Reconstruction) (1980) *Decree No 571: Law on Education in Indigenous Languages on the Atlantic Coast*, translated in Ohland and Schneider (eds) (1983), 79-88.

Le Page, Robert B. (1993) 'Conflicts of Metaphor in the Discussion of Language and Race', in Ernst Håkon Jahr (ed) *Language Conflict and Language Planning*, Berlin/New York: Mouton de Gruyter, 143-164.

------ and Andrée Tabouret-Keller (1985) *Acts of Identity: Creole-based Approaches to Language and Ethnicity*, Cambridge: Cambridge University Press.

López, Luis Enrique (1997) 'La eficacia y validez de lo obvio: lecciones aprendidas desde la evaluación de procesos educativos bilingües' [The Efficacy and Validity of the Obvious: Lessons from the Evaluation of Bilingual Educational Proceses], in Julio Calvo Pérez and Juan Carlos Godenzzi (eds) *Multi-lingüismo y educación bilingüe en América y España* [Multilinguism and Bilingual Education in America and Spain], Cuzco, Peru: Centro Bartolomé de las Casas, 53-97.

------ and Ingrid Jung (eds) (1998) *Sobre las huellas de la voz: Sociolingüística de la oralidad y la escritura en su relación con la educación* [On the tracks of the voice], Madrid: Ediciones Morata / Cochabamba, Bolivia: PROEIB-Andes / Bonn: DSE.

McLean, Guillermo (2001) 'Apreciación del estado del arte de la EIB en la Costa Caribe nicaragüense' [An Assessment of the State of the Art in Intercultural-Bilingual Education in the Caribbean Coast Region of Nicaragua], in Héctor Muñoz Cruz (ed) *Un futuro desde la autonomía y la diversidad: Experien-cias y voces por la educación en contextos interculturales nicaragüenses* [A Future Based in Autonomy and Diversity: Experiencces and Voices for Education in Nicaraguan Intercultural Contexts], Xalapa, Mexico: Universi-dad Veracruzana, 121-134.

Miethaner, Ulrich (2000) 'Orthographic Transcriptions of Non-standard Varieties: The Case of Earlier African-American English, in Alexandra Jaffe (ed) *Non-standard Orthography and Non-standard Speech* , Themed issue of *Journal of Sociolinguistics,* 4/4: 534-560.

MISURASATA (1980 [1983]) *Lineamientos Generales / General Directions*, translated in K. Ohland and R. Schneider (eds) *National Revolution and Indigenous Identity: The Conflict between Sandinistas and Miskito Indians on Nicaragua's Atlantic Coast*, Copenhagen: International Working Group on Indigenous Affairs, 48-63.

Morgan, M. (1994) 'Theories and Politics in African American English', *Annual Review of Anthropology* 23: 325-345.

Morren, Ronald C. (2001) 'Creole-based Trilingual Education in the Caribbean Archipelago of San Andrés, Providence and Santa Catalina', *Journal of Multilingual and Multicultural Development* 22(3): 227-241.

Niedzielski, Nancy A. and Dennis R. Preston (2003 [1999]) *Folk Linguistics*, Berlin/New York: Mouton de Gruyter.

Ohland, Klaudine and Robin Schneider (eds) (1983) *National Revolution and Indigenous Identity: The Conflict between Sandinistas and Miskito Indians on Nicaragua's Atlantic Coast*, IWGIA Document 47, Copenhagen: International Working Group on Indigenous Affairs.

O' Neill, Wayne and Maya Honda (1987) 'Nicaraguan English / El inglés nicaragüense', *Wani* 6: 49-60.

Pieterse, Jan N. (1994) 'Globalization as Hybridisation', *International Sociology* 9(2): 161-184.

Rampton, Ben (1995) *Crossing: Language and Ethnicity among Adolescents,* Harlow, Essex: Longman.

Rigby, Carlos (1990) 'Tres poemas de Carlos Rigby', *Wani* 8: 52-59.

Roberts, Peter A. (1994) 'Integrating Creole into Caribbean Classrooms', *Journal of Multilingual and Multicultural Development* 15(1): 47-62.

Romero Vargas, Germán (1992) 'La presencia africana en el Pacífico y el Centro de Nicaragua' [The African Presence in the Pacific and Central Regions of Nicaragua], *Wani* 13: 20-34.

Savery, Ernan (1986) 'Una crónica social orquestada' [An Orchestrated Social Chronicle], *Wani* 4: 40-43.

Schiffman, Harold F. (1996) *Linguistic Culture and Language Policy*, London: Routledge.

Schieffelin, Bambi B. and Rachelle C. Doucet (1998) 'The "Real" Haitian Creole: Ideology, Metalinguistics and Orthographic Choice', in Schieffelin, Woolard and Kroskrity (eds), 285-316.

------, Kathryn Woolard and Paul V. Kroskrity (eds) (1998) *Language Ideologies: Practice and Theory*, Oxford/New York: Oxford University Press.

SEAR (Sistema Educativo Autonómico Regional) *Por la unidad en la diversidad: Costa Caribe nicaragüense / For Unity in Diversity: Nicaraguan Caribbean Coast*, Managua: URACCAN-IPILC (Instituto de Promoción e Investigación Lingüística y Rescate Cultural).

Searle, Chris (1984) *Words Unchained: Language and Revolution in Grenada*, London: Zed Books.

Sebba, Mark (1998) 'Phonology Meets Ideology: The Meaning of Orthographic Practices in British Creole', *Language Problems and Language Planning* 22(1): 19-47.

------ (2000) 'Orthography and Ideology: Issues in Sranan Spelling', *Linguistics* 38(5): 925-948.

Shopen, Tim (1987) 'Some Comments on the English-Spanish Bilingual-bicultural Programmes in Zelaya Sur', *Wani* 6: 89-107.

Silverstein, Michael (2000) 'Whorfianism and the Linguistic Imagination of Nationality', in Paul Kroskrity (ed) *Regimes of Language: Ideologies, Polities, and Identities*, Santa Fe, New Mexico/Oxford: School of American Research Press/James Currey, 85-138.

Skutnabb-Kangas, Tove (1981) *Bilingualism or Not: The Education of Minorities*, Clevedon, Avon: Multilingual Matters.

Sujo Wilson, Hugo (1988a) 'Different Theories about the History of Maypole', *Sunrise* 55/Apr-May.

------ (1988b) 'Let's Respect Our Creole Language', *Sunrise* 56/jun: 6-7.

------ (1991) 'Palo de Mayo: Todos los olores del mundo' [Maypole: All the Perfumes of the World], *Wani* 11: 103-107.

UNESCO (1953) *The Use of Vernacular Languages in Education: Monographs on Fundamental Education*, Paris: UNESCO.

URACCAN (Universidad de las Regiones Autónomas de la Costa Caribe de Nicaragua [University of the Autonomous Regions of the Caribbean Coast of Nicaragua]) (1998) *Mission Statement*, Managua: URACCAN.

Vilas, Carlos M. (1989) *State, Class and Ethnicity in Nicaragua: Capitalist Modernization and Revolutionary Change on the Atlantic Coast*, Boulder and London: Lynne Rienner Publishers.

Woolard, Kathryn (1998) 'Introduction: Language Ideology as a Field of Enquiry', in Schieffelin, Woolard and Kroskrity (eds), 3-47.

Wünderich, Volker (1986) 'Seguidores de Marcus Garvey in Bluefields 1920' [Followers of Marcus Garvey in Bluefields, 1920], *Wani* 4: 33-35.

Yih, Katherine and Alicia Slate (1985) 'Bilingualism on the Atlantic Coast: Where Did it Come from and Where Is It Going?', *Wani* 2-3: 23, 25-26, 55-56.

Appendix

Informants – the roles identified here are those played by informants at the time of the interviews and writings quoted, that are judged relevant to the language attitudes they express.

AB – Angelica Brown, Creole, former leader of the PEIB technical team and leading pro-Creole activist.
DAO and JS – Diana Aristomene Omeir and Joan Sinclair, Creole teachers in the PEIB, and students on the Sociolinguistics and the Language Policy and Planning courses for the Licenciatura (BA) in Intercultural Bilingual Education at URACCAN. The quotation is from an essay on which they collaborated.
FD – Faran Dometz, Creole Moravian priest, former Director of the Moravian College, and member of the technical team preparing teaching manuals for the Literacy Crusade in English.
HSW – Hugo Sujo Wilson: former Director of the Moravian College, former Director in Bluefields of the Centro de Investigación y Documentación de la Costa Atlántica [Research and Documentation for the Atlantic Coast], CIDCA, later Sandinista member of the Regional Autonomous Council, RAAS (Southern Atlantic Autonomous Region), founder member of the Association of Black Nicaraguans formed in the 1980s.
GG – Grace Gordon, Creole teacher in the English PEIB, student on Sociolinguistics and the Language Policy and Planning courses for the Licenciatura (BA) in Intercultural Bilingual Education at URACCAN.
GMcL – Guillermo McLean, then Costeño Mestizo leader of the technical team preparing English primers for the Literacy Crusade on the Coast, currently director of the Instituto para la Promoción e Investigación de Lenguas y Culturas [Institute for Promotion and Research of Languages and Cultures, URACCAN].
JH – Johnny Hodgson, Creole and 'Black' Sandinista leader, later Sandinista member of the Regional Autonomous Council, RAAS.
NT – Nidia Taylor, Creole activist in Cultura Pro-Autonomía [Culture for Autonomy], CPA.
WW – Wesley Wilson, Creole teacher in the PEIB, student on Sociolinguistics and the Language Policy and Planning courses for the Licenciatura (BA) in Intercultural Bilingual Education at URACCAN.

7. Can a Language that Never Existed Be Saved?

Coming to Terms with Oroqen Language Revitalization

LINDSAY WHALEY

1. Introduction

The Oroqen (Orochen) are one of China's smallest officially recognized nationalities with a population of about 7000 according to the 1990 census. In some respects, the situation facing the Oroqen is reminiscent of any number of small ethnic communities around the world. A series of historical developments not favorable to the viability of traditional Oroqen social patterns, as well as pressures to assimilate to a surrounding national culture, have led to the near disappearance of many key markers of ethnic identity: unique dress, subsistence hunting and gathering, shamanistic religion, a clan-based organizational structure, and the Oroqen language. As a result, the youngest generation of Oroqens is now in a transitional period of sorts, one in which identification with traditional culture is made primarily through the memories of parents and grand-parents, yet the greater identification for younger Oroqen is with contemporary Chinese national culture, which is the more immediate basis of their experience. This transition is clear to all Oroqens and has led to a burgeoning interest in the reclamation of some aspects of traditional culture and in language revitalization. The last decade has witnessed several attempts to launch projects toward this end.

While this general scenario does in fact parallel case studies from around the world, it would be a mistake to gloss over some peculiarities of the Oroqen situation, peculiarities that render the possibility of language revitalization highly doubtful and raise questions about how uniformly instances of language endangerment and death can be understood. I mention just four such peculiarities here. First, language shift has occurred at a remarkable pace: in just 50 years, there has been a transformation from 100% fluency in Oroqen with little bilingualism in Mandarin Chinese to near 100% fluency in Chinese and less than 25% of Oroqen being fluent in their heritage language. Second, the Oroqen population is highly dispersed, such that fluent speakers, who probably number only between 1000-1500, are distributed over a dozen different communities. In all these communities, they represent only a small percentage of the population. Third, there is no standard dialect or written form of the language. Finally, in the People's Republic of China people who claim Oroqen nationality are granted a number of special advantages due to their minority status, a fact that has undermined efforts to maintain the group cohesion necessary to recreate a vital speech community (the reasons for this are discussed below). Although there are a host of additional variables that might also be noted as obstacles to language revitalization, these four, at least, are related in that they are directly or indirectly associated with problems in establishing or maintaining an Oroqen ethnic identity.

The notion of an 'Oroqen ethnic identity' is, in fact, a relatively recent construct. Just after the formation of the People's Republic of China in 1949, the newly founded regime, in an effort to draft a workable national policy regarding minorities, established guidelines for demarcating ethnic groups. As a consequence, the Oroqen became designated as an official ethnic entity in China. Prior to this time, the self-understanding of the Oroqen was more that of a cluster of distinct clans related in part by a complex web of kinship, in part by the shared feature of survival through hunting and gathering, and in part by mutually intelligible language. There was not, however, any wider concept of these clans forming a unique ethnic unity, and this is one of the facts that allows us to understand the processes today that counter their attempts at language maintenance and revitalization.

In this paper, I explore the origins of the incongruence between the notion of 'the Oroqen' and the historical self-understanding of the people who are now so designated. In the first section, I provide some historical context. In the second section I outline the implementation of minorities policies in the People's Republic of China and their effect on the use of the Oroqen language. Finally, I highlight the obstacles to language revitalization as the Oroqen people now must ironically rally around a language that never truly existed in the first place.

2. Situating Oroqen Historically

The Oroqen language is part of the Tungusic language family. Languages of this family are found across most of East Asia. The range extends up into the Russian arctic in the north, with the southern most Tungusic languages being spoken in northern China. The internal structure of the family has proven difficult to classify on any firm basis (see Whaley *et al.* 1998), but there is minimally a basic two-way split between a northern and a southern branch; most likely there should be a third transitional branch, which shares some features with each of the other two branches. Within Northern Tungusic, Oroqen, together with Solon, Negidal, and Evenki, comprise the Northwest Tungusic branch. These four languages are closely related. In fact, the names of the four languages are perhaps best conceived of as arbitrary labels assigned to clusters of dialects within a massively complicated dialect chain.

Historically, Tungusic peoples have been nomadic reindeer herders or hunters (Zhao 1991; Zheng 1991). By their very nature, such activities require low population density and tend to give rise to relatively small nomadic communities. In the Tungusic case, the communities were clans organized around two to a dozen families (Qiu 1983).

The clans which have ultimately come to be known as the Oroqen came into China sometime in the seventeenth century, presumably to exploit the hunting grounds of the Hinggan mountains, which at the time were unoccupied by other groups (Fang 1993; J. Sun 1987). While the migration may have had benefits to hunting, it also placed these clans in a region that was much sought after for strategic reasons. Already in the seventeenth century the Qing dynasty of China made efforts to organize the Tungusic clans administratively so that they could levy taxes and conscript soldiers to protect their northern frontier against Tsarist Russia (Hsiao 1962-3). In the twentieth century, northeastern China was occupied successively by the Japanese, Chiang Kai Shek's National Army and by the Eighth Route Army of the Communist Party (Li and Whaley forthcoming).

For any time period it is difficult to determine the number of clans that were hunting in and around the Hinggan mountains. Oroqen has never had a written form, and the oral history of living Oroqen people does not allow one to reconstruct these facts. However, outside sources offer a reasonably good sense. Using geographic regions as his basis, Shirokogorov (1929) recognizes around 4000 people in five clusters of related clans, the very same ones that today are together called Oroqen. One of these he calls the Kumarchen. In 1920 a survey was carried out on the Kumarchen that recognized 43 groups hunting along 32 rivers and tributaries (Inner Mongolia Compilation and Editing Company 1984).

Three comments should be made at this point. First, conflict between major military powers represents a significant development in the formation of what was to become the Oroqen ethnicity. Movement by Tungusic groups in the Hinggan mountains across the Amur river into modern day Russia would likely have been a normal occurrence but was curtailed for strategic reasons. This initiated a geographic division between Russian Tungusic groups and Chinese Tungusic groups. Second, although Chinese Tungusic groups were still nomadic into the 1950s, external administrative control was exerted on them as far back as the seventeenth century. As a result, we begin to see external descriptions of Tungusic peoples based on these administrative units, which, on the one hand, may not have matched Tungusic-internal relationships and, on the other hand, groups the Tungusic clans into large categories that are purely geographical. Finally, the external pressures on the Tungusic clans, especially during the first half of the twentieth century, had dramatic demographic effects; the Oroqen population declined from around 4100 in 1917 to almost half that number in 1950.

3. The People's Republic of China and the Nationalities Policy

The People's Republic of China (PRC) was founded in 1949. Very early in the formation of this new nation, efforts were made to develop a set of policies to give legal standing to minorities within Chinese borders, and in general, the policy makers operated on the assumption that in a communist state all nationalities have equal status (see Dreyer 1976; Fu 1985; Heberer 1989; Mackerras 1994 for good overviews). Hence, article 53 of the 1949 common program of the Chinese Peoples' Political Consultative Conference states: "All minority nationalities have the freedom to develop their (spoken and written) languages, and to maintain or reform their customs, habits, and religious beliefs".

The practical issue of what constitutes a minority arose almost immediately, and beginning in the 1950s, Chinese scholars employed a concept of minorities as nationalities based on Stalin's 1914 monograph entitled *Marxism and the National Question* (Heberer 1989): "A nation is a historically formed stable community of people arising on the basis of a common language, common territory, common economic life and a typical cast of mind manifested in a common culture".

In the early 1950s then, a push was made to identify the minority nationalities in China, and the notion of an Oroqen nationality was born. The appellation itself is of interest. The term is attested in seventeenth century Qing documents, though its reference in such documents is unclear. Sporadic use of the term as a vague designation to some subset of Tungusic hunting clans continues into the twentieth century. It is testimony to the awkwardness of creating a coherent and distinct ethnic group out of these clans that the etymology of the term Oroqen is unclear. It is clearly a Tungusic word that employs the highly productive suffix *-chen*. The suffix is attached to a nominal base to denote a group affiliation. For example, *Ganchen* is a combination of the suffix and the name of a river and means "people from the region of the Gan river". The nominal base of Oroqen, however, is unclear; most favor the hypothesis that it is *oro* which means "near the top of a mountain, mountain"; others suggest the root is *oron* 'reindeer', with a predictable loss of the root final *–n*. Regardless, the debate over the origins of the very name given to the Oroqen nicely captures its artificial nature.

Consonant with an understanding of nationality that is partly based on common territory, the Chinese government in the 1950s began to create autonomous regions, prefectures and counties for minority groups, including the Oroqen Autonomous Banner in Inner Mongolia. Various rights have been accorded to the minority nationalities within autonomous units: 1) administration is placed in the hands of minorities; 2) local languages and writing systems should be employed in these administrative units; 3) the ruling minorities can promulgate their own laws and regulations; 4) they can draft their own production plans; and 5) they can opt for their own path of cultural and economic development. The conception behind autonomous areas, then, has been that they provide for self-rule for minority nationalities, though the reality has often born only faint resemblance to this ideal.

Early in its history, the government of the PRC also aimed at instituting measures that would strengthen minority nationalities and raise their standard of living. For some of the larger minority groups, writing systems were created for use in literacy training, though this did not involve the Oroqen (Sun 1988, 1992; Edmonson 1984; White 1992). For minority groups of all sizes there were efforts at providing health care and education. In the case of the Oroqen, however, the government efforts faced the practical dilemma of providing such services to nomadic hunters. Consequently, government officials encouraged Oroqen clans to settle into villages that would still provide access to hunting grounds, but would also make modern medical and educational opportunities a possibility. Within a decade of the founding of the PRC, full-scale nomadism among the Oroqen had ceased.

The legal standing of minority peoples has also been a matter of some concern since the origins of the modern nation of China. Therefore, within the numerous incarnations of the Chinese constitution, certain rights for minorities have been codified. Despite rather straightforward constitutional language about linguistic and cultural rights for minorities, the actual implementation of such statutes has always been irregular at best. Furthermore, ideas about equality of all nationalities notwithstanding, there has always been a strong undercurrent of assimilatory practices in the People's Republic of China, a fact that has greatly undermined the potentially positive effects of early minority policies (Cheng 1976; Svantesson 1991; Harrell 1993).

Indeed, between 1958-1977 the push towards cultural and linguistic homogenization became increasingly overt, and much pro-minority language was expunged from the constitution. In particular, during the cultural revolution of 1966-1976, minorities were told to renounce their national identities (Heberer 1989). Minority languages and writing systems were decried as backward; in some places it was considered criminal to speak a native language.

At the end of this time, many of the legal protections for minorities were restored, and there was a return to many of the policies favourable to minority peoples. Today, as with most other minorities, Oroqen children attend schools at state expense until they complete their upper level of secondary school; they are admitted into universities with lower passing scores on entrance exams than the Han Chinese majority; there is a quota system in place to guarantee a certain number of minority entrances into universities. Furthermore, the Oroqen are one of many minorities which are exempt from the national one child per family policy. Their children receive monthly subsidies from the state. The Oroqen are often permitted to marry earlier than the law allows for the Han majority and other minorities. Finally, many Oroqen live in government built houses that are of above average size and quality by local standards.

However, government efforts to strengthen Oroqen culture and language have more often than not had the effect of hastening the rate of assimilation into broader Chinese culture. Upon first thought, this fact appears counter-intuitive, especially given official verbiage about minority rights and the slate of special privileges bestowed upon minority nationalities. However, when one takes stock of the social conditions that originally helped shape and preserve Tungusic clan identity, it is easy to see how political actions have led to the speedy loss of language and culture.

Consider some of the following variables of the pre-1949 context for the Oroqen. They were endogamous, geographically isolated in an area of low language and population density. There was a connection between clan membership and language use in the sense that each clan had small linguistic markers to identify it such as unique lexical items or idiomatic pronunciations of certain words. Finally, the Oroqen dialects were well developed for all aspects of traditional culture. No surrounding language had the necessary lexicon for hunter-gathering activities. The conditions represented by these variables held true for centuries, perhaps millennia. They were sufficient to offset the vulnerability of the individual clans to neighbouring languages and cultures.

The buttressing role of these conditions, however, was steadily eroded by the approach to minorities taken by the government authorities of China.

The decision to establish the Oroqen as an official nationality, for instance, had the unintended effect of diminishing the significance of clan structure. The people of Oroqen ethnicity were administered as a unity; the dictates of the central government were applied to this unity. Therefore, it became natural to respond to the state polity as an Oroqen, rather than as a member of a particular hunting group, family or clan.

As an official minority nationality, the Oroqen were, and are, considered distinct from the other Northwest Tungusic groups in China, who are now collectively identified as Ewenki. The official distinction between the Ewenki and Oroqen is clearly artificial as there is more linguistic and cultural variation within the Ewenki minority than there is between certain Oroqen communities and certain Ewenki communities. The understanding of language operates similarly. Though on a purely linguistic basis it makes little sense to speak of a single language called Oroqen that has a well defined set of properties and is distinct from Ewenki, as well as other Northwest Tungusic languages, this is now how the linguistic make-up of the area is conceptualized by the authorities and often by the speakers themselves.

The drive to settle the Oroqen also ultimately had a profound influence on them. Not only did settlement disrupt the fluidity among clan membership, it rapidly led to the need for the development of infrastructure in the regions where the Oroqen lived. In order to institute administrative structures, to build houses and education facilities and to provide medical care, it was necessary to cut roads through the forests and mountains and to extend the railroad system. The development of infrastructure made the exploitation of natural resources in the area easier, but in order to exploit them, it was necessary for people to move into this region of China, which they did in massive numbers. Hence, the Oroqen went from being relatively isolated and numerically dominant in most of the regions where they lived to being in close contact with other minorities and the Han majority. They now represent less than 1% of the population in most of the cities and villages which they inhabit.

Of course, the boom in population and industry in the northeastern portion of China had a negative impact on the quality of hunting. This, coupled with a generally negative view of subsistence hunting in China, led the government to promote agriculture among the Oroqen. As part of this transformation, hunting in groups all but ceased, and today, even hunting by individuals must be carried out clandestinely due to a hunting ban enacted to protect the wildlife of the region.

The special benefits accrued by the Oroqen have also hastened the decline of the Oroqen language and the loss of much of traditional culture, as non-Oroqen have an incentive to marry into the ethnic group. In intermarriage situations, the children are considered Oroqen, though inevitably they are raised speaking Chinese and tend to follow Chinese customs. The privileges given to the Oroqen have also left them with relatively positive feelings towards the Chinese system and with being Chinese, so there is little organized or collective resistance to being Sinicized.

Finally, memories of the period of persecution for minorities during the Cultural Revolution has, it seems, created a hesitancy among the Oroqen to assert themselves too boldly as a distinct nationality. People are well aware that constitutional rights are not secure in a country where the ruling party is above the law. Therefore, despite being forced to fit the mould of a minority nationality, the Oroqen operate in this capacity with the knowledge that a shift in political sensibilities could very well mean that they need to revoke their new ethnic identity as they did during the Cultural Revolution.

4. Language Revitalization

In summary then, the objectification of an Oroqen ethnicity and an Oroqen language arose to meet the expediencies of Chinese minority policy. Prior to the advent of a Chinese nation-state, group identity among the Tungusic peoples of northern China was grounded in smaller cultural units and had a degree of fluidity. There was little need for a more highly demarcated identity that encompassed a large number of culturally similar groups.

Now, as the Oroqens increasingly become aware of their linguistic and cultural assimilation, there is widespread interest in preserving the language. The sense that revitalization is important and desirable is strongest among older fluent speakers, though younger semi-speakers and non-speakers also assent. Yet, importantly, these attitudes must be interpreted in a fuller context. Though people are aware of dialect differences among Oroqen communities and well aware of the linguistic and cultural similarities between the Oroqen and Ewenki, the interest in language revitalization is always framed by the construct of a single, distinct Oroqen language.

As a result, the issue of what constitutes the standard variety of Oroqen becomes significant, yet there has never been a coordinated attempt to determine what this might be. The Chinese government never made an effort to develop a writing system for the language because the Oroqen population was too small; therefore, there is no literary standard or literary tradition to draw on. Also complicating matters is the fact that Oroqen communities are distributed across two provinces, Heilongjiang and Inner

Mongolia, and are found in seven different counties and autonomous regions. This furnishes a large disincentive to develop revitalization efforts that would include and benefit all Oroqen communities since such programs would require approval by a bewildering number of local, regional and provincial authorities. Short of the central government coordinating the effort, it would be unclear who would bear the burden of financing the operation. The three language revitalization efforts which have been initiated among the Oroqen, therefore, have been highly local affairs with the local dialect serving the role of a standard for the language (see Whaley and Li 2000 for a description of Oroqen dialects).

The first, and earliest attempt, began in the township of Xinsheng in Heilongjiang Province (Janhunen *et al.* 1989). Oroqen was introduced into the local school in 1986. A local Oroqen was selected as the instructor, and she taught the language two hours per week to elementary students and middle school students. After several years, the program faltered, primarily due to a lack of funding. However, the program was also handicapped by the lack of any pedagogical material available in Oroqen, the lack of training for the teacher, and the fact that it was difficult to teach an unwritten language in a school setting. Although an effort was made to teach the students phonetic transcription so that they could learn to write Oroqen, this proved to be largely ineffective.

A similar effort was made to teach the Oroqen language in the Oroqen Autonomous Banner using the local dialect in the late 80s and early 90s, with the same limited results. Ultimately, this program was also cancelled. A third program was initiated in Banner in the mid-90s, this time by putting brief language lessons for young children on local TV. The Oroqen speaker selected to teach the lesson was from not from the area, though because of the nature of the teaching, any dialect differences were insignificant. For the lessons she would introduce individual Oroqen words, for example body parts, to a group of children who appeared with her on the television show. The children would repeat the word, the idea being that children watching at home would join in the activity and learn a set of Oroqen words. This program also ended after several months due to lack of funding.

Just as the very notion of Oroqen, either as an ethnic unit and a language, is an external construct that the Oroqen people are now compelled to operate with, so also are their language revitalization efforts constrained by external administrative and political considerations. A peppering of language instruction in the schools or on television, while well intentioned, is unlikely to have much effect on a shift to Mandarin Chinese. However, the sorts of measures that might prove to be more beneficial such as Oroqen immersion schools or developing social contexts that are distinctly Oroqen and involve exclusive use of the language would be seen as separatist acts and quelled by the government. Revitalization must occur without any concomitant loss of a commitment to being a good Chinese citizen. What we find then is a people group that, in one sense, never really existed working to promote a language that never really existed in a context that discourages them from forging a necessary sense of group distinctiveness. While obvious practical considerations such as the lack financial resources and a widely distributed population are barriers to successful revitalization of the Oroqen language, a more profound problem is developing a self-identity on someone else's terms.

References

Cheng, Chin-Chuan (1976) 'Chauvinism, Egalitarianism, and Multi-lingualism: China's Linguistic Experience', *Studies in Language Learning* 1(2): 42-57.

Dreyer, June Teuful (1976) *China's Forty Millions*, Cambridge, MA: Harvard University Press.

Edmondson, Jerold A. (1984) 'China's Minorities', in F. Coulmas (ed) *Linguistic Minorities and Literacy* (Trends in Linguistics, monograph 26), Berlin: Mouton, 63-75.

Fang, Yan (1993) *Heilongjiang Shaoshu minzu jian shi* [A Concise History of the Minority Nationalities of Heilongjiang Province], Beijing: Central Nationalities University Press.

Fu, Maoji (1985) 'Language Policies toward National Minorities in China', *Anthropological Linguistics* 27: 214-221.

Harrell, Stevan (1993) 'Linguistics and Hegemony in China', *International Journal of the Sociology of Language* 103: 97-114.

Heberer, Thomas (1989) *China and Its National Minorities*, Armonk, NY: M.E. Sharpe.

Hsiao, I-s. (1962-1963) *Ch'ing tai t'ung shih* [Complete History of the Qing Dynasty], Taipei: Taiwan Commercial Press.

Inner Mongolia Compilation and Editing Committee (1984) *Elunchun Zu Shehui Lishi Diaocha* [A Survey of the History and Society of the Oroqen], Huhot: Inner Mongolia People's Press.

Janhunen, Juha, Jingxue Xu and Yucheng Hou (1989) 'The Orochen in Xinsheng', *Journal de la Société Finno-Ougrienne* 82: 145-169.

Li, Fengxiang and Lindsay J. Whaley (forthcoming) 'The End of Nomadism: Oroqen History, Migration and Current Distribution', in C. Naeher (ed) *Proceedings of the First International Conference on Manchu Tungus Studies*, Bonn, August 28-September 1, 2000 [Vol. 2: Trends in Tungusic and Siberian Linguistics, Tunguso-Sibirica 9], Wiesbaden: Harrassowitz.

Mackerras, Colin (1994) *China's Minorities: Integration and Modernization in the Twentieth Century*, Oxford: Oxford University Press.

Qiu, Pu (1983) *The Oroqens: China's Nomadic Hunters* (Trans. by Huimin Wang), Beijing: Foreign Languages Press.

Shirokogorov, Sergei M. (1929) *Social Organization of the Northern Tungus*, Shanghai: Commercial Press.

Sun, Hongkai (1988) 'Minorities and Language Planning in China: An Outline', *New Language Planning Newsletter* 3(1): 1-5.

------ (1992) 'Language Recognition and Nationality', *International Journal for the Sociology of Language* 97: 9-22.

Sun, Jinji (1987) *Dong bei minzu yuan liu* [Origins of the Nationalities of the Northeast], Harbin: Heilongjiang People's Press.

Svantesson, Jan-Olof (1991) 'Tradition and Reform in China's Minority Languages', *International Journal of Applied Linguistics* 1(1): 70-88.

Whaley, Lindsay J. (2001) 'Language Loss and Culture Change among Manchu-Tungusic Peoples', in J. E. Terrell (ed) *Archaeology, Language and History: Essays on Culture and Ethnicity*, Westport, CT: Bergin and Garvey, 103-124.

------ and Fengxiang Li (2000) 'Oroqen Dialects', *Central Asiatic Journal* 44: 105-130.

------, Lenore A. Grenoble and Fengxiang Li (1998) 'Revisiting Tungusic Classification from the Bottom up: A Comparison of Evenki and Oroqen', *Language* 75(2): 286-321.

White, Dob (1992) 'The position and role of minority languages and their writing systems in China', International Journal for the Sociology of Language 97:47-57.

Zhao, Fuxing (1991) Elunchunzu Youlie Wenhua [Nomadic Hunting Culture of the Oroqen], Huhot: Inner Mongolia People's Press.

Zheng, Dongri (1991) Dong bei tong gu si zhu min zu qi yuan ji she hui zhuang kuang [The Origins and Social Conditions of the Tungus Peoples of the Northeast], Yanji: Yanbian University Press

8. Language and Intergroup Perception in Sabah

A Case Study of the Rungus Ethnic Community

JEANNET STEPHEN AND VERONICA PETRUS ATIN

1. Introduction[1]

In this case study, we focus on the Rungus ethnic community's perception of the ethnic language 'Kadazandusun'. The ethnic language is currently being taught under the Pupils' Own Language policy of Malaysia from Primary 6 to 12 (ages 9 to 12 years old) pupils of Kadazandusun ethnic origin.[2] 'Kadazandusun' is both the generic ethnic label used to encompass some 40 dialectal and tribal groups in Sabah, including the Rungus, and also the name of a standard language developed from the Dusunic languages. This language is the first ethnic tongue in the state of Sabah, Malaysia to receive institutional support from the government. Recently though, several schools in the Kudat area – where the Rungus community is the major ethnic group – have stopped teaching the Kadazandusun language. When questioned by the inspectorate officer then in charge of the language programme, a Rungus teacher said "it is not our language".[3] One interpretation of this is that the Rungus people are reluctant to learn an ethnic language which is not theirs, or that the Rungus perceive that by learning Kadazandusun, they are being 'kadazandusunized' by the 'more advanced'[4] Kadazandusuns. These reports, whether true or not, indicate

---

[1] We would like to thank all those who have contributed to the writing of this paper especially the CEO and staff of the Kadazandusun Language Foundation for information and materials, and to the Rungus people involved in our questionnaire. We would also like to give our sincere thanks to our editors for having the highest level of patience while working with us on this paper.

[2] The Pupils' Own Language policy in the Malaysia education system allows for a language other than the national language, Malay, to be taught in the school provided it is formally requested by the parents of 15 or more pupils in the school.

[3] This is based on our informal discussion with the officer who was in charge of the program in 2000, Madam Evelyn Annol of the Sabah Education Department.

[4] The Kadazandusun community (i.e. the speakers of the Kadazan Tangara dialect) are considered to be the most 'advanced' amongst the 40-odd non-Muslim ethnic communities in Sabah because they were the first ethnic community to be exposed to literacy and the media (Lasimbang *et al.* 2000). The Kadazandusun ethnic community has also been closely situated near the State's capital, Kota Kinabalu and been politically active as a group.

that the situation warrants further research, to discover whether the Rungus perceive the Kadazandusuns as an equal friend or an imposing foe, and whether there is real resistance to learning an ethnic language that is not one's own, even though it may be related to it.

The purpose of this paper is to explore these questions and report on some of our research findings on ethnicity, language attitudes, and language teaching in the Kudat region of Sabah. For this research we devised a questionnaire and used semi-structured interview questions to arrive at some of the reasons for abandoning Kadazandusun language teaching in this region. While some of these reasons are structural – including the fact that the classes were taught after regular school hours, there were no state exams required for the Kadazandusun language courses, and there was a lack of proper teaching materials – there are other reasons that relate to language categorization and the fact that state policy has placed Rungus under the larger umbrella language group, Kadazandusun. There are thus additional problems associated with teaching a standard language that is linguistically different from one's own variety. In addition, there are various social positions which Rungus speakers take up regarding their relationship and identity with the Kadazandusun language. While some speakers feel that Kadazandusun is clearly related to Rungus, and orient themselves to a more inclusive Kadazandusun ethnic identity, others do not perceive the language this way. The findings we present are still preliminary, and part of their purpose is to indicate further lines of research. These further lines of research will be explained more at the beginning of the conclusion section of this paper.

We will first explain the complex multilingual and multiethnic context in Sabah from our perspectives – ourselves being Kadazandusun, who live and observe this context daily. We will also discuss how the Rungus community perceives issues such as the revitalization of the Kadazandusun language, the legitimization of the Kadazandusun language in a multiethnic and multilingual region, and the Rungus' definition of ethnic identity in multiethnic Sabah. Prior to that final objective, we will outline the socio-historical background of the ethnic label 'Kadazandusun'.

This research stems from our shared academic interest in the fact that the Kadazandusun language had ceased to be taught in some schools in the Kudat district. We hypothesize that this decision was connected to the issue of ethnic identity and ethnic language, which are both major concerns for the ethnic communities in Sabah (Lasimbang and Kinajil 2000). Although our research found other reasons why Kadazandusun was no longer taught, our focus is the ethnic categorization of the Rungus and their perception of the ethnic 'umbrella' term 'Kadazandusun', used to refer to both the people and the language in this region.

Although some people might remark that the ethnic communities in Sabah should be grateful that at least one ethnic language, Kadazandusun, has been granted the right to be taught in school, we will explore some of the issues that have arisen with respect to this language policy. While it is true that not all of the thirty-two ethnic languages can be taught in the education system, what is at stake here is the issue of how certain ethnic groups and languages are categorized and attitudes towards this categorization.

2. The Multilingual and Multiethnic Context in Sabah

According to Grimes (1996), there are 138 languages in Malaysia, of which 54 are indigenous to Sabah. Using a classification system according to which Dusunic dialects are separate if they have 80 to 85 percent or less of shared cognates, Smith (1984) suggests that there are 10 languages in the Dusunic language family, which is of the Borneon stock of the North-western Austronesian superstock. One of these languages is Kadazandusun (Kadazan/Dusun), which is said to have 13 dialects under the Dusunic family of languages. Smith treats Rungus as a separate language within the Dusunic family. Although this classification is already complicated, it nevertheless does not include the other languages spoken by Sabah's Muslim ethnic communities, including the Bajau, Suluk, Bisaya, and Bugis languages (King and King 1984).

On the relationship of Rungus to other Dusunic dialects, King (1984) reports the result of an intelligibility test conducted among Rungus and three of these dialects, based on a lexicostatistical analysis of mutual intelligibility. The three dialects of Dusunic included the Outer Sugut Kadazan (spoken in the area nearer to the Rungus villages), Central Dusun dialect (a prominent Dusunic dialect spoken in villages in the interior parts of Sabah including areas nearer to the Rungus villages), and Kadazan/Dusun (spoken in over half of the 23 districts[5] in the state of Sabah). The findings revealed that the intelligibility scores of the Rungus subjects of the Outer Sugut Kadazan were between 60-72%, thus they were "below the 80%

[5] The twenty-three districts in Sabah encompass hundreds of villages. It is acceptable to say that each district in Sabah is represented by an ethnic community e.g. the Penampang district by the Kadazandusun, the Kota Belud district by the Bajau, the Kudat district by the Rungus, and so forth. Nevertheless, the representation is only by a majority of the population as of course the districts are also multiracial and multicultural, having other ethnic communities alongside the majority.

threshold which defines same or different languages" (ibid.: 290). The intelligibility scores of the Rungus subjects of Central Dusun ranged from 60-71% when a reference tape from Menggaris, a village right on the borderline between Rungus and Central Dusun area, was used. The scores were much lower (39-45%) when reference tapes of Central Dusun from areas farther than the Rungus speaking areas were used. Lastly, intelligibility cross tests between Rungus and Kadazan/Dusun gave scores ranging from 19-50%.

As previously mentioned, the multiethnic and multilingual situation in Sabah is complex. Despite the results of linguistic research that show that Rungus is a different language from the other Dusunic languages, the Kadazandusun Cultural Association (KDCA) in its Constitution states that a 'Kadazandusun' is someone whose mother tongue is one of the 40 dialects spoken in Sabah, and who expresses the traditions, customs and other cultural manifestations, thus treating the Rungus as a Kadazandusun group. The Kadazandusun Cultural Association (KDCA) is a non-political association of 40 indigenous ethnic communities of Sabah, first registered under the Malaysian Societies Act in 1966 as the Kadazan Cultural Association (KCA). The KDCA has focused much of its efforts in the preservation, development, enrichment and promotion of the Kadazan-dusun multiethnic cultures.

We feel it is important to emphasize the roles of the KDCA as an unspoken authority over the non-Muslim ethnic groups. These roles are to identify, plan, organize, implement and coordinate socio-cultural, economic, educational, health and welfare, and women's development programmes for the Kadazandusun community. Thus, over the years the KDCA has had a say in things Kadazandusun in Sabah. Examples include the standard-ization of the Kadazandusun language, the use of the name or label 'Kadazandusun', and research activities pertaining to the culture, history, environment, social and economic issues and current affairs affecting the Kadazandusun community.

3. Issues of Social and Linguistic Categorization

The whole issue of ethnic labels or the nomenclature of the ethnic groups in Sabah is very important to the Kadazandusun community because of the value that ethnic labels have in representing self-perception, inclusion and exclusion, power and prestige (Lasimbang and Miller 1990). In former times in Sabah, formerly North Borneo, the ethnic communities were known by their tribal names such as Gonsomon, Momogun, Tobilung, Tangara, Tatana and others. As far back as the 1920s, North Borneo's ethnic communities were further distinguished by the religion they profess. Thus there were the Muslim ethnic communities who referred to themselves as 'Sama', and the non-Muslim ethnic communities each referring to themselves by their tribal group names (Lasimbang and Miller 1990). This differentiation, through the use of different ethnic labels, made nomenclature (i.e. linguistic and ethnic categorization) a major problem confronting language researchers in Borneo.

As early as 1886, there were problems of 'language labelling' used by various groups amongst the indigenous population of North Borneo (Lasimbang and Miller 1990, cited in Lasimbang and Kinajil 2000: 416). This was further complicated by the differentiations made between indigenous populations by early traders from Brunei, a neighbouring country. The term 'Dusun' in the Malay language means *orchard* and therefore brings the connotation of 'rural' (Banker and Banker 1984). Geographically, compared to the Kadazan community who live in nearby towns with modern amenities, the Dusun people live in areas further from towns such as in the foothills of Mt. Kinabalu. As noted in the early twentieth century, "the Dusun usually describes himself generically as a *tulun tindal* (landsman) or, on the West Coast, particularly at Papar, as a Kadazan" (Rutter 1929: 31). However, what arose subsequently was that the term 'Dusun' refers to someone who is different from a 'Kadazan'. Tunggolou (1999) gives various theories and explanations about the origins and meanings of the terms 'Kadazan' and 'Dusun', which suggest how complicated the issue of nomenclature within the indigenous communities can be in this region.

In 1961, disagreements still persisted amongst the various ethnic communities. It should be noted that the present Kadazandusun Cultural Association (KDCA) was previously known as the Kadazan Cultural Association (KCA) and the change itself is a sign of the historical development of the Kadazandusun community. To emphasise the gravity of the whole issue regarding ethnic labels, it is worthwhile to point out here that there was also formerly a body called the United Sabah Dusun Association (USDA). This body insisted on the full measure of respect and recognition due to the Dusun, and that they would not accept any form of pressure to change their ethnic name (Reid 1997). In 1989, considering that the bickering would not rest and would only jeopardize the development of the ethnic communities concerned, the president of KDCA *Huguan Siou*[6]

[6] The title '*Huguan Siou*' or Paramount Leader is a highly dignified and near sacred term to the Kadazandusuns. It is bestowed to a leader considered worthy of the title by The Delegates Conference of the KDCA. If no leader is considered worthy, the Huguan Siou Office would rather be left vacant.

Datuk Seri Joseph Pairin Kitingan of the non-Muslim ethnic communities saw that the name 'Kadazan' was unpopular as a unifying label for the 40 or so ethnic communities (excluding the Muslim ethnic communities) and announced that the KCA would therefore be changed to the Kadazan Dusun Cultural Association (KDCA). Datuk Seri[7] Joseph Pairin Kitingan is also the president of a political party, Parti Bersatu Sabah and an ex-Chief Minister of Sabah. The Extraordinary Delegates Conference of the KDCA in 1998 bestowed the title of '*Huguan Siou*' to Kitingan, making him only the second person up until now to have received it, after Tun Fuad Stephens, the first Chief Minister of Sabah and a Kadazandusun of mixed parentage.

Again, with the aim of unity in mind, another historic agreement was reached by both KDCA and USDA on 24 January 1995, for the ethnic labels 'Kadazan' and 'Dusun' to be officially known henceforth as 'Kadazandusun' to refer to the ethnic group, and for their language to be known as the 'Kadazandusun' language. From that point on, where the label 'Kadazandusun' is used, it is understood to refer, at least socio-politically, to the whole of the 40 non-Muslim ethnic communities as listed under the KDCA Constitution. This change of ethnic label is seen as an effort to unite all the non-Muslim ethnic communities.

It should now be clear that labels of ethnicity are seriously valued as important markers of ethnic identity, which De Vos (cited in Brass 1996) defines as consisting of the use of any subjective, symbolic or emblematic aspects of their cultures to differentiate themselves from other groups. Despite the intention that the term 'Kadazandusun' should be an umbrella term for the 40-odd non-Muslim ethnic communities, it remains a socio-political term used primarily by the state. The different ethnic labels are still widely used by the various ethnic groups in the region. This issue is emotion-laden and sensitive to the ethnic people involved and could therefore easily fuel debates and arguments. Therefore, it is not surprising that many political parties have formed, based on ethnicity, which further reinforces the divisions. These include the Pasok Momogun, the United National Kadazan Association (UNKO) and the use in the media of the term 'Kadazandusun Murut' or its acronym 'KDM' (Stephen 2000). In addition, there are different cultural associations – including the United Sabah Bajau Association (Bajau), Sabah Murut Association/PMS (Murut), Sabah Kedayan Association (Kedayan), and Sabah Momogun Rungus Association/SAMORA (Rungus) – which are not purely for the purpose of promoting traditional dances and so forth, but more specifically because

[7] 'Datuk Seri' is a State award given especially to statesmen considered to have contributed to the State.

each ethnic community still wishes to express their own ethnic identity.

Lasimbang and Kinajil (2000) point out that the main problem faced by census takers in classifying the ethnic communities in Borneo was precisely the problem of nomenclature since no community wishes to be called differently from the way they know themselves. Divisions in the 'Kadazandusun' group already existed, as demonstrated in the 1996 decision by SAMORA for the Rungus community to be disassociated from the Kadazandusun family. At the time of that decision, the Kadazandusun political arena was going through turmoil and SAMORA's wish was, in our view, a suggestion that it was disappointed with what benefits were given to the other ethnic groups within the larger name 'Kadazandusun'. Nevertheless, the issue of labelling and the imposed 'umbrella' category used by the state poses problems when the 'Kadazandusun' group is given the right to teach the Kadazandusun language in schools. The background leading up to this decision is discussed below.

4. The Teaching of the Kadazandusun Language and the Process of Legitimization

We base the following discussion on Lasimbang and Kinajil's (2000) outline of the legitimization process of the Kadazandusun language. A Kadazandusun orthography has been in existence since the early 1880's, when literacy was introduced to the Penampang populace (who speak Tangara Kadazan) through the school-building efforts of Mill Hill Missionaries (Lasimbang and Kinajil 2000: 416). Reid (1997) observes that the mission schools were well accepted by the people because the local Tangara Kadazan dialect was used to teach them in the first two or three years in school, only shifting gradually by the third or fourth year into English. In 1953, the Kadazan language was introduced into the English newspaper, *Sabah Times*. The year after saw the introduction of the Kadazan language on Sabah Radio, in which the programme ran for 15 minutes daily and was increased to 14 hours per week in 1960. Then, only the Tangara Kadazan and a dialect of Dusun mainly spoken in the interior areas of Sabah were used. Initially, then, the other Kadazandusun dialects or Dusunic languages such as Rungus etc. were not given much exposure in the media. At present, however, under its Various Languages Broadcast programme, Radio Malaysia Sabah airs radio programmes in four ethnic languages: Kadazan, Dusun, Bajau and Murut (Stephen 2002). Rungus songs are sometimes heard playing on air in the Kadazan section.

It was only in 1985, when the Kadazandusun orthography was standardized, based on the standard Kadazan orthography decisions made earlier by KCA in 1984, that elements of pronunciation of the other dialects, including Rungus, were taken into consideration. The Kadazan orthography standardization process involved taking into account the proposal paper by Miller and Miller (1983) titled 'Problem Areas Within the Kadazan Writing System' as well as considering the various comments and suggestions received from leaders of the Kadazan communities (the 40 ethnic groups under KCA) (Lasimbang *et al.* 2000). Some of the problem areas reported were the sound system of the language, since the sounds in the various dialects do differ significantly from each other. Other problems pointed out were the use of hyphens, spelling of particles or clitics and variant spellings. In the same year, children's books from the Kadazan Children's Literature Production Workshop were published using the standardized orthography. In 1987, the standardized Kadazan orthography was used in the update of Antonissen's 1958 Kadazan Dictionary and grammar, and this update was used in the first trilingual KadazanDusun-Malay-English Dictionary published by KCA. The following year, the KCA requested that Kadazan be taught in schools in Sabah, and received a positive response from the Malaysian Minister of Education. In 1989, the year that KCA officially became known as KDCA, it organized the Symposium on Standardization of the Kadazan dialects to examine the issue of standardization of the various dialects. Nevertheless, the old issue of nomenclature, whether to use Kadazan or Dusun arose again, erasing any hope of achieving a consensus on the standardization and the teaching of the language in schools. As Smith remarks: "The problem the Kadazan and Dusun were facing at the time was the issue of standardization of the various dialects. However, when it came to the choice of the name for the language, it seems that each group had conflicting ideas as the issue of identity was foremost in their minds" (2003: 5).[8]

Despite these initial efforts by language enthusiasts to include the Kadazandusun language in the education syllabus, the linguistic situation as Smith describes it led to a delay of the process. After lying dormant for four years, the idea of having the Kadazan language taught in school was revived in 1994 by Tan Sri Bernard Dompok, a Member of Parliament and a Kadazandusun himself. Finally, in 1995, the request was granted. Despite the problem of which name to use, the Sabah Education Department successfully mediated between KDCA and USDA – then the two main cultural bodies of the Kadazandusun ethnic group – persuading both to agree on 'Kadazandusun' as the official name for the standard lan-

[8] Personal copy from the writer, an earlier version of the one published as Smith 2003.

guage to be taught in the schools. In the same year the Kadazandusun Language Foundation (KLF) was set up as a body whose concern is to mobilize the Kadazandusun community towards taking increasing responsibility for the development of the language. In 2000, there were 881 teachers of the various Kadazandusun ethnic groups, teaching the standard Kadazandusun language to 19, 732 children in 440 primary schools in 21 districts throughout Sabah.

As previously mentioned, one of the districts involved is Kudat where the Rungus predominate. Although it is included under the umbrella term Kadazandusun, linguistic research has demonstrated, as we have seen, that Rungus is a different language in the Dusunic family. In contrast to the Kadazan of Penampang area, published materials in the Rungus language appeared only in 1966, in the form of an English-Rungus dictionary by the Protestant Church of Sabah, and religious documents such as bible translations and service books (King 1984: 285).

The development of Rungus orthography and literacy materials also began quite late. Some linguistic work began in the 1960s and 70s (see King 1984: 283). In the 90s, the SIL (Malaysia) conducted more linguistic work on Rungus and the KLF held seminars on Rungus such as the 'Rungus Orthography Seminar' in Kudat (2001) and the 'Rungus Writers Seminar', also in Kudat (2001). It is evident, then, that despite finally agreeing to come under the umbrella term 'Kadazandusun' and accepting the literary development of Kadazandusun, the Rungus are still very concerned about the status of their own language. It would appear, then, that ethnic identity, and language as one of its markers, are important to them. The attachment of the Rungus to their language and their attitudes towards their inclusion under the Kadazandusun umbrella term is the focus of investigation we discuss below.

5. Analysis of the Case Study

The following analysis of the Rungus attitudes towards to both the Kadazandusun label and the standard language is based on field research in the Rungus speaking areas. We gathered data in the Kudat township (where people we interviewed are from various villages in Kudat), and the villages of Tinangol, Lajong, and Tinutudan. These areas were chosen because they were easily accessible. In addition, local residents there were engaged in pro-active languages activities, actively used longhouses in their communities, and had primary schools nearby, where the Kadazandusun language was taught.

In our attempt to find out the perception of the Rungus people on the issues of the label and the teaching of Kadazandusun, we devised a questionnaire to elicit people's views on the processes of language legitimization in a multiethnic and multilingual region, and their definition of ethnic identity in multiethnic Sabah (see appendix for questionnaire). The five questions served as a starting point, from which other unplanned questions were derived. Their purpose was to try to elicit from the Rungus their actual views rather than answers which they thought we wanted from them.

Using this questionnaire, we interviewed community leaders, parents, children and teachers involved in the Kadazandusun language teaching programme. Since neither of us speaks the Rungus language (not being Rungus ourselves but of another Kadazandusun ethnic group) we conducted the interview in Malay, the national language of Malaysia, which also functions as the lingua franca amongst the many ethnic groups in the state of Sabah. Malay is also the language used as the education medium in the Malaysian schools, as well as in printed and electronic media. Thus it is understood by almost everybody regardless of ethnic origin, except for those who did not have access to formal education and had very minimal contact with people of other ethnic groups.

This preliminary case study is based on data from 50 respondents. We interviewed five Rungus community leaders, ten teachers teaching Kadazandusun, and forty-five other villagers from the community longhouse. Thirty of those had children who had been attending the Kadazandusun classes.[9] All the respondents we talked to consider themselves 'Rungus'. This shows that ethnic identity is still significant to them even though the term 'Kadazandusun' has been officially coined and approved by people in authority. This is better explained by an example given by one of the respondents who is a community leader. He explained that on his national identity card, his race is written as 'Kadazan' but in reality he is a 'Rungus'. Prompted to explain his perceived difference between the two ethnic terms, he felt that 'Kadazan' is the term one uses to distinguish race in Malaysia, since people are generally referred to as Malay, Chinese, Indian and 'others' (which most often refers to major ethnic groups in Sabah and Sarawak, namely 'Kadazan' and 'Iban'). 'Rungus', for this informant, is a term to identify one's ethnic group within the Sabahan circle. Although we came

[9] Obviously, this is not a representative sample; recent national census figures show the total population of the Rungus in Sabah to be approximately 40,000. Both writers are now engaged in the second phase of this research that involves a larger number of respondents in more Rungus villages. This bigger coverage is made possible through the Fundamental Research Grant from Universiti Malaysia Sabah.

across only one such case, we feel that it is significant as both of us have the same 'Kadazan' label in our national identification regardless of the fact that we are of another ethnic group coming under the wider label Kadazandusun.

Respondents had varying opinions on the differences between 'Rungus' and 'Kadazandusun' as both language and ethnic labels. Since we did not specifically choose our respondents, we assumed that everyone knew the term 'Kadazandusun'. Surprisingly, we discovered that 3 respondents, who are housewives in their 30s, did not have any idea of the differences between Rungus and Kadazandusun, saying that they never had any prior contact with either Dusun or Kadazan people. This appears to be in direct contradiction to the concept of the umbrella term given by KDCA and would seem to indicate that the KDCA authorities need to do more grass-roots work if they want to successfully unite people as 'Kadazandusun'.

Most respondents perceived differences between 'Rungus' and Kadazandusun, in the lexicon, pronunciation, and sentence structures. We have to make it clear here that when we used 'Kadazandusun' with them we were referring to the standard language. However, some respondents understood us to mean the Kadazan spoken in Penampang and Papar (Tangara or Coastal Kadazan), others thought we were referring to the Dusun spoken in the interior areas to the northern part of Sabah (Central Dusun and Outer Sugut Dusun). Since the standard Kadazandusun is based mostly on Tangara Kadazan and Central Dusun, we accepted both of these responses. Again, however, this shows that not everyone understands the label 'Kadazandusun': these findings therefore contradict our earlier assumption that the label 'Kadazandusun' is understood by everyone. This bears significantly on the issue of processes of language legitimization in a multiethnic and multilingual region like Sabah because although Kadazandusun underwent more than a decade's process to achieve its status today, the abandonment of the Kadazandusun language teaching in Kudat indicates that language and ethnic identity are very intimately linked. To authorities such as the KDCA and others directly related to the legitimization process, it would seem that the legitimization of the Kadazandusun language should benefit all the ethnic communities. However, this study shows that this might not be the case and that the authorities involved failed to disseminate necessary information, such as explaining what the standard 'Kadazandusun' language is and why it was being taught to the ethnic communities, especially in the more rural areas such as Kudat.

We found that the community leaders could most clearly relate to the term Kadazandusun as an umbrella term for the ethnic groups of related culture. These leaders are well aware of the motive of the KDCA to include 40 ethnic groups under the term. They also strongly feel that the myths and legends on the origin of the people (Kadazandusun) count in establishing the relation. They recount this story:

> In the beginning, the ancestors of all those presently known as Kadazandusun people had only one settlement, Nunuk Ragang, presently known as Tampias in the area of Ranau in the interior of Sabah. The name of the place was based on the nunuk ragang tree, a very huge tree that sheltered the people from the sun and rain. As the population grew, food became scarce. The river had considerably eroded its banks and the Nunuk Ragang began to bend lower and lower into the river pool. Many died due to lack of nourishment. Realizing this as a threat to the people, the chief then instructed his people to find new settlements. The Kadazan/Dusun migration movement thus began towards the west to Tambunan, Ranau, Penampang and towards the east to Labuk and beyond to where the Kadazan/Dusuns are found at present. The principal guides for the movement were river tributaries. As the expeditions occurred in groups, they had multi-destinations. Each group formed their own long house for unity and strength against wild beasts and intrusions by other communal groupings.

Apparently, this legend has significance for these community leaders, as it contributes to the sense of belonging among the various ethnic groups, thus promoting unity. The legend of Nunuk Ragang is a common story of origin for the people now known as the 'Kadazandusun'. There are of course various versions of the story, which differ according to ethnic groups. For example, in the Rungus community the name used to refer to the earlier people was 'Momogun', whilst for the Dusun community it is termed as 'the people of Nunuk Ragang'. Because the legend varies across ethnic groups, it was not taken into consideration with regard to nomenclature. The legend will also normally be used to inspire emotions and sentimental values of unity among 'the people' in times of political necessity such as in Kadazandusun politicians' speeches during state elections.

In addition, some community leaders feel that the term Kadazandusun acts as a 'career label'. Using this term, one stands a better chance to get a job both in the government and private sectors, as it is a better-known term to every Malaysian than some of the minority ethnic labels. These leaders are also aware of the scenario of nomenclature in Sabah, and of the negative associations of 'Dusun' that we pointed out earlier. As they point out, 'Dusun' is said to have been the name given to the Brunei people and they feel that it carries negative connotations with rural life, while Kadazan literally means 'people of the township'. Thus, for them, it is not a problem to use 'Kadazan' or 'Kadazandusun' for the sake of unity or for one's benefit.

On the teaching of the Kadazandusun in schools, respondents held different views. Many respondents may have been overly positive in their attitudes toward Kadazandusun, in light of an ideology of unity amongst the ethnic brotherhood, such that no one ethnic community in Sabah would openly say that another ethnic community is bad and that they are imposing unwanted restrictions upon them. This would go against the spirit of brotherhood of the people. In light of this, many felt that teaching Kadazandusun was positive, and an important step in unifying the different ethnic groups in Sabah. Many parents, in particular, welcomed the opportunity for their children to learn the language of their 'close cousins'. Children, they told us, find it fun to learn a language that is similar, but not quite the same as their mother tongue. However, whilst agreeing with and supporting the teaching of the Kadazandusun language, the Rungus, still being loyal to their own Rungus identity, politely suggested that perhaps more Rungus vocabulary be included in the Kadazandusun syllabus, presumably until their own Rungus language can be taught in schools.

Teachers, on the other hand, have two clearly articulated responses. They are of the opinion that Kadazandusun, being the first indigenous language in Sabah taught in schools, may act as a paradigm in setting up a Rungus syllabus in the future. They also felt that teaching Kadazandusun could heighten awareness of the various related languages and cultures. This is a particularly positive response taking into account the difficulties involved to teach an ethnic language. Institutionalizing a language requires manpower, time, and commitment from the ethnic community itself to materialize an ethnic language teaching programme. Others, however, expressed fears that the Rungus language will be left out in the course of establishing the status of Kadazandusun. These views perhaps more adequately reflect the contradictions that exist concerning indigenous language teaching in this area.

This discussion brings us back to the abandoning of the Kadazandusun language teaching in schools. Leaders and parents generally feel that not teaching an indigenous language is a loss to the community. Leaders further articulated their suspicion that the language teaching probably stopped because the standard Kadazandusun language does not contain many Rungus language elements such as lexical items, and they suggest that the authorities should do more to include them. Teachers, too, thought that linguistic differences might have contributed to the abandonment. In cases where the teacher is Rungus not only does he have difficulty in understanding some of the words and sentence structures of Kadazandusun, he also faces the challenge of explaining these to a group of Rungus kids who tend to respond in Rungus (all Rungus teachers we interviewed were male). Teachers of other ethnic Kadazandusun groups, on whose language the standard is based, have a better grasp of the language. Some teachers find the challenge of teaching the standard language to the Rungus kids so great that they quit halfway.

In relation to this, teachers emphasize other problems that arose in the teaching of Kadazandusun. These include the short period of training that they receive (one week of initial training and a few retraining sessions lasting from one to two weeks), which they feel is too short for them to master the syllabus. Also, pupils simply stopped coming to the classes, which the teachers attributed to the fact that the classes were conducted outside of school hours and there is no official exam.[10] Teachers also noted the infrastructure problems that still persist in some parts of Kudat. Since many villages still do not have electricity, some materials for use in language teaching such as CD-ROMs or even cassettes provided by the Kadazandusun Unit in the Ministry of Education (Sabah Education Department) cannot be used. Besides, funding to carry out the programme is limited, to such an extent that some teachers initially bought their own batteries to operate the cassettes. In the long run, however, it became such a problem that they finally stopped using any of those teaching materials.

6. Conclusion

In this chapter, we have discussed the case of the abandoning of state-sponsored Kadazandusun language teaching in certain schools in the Rungus dominated district of Kudat, Malaysia. We wanted to explore the reasons for this failure: whether the Rungus people are simply reluctant to learn an ethnic language which is not theirs, perhaps because the Rungus perceive that by learning Kadazandusun, they are being 'kadazandusunized' by the more 'advanced' Kadazandusuns. We found that the Rungus people in this study support the larger intention of teaching the Kadazandusun language (in the general context of Malaysia), but that locally in Sabah they cannot deny their loyalty to the Rungus language and identity. As the early sections of the chapter demonstrated, this loyalty relates to the very complex social and linguistic categorization issues, which still persist in the region, and to their significance for ethnic groups'

[10] In Malaysia, the education system is very much exam-oriented, so that any subject that does not have an official exam tends to be treated lightly by parents and pupils.

self-perception. The case reveals in a more general way some of the complexities attendant on the granting of language-in-education rights to indigenous peoples in such multilingual areas, especially when they are intended to serve specific political goals – in this case, to unite ethnic groups of the non-Muslim ethic languages in Sabah.

In Sabah, the umbrella term 'Kadazandusun', and the standard 'Kadazandusun' language have been accepted by the ethnic communities in the name of unity amongst all the non-Muslim ethnic communities, and for the developmental advantages this can bring within the larger Malaysian context. From this perspective, some people feel that they have a 'win-win' situation, since no ethnic community is forced to leave behind its own dialect or lifestyles. Rather all – Kuijau, Bisaya, Murut, Rungus, Liwan, or Tobilung – are considered free and are even encouraged to run their own language development projects in their own communities. In this context, the Rungus definition of ethnic identity is being able to call themselves Rungus, being free to have their own ethnic language development projects, while at the same time accepting the umbrella term 'Kadazandusun' for the sake of unity and certain personal benefits. This acceptance is no mean feat given Sabah's complex multiethnic and multiracial history, and ultimately indicates the willingness of the ethnic communities to understand each other mutually and minimize differences for the sake of a united society.

At the same time, the case of the Rungus indicates some potential problem areas worthy of further study. One of these is that, within this larger ethnic identity, the Rungus still desire to have their language recognized within the Kadazandusun syllabus, for instance by including more of its vocabulary. On one hand, one may see this as a reaction of insecurity. However, we prefer to think of it as a normal reaction from an ethnic community whose language seems to be losing importance, in this case compared to the more major languages, which make up the standard 'Kadazandusun' language. There have been comparable complaints or demands from speakers of the other 40 dialects, especially where their language differs significantly from the standard. In our personal view, then, barriers of this kind have yet to be overcome to ensure the success of Kadazandusun language teaching.

From this point of view, the Kadazandusun language revitalization process and its use in school is seen as a potential model and a future point of aspiration for their own Rungus language. The teaching of the Kadazandusun language has paved the way for other ethnic communities in Sabah to start working on their own language, as is the case with the Murut communities, who have now started to have classes for primary school children in Murut dominated areas in Sabah.

As researchers local to the situation, we feel it is appropriate to have the Kadazandusun language in the education system to represent the 40 ethnic communities, since most of the languages involved have fairly high mutual intelligibility scores with the main dialects that form the Standard Kadazandusun (Central Dusun and Coastal Kadazan). We also recognize, however, that it is quite impossible to have all of the ethnic languages taught formally. Nevertheless, our research strongly suggests that having only one ethnic language in schools will not be agreed to, since it does not satisfactorily recognize important ethnic and linguistic distinctions made within Sabah which are not made by Malaysians in general. In other words, there is a fear that the larger ethnic identity does not sufficiently recognize smaller local ones.

In order to encourage communities to preserve their languages, we feel that they should all be encouraged and helped to hold informal language classes in community schools, community halls, churches, or in individuals' houses. Support for this kind of work does come from the Kadazandusun Language Foundation (KLF), the main custodian of Kadazandusun language development. As Ms Rita Lasimbang, KLF's CEO, has reiterated, the KLF has been instrumental in helping to set up the Murut Language Centre, and in Rungus language development, for example by conducting the Rungus Writers' Seminar in the year 2000. KLF hopes that all ethnic languages in Sabah will one day be at par with the Kadazandusun language, but this can only be achieved if the ethnic communities themselves strive to make their languages prestigious in their own eyes.

Finally, we suggest that ethnic communities of the Kadazandusun, specifically those who still do not have any ethnic language development programmes, focus on other means than formal education to revitalize their own ethnic languages, relating it to activities outside school such as documenting their rich oral traditions, and motivating the younger generations to continue learning and speaking the ethnic language.[11]

---

[11] On the issue of confining language revitalisation entirely to formal education, see also the chapters by Patrick, Freeland, Heugh and Stroud in this volume.

References

Antonissen, A. (1958) *Kadazan Dictionary and Grammar*, Canberra: Government Printing Office.

Appell, G. N. (1963) *Myths and Legends about the Rungus of the Kudat District*, The Sarawak Museum Journal.

Banker, J. and E. Banker (1984) 'The Kadazan/Dusun Language', in J. K. King and J.W. King (eds) *Languages of Sabah: A Survey Report*, Pacific Linguistics C78, Canberra: The Australian National University, 297-324.

Brass, P. R. (1996) 'Ethnic Groups and Ethnic Identity Formation', in J. Hutchinson and A. D. Smith (eds) *Ethnicity*, Oxford: Oxford University Press, 85-90.

Forschner, T. (1978) *Outline of Rungus Grammar*, Mimeo. Kudat.

Grimes, B. F. (ed) (1996) *Ethnologue: Languages of the World*, Texas: Summer Institute of Linguistics.

Kadazandusun Language Foundation website. http://www.klf.com.my

King, J. K. (1984) 'The Paitanic Language Family', in J. K. King and J. W. King (eds) (1984) *Languages of Sabah: A Survey Report*, Australia: Pacific Linguistics C78, Canberra: The Australian National University Press, 139-153.

Koisaan (Kadazandusun Cultural Association) *Constitution and Rules*, Kota Kinabalu: Kadazandusun Cultural Association (KDCA).

------ and J. W. King (eds) (1984) *Languages of Sabah: A Survey Report*, Australia: Pacific Linguistics C78, Canberra: The Australian National University Press.

Lasimbang, R. and C. P. Miller (1990) 'Language Labelling and Other Factors Affecting Perception of Ethnic Identity in Sabah', in James T. Collins (ed) *Language and Oral Traditions in Borneo (Selected Papers from the First Extraordinary Conference of the Borneo Research Council, Kuching, Sarawak, Malaysia, 4-9 August)*, Borneo Research Council Proceedings Series (vol.2), Williamsburg, VA: Borneo Research Council, 115-139.

Lasimbang, R., C. P. Miller and J. Miller (eds) (1995) *Kadazan-Dusun-Malay-English Dictionary*, Kota Kinabalu: Kadazandusun Cultural Association (KDCA).

Lasimbang, R. and T. Kinajil (2000) 'Changing the Language Ecology of Kadazandusun: The Role of the Kadazandusun Language Foundation', in A. J. Liddicoat and P. Bryant (eds) *Current Issues in Language Planning* (Special Issue on Language Planning and Language Ecology) 1(3): 415-423.

Lasimbang, R., Trixie Kinajil, Aloysia Moguil and Lena Sipulou (2000) 'The Kadazandusun Language: The Advent of Literacy to the Ascent of Its Teaching in Sabah's Schools Today'. Paper presented at 1st Borneo Language Teaching Conference Organised by University Institute Teknologi Mara, Kota Kinabalu, 7-9 Sept 2000.

Miller, J. and C. Miller (1983) 'Problem Areas Within the Kadazan Writing System', Paper submitted to KCA as reference in updating the spelling system of Kadazan. Unpublished manuscript.

Reid, A. (1997) 'Endangered Identity: Kadazan or Dusun in Sabah (East Malaysia)', *Journal of Southeast Asian Studies* 28(1) (March 1997): 120-136.

Rutter, O. (1929) *The Pagans of North Borneo*, London: Hutchinson.

Smith, K. D. (1984) 'The Languages of Sabah: A Lexicostatistical Classification.', in J. K. King and J. W. King (eds) *Languages of Sabah: A Survey Report*, Australia: Pacific Linguistics C78, 1-49.

------ (2003) 'Minority Language Education in Malaysia: Four Ethnic Communities' Experiences', *International Journal of Bilingual Education and Bilingualism*.6 (1): 1-21.

Stephen, J. (2000) 'The Value of Ethnic Labels in Relation to Ethnic Identity in Sabah: The Case of the Kadazandusun', in M. Leigh (ed) *Borneo 2000, Volume I: Ethnicity, Culture and Society*, Kuching, Sarawak: Institute of East Asian Studies Publications.

------ (2002) 'The Roles of Ethnic Community Broadcasting in Kadazandusun Language Maintenance'. Paper presented at the 7th Biennial International Conference of the Borneo Research Council, 15-18 July, Universiti Malaysia Sabah, Malaysia. Unpublished manuscript.

Tunggolou, R. F. (1999) 'The Origins and Meanings of the Terms "Kadazan" and "Dusun"', http://www.kdca.org.my/kadazandusun_meaning.shtml.

White, Dob (1992) 'The Position and Role of Minority Languages and Their Writing Systems in China', *International Journal for the Sociology of Language* 97: 47-57.

Zhao, Fuxing (1991) *Elunchunzu Youlie Wenhua* [Nomadic Hunting Culture of the Oroqen], Huhot: Inner Mongolia People's Press.

Zheng, Dongri (1991) *Dong bei tong gu si zhu min zu qi yuan ji she hui zhuang kuang* [The Origins and Social Conditions of the Tungus Peoples of the Northeast], Yanji: Yanbian University Press.

Appendix

Question	Purposes
What is your ethnicity?	–to elicit in, hopefully, the most neutral manner, a respondent's perception on his/her ethnic group
Do you think that there is any difference between Rungus and Kadazandusun?	–to obtain response on how the people view the term 'Kadazandusun' (on Ethnic Identity)
What do you think of the teaching of the Kadazandusun language in schools?	–to know people's views on the teaching of Kadazandusun to Rungus people. (on the revitalization and legitimization of the Kadazandusun language).
What is your opinion on your teaching of the language?	–to evaluate the teachers perception on their teaching of Kadazandusun
Why do you think the teaching of Kadazandusun in this school has been stopped?	[to teachers who had stopped teaching the language]-to identify reasons behind the refusal to teach. [to parents and leaders in the affected areas]-to find out the reasons behind the stoppage of the teaching.

9. The Politics of Language Rights in the Eastern Canadian Arctic

DONNA PATRICK

1. Introduction

Languages are often described as 'living things' that are either vibrant, thriving, strong, or surviving; or threatened, dying or dead (Dorian 1989, Crystal 2000, Blommaert and May, both this volume).[1] A small, 'less used', or minority language will 'live' or 'die' depending on a range of factors, including the number of its speakers, its relative geographic isolation (and hence degree of contact with a more powerful language), and its prestige in institutional domains such as the media, schools, religion, or the job market. Indigenous languages are often considered the most 'threatened', since they are spoken by people who have entered into colonial relationships, which tend to favour the use of one or more dominant language varieties.

Of course, languages are used by living speakers; and it is the speakers, not the languages, that live and die. Likewise, it is the speakers who are affected by geographical, political, and institutional constraints and who vary their language use accordingly. Despite this knowledge about language and its relationship to human beings, biological metaphors continue to be used in 'endangered' language discourse. These metaphors are based on the 'biological analogy' described by England (2002: 142): namely that "language diversity is like biological diversity and (...) the disappearance of languages is like the disappearance of species". As England notes, this constitutes a false analogy because the characteristics of languages are neither "genetically endowed nor biologically inherited" (ibid.).

There are additional problems with this analogy which are worth making explicit. For example, if we think of varieties of language as 'endangered species', we would expect them to 'disappear' the way the narwhale or the dodo has. But language varieties do not necessarily 'disappear': instead, while one variety falls out of use, other, new forms might

---

[1] I am grateful for the discussion and comments from the panelists and audience at the *Linguistic rights and wrongs* panel, Sociolinguistics Symposium 14, in Ghent, Belgium. Special thanks are due to Jane Freeland for her detailed comments on this paper.

be created that contain discursive, lexical, or pragmatic features of the old variety. In other words, a language variety, unlike (common conceptions of) an 'endangered species', does not completely disappear. Likewise, when a language falls into disuse, it is not obvious at all that this change impacts negatively upon other languages in speakers' linguistic repertoires, as the extinction of a species might do in an 'ecosystem'. Rather, the other languages that speakers take up simply continue to change and develop. Furthermore, there is no scientific sense in which only the 'strongest' language varieties survive, in a kind of 'linguistic survival of the fittest' in which language varieties that 'adapt' better to their environment somehow win out over competing varieties. This is because it is speakers and not languages that are 'living things'.

What these considerations suggest is that we need to move away from the view that languages are biological 'species' and focus more on the social conditions under which a language is used. Thus, if we are to make use of a biological analogy at all, it would make more sense to focus on the 'habitat' in which a language is used rather than on a language 'species' *per se*. This is because languages are constrained by the social context in which speakers thrive – economically, culturally, and socially.

Alaska provides some examples in which Native languages have fallen into disuse, but a strong ethnic identity is maintained through the use of particular forms of English. In these contexts, speakers of Native languages such as Yup'ik and Inupiaq (both members of the Eskimo-Aleut family) have shifted towards the use of English, and have formed and maintained new Native identity markers through discourse (Hensel 1996, 2001; Kaplan 2001). This is not to say that significant features of these languages have not been lost when people stop speaking them (Woodbury 1993, cited in Hill 2002); but in many Yup'ik and Inupiaq communities, there continues to be a vibrant Native cultural life and ways of expressing cultural beliefs, values, and practices by using distinctive varieties of English, and sometimes by using certain 'Native' terms and phrases (Kaplan 2001).

In southwestern Alaskan Yup'ik communities, for example, Hensel (1996, 2001) describes how English is used to talk about subsistence activities in particular ways that mark one as being 'more' or 'less' Native – as being an insider or an outsider in ethnic group collectivities that centre on land-based activities and practices. This includes discourse that constructs Native identities, and a sense of 'Nativeness' as opposed to 'Whiteness', through the description of such subsistence practices as fishing, which includes the number of fish one catches, how the catch is prepared, and how these practices are valued. Thus, local identities can be constructed through English, but marked through particular local usages of English, which define one's relationship to a place and one's closeness to a local Native community.

In Inupiaq communities in northwestern Alaska, as Kaplan (2001) notes, there are older community members in their sixties who no longer speak Inupiaq, yet identify themselves as Inupiaq, since they feel that they are 'non-Euroamerican'. Certain lexical items and phrases continue to be used in traditional ceremonies among those who no longer speak the language fluently. Use of these forms constitutes a connection to Inupiaq identity, just as the use of particular forms of 'village English' – a variety of non-standard English that is used by Native and non-Native speakers alike – is used to identify strongly with local communities. While there are still many elders in this region who see Inupiaq as a crucial element in Inupiaq identity formation, new ways of using Inupiaq and new forms of English have become part of the signs, symbols, and rituals that are used to perform 'Inupiaqness'. Although *fluency* in Inupiaq is not crucial to performing Inupiaq identity, the language remains important to many Inupiaq. This is witnessed in, among other things, the rise in Inupiaq language courses and bilingual language revitalization programs.

In other Native communities, however, fluency in the Native language has been maintained to a much greater extent than in the western Arctic, and it continues to play a key role in constructing Native identity.

This chapter focuses on one such language situation: that of Arctic Quebec (Nunavik), where virtually all the Inuit continue to speak the indigenous language, Inuktitut, which is closely related to Inupiaq. In what follows, we will examine the issues of language rights, language policy, and language 'survival' in Nunavik. Here the granting of language rights and the implementation of language policies are part of a larger colonial enterprise that has involved complex processes of accommodation and resistance on the part of the Inuit who live there. The discourse of rights – including those relating to land, language, and culture – has become hegemonic among Canadian Aboriginal peoples, in part because procuring rights is seen as the only viable means of retaining some form of autonomy and control (within the constraints of the Canadian state) over local institutions, local governing bodies, and economic development ventures. Therefore, rights discourse, despite being an imposed Western discourse, is taken up in contemporary indigenous struggles as a necessary strategic means to construct and maintain 'ethnic difference' and to garner more political power in ongoing land claims negotiations with the Canadian state. For some groups, language rights have become intertwined with struggles over land rights. For other groups – those not currently involved in land rights struggles – issues of Native-language policy, curriculum, teacher-training programmes, and the like continue to be on the political agenda. Thus language 'survival' and language 'revitalization' are considered crucial for many communities in their efforts to maintain aboriginal identities and in marking their continued resistance to assimilative policies in Anglo-dominant Canada and Franco-dominant Quebec.

In the next section, I will describe the particular political and social context of Nunavik, where Inuit have paradoxically had to engage in Western political and legal practices in order to retain rights to their land and to gain the rights and resources necessary to support their language and traditional cultural practices. In describing this context, I will first introduce the Eastern Arctic and the land claims processes that have produced the territory of Nunavut and the region of Nunavik. In the rest of the chapter, I will examine some of the consequences of this political engagement for Inuit with respect to their language and culture. The overall aim of this discussion is to provide an understanding of some of the sociocultural and sociolinguistic complexities involved in language rights discourse with respect to the Inuit in Nunavik. Through this case study I also hope to shed light on some of the complexities concerning other endangered languages, including the implementation and social effects of language policies stemming from a notion of linguistic human rights.

2. The Context of Inuktitut in the Eastern Arctic

In the eastern Canadian Arctic, the Inuit live under two separate jurisdictions, which are each distinct from those in the western Arctic. One is Nunavut (which translates as 'our land'), the independent, Inuit-dominant Canadian territory which gained its current status in 1999. The other is the region of Nunavik (which translates as 'big land' and is also known as Arctic Quebec and Nouveau-Québec), which is the result of a land claims settlement ratified in 1975. Nunavik is currently the subject of negotiations through which Inuit hope to gain increased political and economic autonomy (something akin to the territorial status of Nunavut) within Quebec (Nunavik Commission 2001).

There are currently about 25,000 Inuit in Nunavut and over 9,000 in Nunavik (numbers which have been increasing fairly rapidly each year due to the high birth rate among Inuit). Both of these regions enjoy a remarkably high rate of retention of Inuktitut as a home language in the face of dominant colonial languages. In Iqaluit, the capital of Nunavut, roughly 60-65% of residents are Inuit, and about 90% of them speak Inukitut (an estimate based on Dorais and Sammons 2000: 93 and more recent census data). There is also some sociolinguistic evidence that Inuktitut is being passed on to children, who use it as their primary language before they become bilingual at school and then tend to favour English (Dorais and Sammons 2000, 2002). In Nunavik, the number of Inuit still using the language is remarkably high, with over 98% expected to continue speaking Inuktitut as a home language all their lives. This rate of language retention, determined on the basis of census data, is considered to be quite stable (Dorais 1997).

In order to understand the political processes for Inuit in Canada and the link between these and the maintenance of Inuktitut, we need to examine both the colonial history of the region and the particular political context that has arisen from this. This context is important because it has provided the basis from which the struggle both for land rights and language rights has arisen. It is linked both to national concerns, specific to the historical and political context of Canada, and to international concerns in the aftermath of the Second World War, the adoption of universal declarations of human rights, indigenous rights, and more recent proposals for international declarations of linguistic human rights.

Generally speaking, the Inuit of the eastern Canadian Arctic were sedentarized later than the Inupiaq, Yup'ik, and other indigenous peoples of the western Arctic. Although there were a few whaling stations in operation in the eighteenth and nineteenth centuries, it was only in the twentieth century that many Inuit came into intense European contact through trade and missionary activity. This was then quickly followed by a process of sedentarization, which began in the late 1950s, as Canada sought to assert sovereignty in the northern territories during the Cold War and the period of American military defence penetration into the region. As a result, many Inuit in their forties and older can still recall living on the land for extended periods of time before permanently settling year-round in government housing. Thus, a great deal of 'traditional' subsistence knowledge and activities have persisted in these regions, along with the indigenous language varieties. Together, these activities and language practices have become the basis of political resistance to assimilation and of efforts to gain control over and to manage Inuit integration into the Canadian state.

In the early 1970s, Inuit of Northern Quebec and of the former North West Territories mobilized to gain increased autonomy and protection for their subsistence activities and culture. The Nunavik land claim falls under the James Bay and Northern Quebec Agreement (JBNQA), ratified in 1975. This and the more recent Nunavut land claim, ratified in 1992, are seen as landmarks in the gaining of increased political power by indigenous peoples in Canada. Admittedly, however, the political and economic autonomy that has been gained through the establishment of both Nunavut and Nunavik has been limited, since these polities still fall under federal jurisdiction – and in the case of Nunavik, under Quebec. This means that even in Nunavut, where Inuit enjoy more power than their counterparts in Nunavik, most of the land and mineral rights still belong to Canada (Kusugak 2000: 21). French is also required as an 'official' territorial language, despite the fact that there are very few French speakers in the region. Although a significant number of Inuit in Northern Quebec opposed the JBNQA, largely on the grounds that it would mean giving away valued land for limited economic and political returns – a topic to which we will return – the rights that were gained in Nunavut have been envied by Nunavik leaders (Nungak 2000) and would be welcomed by many indigenous groups involved in land disputes and struggles for state recognition.

The establishment of Nunavik and Nunavut as political and territorial entities cannot be divorced from the particular sociohistorical context in which they arose. After the Second World War, international attention had turned towards issues of human rights, post-colonial movements, and the use of vernacular languages in education, among other things. Closer to home, the nationalist movement of Quebec was reshaping the Canadian political landscape during the 1960s and 1970s. This period saw the increased participation of Francophone and indigenous groups in political struggles to assert their minority rights and to gain control over institutions in their communities. In Quebec, Francophones mobilized to increase their socio-economic status and control over the economy. Indigenous groups mobilized to affirm their Aboriginal status and to have their rights recognized within the Canadian federation – something on a par with Quebec – as founding peoples of Canada and distinct from members of other cultural groups that arrived as immigrants. In both the French-speaking and the indigenous arenas, therefore, language, culture, and politics had become tightly intertwined (Handler 1988; Heller 1994; Patrick 2003).

This kind of political strategy, which unites political aspirations with linguistic, cultural, and economic ones, has been effective for many First Nations (the name for Native peoples in Canada), including the Inuit. Through a movement towards nation-to-nation negotiations with the federal and provincial governments, Aboriginal groups have secured land rights and achieved greater local authority and autonomy in these jurisdictions. However, it should also be noted, that in addition to the limited gains in autonomy mentioned above, the process associated with this strategy has been an exceedingly slow one, which has often increased frustration and led to direct confrontation in various regions of Canada (see Dickason 1997: 378ff.)

Aboriginal groups, while pursuing land rights and a constitutional place in Canada, have also fought for language rights, not only to preserve Aboriginal languages and cultures, but also to assert increased cultural and institutional control in their own regions (Battiste 1996; Burnaby 2002). In Nunavik, the demand by Inuit to be educated in their own language was granted by Quebec in 1964, with the understanding that French would also be a language of instruction (Trudel 1996). Arguably, this shows how Quebec politics has shaped Aboriginal politics and fostered aspirations for greater political and economic power in the region (Patrick and Shearwood 1999). It also shows that language rights discourse was introduced at a particular time and place, and in a particular national political space, which allowed for the modernization, standardization, and institutionalization of an indigenous language in a remarkably short period of time.

The widespread use of Inuktitut in Nunavut and Nunavik goes hand in hand with its politicization in the Canadian context, and its status as a marker of ethnic difference in the conflicts and accommodations of Inuit in relation to the colonizing interests of Europe, Canada, and the United States. Gaining rights to Inuktitut-medium schooling, Inuit cultural production, and the promotion of Inuktitut in the running of community and regional affairs has also become a crucial part of modern language maintenance efforts. The struggle to have these rights respected – through adequate funding and resource allocation for local cultural production (including art, film, and media production), curriculum and language development, indigenous teacher-training programmes, and the like – has become a part of many modern indigenous struggles. Endangered languages have thus become socially, historically, and politically constructed. Thus, the promotion of language rights and language 'survival' – whether by language activists, educators, linguists, or other concerned individuals – needs to be viewed in this light.

From the above description, the political processes of state formation and the recognition of language rights appear to have had overwhelmingly positive effects in the Eastern Arctic. One could surmise from this that pursuing language rights through political means is preferable, if not crucial, for minority groups who wish to maintain or revitalize their languages. In addition to the increased prestige accorded a language through official recognition is the importance of mother tongue education for achieving school success in particular minority language populations, as indicated by a large body of research (Cummins 1993; Corson and Lemay

1996). However, the assumption that benefits accrue in a straightforward fashion once language rights have been granted, and the view that, in some cases, language rights are a panacea for the plight of dominated or endangered languages need to be more closely examined. Although many speakers of minority languages in particular nation states would greatly benefit from the formal and legal recognition of their languages, the adoption of a rights discourse and collective mobilization around language have important consequences and raise many difficult issues.

The rest of this chapter will be devote to the discussion of these issues around language rights and language 'survival' as they pertain to the language maintenance efforts of Inuit in Northern Quebec. These include the following:

(i) Language rights discourse when adopted as 'linguistic human rights' is an imposed, universalistic discourse that for colonized peoples is both hegemonic and homogenizing. As with other rights that are granted in the process of state formation, language rights discourse produces inherent contradictions in the way language is defined, used, and standardized in the communities receiving the rights.
(ii) As minority or endangered languages gain rights in education and other social institutions, they enter into competition with other languages in the dominant language market; however, if the minority language is not valued as highly as other languages in particular sites such as the workplace, higher education, and other cultural and economic spheres, it risks continued marginalization and potential disuse.
(iii) Language rights alone cannot ensure minority language maintenance or revitalization. As we have seen so far, language rights are granted in particular historical and political contexts. The specificity of these contexts, in addition to the cultural and sociolinguistic contexts of language use, tend to be obscured in language 'survival' and endangered language discourse.

3. The Politics of Language 'Survival' and Rights Discourse

The first point concerns the discourse of linguistic human rights, which is hegemonic and universalizing, and for certain groups. It is therefore an imposed discourse that produces contradictions and inequities in the way that language is standardized, valued, and used. In order to fight for and receive rights, whether they are related to land, development, or institutions, many indigenous groups in Canada and other colonized peoples "are culturally transformed in the discourses and procedures of the state" (Samson 2001: 228). That is, the state structures of ownership, social and linguistic categorization, and institutionalization are often at odds with local customs and beliefs. One part of recognizing an indigenous culture in the discourse of rights is bringing it in line with the unifying homogeneous forces of national and international law, state formation, and nationhood (see Whaley, this volume).

For some collectivities or indigenous groups, this tension in the ways that language is used, categorized, and commodified could pose major problems and lead to divisions and conflicts. For others, like the Inuit of Nunavik, there may be little organized resistance to or public disapproval of the modernization of their language. In other words, although many indigenous groups might contest the variety chosen as the standard and the way that language forms are used and valued, little public conflict may arise in some groups around this issue, as seems to be the case with the Inuit of Nunavik, even though certain individuals may continue to feel that their own language variety or ways of speaking are marginalized or threatened in the larger modernization process (Patrick 2003: 122).

The relatively smooth implementation of a unified language policy and general acceptance of the modernization of Inuktitut may well be crucial to current language maintenance efforts. This is not to say, however, that there are no problems or contradictions inherent in this process. The more a language is modernized and institutionalized, the further it is removed from local cultural and ideological practices. This process can create a dichotomy between modern, Western ideals and 'traditional' Inuit subsistence culture. This is precisely what happened in the granting and defining of land rights in Nunavik, where this dichotomy became heightened and expressed through various Inuit positions. Although land rights are, of course, not the same as language rights, it is useful to examine the parallels between the two and the lived contradictions that arise when different ideological systems come into play.

As political organizations were formed in Nunavik to protect Inuit interests and to facilitate negotiations with larger (federal and provincial) governments, some Inuit found that these organizations were at odds with particular community interests. Locally based resistance has been a fact of political life in this region, and is amply demonstrated in the divisions that arose in the early 1970s, when three communities – Puvirnituq, Ivujivik, and Salluit, forming about one third of the Nunavik population – refused to sign the James Bay and Northern Quebec Agreement. Ironically, the Agreement was negotiated to win compensation and subsistence rights for 'traditional' Cree and Inuit, who stood to lose some of their hunting grounds to flooding and to suffer other unknown effects on the environment. Yet the Agreement itself and the process that it involved have moved Inuit further away from their 'traditional' practices and towards more corporate models of development.

The opposition that was mounted to the land settlement was originally based on alternative practices and ideologies that were at odds with the capitalist ones inherent in a discourse about land 'ownership' and 'rights', which defined the parameters of resource extraction. In the three dissident communities, a strong representation of elders, concerned with preserving subsistence activities and local ecologies, coalesced around community ideologies of cooperative development (which figured in the founding of retail 'co-op' stores and arts production co-operatives in the 1960s, see Mitchell 1996). While some Inuit were thus concerned with the preservation of Inuit practices, which had persisted over time, others were more concerned with negotiating an equitable redistribution of wealth and resources, which is part and parcel of modernization and land rights treaties. This resulted in further divisions in the three dissident communities: people were caught between the desire to maintain 'traditional' Inuit land-use ideologies and practices and the need to negotiate a strong settlement that would favour Inuit community-based interests. That is, if the Inuit were to 'lose' some of their land to development, then it would be necessary to secure stronger bargaining powers within the modern state than what the Inuit had been negotiating under the James Bay and Northern Quebec Agreement. The recognition of these contradictions led to the creation of a separate political organization, which was opposed to the dominant Inuit one, and had as its goal the winning of a better deal with Canada and Quebec; that is, to be able to "make laws, be self-supporting financially, raise taxes and claim royalties from any activities in the territory" (Sivuak 1980, cited in Mitchell 1996: 354).

The point here is that once indigenous groups accommodate themselves to larger state structures and engage in modern political discourse, tensions and divisions arise which result in contradictory positions. These same tensions can be seen in contemporary Inuit politics in Nunavik, some thirty years later, where modern corporate structures and the interests of corporate development are at odds with local 'traditional' stances and the preservation of the local Inuit economies and ecologies. Similarly, languages can be seen to operate in speech economies, where traditional local language practices are at odds with those valued in modern institutional arenas, such as schools and government offices. Just as there are concerns with the redistribution of wealth once land is commodified in a market economy, so too are there concerns with the distribution of language resources in schools and the implications of this for community members. This brings me to the second issue that needs to be addressed here: the formation of language markets and the question of language 'survival'.

4. Dominant and Alternative Language Markets

Once endangered languages gain rights in education and other social institutions, they enter into competition with dominant languages, which are themselves often attractive to minority language speakers, given their association with social mobility, cultural prestige, and the like. Metaphorically speaking, this form of competition operates in a 'language market', a concept based on Bourdieu's notion of 'linguistic capital', where different language varieties are ascribed different values within a given market. Language is thus seen as "a symbolic asset which can receive different values depending on the market on which it is offered". Knowledge of a language, like other forms of cultural knowledge, thus "functions as linguistic capital in relationship with a certain market" (Bourdieu 1977: 651-652). If that market is the school, then the language varieties used as the media of instruction will have a high currency – they are the languages one needs to master in order to pass tests, write highly valued prose, and speak according to norms reflecting 'standard' usage. The school not only legitimizes language, it increases its actual value for speakers.

School languages thus operate in a dominant language market, where the standard language varieties are valued in political, economic, legal, and cultural spheres. School languages thus have value outside of school: in the job market and in other arenas of formal and informal communication, including community events, government services, and the media. For speakers of endangered languages, then, gaining the right to legitimize their language in education automatically provides a market for this language in curriculum development, teacher training, interpretation, translation, and the like.

Nevertheless, if young people leaving school see that increased employment and life opportunities depend on knowing some other language, then the dominant language market might in effect be at odds with the endangered language, which is subject to competition. Schools may indeed be under pressure to promote the use of a more dominant (usually European) language, since this is what is valued in higher-paying jobs, higher education, and in wider forms of communication in which the minority speakers wish to – and indeed have a right to – engage.

This does not mean that bi- or multilingualism cannot operate to sustain both dominant and minority languages. The minority language can be valued in important ways, particularly in local contexts, in local economic, cultural, and interactional activities. The challenge for the school is to balance the symbolic sources of power in school-based activities in such a way that the local language is not undermined, but the highly-valued standard forms are nevertheless clearly and effectively taught. The tension in this market is the inequitable distribution of power among languages outside the school. Dominant hegemonic forces weigh heavily, especially on young people who become more oriented to Anglo-dominated culture.

The language market, described above, is in fact a dominant linguistic market, in that there is a social consensus regarding the value accorded to language varieties, including a tacit acceptance of the symbolic domination of particular prestige language forms. That is, in the dominant market, the legitimized language varieties used in schools, the dominant media, and other state institutions are accorded a higher social value than vernacular forms.

We might, however, take exception to the view that there is only one market operating for the Inuit and other indigenous groups, who still engage in alternative economic and cultural practices that are in opposition to those promoted by the state. Thus, an 'alternative marketplace' may exist which does not operate by the rules of the dominant linguistic market and "in which alternative or opposing linguistic forms are generated and maintained" (Woolard 1985: 740). In one sense, too much emphasis has been placed on formal institutions in social reproduction, and more attention should be given to economic relations "and on the informal structures of experience in daily life" (ibid.: 742; see also Heugh and Stroud, this volume). Alternative markets are vernacular markets, where local language varieties operate under a set of cultural values and ideologies different from the dominant institutional and corporate sphere. It is these markets that need to be considered if we are to understand how and why vernacular languages continue to exist.

'Alternative markets', or markets that operate with different sets of resources and rules (Heller 1995a, 1992), can continue to operate in colonized areas, where non-capitalist economies flourished prior to contact but have become more or less co-opted by an imposed capitalist sector. This overlap between the Inuit and non-Inuit economic practices and the ideologies that constitute subsistence activities is clearly demonstrated in the rising costs of buying the food and materials needed to hunt or fish. For example, Dorais (1997: 53) notes that the cost of purchasing and operating a snowmobile for two or three seasons in Nunavik is about CDN

$15 000, a figure which will continue to rise as production and transportation costs increase.

Despite this co-optation, the local vernacular language is still widely used by speakers in alternative 'traditional' practices. One question concerning endangered languages is to what extent an alternative market can support a vernacular language in the face of modernization and unfair competition in a dominant market. Another is what effect the tensions and contradictions between these two markets have on the value and the continued everyday use of the endangered language.

If we return to the previous section, we can recall the contradictions arising in the ways Inuit engaged with and resisted co-optation into a land-rights discourse – a discourse that threatened to undermine their way of life, which, ironically, formed the basis of their having land rights in the first place. Language varieties in Nunavik and in similar colonized contexts are operating with the same set of contradictions. It is these parallels and contradictions that construct the complex lived realities and multifaceted identities of speakers (see Freeland, this volume). While these two 'markets' or opposing systems may represent oppositional constructs, they do not form a simple dichotomy: the 'Inuit way of life' and the 'White people's way of life' overlap in complex ways. What does this mean for language 'survival' in the midst of these forces, tensions, and contradictions?

5. Social Context and Language 'Survival' Discourse

This brings us to the third and final issue, the future of endangered languages and how one is to understand the prospects of such languages, given what is required to keep them in use. Many people, including linguists, applied linguists, language educators, and activists are interested in the maintenance or revitalization of languages. Many more people are in favour of granting language rights to particular groups for reasons of social justice or for such pedagogical reasons as providing easier access to schooling for children, who are often disadvantaged socially and economically. However, as this chapter has shown, language rights are granted in particular cultural, historical, and political contexts, and in the discourse of language 'survival' and language rights, these contexts tend to be obscured. The business of granting rights, formulating language policy, and creating environments for speakers to continue to use minority languages and pass them on to their children is complex and contradictory, and granting language rights alone cannot ensure minority language maintenance or revitalization. Nevertheless, 'small' languages will continue to persist and be used in a variety of ways and forms, in informal and formal interactions, and in local, national, and international contexts.

Recall that in Nunavik, the James Bay and Northern Quebec Agreement (1975) secured Inuktitut language rights in education and administrative domains. This is one important arena in which certain protections, status, and support can be allotted to indigenous languages (although, as we have seen, this process is not without its own set of difficulties). In addition to this modern language economy in Nunavik, there remains the 'traditional' harvesting economy, where more traditional, local forms of Inuktitut are valued. Let us now look more closely at this traditional economy, through the following example of how language is valued in the construction of Inuit identities and oppositional culture.

Traditional Inuit ideologies and cultural values – including those that grant importance to the Inuit diet of 'country' food such as caribou, seal, walrus, and whale meat – have been communicated in Inuktitut over generations. The use of Inuktitut in harvesting this food has also persisted in Nunavik, largely due to late sedentarization and concomitant political processes that arose after the Second World War. However, Inuktitut has also persisted because the relationships and human interaction in colonial settings have contributed to the construction of group boundaries, producing lines of solidarity based largely on ethnicity. In this context, Inuktitut has proven to be of great value in constructing and maintaining boundaries in face-to-face communication, which in effect militate against challenges to harvesting activities and other Inuit practices from a Euro-Canadian presence and dominant Euro-North-American ideologies.

This can be seen, for example, in the harvesting of beluga whales, which are highly valued in Inuit culture as both a food and a cultural resource. For Euro-North-Americans (and in Western discourse, generally), beluga whales (i) are an endangered species, as reflected in the quotas that the Canadian government imposes on the number of whales hunted each year; and (ii) have meat that is very high in fat (and hence of little value as food). For the Inuit, in contrast, the beluga whale and its fat are highly valued and considered to be the favourite food of many Inuit. The harvesting of whales has gone on for centuries; and the rituals, meanings, and spiritual significance of catching one of these animals is closely linked to Inuit identity. The use of Inuktitut during harvesting – seeking the whales out, killing them, bringing them to land attached to small boats – operates to exclude non-Native bystanders from both participating in and challenging these activities. In other words, the language bound up in the actual animated activity of harvesting and butchering the beluga can act as a barrier to outsiders in social group interaction and at the same time serve to prevent oppositional Euro-North-American ideologies from being expressed.

Dividing up the meat of a whale, given the shared cultural associations with this activity, creates a joyous, excitable occasion, which is not conducive to intervention by outside observers who might be opposed to the practice. In the Arctic Quebec harvesting economy, therefore, Inuktitut is a valuable resource for keeping local ideologies circulating. The language maintains a dominant role in these cultural, ideological, and economic activities, helping to maintain them. In fact, English or French have no 'front stage' role at all, although they may have a 'back stage' role, in procuring the means to harvest the whale: the boat, the gas, the ammunition, and other tools. This is because in modern Inuit life, the harvesting economy is dependent on the market economy, and dominant languages are often needed to procure the cash (whether it is through wage labour or through regional government programmes set up to support hunters).

In other interactional encounters in Arctic Quebec (see Patrick 2000 and 2001) I observed that Inuit sometimes prefer to use their own language in certain intercultural encounters in everyday community settings. This preference appears to stem from relations of solidarity and inclusion, or from particular social meanings attached to Euro-Canadian language (usually French) that militate against its use in certain contexts. Put another way, Inuit sometimes use Inuktitut (usually in encounters with French interlocutors) as a way to avoid excluding their friends or other community members, who are listening to the interaction. Inuktitut is sometimes also favoured in politically-charged environments, where maintaining group attachments distinct from Euro-Canadian groups is consciously preferred, as I noted during a period of local resistance to hydroelectric development on Inuit land in the early 1990s.

This distancing of Inuit from the use of French was specific to the socially charged atmosphere, which worked to create clearly defined boundaries around Inuit and Cree interactions in a multilingual northern community. In this context, native language use increased and the English lingua franca became the language of inclusion, when inclusion of non-Native language speakers was desired. In certain situations, the use of French was sometimes avoided (to an even greater extent than usual) by the new generation of Inuit who were schooled in French or by those who had spent time in southern Quebec. The dynamics of having two dominant languages and two ethnic groups in relatively small northern communities appears, at particular moments, to have worked in favour of the use of Inuktitut, although more investigation of this is required.

The point here is that sociolinguistic encounters and the dynamics between ethnicities, cultures, and social networks shape the language choices that speakers make, consciously or unconsciously. In Nunavik, these dynamics have tended to favour the indigenous language in certain contexts. This, coupled with the other aspects of social context discussed in this chapter, creates a specific environment for language learning and social reproduction, where Inuktitut is still widely used and passed on to children. Language 'survival' discourse, which focuses on preserving culture and identity as essentialized constructs and uses these as primary justifications for 'saving' indigenous (and other minority) languages, tends to obscure the complexity of the socio-political context in which languages are valued.

In light of this, language rights and the valuing of language varieties in institutional spheres are only one part of intricate webs of relations and social patterns which are necessary to maintain or revitalize minority languages within nation states.

6. Conclusion

In this chapter, we have seen that the use of Inuktitut has been linked to political engagement at particular historic moments and bound up with local economic and cultural practices, cultural ideologies, and local constraints in face-to-face interaction that favour the maintenance of the language. What this means is that the clash between the "'two worlds' of hunting camps and government sponsored settlements" (Samson 2001: 229) does not necessarily lead to an erasure of the indigenous language and culture, but may shape new identities and new ways of using, defining, and valuing indigenous languages (see Freeland and Darnell, both this volume). The challenges posed by the provision of rights – to actually place colonized or dispossessed peoples on a more or less equal footing with the dominant state – are the subject of ongoing political struggles and will continue to create contradictions in the ways language and culture are valued and used by the indigenous people involved.

Winning or breaking even in a language competition – created through the granting of language rights and the subsequent inclusion of the minority language in a dominant market – is an almost unreachable goal for many indigenous languages. Some national minorities, such as the Québécois, the Flemish, or the Catalans can successfully promote their languages in the same market as more dominant languages. This is not so easy for Aboriginal groups, which in Canada are also considered to be national minorities, given that they were "historically settled, territorially concentrated, and previously self-governing [before they became] incorporated into a larger state" (Kymlicka 1998: 30). These groups are faced with a much greater struggle than that faced by the Québécois in trying to create a societal culture which favours the minority language in public spheres, including political, economic, legal, academic, military, and cultural institutions (Kymlicka 2001: 156). In Nunavut and Nunavik, Inuit also face significant hurdles in seeking to legislate Inuktitut as the language of the workplace, as was done in Quebec with the language laws of the 1970s.

In the eastern Arctic, increased Inuit control over curriculum development in schools and the promotion of Inuktitut in government, bureaucratic, and other institutional arenas have greatly reinforced Inuktitut as a valued language for speakers. The concept of an Inuit nationhood and aspirations towards these goals (despite the contradictions) may also have fostered positive attitudes toward Inuktitut. But at least as importantly, the language is still valued in everyday interaction, in Inuit cultural practices and harvesting activities, in the formation and maintenance of group identities, and in many spheres of everyday cultural practice. Together, these circumstances have led to a guarded optimism about the continued widespread use of Inuktitut in the region (Dorais and Sammons 2002).

As we have seen, this case also sheds light on the socio-political complexities of language survival, the granting of language rights, and the implementation of language policies in modern nation states. The granting of language rights is extremely important for many indigenous groups who seek resources to develop their own education and cultural programmes. Yet, these processes are often a part of larger colonial enterprises, which create their own forms of domination of particular people who are negotiating their place in the new and emerging forms of governance. The political arena in which language rights operate is often contradictory and complex and not to be overlooked in our understanding on how minority languages persist.

References

Asch, Michael and Patrick MacKlem (1991) 'Aboriginal Rights and Canadian Sovereignty: An Essay on *R. v. Sparrow*', *Alberta Law Review* 29(2): 500-520.

Battiste, Marie (1996) 'Post-colonial Miqmaq Language Development Strategies', in Sylvie Léger (ed) *Towards a Language Agenda: Futurist Outlook on the United Nations*, Ottawa: Canadian Centre for Linguistic Rights, 467-489.

Bourdieu, Pierre (1977) 'The Economics of Linguistic Exchanges', *Social Science Information* 16(6): 645-68.

Burnaby, Barbara (2002) 'Language Policies in Canada', in J. Tollefson (ed) *Language Policies and Education: Critical Issues*, Mahwah, NJ: Lawrence Erlbaum, 65-86.

Corson, David and Sylvie Lemay (1996) *Social Justice and Language Policy in Education: The Canadian Research*, Toronto: OISE Press.

Crystal, David (2000) *Language Death*, Cambridge: Cambridge University Press.

Cummins, Jim (1993) 'Bilingualism and Second Language Learning', *Annual Review of Applied Linguistics* 13: 51-70.

Dickason, Olive P. (1997) *Canada's First Nations: A History of Founding Peoples from Earliest Times*, Second Edition, Oxford: Oxford University Press.

Dorais, Louis-Jacques (1997) 'The Aboriginal Languages of Quebec, Past and Present', in Jacques Maurais (ed) *Quebec's Aboriginal Languages: Theory, Planning, Development*, Clevedon, UK: Multilingual Matters, 43-85.

------ and Susan Sammons (2000) 'Discourse and Identity in the Baffin Region', *Arctic Anthropology* 37(2): 92-110.

------ (2002) *Language in Nunavut: Discourse and Identity in the Baffin Region*, Iqaluit: Nunavut Arctic College, Québec: GÉTIC, Univerisité Laval.

Dorian, Nancy (1989) *Investigating Obsolescence: Studies in Language Contraction and Death*, Cambridge: Cambridge University Press.

England, Nora (2002) 'Commentary: Further Rhetorical Concerns', *Journal of Linguistic Anthropology* 12(2): 141-143.

Francis, Daniel and Toby Morantz (1983) *Partners in Furs: A History of the Fur Trade in Eastern James Bay 1600-1870*, Montréal/Kingston: McGill-Queen's University Press.

Grant, Shelagh (1988) *Sovereignty and Security: Government Policy in the Canadian North 1936-1950*, Vancouver: UBC Press.

Handler, Richard (1988) *Nationalism and the Politics of Culture in Quebec*, Madison: University of Wisconsin Press.

Heller, Monica (1992) 'The Politics of Code-switching and Language Choice',

Journal of Multilingual and Multicultural Development 13(1-2): 123-142.

------ (1994) *Crosswords: Language, Education and Ethnicity in French Ontario*, Berlin/New York: Mouton de Gruyter.

------ (1995) 'Code-switching and the Politics of Language', in Lesley Milroy and Pieter Muysken (eds) *One Speaker, Two Languages*, Cambridge: Cambridge University Press, [page numbers missing]

Hensel, Chase (1996) *Telling Our Selves: Ethnicity and Discourse in Southwestern Alaska*, New York/Oxford: Oxford University Press.

------ (2001) 'Yup'ik Identity and Subsistence Discourse: Social Resources in Interaction', *Etudes/Inuit/Studies* 25(1-2): 217-227.

Hill, Jane H. (2002) '"Expert Rhetorics" in Advocacy for Endangered Languages: Who is Listening, and What Do They Hear?', *Journal of Linguistic Anthropology* 12(2): 119-133.

Kaplan, Lawrence D. (2001) 'Inupiaq Identity and Inupiaq Language: Does One Entail the Other?', *Etudes/Inuit/Studies* 25(1-2): 249-257.

Kusugak, Jose (2000) 'The Tide Has Shifted: Nunavut Works for Us and It Offers a Lesson to the Broader Global Community', in Jens Dahl, Jack Hicks and Peter Jull (eds) *Nunavut: Inuit Regain Control of Their Lands and Their Lives*, Copenhagen: IWGIA, 20-28.

Kymlicka, Will (2001) *Politics in the Vernacular*, Oxford: Oxford University Press.

------ (1998) *Finding Our Way: Rethinking Ethnocultural Relations in Canada*, Oxford: Oxford University Press.

Mackey, Eva (1999) *The House of Difference: Cultural Politics and National Identity in Canada*, London/New York: Routledge.

Mitchell, Marybelle (1996) *From Talking Chiefs to a Native Corporate Elite: The Birth of Class and Nationalism Among Canadian Inuit*, Montreal: McGill-Queen's University Press.

Morse, Bradford W. (ed) (1991) *Aboriginal Peoples and the Law Indian, Métis and Inuit Rights in Canada*, Ottawa: Carleton University Press.

Nunavik Commission (2001) *Amiqqaaluta/Let Us Share: Mapping the Road toward a Government for Nunavik*, Report of the Nunavik Commission, March 2001.

Nungak, Zebedee (2000) 'Pigatsipivigut-You Attain, Therefore We Attain', in Jens Dahl, Jack Hicks and Peter Jull (eds) *Self-determination in Nunavut: Inuit Regain Control of Their Lands and Their Lives*, Copenhagen: IWGIA, 142-144.

Patrick, Donna (1994) 'Minority Language and Social Context', *Etudes/Inuit/Studies* 18(1-2): 183-199.

------ (2000) 'Language Markets and Minority Language Maintenance in an Arctic Quebec Community', *Texas Linguistic Forum 43, Proceedings from the 6th Symposium about Language and Society – Austin*, 452-461.

------ (2001) 'Languages of State and Social Categorization', in M. Heller and M. Martin-Jones (eds) *Voices of Authority: Education and Linguistic Difference*, Westport CT: Ablex, 297-314.

------ (2003) *Language, Politics, and Social Interaction in an Inuit Community*, Berlin/New York: Mouton de Gruyter.

------ and Peter Armitage (2001) 'The James Bay and Northern Quebec Agreement and the Social Construction of the Cree 'Problem'', in Colin Scott (ed) *Aboriginal Autonomy and Development in Northern Quebec and Labrador*, Vancouver: UBC Press, 206-232.

Patrick, Donna and Perry Shearwood (1999) 'The Roots of Inuktitut-language Bilingual Education', *Canadian Journal of Native Studies* 19(2): 249-262.

Samson, Colin (2001) 'Rights as the Reward for Simulated Cultural Sameness: The Innu in the Canadian Colonial Context', in J. Cowan. M-B Dembour and R. A. Wilson (eds) *Culture and Rights: Anthropological Perspectives*, Cambridge: Cambridge University Press, 226-248.

Shearwood, Perry (2001) 'Inuit Identity and Literacy in a Nunavut Community', *Etudes/Inuit/Studies* 25(1-2): 295-307.

Tester, Frank J. and Peter Kulchyski (1994) *Tammarniit (Mistakes): Inuit Relocation in the Eastern Arctic, 1939-1963*, Vancouver: UBC Press.

Trudel, François (1996) 'Aboriginal Language Policies of Canadian and Quebec Governments', in J. Maurais (ed) *Quebec's Aboriginal Languages: History, Planning and Development*, Clevedon: Multilingual Matters, 101-128.

Woodbury, Anthony (1993) 'A Defence of the Proposition, "When a Language Dies, a Culture Dies"', in Robin Queen and Rusty Barret (eds) *SALSA 1, Texas Linguistic Forum 33*, Austin: University of Texas Department of Linguistics, 102-130.

Woolard, Kathyrn (1985) 'Language Variation and Cultural Hegemony: Toward an Integration of Sociolinguistic and Social Theory', *American Ethnologist* 12: 738-748.

10. Language Rights and Linguistic Citizenship[1]

CHRISTOPHER STROUD AND KATHLEEN HEUGH

1. Introduction

In recent years, Linguistic Human Rights (LHR) as a *sociolinguistic* phenomenon has come under heavy critique from a number of different directions.[2] Pennycook (1998) points to the potential problems of working with a *universal* notion of rights; Blommaert (2001) argues that LHR approaches do not gel with what we know about language in society, correspond to experiences with linguistic pluralism, nor are they empirically sustainable. Stroud (2001), as does Freeland (2002, 2003), critiques the notion of LHR by pointing to the essentialist assumptions of language and identity that underlie it, as well as its problematic assumptions on the working of the nation-state. Other work shows that the assumption that speakers of minority languages need legal protection from encroaching languages of power sometimes distorts the reality on the ground; ex-colonial languages can be productively appropriated by minority speakers into local multilingual repertoires to serve a range of local functions (e.g. Stroud 2002; Blommaert, this volume). In this chapter, we add to this liturgy of problems by arguing – with examples from Southern Africa – that the LHR paradigm is *in principle* unable to get to grips with the very problem it is meant to address, namely the linguistic barriers which hinder equitable political participation for linguistic minorities. This is because the notion of linguistic human rights is framed within a *liberal* understanding of citizenship which does not effectively

[1] Many people have given us valuable comments on earlier versions of this chapter. We would particularly like to thank Paul Bruthiaux, Kenneth Hyltenstam, and Anne Pakir. Barry Streek and Xola Mati have provided very useful historical detail and Anthony Johnson has offered political commentary which strengthens the South African material. Lionel Wee, Jane Freeland and Donna Patrick have read numerous drafts and consistently given us many invaluable suggestions and critical comments which have helped improve the paper immensely.

[2] We wish initially to emphasize and reaffirm our commitment to the moral imperative behind the linguistic human rights paradigm. The point of our critique is that we do not believe that LHR is the best means to attain goals of social, political and economic equity for linguistic minorities.

knit language into general principles of good governance and citizenship. Janoski (1998) in discussing citizenship identifies four types of rights: legal, political, social (e.g. access to health care and education), and participation rights. Prevailing historical and ideological conditions have intersected with the notion of rights, resulting in 'traditional', 'liberal' and 'social democratic' approaches to rights (McGroarty 2002: 25, after Janoski op cit.). The effects of globalization and the spread of the western liberal paradigm in conjunction with development aid and capitalism, have given heaviest weight to a liberal interpretation of rights (particularly in recent practices in Africa). Subsequently, we shall argue that within a LHR context, citizenship rights are de facto restricted to legal and political rights, and where their more practical manifestation is required, in the social and particip-atory contexts, there is a singular lack of planned provision. The results are in evidence in US language planning (see Wiley 2002), in Australia (Moore 2002) and in recent developments in the language planning of the Pan South African Language Board (PANSALB) (Heugh forthcoming).

More specifically, we agree with those critics of the liberal concept of citizenship who claim that it does not address political constraints on the exercise of human rights (see also McGroarty op. cit.; Wiley op.cit.), nor entertain a conception of the role of citizenship in governance, the contingent materiality of rights, the linkage between civil and political society or the implications of globalization. One implication of this is that LHR discourses, far from being able to accommodate linguistic diversity, actually reinforce trends towards *reduction* of the world's languages in favour of large metropolitan languages.

In section 4, we therefore develop an alternative and competing political understanding of language and society in a notion of *linguistic citizenship* (Stroud 2000, 2001, 2002). The reference to citizenship (as opposed to rights) in relation to language indicates that language issues need to be politically theorized in broader terms as "a relationship between rights, responsibilities and participation crucial to any form of governance" (Faulks 2000: 146). We understand linguistic citizenship as a post-liberal paradigm concept with ideological affinities to ecological citizenship, feminist citizenship and sexual citizenship. Just as ecology, feminism and sexuality were made invisible and ruled out of the abstract liberal conception of citizenship, so have the realities of language in governance been distorted in narrow liberal LHR discourses. Just as notions of post-liberal citizenship stand for an increasing *visibilization* of minorities and issues traditionally ignored in abstract liberal citizenship, so does linguistic citizenship aim to make visible the sociolinguistic complexity of language issues for minority speaker participation in governance. Linguistic citizenship assumes a relationship between language, state, market and civil society markedly different to LHR, emphasizing the importance of language as a rich *resource* in linking civil rights to political rights in the pursuit of participatory citizenship. Whereas the concept of language as a resource (Jernudd and Das Gupta [1971] 1975: 211; Ruiz 1984) has been present in the literature for thirty years, and absorbed in much of the literature on language and the economy (e.g. Coulmas 1992; Grin 1996a, 1996b) there have been few examples of language planning within this perspective, especially in relation to minority languages. In this chapter, we offer linguistic citizenship as an alternative that makes allowances for social and participatory rights alongside legal and political rights, and in addition builds on the concept of language as a resource.

We develop our argument primarily with data from South Africa, where language has long been a site of struggle. From the earliest days of settlement when Afrikaaners successfully contested the imposition and hegemony of English, to the historically more recent use of Bantu mother tongue education in the production of 'docile bodies' (cf. Pennycook 2002), control of language policy has been an important tool of *governmentality* (Foucault 1991; Pennycook 2002). It is therefore hardly surprising that the negotiated settlement at the end of apartheid and a constitution proclaiming 11 official languages was widely heralded as a significant milestone of liberationist politics.

The architects of the South African constitution were strongly influenced by liberal politics in addition to the view of an erstwhile revolutionary, populist movement (the ANC). A central feature of the constitution is a liberal Bill of Rights, which, although foregrounding individual rights, also makes provision for group rights (Johnson 2003). It allowed for the setting up of a Pan South African Language Board (PANSALB) to oversee the language rights of all, but especially those of African and other 'previously marginalized' people. In addition it was to create the conditions for the development and promotion of African languages.[3] The official acknowledgement of African languages would not only give symbolic

---

[3] Legislation for the establishment of this language board included the orientations of both language as a right and language as a resource. However, implementation resorted mainly to parallel/monolingual ethnolinguistic planning under the guise of a rights-based approach. Language issues have consistently figured in South Africa as a ready tool in the hands of political actors entangled in the daily dynamics of power struggles and political positioning.This is now accentuated by the philosophical framework of linguistic human rights (LHRs) which arose from the rights-based constitution (Heugh 2003, forthcoming).

prominence to marginalized communities, but would also comprise an important means of political participation.

However, almost ten years down the line, the bitter fruits of this initiative are ripe for the plucking. Far from reconstituting linguistic markets and relocating linguistic legitimacy to the African languages, the current politics of language is instead contributing to the traditional linguistic disempowerment of African language speakers. In what follows, we will attempt to detail some of the fundamental inadequacies of the LHR paradigm.

2. Linguistic Human Rights

LHR discourses do not sufficiently address the role of language issues in governance, nor correctly conceptualize the socio-economic fabric of language, how language links civil and political society, or the implications of globalization for a politics of language. Furthermore, LHR rests upon a notion of group collectivism that is itself arbitrary and essentialist.

2.1. LHR and the State

McGroarty notes how the provision of linguistic rights is impacted by "distinctive national and local socio-political settings, all of which are variously permeable to innovations depending on a host of local, regional and national values and circumstances" (2002: 33). In modern South Africa, traditional ethno-linguistic structures and mythologies constituted through colonialism and apartheid comprise a web of unequal power relationships within which the provision of linguistic rights becomes entangled. LHR discourses reproduce these power inequalities in ways that typically render invisible those speakers furthest from these centres of power. Furthermore, these traditional structures of power channel discourses of diversity into predetermined cultural and linguistic identities that serve to transport arbitrary constructions of linguistic identities from one system to another.

One example of how rights-based attempts to accommodate diversity and difference within traditional structures of power reinforce the hierarchical distribution of languages and their speakers along historically exclusionary fault-lines of power and privilege is that of the differentiated treatment of Northern Ndebele (*SiNdebele*) and Southern Ndebele (*isi-Ndebele*).[4] The new constitutional arrangements preserved the status of

---

[4] Southern Ndebele, like most of the other Nguni languages uses a prefix beginning with the lower case 'i' in 'isiNdebele', 'isiXhosa', 'isiZulu'. Northern Ndebele, which has features of both Nguni and the Sotho cluster of languages,

'official languages' during apartheid at national level as well as in each of apartheid's (ethnically conceived) 'independent homelands' and 'self-governing states' for Africans. Eleven languages were therefore given official status in the post-apartheid constitutions, including English, Afrikaans and nine of ten other languages, which had previously had 'official recognition' and featured regularly in government census data prior to the allocation of nine homelands. The tenth formerly 'officially recognized' language, Northern Ndebele, was however not given official status in post-apartheid South Africa. Its speakers now claim that this was because they were the only 'officially recognized' linguistic community which was not given a territorial base and hence their language did not achieve official status anywhere.[5] Far from being compensated now for their apparent exclusion during apartheid, however, they have been further marginalized by the new liberal government. The 'official recognition' of N. Ndebele during the early phase of apartheid has now been further diminished, since this category is no longer in use, and N. Ndebele does not feature as one of the basket of 'official languages'. Arbitrary linguistic identity (and status) are thus transported from one system to another. An alternative to the exclusion of Northern Ndebele may have been to offer an inclusive identity for both Northern and Southern Ndebele, and have as the eleventh official language, a Ndebele (sub)cluster.

Another example of the persistence of traditional structures of power comes with the name given to one of the official languages identified in the 1993 interim constitution, *Sesotho sa Leboa* (Northern Sotho), and the most powerful of the languages in Limpopo Province. During apartheid N. Sotho was often referred to as *Sepedi*, which is the largest variety of the N. Sotho sub-cluster of Sotho. Refinements to the 1993 constitution were concluded in 1996, by which time influential speakers of *Sepedi*, including parliamentarians, had successfully lobbied to have *Sepedi* replace the more inclusive *Sesotho sa Leboa.* Immediately, speakers of another smaller variety of *Sesotho sa Leboa*, *Khelovedu*, insisted that their

---

has a preferred orthographic convention beginning with uppercase S, thus SiNdebele, but keeps the uppercase N immediately after the prefix. In the Sotho cluster, the preferred convention now is an uppercase prefix followed by lowercase as in Sesotho, Setswana, Sesotho sa Leboa, etc.

[5] The politics in the northern part of South Africa, and tensions between speakers of N. Ndebele many of whom resided in the homeland called Lebowa (a predominantly Northern Sotho area), and those who resided in KwaNdebele, are too complex to explain here. There is nevertheless justification for the claim of exclusion, since N. Ndebele speakers interpret the official status of isiNdebele to exclude SiNdebele.

language similarly receive official status. In this case, PANSALB swiftly advised government to reinstate *Sesotho sa Leboa* as the official language and immediately adopted a PANSALB policy of using the more inclusive name.

There are several levels at which one might wish to analyze the different responses to the claims of the N. Ndebele and the speakers of *Khelovedu*. The first has to do with traditional (pre-colonial) ideas of power and significance. Queen Modjadji, the Rain Queen of the *Khelovedu*-speaking *Valovedu* people, exercized significant traditional power, including, it was believed by many, over weather patterns. Influential ANC politicians in parliament and senior PANSALB staff did not wish to risk the displeasure of the Rain Queen. Rev. Molomo, the primary spokesperson of the Northern Ndebele, on the other hand, did not carry similar appeal/cultural capital.

A second layer of analysis reveals entirely contrary (arbitrary) decisions to similar linguistic challenges. The architects of the interim and final constitutions appeared to have inconsistent rules for the identification of languages. While a relatively inclusive term, *Sesotho sa Leboa* (including *Sepedi*, *Khelovedu* etc.) was used in the 1993 version, it succumbed to the narrower, exclusive interests of *Sepedi*-speakers in the 1996 constitution. With respect to Ndebele, however, a narrow exclusive decision was taken to identify only *isiNdebele* in both the 1993 and 1996 constitutions. The 1993 constitution, in addition, named a number of minority languages used by recent immigrant communities, but left the indigenous Khoe and San languages entirely invisible. The 1996 constitution partially rectified this omission by including the following: 'Khoi, Nama and San languages' for lesser attention than the official languages. The issue of Nama has similarities with *Sepedi*. Nama is a sub-set of the Khoe languages, and by so identifying it, raises its status over other Khoe languages, such as Gri and !Ora, which were not named in the document. The San languages were all thus individually invisibilized.

What these examples show is that there was no clearly equitable or systematic set of rules governing language planning choices as the constitutions were being written. The constitution writers were neither applying a rule of using the more inclusive language name nor one which systematically identified each of the languages which would fall within the more inclusive name/language cluster. Having slipped up by omitting the Khoe and San languages in the first instance, one might have imagined that they would have sought advice concerning the currently accepted orthographic conventions (Khoe vs. Khoi) and investigated the relationship amongst Khoe, Nama and San. Such examples are a reflection of the arbitrary nature of decision-making, overlaid by (pre-) colonial and apartheid monolingual conceptions about and practices concerning language identity, exclusion and invisibilization.

Arbitrary and limiting conceptions of language are also leading to an enforcement of cultural identities that do not reflect the perceptions of local speakers, and a delimitation of linguistic identities that jar with constructs of language entertained by the community. When the Northern *Ama*Ndebele National Organization (NANO) lobbied parliament and PANSALB to accord official status to *Si*Ndebele, the Board agreed to provide limited financial assistance on condition that it could be proved that *Si*Ndebele was a language *separate* from *isi*Ndebele. The community thus finds itself actively contesting an earlier classification of *Si*Ndebele as a variety in a larger cluster of Ndebele languages, and has invested in the development of a distinct orthography, grammar and school glossary. One consequence of this is the production of division and conflict both within and between the designated linguistic groups themselves. This situation brings to mind Alexandra Jaffe's claim that "forms of language activism that reproduce a dominant language ideology also reproduce the structures of domination" (1999: 28), drawing attention to the "dilemmas, ambiguities and limitations of forms of resistance that do not challenge the premises of dominant models of power and value" (ibid.: 247).

The preceding examples underscore the extent to which language is a constructed and contested object, the socio-historical outcome of debate, legislation, competing ideologies and social conflict – processes that do not explicitly figure as constitutive of language in the LHR paradigm. They illustrate general problems with the LHR discourse. The notion of language rights endorses an ethno-linguistic stereotyping in the form of monolingual and uniform identities. It forces groups of speakers to work actively to differentiate themselves from others, by claiming unique linkages of language and identity so as to gain political leverage in the competition for scarce resources. The LHR approach thus lends itself to strategies of enhancing the role and importance of minority languages that "are structured willy-nilly around the same received notions of language that have led to their oppression and/or suppression" (Woolard 1998: 17) exacerbating problems of *linguicism* (Phillipson and Skutnabb-Kangas 1986; Phillipson 1992) that motivated the rights paradigm in the first place. Furthermore, within the LHR paradigm, a linguistics of standardization, officialization and intellectualization reconstructs minority languages in the image of official standard languages so as to embody the social ideologies, class differences and standard/non-standard distinctions common to prestigious languages and, at the same time, levels multi-layered and complex blended identities of minority speakers almost to political insignificance.

Although linguistic human rights discourses are subject to all the exigencies of how power is exercised in any particular nation-state, there is little, if any, mention of language as a construct formed through processes of political power, nor of the ways in which technologies of language description themselves impose specific political definitions of linguistic realities. Because of this, there is very little manoeuvre room for disadvantaged groups to contest the status quo.[6] Although marginalized linguistic communities may express opposition to hegemonic decisions, whether or not they will be successful depends upon the extent to which the structures of power, as these devolve to a few significant individuals, find it in their interest to accommodate possible change.

2.2. The (im)materiality of LHR

Another problem with the exercise of LHR in South Africa is that it is plagued by problems of material contingency. According to PANSALB statistics, although 36% of those asked claim to understand English (PANSALB 2000: 180), only 12% of people use English as a lingua franca of their first choice, and these are predominantly in three of the nine provinces (ibid.: 30). Thus, almost by definition, most people will seldom use English and then only for minimal functions. In a participatory citizenship, community members should be able to use their own language in the pursuit of their political, social and economic rights. However, in South Africa, the formal (linguistic) market gives preference to speakers of English, and it should come as no surprise that more than 50% of non-English-speaking South Africans report that they feel linguistically disadvantaged in job interviews for the formal sector (ibid.: 62-63).

---

[6] There are countless examples of linguistic invisibilization in South Africa. Marginalized speakers of Khoe and San languages in the Northern Cape were lured by meager socio-economic rewards during apartheid into identifying themselves as a sub-set of Afrikaans-speaking 'coloured' people. This amounted to a form of coercion in which Khoe or San identity was hidden. The post-apartheid Northern Cape government sought to clarify its language policy and contracted one of these authors, Heugh, for this purpose in 1997. The administration, in favour of an English mainly policy despite only 1% of people being proficient in English in this province, claimed that there were no local speakers of Gri, a Khoe language. Cursory research, however, uncovered scores of speakers of Gri within days. The presence of other Khoe and San speakers: Nama, Khwe, !Xun and ǂKhomani, while acknowledged, was not reflected in provincial language statistics at the time.

Clearly, the LHR paradigm has not been able to provide for the realization of social rights or minority speaker participation. One reason for this is that no provisions are made for the socio-economic and other forms of material existence that this would require. Although the legislative acknowledgement of linguistic diversity, and recognition of African languages is important, merely granting official recognition to these languages does not come to grips with the widespread perception among their speakers that the languages are a liability rather than a resource. Fraser (1995:85) has coined the notion of *bivalent collectivity* to refer to those groups for whom "neither [i.e. socio-economic maldistribution nor cultural recognition is] an indirect effect of the other, but ...both are primary and co-original". Linguistic communities are typically bivalent collectivities in that *both* recognition of a language and the economic viability of its community of speakers need to be attended to in order to bring about productive use of a language.

An important material resource for minority language use is the use of the language itself to generate socio-economic wealth. In the South African context, those who remain outside the formal sector are predominantly people whose socio-economic transactions do and will take place in other languages. Analyses of vernacular and multilingual use in informal markets reveal the intricate socio-political mechanisms whereby language as a resource is embedded in social structures of consecration, expertness and apprenticeship, giving rise to mutual supportive economic networks.

The West African women's markets are a case in point of how practices of multilingualism comprise material resources. Titi Ufomata's (1998) account of the role of women's discourses in Nigerian, especially Yoruba markets, presents a view of African women and language not often acknowledged in the discourses of power and poverty. Women, despite the encumbrance of husbands, take charge of their own economic independence and engage in trading activities. Women use local, regional and sometimes pidgin languages in ways that reinforce their own carefully structured market-based social and welfare systems. Whilst they function multilingually, English, the language of the formal economy, is not a regular feature of the markets. English is certainly seldom the language of their clients. Young women are inducted into markets via apprenticeships that include the teaching and learning of unwritten codes of conduct in local languages. Regular contributions into a central fund are reserved for social welfare purposes or used as 'loans', to newly inducted traders who need the start-up capital for their stalls, which will be repaid to the market fund.

Ufomata (ibid.) argues that 65% of the Nigerian economy arises from the informal sector of which the markets comprise a significant and growing part. She points to both the self-regulatory aspects of the market, and to Levine's analysis (1970: 179) of traditional gender politics amongst the Yoruba that allow women perhaps greater mobility and economic autonomy than is the case for many other women in Africa. An irony here is that although the markets are defined as outside the formal economy, they demonstrate regulatory features of a formal system. Yet they exist independently of and beyond the delimitations of a narrow, English- or French- and male-dominant formal economy. The intersection of local languages and economic autonomy offers alternatives to the male oriented formal sectors which elsewhere frequently render women invisible, dependent and inferior. Importantly, however, this is possible because community members themselves are effectively rejecting the narrow systemic language categories promoted by LHR discourses, and replacing these with their own control over linguistic exchanges.

2.3. LHR in Intimate and Local Contexts

The previous section showed how informal multilingual networks link linguistic practices to resource distribution of a clearly material and economic kind. Interestingly, material networks of this type are also implicated in aspects of individual and group welfare relating to the consolidation of trusting social relationships, the exploration of new gender identities and the development of responsible socio-political roles and identities. Ufomata's (1998) West African women's markets are again a case in point. What is obvious, from both her analysis and the voices that she releases in her stories, is that market women judiciously guard their independence from their husbands as a mechanism to ensure the future of their children and their own economic survival. She discovers that the marketplace is also a space in which women reveal their control over reproduction, a matter not disclosed to their husbands. Control over their lives as expressed through discourses in local languages is manifested in the highly regulated space of the market.

Insights such as these cannot be accommodated in LHR paradigms. This is because the structural concept of language that it endorses governs the flux and hybridity of language use in informal, intimate contexts that are not part of the legitimate market. The important functions and resources of unofficial, local varieties, and the broader perspective on language as performance and linguistic repertoire, lie outside the purview of the LHR paradigm. In fact, the LHR paradigm has a tendency to lock discourse on language along a set of parameters that heavily constrain what can be said about language. For example, debates about mother-tongue education and bilingual education in South Africa are often interpreted as based on a narrow monolithic view of language and identity, leading some critics (e.g. Makoni 1995, 1996, 1998) to argue that in the metropolitan and township environments, students speak a (mixed or fluid) variety of languages, which does not correspond with standard written forms, and thus renders mother-tongue education problematic.[7] However, the reality of language practices in educational contexts shows that this very fluidity is *indeed* productively and performatively reconstituted in linguistic repertoires that span many ways of speaking, even incorporating more formal varieties – as in the following example.

During the mid-1980s, pupils in many schools were resistant to the teaching of Afrikaans as a subject, even in conservative 'white' English medium schools. The degree of prejudice in one such school was particularly acute until the arrival of an unconventional teacher, 'Lappies' Labuschagne. As a new teacher, he was given the most difficult of classes to teach, literally the lowest streams with uncooperative pupils. Having assessed the situation he drew on his intimate knowledge of a 'non-standard' hybrid language (including elements of Zulu and Afrikaans) called 'Tsotsitaal' from the working class outskirts and townships of Johannesburg. This is a language used by (would-be) gangsters and rebellious township youth. Labuschagne taught pupils the basics of Tsotsitaal, which obviously included Afrikaans, introduced them to the poetry of the Soweto literary fringe, and immediately gained the admiration of the pupils who believed that their learning of Tsotsitaal gave them valuable cargo. He kept up with the requirements of the Afrikaans syllabus, had converts to poetry, and retained the incentive and reward of Tsotsitaal. It was not long before other pupils, in this otherwise deeply prejudiced (racist) community at the height of apartheid, were clamouring to get into this teacher's classes to learn the language of black township youth.

This example illustrates how spoken linguistic varieties which may display marked differences from the standard written varieties are used effectively: to validate the pupils' own resources, add to their resources, and also as a strategy to provide a positive context for the teaching and learning of the standard written variety. The important point is that these educational and personal stances are accomplished through local forms of language that create intimacy and solidarity among speakers. The use of the elaborate resources of informal and hybrid varieties of African languages, including Afrikaans, as well as codeswitching between the

[7] The conclusion that mother-tongue education (MTE) is therefore useless does, of course, not follow from this.

varieties, admit speakers of various degrees of proficiency into the activity, as well as incorporating multilinguals speaking syncretic varieties of a language, comprising loans, transfers and codeswitches. This multi-*refunctionalization* of local verbal resources and repertoires provides the means for speakers to reposition themselves and their identities in relation to official narratives, in the process opening up avenues of (political) action otherwise unavailable. The processes not only create novel political and ethical positions, but reconfigure the meaning of speaking in these particular languages.

The importance of informal and at times stigmatized local varieties in intimate contexts of this type challenges the emphasis of LHR discourse on formally sanctioned and publically recognized linguistic practices. Language or educational policy based within LHR paradigms, with their narrow conception of ethnolinguistic identity do not fit complex and ever shifting identities, and there is no sense in which facts such as these can be productively employed in educational contexts within the LHR paradigm. In other words, languages like Tsotsitaal are not legitimated in the rights paradigm, their speakers and their speakers are thus marginalized.

2.4. LHR in Local, Regional and Global Arenas

LHR discourses have increasingly come to assume the role of panacea for global injustices implicating minority languages (cf. Kontra *et al.* 1999; Kymlicka 1995; Skutnabb-Kangas and Phillipson 1994). Yet, the LHR paradigm works not only with a narrow understanding of language in systemic terms, but also with a very *local perception* of relevant language delimited by national territorial borders. The UN Declaration on the Rights of Persons Belonging to National or Ethnic, Religious and Linguistic Minorities states that "[s]tates shall protect the existence and the national or ethnic, cultural, religious and linguistic minorities within their respective territories.." (Office of the High Commissioner for Human Rights 1992, Article 1.1). In the African context, the sociolinguistic reality, akin to what we find in many multilingual ecologies in the world, tells another story. Millions of speakers, rather than being divided by their multilingualism in African languages, are actually linked into regional speech communities through linguistic continua (see also Prah 1995), demonstrating the point that "purely linguistic demarcation of language or dialects…does not translate into actual boundaries of communication" (Djité 1993: 150). Speakers, who to all intents and purposes speak different languages, often do manage to communicate in practice: Xhosa speakers in the Southern part of South Africa can understand speakers of Zulu, Swati and Ndebele, which are also mutually comprehensible across the Mozambique, Zimbabwe and Swaziland borders. Similarly, Changana from Mozambique is understood by speakers of Tsonga in South Africa, and Shangaan in Zimbabwe, etc. The existence of these multilingual networks helps local communities to find ways of articulating global and regional social interests, comparable to more officially sanctioned enhanced cooperation across boundaries, or simplify the flow of contacts, goods and services between countries.

The Cameroon linguist Chumbow (1999) has pointed out that trans-border languages have "lasting advantages for national development, peaceful co-existence and international cooperation" (ibid.: 58). He argues that national borders ought to be *reconceptualized* as meeting places instead of the situation today, where "contacts at the borderline are more often contacts of conflict rather than for harmony" (Asiwaju 1984 quoted in Chumbow 1999: 56). In modern African states, a positive policy option towards borders is not policing but management through legal instruments of cooperation and the expansion of "the principle of simplification of the boundary function" (Boggs 1940). This means that the function of borders "as lines of demarcation, division and separation should be modified for them to assume a simpler function as lines of productive contact" (Chumbow ibid.: 58). In the Southern African context, the to and fro migration of languages and speakers across borders underscores the potentiality for such a revised perspective on national borders.

Prior to 1997, the prevailing wisdom was that most visitors who intersected with the South African economy were tourists, and speakers of English, followed by German, Dutch and French. Research focussing on language and the economy and conducted during 1997 investigated the language profile of visitors to SA and included land, sea and air ports of entry. At the time the immigration officials had not analyzed data from this perspective. The Department of Home Affairs nevertheless designed a software package to provide a statistical analysis of the nationality of visitors. The data from international airports demonstrated some congruence with the perception of the tourism industry: that apart from English-speakers, visitors were most were likely to speak: German, followed by French, Dutch, and then Portuguese.

However, when these data were cross-tabulated with visitors arriving through border posts between SA and its neighbours, it emerged that the greatest number of visitors were in descending order, speakers of: Sotho (810 000), Portuguese (328 000), Swati (265 000), German (241 000), Tswana (224 000), Shona (221 000), Ndebele (113 000), French (92 000) and Chichewa/Njanja (62 000) (Heugh 1997). The mining industry has for years depended upon migrant labour from Mozambique, Swaziland

and Lesotho. Citizens from these countries, who in fact participate in the formal economy of SA, were not counted as 'visitors' or contributors to the economy. Interviews at the Oshoek border post with Swaziland confirmed that the purpose for most travellers was economic: trading with, purchasing supplies from, or supplying labour to, the South African formal sector.[8] Prior to this, official cognisance was only taken of visitors to SA who speak European, or sometimes Asian, languages. Speakers of African languages remained invisible. They were not recognised as significant to tourism, thus, the economy.

The point is that LHR solutions cannot be detached from issues of speakers' participation in local and wider arenas (such as the ecology of languages, see Mühlhaüsler 1996). Where governments adopt a narrow nation-state conception of citizenship and linguistic rights generally, the linguistic versatility of multilingual portfolios and their implications for participatory citizenship is ignored.

3. LHR and the Problematic Nature of Liberal Citizenship

In the preceding sections, we have noted that despite the avowed intention of LHR, the South African context offers irrefutable evidence of post-colonial reproduction, and even exacerbation, of existing inequity, where arbitrary decisions on linguistic categorization, and monolingually based ethnolinguistic stereotyping have deprived speakers of the exercise of their political and legal rights. Those furthest from the centre of power are likely to be rendered invisible, their cultures and identities distorted, and made right-less. Furthermore, the rights-based orientation of PANSALB, has failed to recognize or grasp the potential of multilingual channels of communication which not only allow people to cross linguistic divides circumscribed by parallel and monolingual identities, but that, by so doing, simultaneously contribute in important ways to the socio-economic well-being of the community. Structural ideologies and constructs of language that ignore everyday language as *practice* do not acknowledge how intimate uses of non-standard (and officially non-legitimate) ways of speaking comprise important resources for generating alternative narratives of self and society. And finally, the spatially constrained nature of the LHR paradigm does not do justice to the spread and complexity of speakers' participations in translocal networks of communication, linking local, regional and global arenas.

All of these problems effectively hinder the participation of linguistic

[8] Babazile Mahlalela carried out the fieldwork research at Oshoek during 1997.

minorities in democratic governance, excluding speakers of African languages from social and participation rights. Our contention is that these shortcomings, far from comprising temporary mishaps, can be traced directly to the notion of liberal citizenship on which LHR paradigms draw. This is because of the specific relation between state, market, civil society and language that liberal citizenship assumes, and which is becoming increasingly difficult to uphold in today's postmodern and globalized world (Faulks 2000, Mutua 2002).

3.1. Liberal Citizenship and Nation-state

A foundational assumption of liberal citizenship is that its exercise requires a constituency of commonality – it is about belonging and participation. Traditionally, commonality is defined either in terms of *nationality* – a shared history, destiny and common culture (e.g. Miller 1995), residency in a state (e.g. Oommen 1997), or similar such grounds for establishing a sense of commonality. In most contexts, citizenship is tightly tied to the notion of the nation-state, which provides the territorial, ideological and institutional demarcation of inclusive and/or exclusive citizen status. Visible manifestations of such a concern are readily apparent in such phenomena as immigration controls, residency requirements and the like, which privilege citizens over non-citizens.[9] In most nation-states, cultural discourses on language are rhetorically and mythologically used to bolster the political discourse of the unity and homogeneity of the State (cf. Stroud 1999 on the use of language as part of cultural politics by Samora Machel in newly independent Mozambique). This implies that the exclusionary nature of a notion of citizenship grounded in nationality (and its corollary, the national language) is also potentially at work in LHR discourses, and in fact, the example we have provided here is just one of the many of how the development of nation-states goes hand in glove with the disempowerment of linguistic minorities (cf. May 2001 and Wright, this volume).

A tenet of liberal citizenship is the abstract and apolitical nature of citizenship and attendant rights, the rationale being that all individuals are equal before the law and that private life, social habit, class, gender, sexuality, ownership of property, etc are the private concern of the individual and should be protected form the political interference of the public sphere.

---

[9] The exclusionary nature of a nationality-based citizenship is obvious. Less obvious, but just as problematic nevertheless, is how the concept of the nation is bound up with notions of gender and class, for example, in the way in which women in many countries are not expected to do national service or the fact that officers are mostly recruited from the upper classes (cf. Faulks 2000).

The nation-state, which requires homogeneity and unity can only, with difficulty, accommodate social and cultural varieties. As Faulks (2000) notes, the underlying, but seldom stated rationale for this, is the protection of the (neo)liberal market economy. However, the *apolitical* nature of liberal citizenship, with its concern to constrain the effects of state power, means that it does not theorize the way in which power and its effects are contested, reflexively constituted, and dispersed unevenly among different social groupings on the basis of class, gender or ethnicity (see also May 2001: 11; Mutua 2002). With respect to the *abstract* nature of liberal citizenship, various approaches have been proposed on how to reconcile liberal citizenship with a politics of difference and diversity. Kymlicka's notion of *multicultural citizenship,* comprising a set of principles for acknowledging the rights of different groups, is quite likely the best-known among them (Kymlicka 1995). However, Faulks (2000), among others, has drawn attention to a number of problems with a group-based/collective citizenship (see also May 2001; Stroud 2000). In principle, (neo)liberal attempts to manage diversity seem not to want to question the viability of trying to accommodate difference in a framework that is fundamentally constructed around explicit denial of difference in the interests of commonality. This is particularly evident in countries where official multilingual policies are implemented, but, as we have seen in the case of South Africa, certain groups remain excluded.

3.2. Liberal Citizenship and Materiality

Because of the integral relationship between the free market and liberal citizenship, one of the major issues in liberal citizenship is whether and to what extent individuals are able to fully exercise their civil and political rights. In South Africa, the limitations of the liberal human rights framework of government policy are becoming increasingly obvious. Patrick Bond captures the nature of the changes in South Africa in the title of his book (2000): 'Elite Transition: From Apartheid to Neoliberalism in South Africa'. Two other authors (Alexander 2002; Terreblanche 2003) are among the most critical. Sampie Terreblanche, an economist, has for several years monitored the effect of the ANC's dovetailing of the human rights framework with liberal capitalism in South Africa. In order for individuals to exercise their rights as citizens, they must have access to adequate material and economic resources. Terreblanche argues that the gap between the rich and the poor has widened, not narrowed, since the ANC gained power in 1994. Countless victims of the untamed workings of market forces are in practice denied exercise of their rights – such as the unemployed, who according to unofficial sources reach as high as 45% of the population. In essence his argument is compatible with other post-colonial theory which points to the reproduction or reinvention of (pre-) colonial institutions and the consolidation of inequitable conditions. The conclusions of both Alexander and Terreblanche are that civil society needs to shake off the disempowering yoke of liberal capitalism and ethnically conceived practices and choices in order to become revitalized.

3.3. Liberal Citizenship and Intimacy

In recent post-liberal debate, the idea of an abstract and independent citizen – laid down in a limiting notion of the nation-state that restricts the import of citizenship to narrow, public/formal relationships – has been challenged by the local, informal social and interdependent nature of civil and political participation. Post-liberal debates on citizenship, particularly analyses of feminist citizenship, are exploring the connection between civil, political and social rights, and the interconnection between state, market and civil society in this context (Sim 2000).

One major dimension in this debate has been a critical reappraisal of the liberal distinction between a public and private sphere (e.g. Pateman 1989), suggesting the desirability of a politicized and democratised private sphere. Lister (1997: 70-72) has argued that liberal citizenship is a disembodied citizenship – an abstract and contractual relationship – that ignores the importance of body, emotion and sexuality and other interdependent needs, as well as the qualities of compassion and care necessary for a full participatory citizenship. Giddens (1994: 195) has said:

> There are structural conditions in the wider society which penetrate to the heart of the pure relationships; conversely, how such relationships are ordered has consequences for the wider social order. Democratization in the public domain, not only at the level of the nation-state, supplies essential conditions for the democratizing of personal relationships. But the reverse applies also. The advancement of self-autonomy in the context of pure relationships is rich with implications for democratic practice in the larger community.

Plummer (1999, quoted in Faulks 2000) has coined the term 'intimate citizenship' to refer to the types of activities sustained in private, caring contexts of solidarity that are crucial to further democratization and conceptualization of citizenship.

3.4. Liberal Citizenship in Globalization

The notion of liberal citizenship has been subject to considerable rethinking in the wake of increasing globalization. Predictions about the dismantling of the nation-state in Africa (e.g. Fardon and Furniss 1994) pose problems for theorists such as Miller (1995) or Oommen (1997) who require shared common national or institutional belonging among community members for a notion of citizenship to be meaningful. Soysal (1994: 1) suggests that a rights based approach should supersede ideas of citizenship, claiming that "a new and more universal concept of citizenship has unfolded in the post-war era, one whose organizing and legitimating principles are based on universal personhood rather than national belonging", and proclaiming "a deterritorialized expansion of rights despite the territorialized closure of politics" (ibid.: 157). Other authors question whether rights can be deterritorialized and abstracted from wider functions of citizenship such as participatory democracy. Faulks (2000: 145) argues that "[r]ights do not ensure development of participatory networks that are necessary to sustain institutions of governance". And as Mazrui (2002) has warned – in a particular interpretation of the problems posed to citizenship by globalization – transnational processes and structural adjustment are shrinking the elite in Africa, as well as advancing the abandonment of the continent by the West. He argues that this puts renewed pressure on Africa to look inward to itself for development rather than depending on outside powers, thereby simultaneously reinstating the importance of the local in the African context. In a similar vein, Arnold (1989: 127) calls attention to how "a policy of particularities, big or small, that is, of development arenas whatever their size, number of people involved or language used, corresponds without doubt to the reality and spontaneous social dynamics of Africa".

As we saw above, South Africa demonstrates the simultaneous importance of the immediate and local and of the transnational or regional. This raises the question of how to reconcile local, global and regional idioms (cf. Kymlicka 1995); Heater's (1990) notion of *multiple citizenship* is one possibility, as it acknowledges the importance of the local context for the exercise of citizenship in Africa while at the same time extending the reach of citizenship responsibilities beyond the state.

In conclusion, we need to entertain a new post-liberal understanding of citizenship, and that understanding will carry extensive implications for language and linguistic minorities. The theoretical language of a post-liberal citizenship needs to refer to *power*, *participation* and *agency* for governance. The idea of language and multilingualism as a resource in the betterment of governance and the attainment of equity highlights the need to envisage an alternative politics of language, sensitive to the workings of power in language, that builds on the agency of its speakers, and that consolidates and helps link the participation of speakers in intimate, local and trans-local communities. In the following section, the notion of linguistic citizenship will be offered as one way towards such an alternative.

4. Linguistic Citizenship: A Politics of Language for a Post-liberal Citizenship

Linguistic citizenship pertains to a view of language as a symbolic, material, intimate and global resource in the service of participatory governance. Language as a *symbolic resource* emphasizes *actorhood* through the way in which citizens choose to represent themselves as speakers and members of speech communities in structures of power and resistance in ways that carry political implications. Language as a *material resource* highlights the role of language as a political and economic site of struggle, playing an integral part in the reconceptualization of the role of informal economies in developing contexts. Language as a *global resource* acknowledges that language is one of the main ways in which more global and regional concerns are interpreted and negotiated locally. And finally, language as an *intimate resource*, embodies respect for diversity and difference, recognition of multiple and shifting identities and the deconstruction of localized national and exclusionary identities in the service of transnational/ regional cooperation and security.

4.1. Language as a **Symbolic** *Resource: Deconstructing/Reconstructing Language*

It is imperative that language minorities themselves (re)capture a voice in the political discourse on language. Minority speakers must be able to politicize their own knowledge and representations of language and language use; to decide on contending definitions of what languages are for them and what they mean; to advance matters of language as relevant to and determinate of a range of social issues – policy issues and questions of equity. One problem, however, is that much current theorization of language and politics is often unavailable to those communities who are theorized and in many cases, such theory fails to provide any clear basis for political action. Furthermore, what at first blush seems like purely technical linguistic work in determining the boundaries of a variety is, in point of fact, an activity infused with political significance. The problems with a LHR discourse noted above point to the fact that issues in the distribution of power and economy in society, and ultimately, issues of democracy, equity and people's participation are vital framing conditions within which language theorization must be situated.

Current forms of social production and distribution of knowledge around language need to be critically examined as to how far they contribute to characterizations of language relevant to linguistic citizenship. Particularly pertinent in this respect is how applied linguistics should relate to the "pluralization of authority" (Rampton 1997: 249), so as to avoid the recontextualization of speakers' multilingual realities into master narratives of linguistic authority. Roberts (1997:5) argues that in order to counteract this linguists need to pay close attention to how speakers themselves conceive of their languages, and as a matter of course build their descriptions around these, thereby "integrat[ing] the investigation of fundamental linguistic processes with dialogue with the community and the professions".

4.2. Language as a **Material** *Resource*

Linguistic citizenship also highlights how multilingually constructed markets outside of the formal comprise the foremost means whereby marginalized speakers engage with a transformative politics of recognition and redistribution. We take the notion of linguistic citizenship as a way of addressing more explicitly the linkage between economic and material (re)distribution and political participation, on the one hand, and ethnic and linguistic identity and language resources, on the other. In South Africa, the political leadership, and the upper echelons of education and the economy, and PANSALB, which chose LHR as its panacea, have all missed the possibilities which a *resource-based* approach can offer in terms of maximizing existing linguistic repertoires as well as neutralizing ethnolinguistic conflict.[10] In blatant contradistinction to this, linguistic agents on the ground, often at the margins of the formal sectors, have discovered and are exploiting the potential of multilingual exchanges. The exercise of choice in several African countries outside the confines of the formal sector is what leads us towards the notion of linguistic citizenship. A recognition of linguistic cargo, its utilization in education and in the informal

---

[10] The resource-based approach offered an alternative, inclusive language planning paradigm which acknowledged the continua of languages. Instead, a narrow interpretation of language rights attached to essentialist and ethnically bounded language systems predominated. For example, a resource-based approach would have concentrated resources on dictionaries inclusive of all the varieties within respective language clusters such as Nguni and Sotho. The ethnolinguistic approach furthered linguistic balkanization by selecting only the official language varieties and for separate dictionaries. This, coupled with the exclusion of other varieties accentuated the practices of the past, and inevitably contributes to conflict (Heugh 2003, forthcoming).

economy may revitalize not only civil society but also the African Renaissance – but from the grassroots rather than from above.

The lack of material support for African languages in formal markets is a consequence of the way in which these markets are politically defined so as to exclude large spheres of economic activity on the margins of state control. In developing a notion of language as tied to material resources, ways need to be found of transposing this potentiality onto formal markets – or redefining formal markets. This would comprise a timely strategy for South Africa, where new discourses of *entrepreneuralism* are the order of the day. The failure of both the English language dominant formal sector and the large civil service to accommodate approximately 45% of the potential workforce has led to curriculum changes in secondary school that emphasize the development of skills necessary for self-employment. In other words, the question that remains is how the informal and horizontal linguistic markets might penetrate and mediate the vertically configured LHR based structures for language planning and development?[11] The women's markets offer alternative, highly regulated socio-economic systems with in-built educational functions. What such examples show is the potential for and flexibility of alternative linguistic resources owned in sub-cultures to articulate from below with formal and highly regulated sectors. Unofficial language markets are producing resources alongside of, outside of, and sometimes for official markets.

4.3. Language as an **Intimate** *Resource*

Linguistic citizenship draws attention to ways in which the issue of the active participation of language minorities in a community needs to articulate with a range of salient issues in a broader, more ecological citizenship discourse. It highlights how representations, practices and ideologies of language and society, as well as attendant rights and political stances, emanate from the multilingual practices and resources of speakers' local, socio-economic and cultural networks. The fluidity with which speakers view boundaries between variants in their languages (as shown in codeswitches, loans and other syncretic phenomena) provides important information about the complex and shifting communities that they live within, and the multiplicity of allegiances that they assemble around perceived and constructed common variants.

Processes such as standardization are crafted from the specific understandings of language held by dominant elites, and traditionally deployed

---

[11] Cf. Bruthiaux (2002) and Veloso (2002) for some suggestive examples of how this might be made possible.

in the spread and consolidation of prestigious varieties of language. When applied to 'minority' languages, standardization serves to remodel these languages in the image of the dominant language. Hornberger and King (1998) note that one of the problems connected to standardization is that speakers may oppose norms that differ from their own practices and/or that they conceive to be inauthentic. An important role of experts would be to authenticate different narratives or versions of language and culture, by crafting novel resources and new social meanings into legitimate and authoritative repertoires. One way in which this may be accomplished is through a 'broadening of the standard' so as to encompass forms of speech previously excluded as being substandard and impure. An inclusion of and focus on stigmatized variants broadens the linguistic database for standardization. It has the added advantage of extending the possibilities for participation and thus transforms the standardization process into a 'site of struggle'. This lends transparency to the political and social processes implicit in standardization work, and highlights how standardization has traditionally functioned to downplay and distort the socio-symbolic and political importance of linguistic differences.

The concept of linguistic citizenship has far reaching implications for education. To accommodate it, current education systems will need to be redefined so as to develop in an integrated way different kinds of competency: those which allow people to communicate across different languages in addition to those which give adequate access to the written variety of languages most likely to be used in local, regional and national political and economic activity. Luke (1996: 332) sums up admirably this sentiment: "what is needed is a pedagogy which …offers social and cultural strategies for analysing and engaging with the conversion of capital in various cultural fields".

4.4. Language as a **Global** *Resource for Peace, Harmony and Security*

The notion of linguistic citizenship highlights the potential of language, particularly multilingual practices, to address one of the more pressing problems of globalization, namely how to manage the reconciliation of conflict between local, national and transnational trends. Furthermore, the multinational nature of the majority of states suggests that the basis of universal citizenship must be participation across national/ethnic/language groups – in order to accommodate various voices in participatory processes of democracy, to devolve power and to build solidarity within and across groups in a society (Faulks 2000). Linguistic citizenship may promote the formulation of political stands on language issues that are common to oppressed speakers in general. It encourages commonality *of* action and commonality *in* action across segments of society and across national borders rather than a politics based on in-group characteristics of a more essentialist character.

The porous borders between South Africa and its neighbours since the demise of apartheid offers the possibility of what Mazrui refers to as horizontal inter-penetration (2002: 276ff). A significant increase in numbers of people migrating to the country, including West African women with highly specialized expertise in the educational, social responsibility and economic autonomy of the marketplace, offers the transference of 'indigenous knowledge'. Whilst unemployed South Africans often complain that the 'amakwerekwere'[12] are taking their jobs, the women traders point out that this is not so. Interviews with women traders from the north argue that they are bringing skills and experience which they are happy to share with South African women in order to deliver them from the cycle of dependency-poverty in relation to a failing formal economy. The extent of migratory patterns throughout Africa, impossible to control or measure, accomplishes what Mazrui calls for in the spread of indigenous resources and skills.

Concerted regional cooperation on matters of linguistic description (see Alexander 1992 on harmonization) based on the structural convergences that have developed across language systems in contact may help unify speakers and languages around common, regional norms.

5. Conclusion

One of the greatest challenges to participatory citizenship is language. The LHR paradigm, based in the liberal notion of citizenship, does not achieve its objective, namely redressing inequality. LHR defaults to exclusionary practices via top-down policy-making where it is conceived in terms of the nation-state that is ideologically national. LHR discourses do not address the material and symbolic foundations necessary for the exercise of linguistic rights, nor adequately theorize the relationship between civil and political society, or the effects of globalization on language. The paradigm does not provide sufficient space for the realization of social rights, especially meaningful access to education, or for the participation of minority communities themselves. We also argue that where a liberal conceptualization of rights prevails, the most marginalized are often excluded even from legal and political rights.

[12] A pejorative term for immigrants/refugees from other African countries.

The alternative notion of *linguistic citizenship* is a way of drawing attention to the importance of an alternative conception of language and language use for a truly transformative, participatory, extended and in-depth notion of citizenship. We have argued, therefore, that linguistic citizenship is a broader and more inclusive notion than is linguistic human rights. It refers to the role of language in power, access and equity in a democratic framework of participatory citizenship that concedes the intimate bases of politics and security and harmony through global links. The notion of linguistic citizenship articulates well with other post-liberal theories of citizenship. Linguistic citizenship carries a critique of the legitimacy of majority speaking, official-language society's validation of language practices solely in terms of the formal, public sphere and a systemic construct of language. It attends to how speakers' representations and concepts of language could provide a basic building block for a politics of language, particularly with respect to the role that such representations and practices play in promoting more equitable, intimate, democratic and materially supported forms of participation within and across national borders.

References

Alexander, Neville (1992) 'South Africa: Harmonising Nguni and Sotho', in Nigel Crawhall (ed) *Democratically Speaking: International Perspectives on Language Planning*, Cape Town: National Language Project, 56-68.

------ (2002) *An Ordinary Country: Issues in the Transition from Apartheid to Democracy in South Africa,* Pietermaritzburg: University of Natal Press.

Arnold, T. (1989) 'Le multilinguisme facteur de developpement ou le paradox francophone en Afrique', in Robert Chaudenson and Didier de Robilliard (eds) *Langues, economie et développpement* 1, Aix-en-Provence: Institut d'Études Crèoles et Francophones, 115-131.

Asiwaju, Anthony I. (ed) (1984) *Partitioned Africans*, Lagos: Lagos University Press.

Blommaert, Jan (2001) 'The Asmara Declaration as a Sociolinguistic Problem: Notes in Scholarship and Linguistic Rights', *Journal of Sociolinguistics* 5(12): 131-142.

Boggs, S. Whitemore (1940) *International Boundaries: A Study of Boundary Functions and Problems*, New York: Columbia University Press.

Bond, Patrick (2000) *Elite Transition: From Apartheid to Neoliberalism in South Africa*, London: Pluto Press.

Bruthiaux, Paul (2002) 'Hold Your Courses: Language, Education, Language Choice and Economic Development', *TESOL Quarterly* 36(3): 275-296.

Butler, Judith (1990) *Gender Trouble: Feminism and the Subversion of Iden-*

tity, New York and London: Routledge.

Chumbow, Beban (1999) 'Transborder Languages of Africa', *Social Dynamics* 25(1): 51-69.

Coulmas, Florian (1992) *Language and Economy*, Oxford: Blackwell.

Djité, Paulin (1993) 'Language and Development in Africa', *International Journal of the Sociology of Language* 100/101: 149-166.

Fardon, Richard and Graham Furniss (eds) (1994) *African Languages, Development and the State*, London: Routledge.

Faulks, Keith (2000) *Citizenship*, London and New York: Routledge.

Foucault, Michel (1991) 'Governmentality', in Graham Burchell, Colin Gordon and Peter Miller (eds) *The Foucault Effect: Studies in Governmentality*, Hemel Hempstead: Harvester Wheatsheaf, 87-104.

Fraser, Nancy (1995) 'From Redistribution to Recognition: Dilemmas of Justice in a Post-socialist Age', *New Left Review* 212 (July/August): 69-91.

Freeland, Jane (2003) 'Intercultural-bilingual Education for an Inter-ethnic, Plurilingual Society? The Case of Nicaragua's Caribbean Coast Region', *Comparative Education* 39(2): 239-259.

Giddens, Anthony (1994) *Beyond Left and Right*, Cambridge: Polity Press.

Grin, François (1996a) 'Economic Approaches to Language and Language Planning: An Introduction', *International Journal of the Sociology of Language* 121: 1-15.

------ (1996b) 'The Economics of Language: Survey, Assessment, and Prospects', *International Journal of the Sociology of Language* 121: 17-44.

Heater, Derek (1990) *Citizenship*, London: Longman.

Heugh, Kathleen (1997) 'Data Collection on the Linguistic Profile and Linguistic Needs of Foreign Visitors at the Major Points of Entry to South Africa', Unpublished Report for the Telephone Interpreting Service for South Africa Steering Committee, Department of Arts, Culture, Science and Technology, Pretoria.

------ (2003, forthcoming) 'Can Authoritarian Segregation Give Way to Linguistic Rights? The Case of the Pan South African Language Board', *Current Issues in Language Planning* 4(4).

Hoffman, John (1995) *Beyond the State: An Introductory Critique*, Cambridge: Polity Press.

Hornberger, Nancy and Kendal King (1998) 'Authenticity and Unification in Quichua Language Planning', *Language, Culture and Curriculum* 11(3): 390-410.

Jaffe, Alexandra (1999) *Ideologies in Action. Language Politics on Corsica*, Berlin and New York: Mouton de Gruyter.

Janoski, Thomas (1998) *Citizenship and Civil Society: A Framework of Rights and Obligations in Liberal, Traditional, and Social Democratic Regimes*, Cambridge: Cambridge University Press.

Jernudd, Björn and Jyotirindra Das Gupta [1971] (1975) 'Towards a Theory of Language Planning', in Joan Rubin and Björn Jernudd (eds) *Can Language Be Planned?*, Honolulu: East-West Center, The University Press of Hawaii, 195-215.

Johnson, Anthony (2003) Personal Communication.

Kontra, Miklos, Robert Phillipson, Tove Skutnabb-Kangas and Tibor Várády (eds) (1999) *Language: A Right and a Resource. Approaching Linguistic Human Rights*, Budapest: Central European University Press.

Kymlicka, Will (1995) *Multicultural Citizenship*, Oxford: Oxford University Press.

Levine, Robert (1970) 'Sex Roles and Economic Change in Africa', in John Middleton (ed) *Black Africa. Its People and Their Culture Today*, London: Macmillan, 174-180.

Lister, Ruth (1997) *Citizenship: Feminist Perspectives*, Basingstoke, Hants: Macmillan

Luke, Alan (1996) 'Genres of Power? Literacy Education and the Production of Capital', in Ruqiya Hasan and Geoff Williams (eds) *Literacy in Society*, London and New York: Longman.

Makoni, Sinfree (1995) 'Some of the Metaphors about Language, in Language Planning Discourses in South Africa: Boundaries, Frontiers and Commodification', *Per Linguam* 11(1): 25-34.

------ (1996) 'In the Beginning Was the Missionaries' Word. The European Invention of an African Language: The Case of Shona', Paper Presented at the Colloquium on Harmonising and Standardising of African Languages for Education and Development, University of Cape Town, 11-13 July.

------ (1998) 'African Languages as European Scripts: The Shaping of Communal Memory', in Sarah Nuttall and Carli Coetzee (eds) *Negotiating the Past: The Making of Memory in South Africa*, Cape Town: Oxford University Press, 242-287.

May, Stephen (2001) *Language and Minority Rights: Ethnicity, Nationalism and the Politics of Language*, Harlow: Pearson Education Limited.

Mazrui, Alamin (2002) 'The English Language in African Education: Dependency and Decolonization', in James Tollefson (ed) *Language Policies in Education: Critical Issues*, Mahwah, NJ: Lawrence Erlbaum Associates, 267-281.

McGroarty, Mary (2002) 'Evolving Influences on Educational Language Policies', in James Tollefson (ed) *Language Policies in Education: Critical Issues*, Mahwah, NJ: Lawrence Erlbaum Associates, 17-36.

Miller, David (1995) *On Nationality*, Oxford: Oxford University Press.

Moore, Helen (2002) "Who Will Guard the Guardians Themselves?' National Interest versus Factional Corruption in Policymaking for ESL in Australia', in James Tollefson (ed) *Language Policies in Education: Critical Issues*,

Mahwah: Laurence Erlbaum Associates, 111-135.

Mühlhaüsler, Peter (1996) *Linguistic Ecology: Language Change and Linguistic Imperialism in the Pacific Region*, London: Routledge.

Mutua, Makau (2002) *Human Rights: A Political and Cultural Critique*, Philadephia: Pennsylvania University Press.

Office of the High Commissioner for Human Rights (1992) 'Declaration on the Rights of Persons belonging to National or Ethnic, Religious and Linguistic Minorities', Adopted by General Assembly Resolution 47/135 of 18 December, Geneva, Switzerland, http://193.194.138.190/html/menu3/b/d_minori.htm

Oommen, T. K (1997) *Citizenship, Nationality and Ethnicity*, Cambridge: Polity Press.

PANSALB (2000) *Language Use and Language Interaction in South Africa: A National Sociolinguistic Survey*, Pretoria: Pan South African Language Board.

Pateman, Carole (1989) *The Sexual Contract*, Cambridge: Polity Press.

Pennycook, Alistair (1998) 'The Right to Language: Towards a Situated Ethics of Language Possibilities', *Language Sciences* 20(1): 73-87.

------ (2002) 'Language Policy and Docile Bodies: Hong Kong and Governmentality', in James Tollefson (ed) *Language Policies in Education: Critical Issues*, Mahwah: Lawrence Erlbaum Associates, 91-110.

Phillipson, Robert (1992) *Linguistic Imperialism*, Oxford: Oxford University Press.

------ and Tove Skutnabb-Kangas (1986) *Linguicism Rules in Education*, Roskilde: Institute VI, Roskilde University Centre (3 volumes).

Plummer, Ken (1999) 'Inventing Intimate Citizenship', Paper presented at the conference '*Rethinking Citizenship*', University of Leeds.

Prah, Kwesi (1995) *African Languages for the Mass Education of Africans*, Bonn: German Foundation for International Development.

Rampton, Ben (1997) 'Retuning in Applied Linguistics', *International Journal of Applied Linguistics* 7(1): 3-25.

Roberts, Celia (1997) 'There is Nothing So Practical as Some Good Theories', *International Journal of Applied Linguistics* 7(1): 66-78.

Ruiz, Richard (1984) 'Orientations in Language Planning', *Journal of the National Association for Bilingual Education* 8: 15-34.

Sim, Birte (2000) *Gender and Citizenship: Politics and Agency in France, Britain and Denmark*, Cambridge: Cambridge University Press.

Skutnabb-Kangas, Tove (2000) *Linguistic Genocide in Education- or Worldwide Diversity and Human Rights*, Mahwah: Lawrence Erlbaum Associates.

------ and Robert Phillipson (eds) (1994) *Linguistic Human Rights: Overcoming Linguistic Discrimination*, Berlin: Mouton de Gruyter.

Soysal, Yasemin (1994) *Limits of Citizenship*, Chicago, IL: University of Chicago Press.

Stroud, Christopher (1999). 'Portuguese as Ideology and Politics in Mozambique: Semiotic (Re)constructions of a Postcolony', in Jan Blommaert (ed) *Language Ideological Debates*, Berlin and New York: Mouton de Gruyter, 343-380.

------ (2000) 'Language and Democracy: The Notion of Linguistic Citizenship and Mother Tongue Programmes', in Karsten Legère and Sandra Fitchet (ed) *Talking Freedom: Language and Democratization in the SADC Region*, Windhoek: MacMillan, 67-74.

------ (2001) 'African Mother-tongue Programmes and the Politics of Language: Linguistic Citizenship versus Linguistic Human Rights', *Journal of Multilingual and Multicultural Development* 22(4): 339-355.

------ (2002) 'Framing Bourdieu Socioculturally: Alternative Forms of Linguistic Legitimacy in Postcolonial Mozambique', *Multilingua* 21: 247-273.

------ (forthcoming 2004) 'The Performativity of Codeswitching', *International Journal of Bilingualism* 8(2).

Terreblanche, Sampie (2003) *A History of Inequality in South Africa 1652-2002*, Pietermaritzburg: University of Natal Press.

Ufomata, Ttitilayo (1998) *Voices from the Marketplace: Short Stories*, Ibadan: Kraft Books Limited, University of Ibadan.

Veloso, Teresa (2002) 'Becoming Literate in Mozambique – the Early Stages in Sena (*Cisena*) and Shangaan (*Xichangana*)', *Perspectives in Education* 20(1): 79-96.

Wiley, Terrence (2002) 'Accessing Language Rights in Education: A Brief History of the U.S. Context', in James Tollefson (ed) *Language Policies in Education: Critical Issues*, Mahwah, NJ: Lawrence Erlbaum Associates, 39-64.

Woolard, K. (1998) 'Language Ideology as a Field of Inquiry', in Bambi Schieffelin, Kathryn Woolard and Paul Kroskrity (eds) *Language Ideologies: Practice and Theory*, New York: Oxford University Press, 3-47.

11. Language Rights, Democracy and the European Union

SUE WRIGHT

1. Introduction

Much of the current debate on language rights has focused on strategies for groups where there are speakers who are not able to use their own language in education, in contact with their state's bureaucracy or within their legal system, and are thus disadvantaged (de Varennes 1996). Other work has campaigned to aid the survival of languages where speakers are few in number and diminishing, and it seems likely that the language will disappear when the older generation that speaks the language dies (Skutnabb-Kangas 2000). These language rights issues are, of course, linked to two macro-political phenomena that have affected individuals in many ways beyond the purely linguistic and which have been hard to counter in any sphere. The first issue derives from the growth of the nation state, the penetration of state institutions into every aspect of citizens' lives and the state authorities' preference, if not requirement, for the ensuing contact to be in the state language. The second issue derives from the intensity of the interconnectedness, the velocity of flows, the networks and systems of interaction and exchange (Held *et al.* 1999: 27) of the modern world. Few groups are so isolated that their members do not know of events and attitudes outside. Their community desire to participate in these networks and flows is likely to be to the detriment of group specificity and in particular to the survival of languages that do not have the written forms needed for education and which are not currency in the exchanges.

This chapter looks at how these two macro-political phenomena reappear in different guises in another aspect of the language rights question, the ceding of political power to agencies higher than the state and the problems of constituency, access and consultation that are attendant on this.

We could argue that the advent of the nation state in Europe and the spread of national languages actually constructed linguistic minorities. Prior to the concept of nation there was no majority to define minority. There might have been powerful groups and less powerful groups, conquering groups and conquered groups in the feudal world, but political boundaries were liable to change through marriage, inheritance and war, and the speakers of related vernaculars along the dialect continua could come under one then another authority. The state in the person of the monarch was rarely in contact with subjects, who did not need to be consulted and who could be contacted through the hierarchies of feudalism, if there was ever need. The development of the nation state and the strategies of nation building changed this situation radically. The rights and duties of the citizen: education, conscription, welfare, taxation, political participation, presume a cohesive national group that sees itself as such. An important element of this political concept has always been citizens' acceptance of the national language, codified and standardized so that it can be acquired in education, and which provides the community of communication, the forum in which national life can take place. Of course, reality rarely conformed to the ideal and national cohesion was broken both by groups that had no desire to be co-opted into national groups, which they did not see as their natural home and which remained culturally and linguistically separate, or by the centre refusing admittance, full integration and rights to certain categories. For whichever reason, the unificatory process inherent in nation state building and its partial realization created the category 'linguistic minority'.

The nation state is a political experience that all European Union citizens share and which we bring to our understanding and expectations of the supranational experiment in which we and our governments are now engaged. Knowing our socialization and our resulting preconceptions, it is easy to understand some of the difficulties that accompany the construction of this political union. Our experience necessarily frames our expectations of how a polity ought to be, and in this chapter I intend to explore the issue of community of communication from this perspective. We could usefully relate the problems of language, access and exclusion that are arising in a supranational polity that aspires to be democratic to the stock of knowledge we already have about these issues from our experience of the nation state. Our past ought to alert us to the dangers inherent in allowing the development of patterns of inclusion and exclusion.

The first section sets out the reasons for the commitment to multilingualism within the European Union, reviews the linguistic regimes in its institutions and shows how the ideal of multilingualism has been almost impossible to maintain and is only partial in any case. In the second section I advance the argument that democracy is intimately bound with language and can only function fully in a community of communication. My question is whether blocks to communication can be seen to play any role in the perceived democratic deficit of the EU. The final section shows how EU citizens disregard official policies to promote multilingualism and how we may be in danger of reproducing the majority and minority divisions of the nation state era in current language driven inclusion and exclusion.

2. Present EU Policy: *A Commitment to Multilingualism in the EU Institutions and Bureaucracy. Failures and Apparent Inconsistencies*

The multilingualism of the European Union is rooted in the decisions taken in the earliest phase of the European Project that all official languages of the member states should be official languages of the European communities. Article 217 of the Rome Treaty gave the institutions of the EEC the right to determine their working languages. In 1958, Regulation Number 1 decreed that all four languages should be working languages. Since 1958 each enlargement has followed the same rule; an official language of any country that joins becomes an official and working language. Thus English, Danish, Spanish, Portuguese, Greek, Swedish and Finnish have each in turn become official and working languages. There are at present 11 official and working languages. The Irish agreed to a particular status for Irish, which is an official but not a working language.

The reasoning behind the multilingualism of the EEC was firstly symbolic; the equality of member states needed to be acknowledged and respected. Secondly and equally, it was felt that the texts of Community legislation that would become law in all the states must be published in a language that citizens could understand. This transparency was held to be a fundamental requirement that any democratic system must respect. There has to be legal certainty and judges, litigants and defendants have to be able to grasp the full import of the laws that affect them or which they are called upon to implement. Thus, it was argued, citizens must have the right to communicate with the institutions of the EEC (later EC and EU) in any of the official languages and receive a response in the same language. However, these fundamental principles have proved both unworkable and flawed.

If Article 1 of Regulation Number 1 of the Rome treaty declared all official languages to be working languages, Article 6 allowed a fudge on the issue by giving the institutions the right to stipulate which languages could be used in different situations. Only formal documents from the Council and Commission are routinely published in all eleven languages. In the early period of the six-country EEC, the custom was to use French as the *de facto* working language in the Commission and the Council. Since the accession of the UK and the Scandinavian countries that used English as their working language in EFTA, English has challenged French in this role and its use is reported as increasing (Schlossmacher 1992; Wright 2000). The attempts of the German speaking states (that actually have the largest number of speakers of any one language) to gain acceptance for German as a *de facto* working language in the Commission have not been successful.

The European Parliament is the only institution which claims to adhere fully to the plurilingual principle, but even here the commitment is only fully maintained in formal sessions. In the working groups English and French are used with some interpreting support. For informal meetings, casual lobbying and forming alliances, an MEP who did not know one of the two working languages would be hampered and frustrated and would rely heavily on an assistant who would then have a gate keeper role. MEPs who cannot read English and French with ease also report disadvantage in that, even where working documents are available in translation in their language, they are usually obtainable first in English and French. There is thus less time to prepare a response and research evidence for an argument if a team is not working in these two languages (Wright 2000).

The commitment by the institutions to assure exchange in the applicant's language is also proving hard to guarantee. Those who telephone or present themselves at the offices of the institutions cannot be sure that they will be able to use their state language. Only when translation services can be used can this right be assured. Shuibhne (2001) reports on a further development. In a case under review at the time of writing, a Dutch company has challenged the practice of the Office for Harmonization of the Internal Market (Trade marks and designs), which only guarantees communication in English, French, German, Italian and Spanish. An application for a community trademark may be filed in one of the eleven official languages but must specify a second language from the list and this may be used in correspondence. Shuibhne suggests that the practice in the OHTM is significant in that it recognizes that the basic right of citizens to deal with the EU in their own language appears to have become discretionary. This is also the case in the commitment to publish laws in all the languages of the Union. The judgements of the ECJ and the Court of First Instance are published (mostly) in all 11 languages. But an increasing body of other law including staff cases are published only in the language of the case. Shuibhne (ibid.) suggests that litigants may well be prejudiced by "the limited linguistic availability of this case law".

The difficulties of providing for equal treatment for 11 languages are clear. From time to time different groups have raised the possibility of introducing a limited number of official languages after the model followed by the UN and other international bodies. The Political Affairs Committee proposed a simpler linguistic regime in 1982, arguing that Europe must be politically articulate and capable of representing its interest both internally and externally as clearly as possible (paragraph 5. Opinion of the Political Affairs Committee adopted 26/02/82). It was of the opinion that this could not be done in a Tower of Babel and that the number of official languages should be limited. The idea was rejected. Under the French presidency of the Union in 1994, Lamassoure introduced the proposal that there be 5 working languages. Again the proposal was rejected.[1] Now the idea is being debated again. Given the present cost to the European Union of the Translation and Interpretation services (686 million Euro per year, reported in *l'Express* 29/1/2002) and the present creaking in the system, it is hard to see that a strict commitment to multilingualism could continue when there is enlargement. As the accession countries join, the number of languages could rise to 21 if they all claimed the right to be treated according to the present language regime. Translation pairs would then rise to 420 and each fully interpreted meeting could need as many as 210 interpreters. However, despite these practical difficulties the EU, in the form of the European Parliament, again confirmed its commitment to absolute parity of national languages in a Parliamentary Resolution passed 12/12/2001. This stated that the parliament:

1. Reiterates its attachment to language diversity in the EU and considers that all European languages are of equal cultural value and are an integral part of the various European cultures; …
3. Voices its support once again for the equality of the official languages and the working languages of all the countries making up the EU;
4. Believes that a reduction in the number of EU working languages would entail a reduction in democratic and social rights and help accentuate the 'democratic deficit' of the EU;
5. Voices its determination to fight any attempt to introduce discrimination between the official languages and the working languages of the EU;

---

[1] The French government and power elites are among the most committed supporters of unity and diversity as well as the originators of this suggestion. This is not as contradictory as it appears at first, if we understand that the commitment to pluralism is a defence of French in the face of English spread rather than a commitment to full pluralism which would be at variance with France's policy on its own linguistic minorities. For a good illustration of this see the French Ministry for Foreign Affairs *Vade mecum en 10 points* which instructs French bureaucrats and politicians to use French in all situations. This shows little regard for the rights of other language users.

If multilingualism is proving unworkable because of the sheer scale of the operation, it is also under attack because there is an element of intellectual dishonesty in the issue. The multilingualism from the EEC era down to the present EU has always been presented within a discourse that talks of rights, equality and fairness. But linguistic rights in the EU context cannot be seen as a desire to respect human rights. The commitment to providing laws in the language of the citizen is not total. It does not extend to those whose languages were eclipsed in the nation-building era and who are now deemed speakers of minority languages. The argument that citizens have a fundamental right to be able to read laws in their own language and use it for all contact with all European institutions has angered many of those who are deprived of this entitlement. Some groups (e.g. Catalan speakers) petitioned to have the same linguistic rights as others but were refused.[2] The argument for equality thus seems intellectually flawed and such groups wonder why they are expected to accommodate if it is not deemed reasonable for others. Commitment within the EU has actually been to national language rights not individual language rights. Thus the assurance that the institutions will communicate with citizens in 'their language' is not total.

Minority language groups have drawn from the Community's stance to make their own case for basic language rights, and it is logically difficult to counter their argument. It is hard to see why multilingualism at Community level can be presented as positive, a sign of vitality, diversity and creativity, whereas at national level it is divisive, economically disadvantageous and limiting.[3] It is hard not to conclude that recognition of citizens' democratic rights was secondary to a care for state sovereignty as the prime motivation for the language regime of the EU, and that EU language laws are not grounded in language rights. Equality appears an untouchable ideology, but the present legal situation fails equality on

---

[2] The Catalans were supported by a European Parliament Resolution in December 1990, but blocked by the Council and Commission.

[3] The French provide clear examples of this double think. The debate in the press at the time of the refusal to ratify the Charter for Regional and Minority Languages gives ample examples of the majority's disapproval of minority languages. The debates at the time of Maastricht, the passing of the Toubon law or the negotiations on cultural exception provide plentiful examples of French support of multilingualism in supra or transnational settings. The French are not in isolation in this. Other member states exhibit similar attitudes. The Greeks are very protective of Greek in the EU. They were the chief objectors to the 1995 proposal. At the same time linguistic minorities in Greece are under pressure to conform linguistically.

grounds of both effectiveness and fairness. Equality is not being served when we have a paper commitment to multilingualism which is not the reality and which makes some political representatives (those who can use English and French) more effective than others (those who cannot). And, when equality seems to decree that language rights are absolutely essential for some at any financial cost but not appropriate for others, its moral force is diminished.

We have to conclude: that the commitment to language equality in the European Union is only respected in a minority of situations, primarily because it is difficult, expensive and time consuming; that some language groups (French and English speakers) are advantaged by practices that are not acknowledged as existing and for which counterbalancing measures have in consequence not been developed; and that the commitment to the citizens' right to use their languages is partial. Only speakers of the official languages of the nation states have a right to use their language and thus those who are minorities in the nation state system find themselves once again disadvantaged, this time at EU level.

3. Democracy is Intimately bound with Language and Functions only in a Community of Communication

If Europe aspires to be anything more than a trading union run by plurilingual cosmopolitan patricians and technocrats, then we do need to take into account who can communicate with whom. A key issue for the European Union is whether democracy can function within a community which does not possess a forum or a demos, i.e. the means or the space to discuss and debate.

Europe has three democratic traditions: face to face participatory democracy as practised in Ancient Athens,[4] Anglo-Saxon liberal representative democracy and 'Continental' weak communitarianism which originated in French political thinking. In each of these models communication is central to their good functioning. The tradition of direct democracy is highly discursive, the ability to use language expertly to persuade others of one's case paramount. This was particularly true in the Athenian model. No advantage accrued from statecraft built up over years of experience in a certain post; no influence derived from an individual's position in a hierarchy. All political authority depended on the individual citizen's ability

[4] Participatory democracy has only a few further examples in the European context, among them the Icelandic Althing, the Swiss cantons, certain medieval city states in southern France and northern Italy.

to develop and sustain an argument, to support it with evidence, to analyze and to advocate (Lloyd 1992). Liberal representative democracy is characterized by its two party adversarial system, first past the post voting procedures and recognition that there is an interplay between interest groups. It is commonly associated with a commitment to free market economics. Without the oxygen of debate, transparency of information and clarity of how interests are being represented, this political solution soon deteriorates into croneyism. The 'Continental' model of weak communitarianism is characterized by multi-party, proportional representation with its resultant, not always stable, coalitions, and a greater tendency to state intervention and support. Without a functioning community of communication, the danger of this model is that elites may reify 'the people', interpret their will without proper consultation and exclude them from input to policy making. Power in each kind of democracy is thus mediated and policed through language. Communication, in the form of debate, consultation and reporting back, is central to them all. Where another form of government may use coercion on its citizens, a democracy must persuade. Members of a democracy are citizens not subjects and have the right and duty to participate in governance. Even where this participation is minimal (voting once every 'n' years), it is language dependent and the voters need to understand the platforms of those who seek power and the interests of competing groups if they are to make an informed choice.

The European Union has declared its commitment to democracy. Commitment to democratic procedures is a condition of membership. The tests for entry for Spain, Portugal, Greece and currently the ten accession countries demonstrate this prerequisite clearly. It is thus rather curious that the EU itself is actually rather deficient in many of the defining variables of a democratic state. Of course, the EU's departure from the general democratic trend is, in part, because it is a young polity, still to find its final shape, and, in part, because it is novel and without precedent. It is not a state in the old nation state sense of the term and the kind of state which it is becoming is not at all clear (Weiler 1997; Habermas 1997; Grimm 1997). So our first difficulty when enquiring whether the EU is democratic is caused by the question a democratic 'what?'. We are attaching an adjective to an entity which is not a fully evolved polity and, indeed, may never be. At best we can say that the EU is *sui generis*, a supra-national polity in formation. Even so, it does seem worrying that the EU contravenes the classic democratic ideal of the separation of executive and legislative powers, is far from transparent and is not directly accountable to the citizen (Castiglione 1995; Duverger 1991; Bellamy 1996).[5] Many of these

---

[5] The EU is organized according to criteria which Lively (1975) describes as

problems were discussed in the 2002-3 Convention on the future of Europe, presided by Valéry Giscard d'Estaing.

There is, however, one challenge for democracy that has not yet been fully acknowledged. The language issue would seem to present a further hurdle to be overcome before the EU can be actively democratic. This issue might prove the most intractable of all, but it is not being widely discussed. All the traditions of democracy on which Europeans draw and all their personal experience of the nation state model of representative democracy lead them to expect that membership of a democratic polity will involve them in complex patterns of communication. This may be direct from the political class to the voters through meetings, on the doorstep, in political broadcasts and over the Internet or mediated through journalists' presentation of the issues in the press, on television and on radio. The ideal democratic context, admittedly very rarely attained, entails free and simple access to uncensored information from a number of sources; an electorate skilled enough to evaluate evidence and decide upon issues; a public forum where facts and opinion can be exchanged; the frank admission of sectional interests and a social norm which frowns on apathy. Although none of the fifteen member states can claim to have achieved this ideal, they have, nonetheless, a tradition of nation wide debate at times of referenda and elections.[6] In some countries these roots are deeper than in others, but it is the practice which they all now follow. And, moulded by this nation state tradition, Europeans tend to expect that their fellow voters in their polity will constitute a reasonably homogenous populace[7] who will receive similar images and information through national media, will have similar schema for organising them and will be able to participate in the nation wide debate.

This model does not easily transpose to the EU. There is no European *demos* as such, conceiving itself as a unity, recognising interdependence

---

'weak' democracy. In his typology of democratic arrangements, the situation in which rulers are chosen by representatives of the ruled is minimalist democracy, only one category away from benevolent dictatorship. This is broadly the regime which pertains in the Commission and the Council, with both being nominated by national governments. The fact that neither can be removed by a European electorate runs against normal democratic tradition.

[6] In the UK, for example, a few febrile weeks of party political broadcasts, political punditry, vox pop interviews, opinion polls and public debates precede national elections.

[7] Even if this community of communication is achieved through asymmetric bilingualism and the greater effort made by minority groups to contribute to majority language medium debate.

between social groups, promoting a civil society in the Habermasian sense and developing a forum for debate (Habermas 1992). Achieving consensus on European issues through transnational consultation and exchange of opinion has not been the experience of the peoples of the EU.[8] In the view of some commentators this is the fundamental weakness of the EU, for where there is no negotiated consensus for laws, they may be challenged (Bankowski and Scott 1996). The link between the EU's multilingualism and its democratic deficit is not often examined or referred to explicitly,[9] but a very strong argument can be made that lack of direct channels of communication are a major factor in the perception that such a deficit exists. Indeed the transparency issue might well be a linguistic issue as much as a system and distance issue.

Among all the reasons for the EU's democratic deficit, it is this problem caused by the lack of a community of communication which is least likely to be addressed in the near future. Some of the reasons for the silence stem from the way that national identity and pride are closely bound up with language. The nation state tradition, which imposed linguistic and cultural homogeneity from the centre, blocks any parallel development at supranational level because of the meaning that languages have acquired as symbols of membership for national communities. To protect the national languages a very powerful discourse invoking equality has been developed. Challenging the ideology which has shaped the debate is not easy. One does not want to be the 'baddie' who is against 'equality', which is *per se* positive and desirable. The alternative is unthinkable, a loss of heritage and a monochrome monolingualism, shades of Brave New World. But this is a *reductio ad absurdum* of the argument.

---

[8] The practice in all European elections to date has been for national political groups to run national campaigns from national perspectives, with a major focus on national issues. Unsurprisingly the voters have often used the European elections to register their opinion on national governments midterm. However, once elected to parliament MEPs seem to shrug off the national and have started to vote increasingly in party rather than national groups (Hix 2000).

[9] Politicians and political scientist tend to disregard this aspect of the subject. The UK Research Council for the Social Sciences, the ESRC, recently funded a multi million pound programme, entitled 'One Europe or Several'. A number of research teams investigated aspects of integration and convergence. There was no specific project dealing with communication or language. I asked panel members at one of the concluding conferences of the programme (e.g. Westminster 24/3/2003) whether they felt language might play a role in democratic deficit. Some admitted they had not considered language but that it might be a factor in exclusion; most ducked the question.

A viable solution to our need for intragroup debate and exchange is to adopt a single lingua franca. Given the strength of group identity inextricably linked with the national languages as the mother tongues of the majority of their citizens, it is hard to envisage that they would be eclipsed by this auxiliary language. They would remain as language of socialization with all that means. We are not talking about language shift here, we are simply talking about agreeing on one auxiliary language and using it. But this has not been possible and we are not even likely to have the debate. For one language to be chosen as lingua franca relegating the others to secondary status within the Union is too difficult in terms of prestige while the nation state ethos remains strong.

4. Plurilingual Policies and the Spread of English

The need to plan for intragroup communication was recognized from the very beginning of the European project and the educational policy solution at Community level was to promote personal multilingualism. In the early days of the EEC, with only 4 official languages, this would theoretically have been possible. A universally accepted policy which divided each population up into three equal sections learning three different pairs of languages would have created a community where each citizen could have communicated with all the others and where strict equality among languages could have been observed.[10] In the event such policies remained at discussion stage only. Now, with 10 other languages to learn, personal multilingualism is inadequate as a policy if we wish to ensure that any single individual can communicate with any other. A hierarchy of languages would have to be established and a language (or languages) agreed as the preferred foreign language in all the member states' school curricula to keep communication channels open. With the accession of ten further member states there will be 20 languages to learn. The multilingual model will then become even less viable. There is, however, no suggestion that one language might be designated as preferred foreign language in education and thus ultimately as lingua franca. The Commission, bound by the commitment to absolute equality of official languages in the 1958 Treaty and to cultural diversity in the 1993 Treaty of European Union and reluctant to wound the sensibilities of any national group, could not and would not act otherwise in this matter. It continues to support

[10] It would have been a community where any individual could have communicated with any other (either with one interlocutor in the pair using their L1 and the other their L2 or L3 or with both interlocutors using the L2s or L3s).

diversity in the modern languages curriculum and only funds programmes which support that diversity.[11]

These programmes are generally failing to promote multilingualism and this should not surprise us. The miserable results of language learning within the classroom unsupported by any clear motivation are well documented (Gardner and Lambert 1972; Rubin 1981; Seliger 1983; Byram 1989). For most people there has to be demonstrable material advantage (extrinsic motivation) to repay the effort necessary for foreign language acquisition. Where there is clear reward, where mastery of a foreign language gives access to knowledge or brings economic advantage, then it is more likely that large numbers of people will develop foreign language competence. Language learning is often a clear example of the market at work. Languages are, of course, also learnt for intrinsic reasons. When this happens, there are usually questions of identity in play and a different ideological underpinning. For example, in nineteenth century nation building many citizens cooperated in the drive to spread the national language, seeing language shift as patriotic and the cohesion of a single community of communication necessary in the new order. However, there is no ideological commitment to European integration on a scale comparable to commitment to nation building and language policies that had this aim as their main purpose have been unable to convince students and their parents.

This support for multilingualism means that the discourse on language education in EU policy circles tends to an impracticable idealism which would have school children learn several languages and have members of the multilingual networks of the EU rely on relay translation and interpretation, passive understanding of each other's language and a multitude of comprehension/communication strategies in languages where knowledge is only partial.

The reader will now remark, and quite rightly, that this description does not appear to approximate in any way to what is actually happening in the education systems of the EU. The practice in the various state education systems is that all are providing tuition in one foreign language to the virtual exclusion of all the others. Although not officially designated

---

[11] It does this mainly through the LINGUA programme introduced in 1990 to 'improve language competence throughout the 12 Member States'. LINGUA has as its brief the promotion of *all* the national languages and seeks particularly 'to encourage the teaching and learning of the less widely used languages of the European Community' (*Lingua News* No 2 January 1991, p.1).

as preferred foreign language in education, English has achieved that status. In 2000 more than 90% of European secondary school children who do not have English as their mother tongue were learning English as a foreign language.

EU secondary school children (not Ireland and UK) learning English		
1991–1992	83%	(Eurostat 1994).
1992–1993	88%	(Eurydice 1996)
1996–1997	89%	(Eurydice 1998).
1998–1999	91%	(Eurydice 2000)

As some students may have learnt in the past and have given up the subject and as the trend is rising, this suggests that only a handful of Europeans will leave school in the twenty first century without having had some instruction in English.[12] In contrast, the Anglophone countries are not supporting foreign language learning enthusiastically. Ireland does not make foreign language learning compulsory and does not offer a foreign language in primary. The UK does not provide a foreign language systematically on the primary curriculum. The situation seems set to worsen as, at the time of writing, the British Government's Green Paper on the reform of the 14 to 19 school curriculum for secondary schools is proposing that foreign languages should no longer be core subjects on the secondary school curriculum for England. This would reduce the number of years of compulsory foreign language study to three (from a base already one of the lowest in the Union). This lack of enthusiasm for foreign language learning means that the relentless move to English is and not even softened by English mother tongue speakers' mastery of other languages of the Union.

So it seems that the language issue is resolving itself in a piecemeal and incremental way. The pressure that tens of thousands of parents and students have brought to bear on the education services of the member

[12] In the early 1990s the dominance of English was strongest in the countries in the Germanic continuum/in the north of the continent. For example in Sweden all secondary school children were learning English in 1992-1993 and the figure was over 90% in Denmark, Germany and Finland, over 80% in the Netherlands and Austria. The percentages fell to 66% in Italy, 64% in Greece and 52% in Portugal (Eurydice 1998). By the 2000 report this geographical difference was beginning to disappear.

states to study one particular foreign language has made the personal multilingualism goal unworkable. EU top down policy to promote diversity seems not to have been able to withstand bottom up pressure from parents and pupils who see the acquisition of English as necessary for the realization of educational and professional ambitions in a transnational world where English has become the medium of exchange. This state of affairs will be unpalatable in some quarters. Many in Europe will be as unenthusiastic about the spread of English as they will be about the way it has imposed itself through market forces.

5. Conclusions

The situation is thus contradictory and the very opposite outcome to what is desired seems to be developing:

1. The multilingualism of the EU both within its institutions and in its relations with its citizens is partially a myth and likely to become harder to sustain with enlargement.
2. In any case the commitment to allow citizens to deal with the polity in their own language is not absolute and only applies to the speakers of the official languages in each state.
3. The EU is committed to democracy but is itself deficient in a number of the basic requirements of a democratic polity, including the space and medium for debate.
4. The majority of the citizens of the member states have made their own decisions on how to respond to the need to communicate across borders. They have rejected the EU call for diversity in the FL curriculum[13] and have chosen to learn and have their children learn English. This choice stems from extrinsic motivation, a conviction that English is currently the language that will contribute most to their life chances.

If this is the reality we should move the debate forward. It seems anachronistic to continue to promote old style cosmopolitan multilingualism of the major official nation state languages. This is top down language planning without bottom up interest or commitment and, on the evidence of all former such attempts, is doomed to failure. It seems foolish to deny the

[13] Of course now that English learning has spread we are witnessing English plus. Those who understand the concept of cultural capital have made sure that their children have the basic requirement – English plus another foreign language useful in their context This does not mean that a language is learnt instead of English.

growing dominance of English in policy formulation, and not seek palliative measures for the imbalances and inequalities it produces. In particular, we should examine

- whether there is any other way of creating the community of communication that a democratic European Union appears to need
- what policies could attenuate the inherent inequity in present and future practice
- what we should beware of in order not to reproduce the inequalities of the nation state era (i.e. a new set of minorities, this time in the supranational political context)
- and what, if anything, could make the spread of English more acceptable.

Van Parijs (2001) has opened the debate on the first point. He presents the problem of justice and multilingualism within the stark structures of philosophical reasoning. Where there are groups in contact that speak different languages, there are only three possibilities that are fair:

> No individual may learn another's language
> All individuals learn all languages of all other groups
> All individuals learn a single lingua franca, which is not the mother tongue of any of them.

Pushing the choices to their logical conclusion he shows the absurdity of the first two propositions. The third is not absurd and provides a solution. Indeed the idea has been proposed in EU circles on a number of occasions. In 1974 Patija and Van der Hek suggested reintroducing Latin as the language of the Europe parliament, taking the model of Israel, where the sacred language has become the language of the state. This suggestion did not find favour, perhaps in part because it favours the Romance language speakers and perhaps in part because of Latin's association with the Catholic Church.

The other possibility is to adopt one of the planned languages. Over the last decades the Esperanto Association has lobbied the EU to consider Esperanto as the solution to its communication dilemma. Intellectually this would be a solution that fulfilled the criteria of justice and efficiency but was never even close to capturing a constituency. There are perhaps again two reasons for the refusal to consider an artificial language. First, those who acquire English have expectations that they will be able to use it in other transnational settings outside Europe. An artificial language used in Europe would have to become a global lingua franca to be able to compete. Second, those who reject artificial languages cite the lack of an associated culture as a reason for not wanting to learn them. This is interesting since this lack of attachment to any territorial group seems a convincing argument for promoting a language such as Esperanto as international lingua franca.

It seems highly unlikely that any serious candidate for lingua franca[14] in Europe will challenge English.[15] This being so, the fairness criterion that the lingua franca should not be a language of a constituent group is bound to be contravened.

So what can be done to make the situation fair if the language of one group within the EU provides the lingua franca used increasingly within the institutions and in much transnational contact? Van Parijs (2001) argues that the existence of a language in common is of benefit to all participants. Since a lingua franca is a common good, he suggests that all should contribute to the costs. This could be done, he suggests by moving the cost of acquisition away from those who have to expend effort to acquire it to those who already have it. He points out that those who are mother tongue English speakers are spared the opportunity costs as well as the actual expense of acquisition. They are at an advantage because they do not need to pay for translation and interpretation and do not need to wait for the translated text. In addition, they are able to exploit a very profitable TESOL industry and actively seek revenue from their privileged language situation. Van Parijs suggests that it is here that here that some recalibration could take place. He makes the case that English speakers within the EU be asked to contribute to funding English acquisition since they benefit from it. However, this is not a debate that the EU can have it while remains committed to a policy of strict language equality within the institutions and promotion of diversity in foreign language education.

The third point in the argument concerns transcendence. When one

[14] The suggestion that there should be several lingua francas is illogical according to Parijs. It is highly inefficient for all to learn several lingua francas and it is the cause of fracture if different groups learn different lingua francas. The proposals for five working languages etc mentioned above serve a political agenda rather than a communicative rationale.

[15] In 2001 the Swedes held the presidency of the European Union and initiated a cyber debate on the following question, "Today the Union has 11 official languages. Enlargement of the EU makes the language issue acute. Should every country be entitled to use its language(s) or should the number of languages be limited?" The response was limited (100 exchanges with many from the same authors). The exchanges were overwhelmingly in English.

first comes to the language debate, the plurilingual argument seems to have the moral high ground, with a monopoly on positive terms, such as 'equality' and 'respect for difference'. In my early thinking on the spread of English I had included human rights as a valid argument of the anti-English camp in the classic way, accepting the argument that English is a threat to the continued existence of small languages and to the right of such speakers to continue to use their languages in all situations and domains. But on reflection, I think that perhaps there is a stronger case to be made for including rights under the pro-English rubric. Excluding any one from learning English through artificially restricting provision in the education system would seem to be a rights issue. If English instruction is withheld from schoolchildren for ideological reasons (e.g. to promote diversity in foreign language learning in the EU) can this be justified if it excludes them from a community it would be to their advantage to join? The case for withholding a skill from some, which so many others now have, seems to me to be difficult to argue. If the individual who through their language learning is contributing to the maintenance of a heritage or to a centuries-old-cross frontier relationship has freely chosen to follow this course, there is no rights issue. However, if an education system limits choice in foreign language acquisition for 'unity in diversity' goals and children are excluded for ideological reasons from learning English, then there may well be a rights issue. The children persuaded or directed to learn another language apart from English and thus as adults excluded from participating in all the networks and forums which increasingly use English (the international research community, transnational commerce, NGOs, supranational politics, as well as the institutions of the EU) are ultimately not served well. Perhaps it should be argued that it is a human right to learn the language of power and that to be excluded for whatever reason will make new disempowered linguistic minorities.

Perhaps these opposing views on what is required for a proper acknowledgement of language rights stem from the dual nature of language. On the one hand, language is communication. Utilitarian, it permits association, planning, a common project and the execution of plans. On the other hand, language is bound closely with identity (see also May, this volume). Symbolic, it embodies who we are, enmeshes us in our group and, more than any other attribute, constructs its boundaries. Thus there is likely to be conflict where we need to use one language to accomplish the projects that take us outside our group, but another to maintain our identity within it.

This seems to be the crux of the problem in the EU. At a philosophical and policy level, the EU needs to respect the identity dimension of language and cannot be seen to condone or promote a hierarchy where one group's language is promoted above another. At the pragmatic level the growing networks of the EU need a medium of communication, and strict language equality cannot deliver this. Thus where the need to lobby, to defend one's interest, advance one's cause, argue one's case is paramount, people tend to do this in the way most likely to succeed and if this means using the language that will reach the greatest number, the pragmatic solution is accepted. The medium is secondary to the message. However, where the desire to underline group solidarity and membership is more important, then people tend to insist on the right to use their own language. The message becomes secondary to insisting on the medium that is symbolic of identity and demonstrates prime group membership. This explains the mismatch between discourse and practice in the EU. Political rhetoric stresses the symbolic and reiterates the commitment to unity in diversity; every day practice is pragmatic and people use the language in their repertoire that will best further their projects, access the knowledge they require, make the contacts they need and realize their ambitions. If in a multilingual group this has to be the lingua franca, it will be employed.

This argument and the position that it leads me into may be attacked as promotion of English from a mother tongue English speaker, but this is far from my intention. I believe that there are social, economic and political frameworks that must be acknowledged. We can at one level dispute their fairness but in practice we can only act within their parameters. It is thus a desire to understand language practices that challenge current policy stances in the EU and a wish to contribute to a regime that facilitates democratic exchange that motivate this chapter.[16] In pursuit of these aims I would like to put the following points on the agenda for discussion.

Do we really have a model for managing multilingual democracies? The confederal arrangements of Switzerland are always given as an example but the Swiss have not solved the problems of supra-cantonal political association. Where the constituent groups come together in institutions at state level, German is the dominant language and any politician or bureaucrat who cannot speak it is disadvantaged (Département fédéral de l'intérieur 1989). The other examples of successful multilingual polities that are routinely given have also tended to gravitate to a dominant lingua franca at the highest level of political activity (India and South

[16] The hope that consultation and discussion websites could be multilingual has proved overly optimistic. On the Convention chat group web site, for example http://europa.eu.int/futurum/forum_convention/. 83% of the exchanges were in English during the four weeks that I monitored it in spring/summer 2002 (9/8/2002 to 7/9/2002).

Africa, see Stroud and Heugh, this volume). Examples used in the past have broken down completely (Yugoslavia, the USSR) or to have moved to much looser political arrangements (Belgium, Canada). It does seem a desideratum of a stable polity that its citizens imagine themselves to be in a community where communication is possible among all (Anderson 1983). I have not yet seen an argument backed by evidence that shows how those in a multilingual setting that do not have the language of power make their voices heard and defend their interests. Van Parijs' model cuts through the murk here. It is no use if a group has the right to speak in its own language if there is no concomitant legislation that guarantees them the right to be understood.

If it is true that complete multilingual democracy is a myth, does this mean that the alternative is a European Union threatened with English language imperialism as Phillipson (1992, 2000) Skutnabb-Kangas (2000) and others have warned? Does increasing use of English as a lingua franca necessarily entail a capitulation to the philosophies and economic regimes of the states for whom it is a first language? To accept these propositions wholesale would seem to me to be highly essentialist. Of course, it would be wrong to suggest that any natural language could be neutral, and, in the case of English, the legacy of British colonialism and the actuality of American super power dominance make this doubly difficult.[17] However, there is an argument to be made that a language ultimately becomes the possession of those who use it. Pennycook (2000) makes the point that groups have appropriated English for their own purposes, often counter to the Anglophone interests that first promoted it among them. Canagarajah (1999), another key figure in the debate on appropriation, argues that refusing to engage with English unilaterally would let its power go unchallenged. Why should non-English speaking regions and states deprive themselves of the means to interact with other communities? Why should they ghettoise themselves if the language that would serve their interests is English? He believes that non-native speakers of English benefit from the growth of English as a lingua franca, but only if they appropriate the language and in using it make it their own.

---

[17] And as new regions of the world join the English lingua franca network, it is again very evident how language learning tends to be ideologically bound. ELT in Eastern Europe in the late twentieth and early twenty-first century is a complex tale which involves US Peace Corps volunteers, small business consultancies, and resource centres funded by Soros and missionary Christian groups. The close ties between the language and neo-liberalism are clear and many have argued that the discourse of neo-liberalism (in or from English) paves the way for the reality (Bourdieu and Wacquant 2001, Fairclough, 2000).

There are few in Europe who, in Canagarajah's meaning of the term, are appropriating English and making it their own. In Europe at present, English almost always remains auxiliary and there is good reason to think that it will be confined to that role given the deep roots and high prestige of the other languages. The great difference between the present phenomenon and the imposition of a single national language on nation states in the nation building era stems from the fact that English is at present learnt only as a lingua franca for utility and access to knowledge and markets. But even in that position, if it becomes the language that permits political association within the Union, the actual circulation of 'people' and 'services' as opposed to the less linguistically loaded 'goods' and 'capital', it will inevitably lose some of its close identification with the nation states for whom it is a national language. It can never be a neutral[18] medium but it can **also** become the medium of European transnationality and belong to all those who use it in this way.[19]

Since at the moment there appears little chance that English will replace any learners' mother tongue as a first language, learners' competence in the foreign language may remain quite limited both in sophistication and in the domains in which the learners can operate. This is both a bad and a good thing: bad in that a political community that can only communicate in an auxiliary language may well be hampered until competence in certain domains comes through repeated use; good in that if English remains an auxiliary language, in second place to Europeans' first languages, diversity and heritage are preserved. This, of course, is in the short term and what happens in the longer term is quite unpredictable. Siguán, the Catalan sociolinguist, (1996) has pointed out the danger inherent in this situation and sketched the worst-case scenario. As individuals expend

---

[18] While accepting the argument that a language can be adopted as a strategy and then be appropriated by its users, I think we should be wary of accepting any claim that a language can be neutral. The socialization role of the mother tongue and the homogenising function of national languages show that language is a major factor in inclusion and exclusion. The rise and fall of lingua francas throughout history show that they are closely allied with political, economic and cultural dominance. All this makes neutrality unlikely.

[19] The non-essentialist nature of language has been clearly demonstrated by the pan European peace movement active in 2002-2003. Groups from different states opposed to the Anglo-Saxon invasion of Iraq networked to exchange information and co-ordinate protest. Transnational communication among the anti-war groups was mostly in English, the medium of the object of their protest. This was as true of groups networking in the Muslim world (e.g. Sabawoon Online) as of those networking in Europe and America (e.g. APC.org).

immense effort to acquire and perfect a foreign language and less time mastering their own and acquiring high levels of mother tongue literacy, there may come a point when the individual feels more confident in the second language than the first which then becomes dominant. And if Europeanization and globalization together with new modes of travel and information exchange continue to bring about contact on an unprecedented scale, then the patterns of communication that would result might contribute to tipping the balance to a wholesale shift to English.

The best-case scenario, on the other hand, would be the development of a stable diglossia in which political debate and interaction with and within the institutions of the polity took place in an acknowledged language to which all citizens had right of access and in which they acquired competence during their education. No one would thus be excluded and the present hierarchy would be attenuated, at least in so far as it resides on the cultural capital of knowledge of English. At the same time, the Europeans would continue to learn their languages of primary association and socialization. The diglossia would be stable since the supranational language would not be a medium that would routinely fulfil the symbolic identity functions of language, would not be the usual language of affect, socialization or creativity for non MT speakers. Personal bilingualism would be the norm. There would thus be greater equality among the speakers of the official state languages and those of the languages eclipsed in the era of nation state building. We would all be minorities within the EU and the concept of linguistic minority within the polity would become redundant. This is true in a limited way even of English mother tongue speakers who would need to become bidialectal as international English developed.[20]

Political scientists have made the point that constituency and representation came to have different meanings in the late twentieth century. Held *et al.* (1999) noted the inconsistencies and tensions that resulted from a political situation where political power mainly resided with the nation state but where economic power was mostly transnational. I would develop this and say that in the European Union this fundamental difficulty is exacerbated because some political power is now transnational but the demos is still only national. Economic power is mediated through money and can cross cultural and linguistic divides without provoking major social change. Democratic political power, however, is mediated

[20] Understanding the rules and constraints of English as a lingua franca and English MT speakers' need to learn to accommodate are recent focuses of research. See, for example, Seidlhofer 2001.

discursively through language and is constrained by linguistic barriers. Numerous individuals have already overcome these barriers. Putting in place policies to extend this to all citizens to overcome the current social division is going to demand immense social and individual effort, an ability to debate the issues, and, most difficult of all, a successful challenge to the tradition that equated loyalty to the official national language with loyalty to the state. English is, of course, far from being the perfect solution to intra-group communication in Europe, since it is one of these official national languages. However, it seems inevitable that English will be the *de facto* if not *de jure* solution in the foreseeable future, now that it is the most frequently taught foreign language in the education systems of the EU.[21]

The debate at the moment seems to have stalled, in part because there is still lip service being paid to policies, which are widely disregarded, and in part because the issue is being framed in terms of group (state) rights rather than in terms of individual rights.

References

Anderson, B. (1983) *Imagined Communities*, London: Verso.

Bankowski, Z. and A. Scott (1996) 'The European Union?', in R. Bellamy and D. Castiglione (eds) *Papers Presented at the 22nd Conference of the UK Association for Legal and Social Philosophy*, Aldershot: Avebury.

Bellamy, R. (1996) 'The Political Form of the Constitution: the Separation of Powers, Rights and Representative Democracy', in R. Bellamy and D. Castiglione (eds) *Constitutionalism in Transformation*, Oxford: Blackwell.

Birch, A. (1993) *The Concepts and Concepts of Modern Democracy*, London: Routledge.

Bourdieu, P. and L. Wacquant (2001) 'New Liberal Speak', *Radical Philosophy* 105.

Byram, M. (1989) *Cultural Studies in Foreign Language Education*, Clevedon, Multilingual Matters.

Calvet, L.-J. (1993) *L'Europe et ses langues*, Paris: Plon.

Canagarajah, S. (1999) *Resisting Linguistic Imperialism in English Teaching*, Oxford: Oxford University Press.

Castiglione, D. (1995) 'Contracts and Constitutions', in R. Bellamy, V. Bufacchi and D. Castiglione (eds.) *Democracy and Constitutional Culture in the Union of Europe*, Lothian Foundation Press.

---

[21] This is not yet the case for the whole adult population. A recent Eurobarometer survey reported that only 41% of all non-MT English speakers reported that they could use English to some degree.

De Varennes F. (1996) *Languages, Minorities and Human Rights*, The Hague: Martinus Nijhoff.

Duverger, M. (1991) 'L'Europe balkanise, communautaire ou domine?', *Pouvoirs* 57: 129-142.

Eurostat. *Year Book 1993*, Brussels: Office for Official Publications of the European Communities.

Eurydice (1996) *Key data on Education in the EU*, Brussels: Office for Official Publications of the European Communities.

------ (1998) *Key data on Education in the EU*, Brussels: Office for Official Publications of the European Communities.

------ (2000) *Key Data on Education in the EU*, Brussels: Office for Official Publications of the European Communities.

Fairclough, Norman (2000) *New Labour, New Language*, London: Routledge.

Fontana, B. (1992) 'Democracy and the French Revolution', in J. Dunn (ed) *Democracy – the Unfinished Journey*, Oxford: OUP.

Gardner, R. and W. Lambert (1972) *Attitudes and Motivation in Second Language Learning*, Rowley MA: Newbury House.

Grimm, D. (1997) Does Europe need a Constitution?, in: P. Gowan and P. Anderson (eds.) *The Question of Europe, London: Verso.*

Habermas, J. (1992) *Faktizitat und Geltung: Beitrage zur Diskurstheorie des Rechts und des Demokratischen*, Frankfurt-am-Main: Suhrkamp.

------ (1997) *A Berlin Republic: Writings on Germany*, translated by Steven Rendall, Nebraska: University of Nebraska Press.

Held, D., A. McGrew, D. Goldblatt, and J. Perraton (1999) *Global Transformations*, Cambridge: Polity Press.

Hix, S. (2000) *Legislative Behaviour and Party Competition in the EU: An Application of NOMINATE to the Post-1999 European Parliament*. ESRC One Europe or Several Working Paper.

Lively, J. (1975) *Democracy*, Oxford: Blackwell.

Lloyd, G. (1992) 'Democracy, Philosophy and Science in Ancient Greece', in J. Dunn (ed) *Democracy – the Unfinished Journey*, Oxford: Oxford University Press.

Pennycook, A. (2000) 'English, Politics, Ideology: From Colonial Celebration to Postcolonial Performativity', in T. Ricento (ed) *Ideology, Politics and Language Policies: Focus on English*, Amsterdam: John Benjamin.

Phillipson R. (1992) *Linguistic Imperialism*, Oxford: Oxford University Press.

------ (2000) 'English in the New World Order: Variations on a Theme of Linguistic Imperialism and 'World' English', in T. Ricento (ed) *Ideology, Politics and Language Policies: Focus on English*, Amsterdam: John Benjamin.

Pool, J. (1991) ' The Official Language Problem', *American Political Science Review* 85: 95-514.

Rousseau, J.-J. (1954) *The Social Contract*, trans. W. Kendall, Chicago: Henry Regnery.

Rubin, J. (1981) 'The Study of Cognitive Processes in Second Language Learning', *Applied Linguistics* 2(2): 117-131.

Schlossmacher, M. (1994) 'Die Arbeitssprachen in den Organen der Europaischen Gemeindschaft', *Sociolinguistica* 8: 101-122.

Seidlhofer, B. (2001) 'Closing a Conceptual Gap: The Case for a Description of English as a Lingua Franca', *International Journal of Applied Linguistics* 11(2): 133-156.

Seliger, H. (1983) 'Learner Interaction in the Classroom and Its Effects on Language Acquisition', in H. Seliger and M. Long (eds) *Classroom Oriented Research in Second Language Acquisition*, Rowley Mass.: Newbury House.

Shuibhne, N. (2001) 'Language Rules, Language Rights and the EC Administration', Paper given at the workshop *Linguistic Diversity and European Law*, 12/13 November 2001, European University Institute, Florence.

Siguán, M. (1996) *L'Europe de Langues*, Barcelona: Mardaga.

Skutnabb-Kangas, T. (2000) *Linguistic Genocide in Education or World-wide Diversity and Human Rights?*, New Jersey: Lawrence Erlbaum.

Touraine, A. (1997) *What Is Democracy?*, trans. D. Macey, Boulder CO: Westview Press.

Van Parijs, P. (2001) 'Linguistic Justice', Paper given at the workshop *Linguistic Diversity and European Law,* 12/13 November 2001, European University Institute, Florence.

Weiler, J. (1997) 'Legitimacy and Democracy of Union Governance', in G. Edwards and A. Pijpers (eds) *The Politics of European Treaty Reform*, London: Pinter.

Wright, Sue (2000) *Community and Communication: The Role of Language in Nation State Building and European Integration*, Clevedon: Multilingual Matters.

12. Ideological Dilemmas in Language and Cultural Policies in Madrid Schools[1]

LUISA MARTÍN ROJO

1. Introduction

> *(Ordinary thinking) "it contains Stone Age elements and principles of a more advanced science, prejudices from all past phases of history at the local level and intuitions of a future philosophy which will be that of a human race united the world over". (A. Gramsci 1971: 324; from M. Billig 1991: 21).*

During the last decade, schools in the Madrid autonomous region have become multiethnic and therefore multilingual settings. The growing presence of children and teenagers from an immigrant background, in addition to other significant social changes in the education system, such as the extension of compulsory schooling to age 16 and improved access for socially excluded groups or minorities, have led to a situation where, as the legislation indicates today, 'diversity is the rule' in schools and colleges (Regional Plan of Compensatory Education, Community of Madrid, 2000). The research project on which this paper is based arose from a need to understand how this new linguistic diversity is managed, and its social and educational consequences in schools. After all, the study of how diversity is tackled is inseparable from the study of social inequality, and it is this interrelationship that we explore here. This issue, as we shall see, opens up ideological dilemmas for our societies. In order to overcome them, we need to revisit many notions including language skills and identity (along the lines set out by Stephen May in this volume).

Much sociolinguistic research has focused on how linguistic resources are socially controlled and distributed through the education process, and has shown that the way this task is carried out influences the social position and life choices of students (from early works by Labov 1969;

---

[1] This research was financed by the Education Department of the Madrid Autonomous Region (*Proyectos de Investigación en Humanidades y Ciencias Sociales Nº ref.: 06/0122/2000 (2000-2001)*), and received the Second Prize for Social Research from Caja Madrid (2002). Design of the study (definition of objectives and hypotheses, design of the method, observation and interviews guidelines, and the analysis protocol), the coordination of the fieldwork, and the integration of the conclusions were carried out by the author of the present chapter.

Bernstein 1975; and Gumperz 1981 to the more recent work of Heller 2002; Cummins 1997; 2000; Skutnabb-Kangas 2000; and Tusón 2002; Tusón and Unamuno 1999). Schooling involves teaching in the socially legitimated languages forms and varieties characteristic of domin-ant, high status social groups and sectors. Access to this linguistic capital controls students' access to other resources (economic, labour, social, educational, and symbolic) and their social mobility.

Consequently, the way students are taught language skills cannot merely be brushed aside. Acquiring the language which is the medium of education, or its dominant variant, for those on the lowest rungs of the social scale, can certainly palliate social exclusion and enable integration in school. At the same time, however, mastering and competing in a language or variant different from one's own requires additional effort, and so creates inequality. Moreover, unless the underlying situation of social inequality and discrimination is modified, the partial or total acquisition of the dominant language will not in itself prevent social exclusion. As several sociolinguistic studies have shown (starting with Labov's very first study on non-standard English, 1969), the demand that students master and use a given language or variant can exclude or limit a particular sector of the population (social class, ethnic group or gender), and lead to social closure (social domination), constraining access to important social domains such as education. These studies have also shown how such language demands can produce even more perverse effects. In fact, sociolinguistics, sociology and social psychology have revealed the ideology and objectives (assimilative or integrative) that implicitly or explicitly underlie this teaching, and their evident effects on the target student population (see, for example, Labov 1969; Kroch and Labov 1972; Lambert, and Taylor 1986; Bourdieu and Passeron 1977; Bourdieu 1998; Cummins 2000, Heller and Martin-Jones 2001). Often, the teaching of the legitimated language variety implies discrimination against other varieties, in the way it reproduces prevalent linguistic and social values; for instance, the opposition between 'higher', 'cultured', 'elaborated' and 'correct' varieties vs. 'lower', 'uncultured', 'basic or limited' and 'incorrect' varieties, and between languages 'useful' for 'the expression of a culture' and 'worthless' languages that are not seen as 'suitable' for the same purpose (Bourdieu 1982; Martín Rojo 1997). The reproduction of this value scale may even stand in the way of its own goals, impeding the acquisition of the standard varieties and simultaneously encouraging negative attitudes towards learning.

All of this shows that the relationship between equality and diversity is far from simple and that the mere suppression of one of the terms of this opposition (diversity) is not enough to achieve the other (equality). Furthermore, social, political and cultural changes deriving from globalisation highlight the controversial effects of this relationship on a daily basis. These changes have introduced additional elements that further complicate the relationship between diversity and inequality, making it impossible to consider maintaining diversity and achieving equality as separate, even divergent, issues, but as one and the same task.

Nowadays, schools are a key site for observing these changes, as well as how institutions, in this case in the Madrid region, handle the transformation of a formerly homogeneous and predominantly monolingual society into one that is socially, culturally and linguistically diverse. This context also allows us to study how the valuation of the dominant language as a shared and legitimating code coexists with claims for the support of minority languages (regional, native or imported through immigration). These minority claims are not only part of a process of identity building, but also of an incipient perception that the languages in question constitute symbolic capital, a resource to be preserved (see Heller 1999, for an analysis of these changes).

The analysis of educational discourses and practices in this article aims to show how prominent among the manifestations of these changes is the incipient spread and gradual rooting of discourses and ideologies favouring the protection of and respect for diversity in all of its forms. Nevertheless, these discourses and ideologies coexist and often conflict with earlier and more deeply-rooted ideas, such as the perception of diversity as a threat to national unity, the defence of cultural and linguistic assimilation as a prerequisite and strategy for achieving equality, and the interpretation of difference as deficit. Moreover, even where there is recognition of cultural specificity and linguistic heritage, it is not usually accompanied by any real questioning of the subordination of minority cultures to the dominant culture, and so leads to the social segregation of minority groups. In the case of Madrid region we will examine here, this situation has given rise to many contradictions and inconsistencies, in legislation, in the discourses of professionals and academics, and in educational practice.

These issues are of particular interest in the Spanish context. The current Spanish political system (which includes 17 administratively Autonomous Regions) has ostensibly recognised linguistic diversity and the right to the restoration of formerly oppressed heritage languages. On the face of it, this might be taken to entail a conception of the nation-state that is more open to cultural and linguistic plurality. However, this issue is still controversial and dealt with very differently in the different regions. There is also a marked difference between regional and Spanish nationalist discourses on the matter. As Grad and Martín Rojo's (2002) study of parliamentary debate has shown, outside the bilingual regions little importance is given to linguistic and cultural diversity (see also, Martín Rojo 2000). Specifically, in the Madrid region – where the regional and the Spanish nation-state identities largely overlap – there is a general tendency to consider homogeneity and the linguistic and cultural assimilation of immigrants as desirable social goals. According to a survey carried out by a popular radio station in the early months of 2002, a broad majority believed that immigrants should conform, both linguistically and culturally, to the norms of the majority group. Public debate over that year indicates that this tendency is steadily increasing. The government representative for immigration issues, Mr. Fernández-Miranda, declared in the Spanish Parliament that multicultural coexistence is a danger for 'our' democratic culture (February, 26, 2002). This stance is even observable to some extent in autonomous communities that enjoy rights to their own language. As we will see later, while the goal of assimilation clearly indicates that immigrant languages and cultures are accorded a lesser status, it is presented, paradoxically, as a way of bringing about equality of opportunity (section, 6; for the study of this "discourse of equality at the expense of diversity", see also, Bourdieu 1998; Bourdieu and Passeron 1977; Skunabb-Kangas 2000; and Martín Rojo *et al.* 2003).

2. Theoretical Framework

The analysis was approached from two angles. Firstly, from a sociolinguistic perspective, daily linguistic exchanges in schools (in classrooms and playgrounds) were recorded and analysed. These exchanges take place in the dominant language; they enable social agents to carry out their activities, as well as to project social images of diversity, education and themselves. Thus, the analysis focuses upon how these exchanges produce and reproduce the institutional and educational practices of the schools, which in their turn facilitate the implementation of specific educational models, and allow different spaces for diversity. Secondly, and following a discourses analysis perspective, the analysis focuses on the hegemonic ideologies and social representations these daily linguistic exchanges convey, and in their social consequences: that is, how these educational practices are constrained by and at the same time shape the social order (for example, failure in teaching or learning the dominant language will hold back students' qualifications and general progression and lead to the marginalisation of individuals and groups).

Particular attention has been paid to the institutional context because the preferred model of linguistic education in a community not only reflects the community's educational objectives but also the social groups it serves, the ideologies it sustains and the type of society it aims to reproduce. The implementation of educational legislation, linguistic policies and planning regulations not only derives from a social order, it also feeds back into it. By analysing the institutional conditions, we could therefore reveal the relationship between legislation and its effective implementation. In this case, the speed of economic and socio-political change in Spain, especially in the Madrid region (which is a major employer of foreign labour), has resulted in a frequent shortage, both in government and in the schools, of the human, financial and time resources needed to cope with the integration of immigrants. Educational policies have therefore suffered from a certain degree of improvisation, uncertainty, and a tendency to adopt simultaneously methods and procedures that lead to incompatible objectives.

To these ends this research applied two analytical frameworks, *sociolinguistic ethnography* and *critical discourse analysis* (CDA). *Sociolinguistic ethnography* (Heller 1999) is interested in the social regulation of communication in the development of social activity through language use, and in cross- and intercultural interactions in socially relevant domains such as schools. *Critical discourse analysis* has permitted the examination of the social and political effects of discourse and the value socially attributed to it (on this conception of discourse and what the emergence of this field of study means, see, among others, Fairclough and Wodak 1997; Chouliaraki and Fairclough 1999; Martín Rojo 2001).

The qualitative methods of *sociolinguistic ethnography*, such as the observation of natural exchanges and the use of in-depth interviews, allowed us to study both how educational practices are carried out and social ties are established, and how these practices and ties are represented through discourse. In order to study this discursive representation, this research merged the ethnographic perspective with Critical Discourse Analysis (CDA). The combination of both approaches allowed us to compare on the one hand the legislation on education for diversity with its actual implementation in schools, and on the other, educational practices with discourses produced about them. For this we observed interactions in classrooms, and contrasted our observations with the discourse produced by the participants about their educational practices, about languages, and about themselves and their interlocutors. Through these comparisons the role of ideologies in the formulation of educational models and in their application can be highlighted.

For both purposes, we studied five schools (2 primary and 3 secondary) for an observation period of between 3 and 4 months (with the exception of one of the schools). Various types of participant observation were used (both passive and complete participation).[2] Each team researcher[3] was in charge of a task-group in each of the primary and secondary schools studied.

The study sample was made up of five schools from the Madrid Autonomous Region. These were chosen, first of all, according to the number of foreign pupils, resulting in the inclusion of schools in which their presence was significant (CP1, IES2), but also of at least two in which they had less presence (IES1, CP2), so that it was possible to compare what occurred in each case. The second criterion for selection was the educational models and programmes implemented, resulting in the inclusion of schools in which the 'Compensatory Education' programme had been implemented and others in which it had not (IES1);[4] it was thus possible to assess the success or failure of this procedure. Likewise, we were interested in observing schools that applied more innovative models, such as the ELCO ('Home Language and Culture Teaching Programme'), and one such institution was included (IES2), even though finally we could not monitor this programme appropriately. Following a third criterion, it was deemed important to include both primary (CP1 and CP2) and secondary schools (IES1, IES1 and IE3), in order to explore if the profile and performance of staff and pupils changed. Finally, a criterion of location was followed: three of the schools were situated in the centre of Madrid (CP1, IES1 and IES2), one outside (CP2), in a relocation area where there was a traditional presence of gypsy pupils, and one in the mountains to the north,

---

[2] Amongst the different types of participant observation we chose to use both passive participation and complete participation. In the former approach, we aimed to be the least intrusive possible, finding a 'blind point' in the classroom and in the playground to appear as marginal participants (in classrooms, a place out of sight for the majority of students was selected, although this was more difficult in more private places or places restricted by a group, such as the playground). In order to carry out complete participation, our most frequent type, the investigators interacted with the students and carried out the activity that they analyzed. For this second type of observation, the researchers were introduced as trainee teachers, which enabled their full participation.

[3] I would like to acknowledge the collaboration of Esther Alcalá Recuerda, Théophile Ambadiang, Aitana Garí, Laura Mijares and Mª Ángeles Rodríguez Iglesias.

[4] I prefer the term 'Compensatory Education', which is closer to the Spanish term 'compensatoria'. 'Remedial learning' refers more broadly to any kind of educational support.

where there is a significant presence of Moroccan immigrants (IE3). This set of criteria resulted in a significant sample that reflects the current situation in schools in the Madrid Autonomous Region.

3. Linguistic and Cultural Ideologies and their Corresponding Educational Models

This analysis was inspired by the model developed by John Berry (Berry 1990; Berry and Samd 1997) to describe the acculturation strategies of immigrant groups according to their attitudes towards their own culture and towards the host society culture, which we have used as a heuristic tool for this analysis. However, since Berry's model was originally developed to systematize individual responses, not group behaviour, group responses or ideologies, we have modified it significantly, following Grad (Grad 2001; for a similar adaptation, see Montreuil and Bourhis 2001). Furthermore, in this research the model was used to explore the ideological orientations of the majority (government, schools, local teachers, and students) towards immigration and, more specifically, to reveal the ideologies underlying such theories as the deficit and difference theories, their corresponding educational policies (above all linguistic), and their implementation.

This model allowed us to systematize clearly the two basic questions which guide this analysis (see table 1):

1. How are linguistic and cultural diversity considered and dealt with in schools? Specifically, how is the maintenance of minority identity and its cultural and linguistic characteristics valued and facilitated?
2. Are deliberate efforts made to establish and maintain inter-group relationships?

Basic questions		Is the maintenance of minorities' identities and their cultural and linguistic characteristics facilitated?	
		Yes	No
Are deliberate efforts made to establish and maintain inter-group relationships?	Yes	INTEGRATION → **intercultural educational models**	ASSIMILATION → *laissez faire* **educational models**
	No	SEGREGATION → **multicultural educational models**	MARGINALIZATION → **Remedial or compensatory educational models**

Table 1: Linguistic Ideologies and Correlative Educational Models

The combination of the answers to these two questions leads to the four ideology types shown in Table 1 (see, for a detailed presentation, Martín Rojo *et al.* 2003; a close systematisation can be found, for example, in McAndrew 2001).

When the answer to the first question is negative and the answer to the second is affirmative, that is, when maintaining linguistic differences is not promoted but inter-group relations are valued (at least, within the framework of the dominant culture), we find an ideology of assimilation. This ideology tries to dilute or eliminate cultural and linguistic differences by imposing the legitimated forms of the majority, usually on the grounds that this will bring about social equality and perhaps, in this case, the welfare and integration of migrants. (Authors such as Bourdieu 1998; Bourdieu and Passeron 1977; and Skutnabb-Kangas 2000 have studied the current consequences of the maintenance of this model originating in the French Revolution). From the linguistic point of view, what is at stake is the replacement of the vernacular (L1) with the dominant language in a given community (L2). This ideology leads to educational models aimed at the cultural assimilation of students (known as *laissez faire*) and to linguistic substitution. The possibility of making any other changes that may affect the school community is not considered. This model can currently be found in Madrid schools, when the number of pupils with 'special needs' is less than 25% per academic stage.

A second ideology arises from a negative response to both questions, that is, maintaining diversity is not encouraged, nor are inter-group relationships valued. This ideology of marginalization is seldom explicitly stated, because to do so would be perceived as socially undesirable and even to violate the fundamental rights of immigrants. However we have often found professionals who maintain that in order to achieve social equality, linguistic and cultural differences have to be eliminated because they are perceived as sources of marginalization. Furthermore, it is claimed that separation into specific groups is a temporary tactic to achieve assimilation. This position leads to compensatory models of education (*educación compensatoria*), of the kind prevalent in the Madrid region.

In Spain there is a legal framework common to all Autonomous Regions, regulated at the time of this study by the *Ley Orgánica de Ordenación General del Sistema Educativo* (LOGSE) [Organic Law Regulating the Educational System] of 1990, passed under the Socialist government. This introduced important changes related to discourse and programmes in relation to equality, sociocultural integration and democratization in the educational system. Nevertheless, the LOGSE opted for Compensatory Education, at a time when the immigration phenomenon was not as significant has it has since become. The recently-passed *Ley de Calidad* [Law on Quality in Education] refers specifically to social inequality and cultural differences, albeit from a more conservative ideology than the previous law. In addition, however, given the devolution of powers to the regions, each Autonomous Region has generated its own legislation for developing the basic laws proposed by central government. Madrid has opted decisively for Compensatory Education (Resolution of September 4, 2000 and the *Plan Regional de Compensación Educativa* [*Regional Plan of Compensatory Education*], 2000)

From a linguistic point of view, this model is highly contradictory: languages are, after all, learned through interaction with their speakers, not through isolation from them. As in the assimilative ideology, diversity is seen as source of a social inequality, and there is an attempt to make it invisible in order to facilitate the learning of the host language and culture. This however devalues and relegates the immigrant's own culture, and actually reinforces segregation to the extent that it fails to achieve the required educational outcomes.

The third ideology in our outline arises from an affirmative answer to the first question and a negative answer to the second. It means that an immigrant's identity and cultural and linguistic characteristics can be maintained, but inter-group relationships are not encouraged. This may be characterised as an ideology of segregation, in which cultural and linguistic differences are respected but remain outside or subordinated to the majority forms. Here, there is some response to the diversity dilemma, but the issue of social inequality remains unresolved. The most extreme expression of this position is reflected in the motto *"Puesto que somos diferentes, vivamos separados"* ('Since we're so different, let's live separately'), which appears, for instance, in France, in extreme right political campaigns (see Todorov 1989). This ideology has led to the emergence of uncritical multicultural educational models which usual include some degree of segregation. In schools in the Madrid Autonomous Region, activities aimed at incorporating the cultural and religious diversity of pupils are limited to parties and other extracurricular activities, so that they do not affect curricular content or the way it is taught. Frequently, not only do they establish an 'us' and 'them' situation, but even show a marked paternalism and folklorization in the way they treat difference; at times, they even appear to teach gypsy and immigrant pupils to represent the stereotype of gypsy or foreigner.

The fourth ideology arises when the answer to both questions is affirmative, that is, when maintaining diversity is favoured, and inter-group relations are also promoted. Here we find an integrative ideology allowing linguistic and cultural difference to be maintained, and the incorporation of new languages and cultures into the host culture. From this perspective, the host community becomes open to a multilingual reality as part of its daily interactions. At the linguistic level, there would be an increasing trend towards bilingualism and interculturalism, with teaching in both L2 and in students' home languages and cultures. Intercultural educational models involve the reorganization of schools and the introduction of changes in curricular content, which have to incorporate knowledge related to the different languages and cultures of the pupils, and to different cultural values, perceptions, concepts, and views. Despite European policies (Resolution A3-03999/92), in Madrid we have not found examples of this type of educational practice, which entails the empowerment of minorities, by means of questioning ethnocentrism, avoiding segregation and seeking common ground and meeting points. The encouragement of mutual knowledge is emphasized, and the development of ways of living together in which everyone is represented and to which everyone has to adapt.

These four ideologies are, of course, theoretical types that can be enriched or constrained in their implementation. Indeed, such nuancing became one of the objectives of this research. In Spain, schools enjoy quite a broad autonomy and freedom to adapt general regulations to their needs. Sometimes, then, rigid models become much more flexible and open to different forms. In other cases, the opposite happens and the implementation of models leads to a metamorphosis in their aims. Whatever model is adopted, society should be ready to give it the human and financial resources it needs and should share to some extent its underlying ideology. A major goal of this research is to reflect on educational regulations and practices, and to help clarify their underlying values, ideologies, and goals.

Finally, it should be pointed out that in order to identify the ideology underlying a given educational model it is necessary to study the results obtained through its application. We have already mentioned how the attention paid to diversity and intergroup relationships is linked to the success or failure of the educational process, both in relation to the majority, who will be educated or not to live in a multicultural or intercultural reality, and to the minority, giving rise to situations of segregation, assimilation integration or marginalization.

Thus, we understand integration as an active process for all the parties involved, which if it is successful will have positive effects at the following levels:

1. academic: improvement of marks and possibilities for advancement of pupils, but also higher quality and more breadth in the curriculum;

2. social: better relations among students, between teachers and students, and among teachers;
3. linguistic: better competence in the second language and the first language of foreign pupils, and the possibility that home students (monolingual) will learn other languages.

It is essential to study the results obtained with the different ideologies and models presented if we are to assess the appropriateness of maintaining them, rejecting them, modifying them or reinforcing them. The analysis of these results helps clarify the meaning or motivation underlying the choice of objectives, target groups and actions of the different educational models and the different theories. Finally, this framework will enable us in the following sections to explore what happens in the Madrid Autonomous Community, and what are the dominant ideologies, models and practices.

4. The Analysis of the Discourses

In this section we will examine the discourse produced both by the government and by professionals, and to a lesser extent by students, and their underlying ideologies.

The government's discourse points to a notion of integration which seems on first reading to be compatible with an intercultural ideology and model, as in the following examples:

> (1) La total integración de las minorías étnicas en el sistema escolar debe ir acompañada del respeto a la diferencia, lo que implica el reconocimiento mutuo de la expresividad y la creatividad de las diferentes culturas que la convivencia plural y democrática exigea la Comunidad de Madrid ... (*Plan Regional de Compensación Educativa*, 12-13).
>
> The full integration of ethnic minorities in the educational context must be coupled with *respect for differences*, implying mutual acknowledgement of the expressivity and creativity of different cultures that are required for plural, democratic coexistence in the Madrid Region (*Regional Plan of Compensatory Education*,12-13).[5]

However, as Esther Alcalá's analysis of the legislation shows (Alcalá, 2002), this concept of integration encompasses different and even contradictory meanings. Thus, despite the fact that intercultural education is

[5] My emphasis. The same applies to all the examples of discourse analyzed here.

presented as the main objective of the *Regional Plan of Compensatory Education*, subsequent decrees elaborating this plan focus almost exclusively on remedial education, and this is targeted exclusively at a particular sector of students rather than the whole community.[6]

> (2) El plan se desarrollará desde el principio de normalización y atención a la diversidad. Es decir, la atención educativa a los alumnos con necesidades de compensación se realizará en el marco de las instituciones y servicios existentes para el conjunto de la población, procurando su adaptación a las características de ese alumnado y su correspondiente aplicación mediante programas específicos.
>
> This plan will be developed according to the principles of 'normalization'[7] and attention to diversity. In other words, educational attention to students needing compensatory education will be provided within mainstream institutions and services, and will be adapted to the characteristics of these students and applied accordingly through specific programmes.

---

[6] Furthermore, as Alcalá's analysis also indicates, even the semantic and syntactic structures in which the process 'integrate' and the noun 'integration' appear show that this measure is understood to be the majority's contribution to a task to be carried out by others, immigrants. As in everyday language, the word 'integration' is often used as a euphemism for 'adaptation' (they have to integrate). To compound the confusion, these students who have to 'integrate' themselves are presented in the discourse in the semantic role of 'beneficiaries' of the beneficient action of others, rather than as agents, ("integration of educationally disadvantaged students").

[7] There are problems in translating 'normalización'. In this context, the term seems to mean to develop linguistic and cultural 'norms', in accordance with what is understood as normal in society, through compensatory education. This meaning, which evokes the idea of the 'norm', is close to the understanding of normalization as a process of 'domestication'. In fact, the process called by Foucault 'normalization' is a narrowing and impoverishment of human possibilities, linked to the exercise of power and its internalization. However, this interpretation seems to contradict the also stated attention to diversity in this context. Even so, it seems clear that the term 'normalization' does not refer here to a process of making the presence of social and cultural differences become the norm (the 'normal' situation). It is in the latter sense that the term is used in Spanish sociolinguistic tradition, where it has come to mean more than standardization (i.e. more than the development of 'norms' of speech and spelling), and seems to refer to a process of making the use of a minority language the norm in contexts formerly reserved for the majority language.

In terms of the proposed model, then, the decrees and measures proposed by the Plan point towards remedial or compensatory goals and are apparently geared towards assimilative goals.

As Alcalá indicates, the fact that these 'specific measures' are targeted at people of highly varied origins all of whom are assigned to a social position of rejection and marginalization ('underprivileged') is one factor that patently reveals a failure to recognise that all groups, communities and social sectors need to be prepared equally to understand and deal with linguistic differences and differences in linguistic and non linguistic usage:

> (3) Las actuaciones de compensación educativa se desarrollarán en centros que escolaricen a minorías étnicas o culturales, en situación de desventaja socioeducativa, a otros colectivos desfavorecidos, con desfase educativo (...) así como con dificultades de inserción educativa y necesidades de apoyo derivadas de la incorporación tardía al sistema educativo, de escolarización irregular, y en el caso del alumnado inmigrante y refugiado, del desconocimiento de la lengua vehicular del proceso de enseñanza (Orden Ministerial del 22 de Julio de 1999, BOE nº 179, de 28 de Julio de 1999).
>
> Compensatory education programmes will be developed in schools teaching students from ethnic and cultural minorities, who are socially or educationally disadvantaged or belong to other underprivileged groups with an educational gap, (...) as well as those experiencing difficulties of assimilation into the educational system and those who need support due to their late incorporation into the system, to irregular schooling, and, in the case of immigrant or refugee students, to a lack of knowledge of the vehicular language used in the educational process (Order of the 22th July 1999, BOE nº 179, 28th July 1999).

In examples like this, we find a discursive strategy of 'association' and a lack of differentiation between different social groups and peoples (van Leeuwen 1996), such that differences and deficits are inextricably linked. On many occasions, the implementation of these compensatory education programmes lumps together students who do not speak Spanish and students with cognitive problems, lack of motivation, curricular gaps, or other problems. People with extremely different needs are therefore grouped together in the compensatory classrooms, except when the number of students enables provision of a separate Spanish as a Second Language programme (known as *castellanización* [Castilianisation]; a term that evokes other assimilationist policies, like the 'Norwegianisation' of the Sámi). Hence, what is proposed is a compensatory model with segregative aims, dressed in integrative language. Legislative discourse as well as that of teachers and students shows that this issue is a controversial one for society at large.

Thus, both in, government and professional discourses these appraisals are at best ambivalent and at worse manifest explicit contradictions. As in the previous example, the coexistence of positions which are hard to reconcile shows how both in legislation and among professionals, positive valuations of difference are more often found in declarations of intent, although they do point towards an emerging discourse valuing cultural and linguistic diversity, at times imported from European Union legislation (Resolution A3-03999/92, DOCE, the 21 January 1993) or academic debate. This however does not trickle down in any significant way into policy or practices.

What we have here is a double standard or 'double discourse' evident for instance among teachers who say that conserving the mother tongue is relevant while at the same time they conceptualize these students not as bilinguals but as merely lacking Spanish skills. Even when speakers advocate the inclusion of other languages and cultures, as in example (4), using the emerging 'ecological' discourse that compares linguistic and cultural diversity with biological diversity, they still end up fuelling existing dilemmas, as we shall see later. Meanwhile, the expression 'language problem' is becoming more widespread: "the students have a language problem" which often appears insurmountable, as in example (5).

> (4) Yo tendría aquí un departamento de chino con profesores de chino, y un departamento de árabe con profesores de árabe; y eso enriquecería nuestra cultura de una manera...notable. Incluso en las religiones. (Profesor secundaria)
>
> I would have a Chinese department here with teachers of Chinese and an Arabic department with teachers of Arabic; and that would…notably enrich our culture. Even in religion. (Secondary school teacher)
>
> (5) otros "van a encontrar el problema del idioma (…) y tengo mis dudas, incluso, de si van a sacar el graduado escolar" [nota de la entrevistadora: las dos niñas chinas – en especial una – quieren ir a la universidad] "encuentran dificultades muy grandes en las asignaturas que tienen como elemento básico la lengua española". (Profesor secundaria)
>
> others say "they are going to come across language problems (…) and I even have my doubts about whether they will graduate" (inter-

> viewer's note: these two Chinese girls – one in particular – want to go to University) "they encounter great difficulties in the subjects whose basic element is the Spanish language". (Secondary school teacher)

As in the previous examples, produced by the same speaker, so here we see the same contradiction between abstract and concrete plans, between legislation and its implementation.

The real life situation in the schools further highlights this contradiction. Often, we find monolingual teachers and students from an immigrant background, who speak more than one language or know other varieties of Spanish. Observation in schools shows how, despite the linguistic capital of the students, the schools remain completely monolingual communities. No other language than Spanish is used, except in small, separate groups, and always outside the classroom. In the classes we observed, teachers do not usually stimulate the use of different languages and their variants, and this is confirmed by our interviews. In certain cases, even the use of Latin American variants of the Spanish language was corrected as wrong and the use of other languages was considered to be done in bad faith: "that's cheating" or "they do that to annoy us or so that we don't understand them". Minority language rights are not recognized, and minority languages are seen as 'regressive' (maintaining the existence of ethnolinguistic differences), and as obstacles to social mobility and 'integration' (understood as assimilation).

In this 'double discourse', characteristic of times of change, we find that although it has incorporated a better appraisal of multilingualism and affects an integrative ideology, the deficit view remains deeply rooted (see Fairclough's (1992) discussion of the phenomenon of 'double discourse' in times of ideological change, which he calls 'heterogeneous discourse').

The genesis of this 'double discourse' is found in the new discourses on difference that are still anchored, in Moscovici's terms (see Moscovici 1961, 1994; Jodelet 1988) in previously held beliefs and specifically in a deeply rooted sense, associated with deficit theory, that difference requires help. We have often observed this among our teacher informants and, judging by recent public debates, also in Spanish society at large.

Equality is then understood in terms of nationalist principles of linguistic and cultural homogeneity. This position is frequently encountered in Spain even among educational sociologists and teachers. Later, I will link the prevalence of these 'double discourses' to emerging ideological dilemmas. In monolingual Spanish regions, it would appear that bilingualism itself is not understood; in fact, some teachers seem to consider it as highly improbable or unlikely. For instance learning Spanish is perceived as incompatible with maintaining the mother tongue, and bilingualism is not seen as a cognitive and social advantage. Linguistic 'competence' is understood according to monolingual criteria, or in terms of some mythical or idealised 'native speaker' (see Rampton 1995 on this concept).[8] However, even in Spanish bilingual communities the situation is far from being simple (Molina and Maruny, in press).

Similarly, the assimilation of the customs, values and particularly the language of the majority is viewed as the solution to all problems of discrimination and social rejection, despite evidence gathered throughout the world that the situation is far more complex. Full assimilation is never possible. The equality discourse therefore leads to covert inequality, and reveals prejudices and social discrimination.

In the lived reality of the schools, social and economic factors come into play, relating to the social and working conditions of teachers, which reinforce a given implementation of the model of compensatory education made by the regional government, and increase rather than palliate the risks entailed. As we see in example (6), although positive value judgments are often made when the issue of difference is dealt with in the abstract outside the classroom, the contrary occurs inside the classroom where teachers do not know how to approach it practically:

> (6) *se comenta/decide en las evaluaciones el ponerles juntos o separados en clase*? "Al principio, en la primera evaluación, (…) las tres niñas estaban juntas (...) o sea estaban por amistad, (…) o los ponían por orden alfabético" Más tarde, algunos profesores se quejaron de que cuando salían a apoyo los chinos "las clases quedaban como muy desperdigadas (…) porque los chinos estaban como más repartidos (…) optaron por ponerlos... situar una clase ideal con los que no eran de apoyo, los flexibles, y luego colocar a los flexibles aparte. Entonces en la segunda evaluación lo que se hizo fue (…) lo que es al lado de la ventana y en medio, los españoles. Y luego, lo que es en la pared a los chinos" [!!!!!]. Están "separaditos; y no hablan con nadie". "Claro, cuando ellos no estaban, la clase era perfecta, porque están todos unificados, bien, el profesor los tenía bien controlados, bien situados, pero cuando venían los otros... se quedaban ahí los chinos solos y luego, pues claro, no los.... no los movían" (profesora 2 del SS3)

[8] Following this, bilingualism is impossible if it is imagined as a simple doubling of two monolingual competences; if 'language X' is also seen as a mark of ethnic belonging, then two national identities may also be seen as incompatible.

> Q: *Do you decide / comment in tests whether to place them in the classroom together or separately?*
> Initially, in the first term (...) the three Chinese girls were together...either because they were friends (...) or because they'd been placed in alphabet-ical order. Later, some teachers complained that when the Chinese students left the class for the compensatory lesson, the rest of the class was very scattered (...) because the Chinese were spread out (...) they decided to put them...to form an ideal class with those who were not in the compensatory programme together, and to separate those who are. So in the second test at the end of the term what happened was (...) the Spanish were over by the window and in the middle. The Chinese were next to the wall [!!!!!!!]. They're completely separate; and they don't talk to anybody. Of course, before they came the class was perfect because everybody mixed, the teacher had them under control, but when the others arrived... the Chinese were left on their own over there and then, obviously, they didn't move them (teacher 2 of SS3).

It is certainly true that in these examples, teachers and the Administration articulate opinions that are simultaneously excluding and prejudiced, tolerant and inclusive (similar variations and contradictions in opinions, attitudes and ideologies have been found by Wetherell and Potter 1988; van Dijk 1987; Billig *et al.* 1988). We can also see how integrating and respectful positions on diversity have positive effects in speakers' face work. But, as Blommaert and Verschueren (1998) observe regarding the concept of tolerance in immigration policies in Belgium, this is often understood in a superficial, patronising way. Furthermore, the incorporation of these inclusive stances raises many related and controversial issues (see section 6). We shall now move to the analysis of the practices.

5. Analysis of Educational Practices

Given this discursive confusion, and our analytical framework, in the design of this research I proposed two main objectives in our study of schools, to try to answer the same two main questions, this time posed in an open manner: "how was maintaining linguistic diversity and inter-group relationships made possible?", and "how were intercommunity relations promoted or not?". In order to do this, different domains within schools were observed, from the organisation of educational projects to the attitudes of students, parents and teachers. From this observation the prevalent linguistic ideologies underlying educational models, practices and discourses were analysed.

The comparative study of primary and secondary schools was undertaken using an observation guide on the following topics:

– the school (the centre and its environment, the student and the teachers, the sociolinguistic order);
– multilingualism and multiculturalism management (the educational project, the rules and their application, the specialized staff etc.); and the teaching of L2 and L1.

In the assessment which follows, of the models applied and the manner of their application. I draw on data on the social and linguistic order in the schools, which it is not appropriate to present here in its full detail.

5.1. A Practical Example: The Management of Multilingualism

The inconsistencies and contradictions stemming from the legislation on this type of education and the adaptations made to it in practice produce standardising and homogenising outcomes that in turn are in most instances assimilative. And it is in the area of language where this is brought out most clearly. In this section, we show the outcomes of the educational models and procedures that we found in the management of multilingualism. Some of the data used in this section are collated from another research project directed in Madrid by Laura Mijares and carried out by both research groups.[9]

The main languages found in the schools were those from the Afro-Asiatic Semitic group, such as Arabic (the Moroccan variety), and some varieties from the Berber family, in particular those spoken in the north of Morocco. There was a notable presence of other African languages (Niger-Congo), especially Bantu languages, such as Bubi and Fang. Sino-Tibetan languages are also represented, such as Mandarin and some varieties from Zhejiang province (Nandian, Quindian and Wenzhou), as well as Austronesian languages from the Malay–Polynesian language family such as Tagalog. Obviously, we noted the presence of European languages, in particular Eastern European ones, such as Polish and Bulgarian, and Romance languages, especially French, the second most important language of communication of immigrants from Africa. Portuguese was also found, and to a lesser extent Italian.

Regrettably, despite the presence of members of the gypsy population

[9] "Multilingual Cities", directed by the University of Tilburg, Holland, and by the Taller de Estudios Internacionales Mediterráneos (TEIM), in the Universidad Autónoma de Madrid (see Broeder and Mijares, 2003).

we were unable to find any trace of one of the most wide-spread European languages, Romany, and its Spanish variety, Caló. In some schools we registered students who are competent in the languages of the bilingual autonomous communities in Spain, although we do not have enough data to establish how many students speak them and how they were learned. We also noted some (varieties of) Pidgin English spoken in Africa, such as Pichi. It is therefore quite common to find among the older, first generation of immigrant students people who are bi- or even trilingual, speaking a native sub-Saharan language, for example, as well as Pidgin and French, or – a frequent combination – Moroccan Arabic, a Berber language and French. Side by side with these are found many varieties of Spanish, particularly Ecuadorian, Colombian, Dominican, Peruvian, Cuban, and the Spanish spoken in Equatorial Guinea and in the Iberian peninsular.

Despite this linguistic richness, nothing seems to indicate that these languages will continue to be part of the linguistic heritage of their speakers, particularly the youngest ones. In fact, pupils say that they use their mother tongue only at home and with their parents, and to a much lesser extent with their brothers and sisters, with whom they often speak Spanish as they do with their classmates and friends. Teenagers sometimes use their mother tongues with their brothers and sisters and class mates, but as these languages are not taught in schools and their use is not stimulated, they master only an oral variety of the language or non-standard dialects, which are not valued as exchange languages. (This happens with some Berber varieties and some of the varieties spoken in the Chinese provinces). All this indicates that they will end up losing these languages without learning more widespread varieties (Classical Arabic, the Moroccan dialect, Mandarin etc).

Because Home Language and Culture teaching programmes (ELCO programmes) run in very few schools, there is no protection policy for these languages in actual fact, and when the programmes are available, they rarely have institutional support, which is provided only for Portugal and Morocco, although this Arabic programme barely functions (see also Fanzé and Mijares 1999). We are far from accepting minority language education as a public good and its state-funded provision as a public right, which as May (2003) indicates, is an important and necessary first step if minority language rights are ever to be established more fully in modern nation-states.

Despite the linguistic capital of the students, schools are completely monolingual communities. Very few teachers showed an interest in the languages known by their students. For that reason we hardly ever saw these languages being used as an educational tool, for instance to encourage classmates to help new arrivals to understand the lessons, or even to stimulate an interest in linguistic and cultural diversity among all students and mutual understanding.

A training programme for teachers seems to be urgent, at least to provide them with the tools to determine whether students' mistakes are loan-translations from their mother tongues or whether they are just normal mistakes at a given stage of L2 acquisition. Such a programme would also encourage teachers to perceive these students as multilingual people, who have simply not completed their learning of Spanish, rather than as people with a deficit who do not know the language used in an educated context.

All of our observations thus far indicate that there is strong pressure to assimilate and that multilingualism is not seen as capital, but rather as a barrier to mutual understanding and to adapting to the educational system. Equality is not achieved, since in order for students to attend special classes in the dominant language, they are steered away from courses that would enable them to get their diplomas and get ahead. These findings show that it is not enough to superficially take on board a discourse in favour of integration. At the same time, adherence to an intercultural model is not possible until some of the dilemmas explained in the following section are tackled.

5.2. Adaptation of the Educational Models: The Different Schools

Still using Berry's model as our heuristic tool for examining ideologies and the handling of language in the schools, we found the assimilating and the compensatory models to be dominant. However, all the schools adapt these models in their integrating efforts.

In secondary school 1 (IES1) compensatory education had not yet been adopted, because of the number of pupils whose parents are immigrants or who are themselves immigrants (less than 25 students with special needs in each educational cycle).[10] In this school, the teachers themselves assume the task of using specific activities within the classroom to bolster the students. There is no segregation in this school. Some complementary activities of a multicultural nature are also carried out. Effectively, then, the assimilation model is implemented, ensuring inter-group relationships (established on the basis of the majority language and customs), but it is

[10] The school has 353 students aged between 14 and 17, according to data from the final term of the academic year 2000/2001. Of these, 60 are of foreign origin, that is, 17% of the total. In IES2 this figure is 20.36%, and in CP1 it reaches 80%.

adapted and enriched with other activities, and, given the number of students (17%), personalised. This tailor-made adaptation obtained relatively good results.

The compensatory model is carried out in the remaining schools examined. This programme does not seek segregation in principle, or at least not openly, but this is what it produces. In fact, if the intended transitory nature of this procedure is not respected, or if students who follow these programmes do not pass or do not get a qualification, this system clearly produces social inequality.

We have however found adaptations of this model, some of which stress segregation, whilst others try to attenuate this effect and to be more integrative. Amongst the most integrative adaptations, one from a primary school (CP1) stands out. Its high percentage (80%) of students from an immigrant background make it one of the most multicultural schools in Madrid. It achieves an integrative adaptation of the compensatory system by means of 'flexible groupings' in which the Spanish language is taught for an hour each day to the whole student body. Groups are identified by colour names, to avoid any identification by level of proficiency in Spanish.

This school (CP1) also has other compensatory education programmes, which we shall not discuss here. The most outstanding feature of this school is the number of students from an immigrant background, which necessarily leads to changes (like the 'flexible groupings') in how the school is run. Their influx can be also attested in the enrichment of the (local and foreign) students' cultural background. In this primary school, students show an impressive knowledge about some languages of Africa and Asia – for instance, names of the languages, systems of writing, usual terms and expressions, etc. – and about the situation of different countries. We have also observed some differences in the subjects they learn (topics like reasons for immigration, poverty in the world are examined), and in some interpersonal norms adopted in class and in the playground (successful strategies of intercomprehension). This, together with the procedures that avoid segregation, suggests that little by little a multicultural and enriching atmosphere, unknown in other schools, naturally occurs.

Although the legislation provides for a weak form of compensatory teaching (for only a limited number of hours, and only in subjects requiring less use of social skills), in the schools we studied we found certain traits that make it worse than the application of this model in other countries. One improvement would be to distinguish clearly between students with curricular gaps and those needing to develop their second language, so that compensatory training could at least be given during specific school periods and be clearly understood as language training (targeted at those who have just joined the school or have another language). This would make it more clearly focused and diminish its segregating effect. The example of 'complementary action' has already been implemented in Catalonia with the *Talleres de Adaptación Escolar* (TAE, School Adaptation Workshops) and in other European countries, with programmes such as PRISMA in the Netherlands. The Madrid Autonomous Community has just announced for the academic year 2002/2003 the introduction of induction classes that will be called *Aulas de Enlace* (Link Classes), as a preliminary step before students are placed in the mainstream teaching programme.

At the time of this research, only the school with the highest number of students from an immigrant background, a school with more than 18 different nationalities speaking a notable variety of languages (IES2), seems to be moving in this direction. In this secondary school, thought is given to the consequences of compensatory teaching and its shortcomings. An effort is therefore made to differentiate students who need preliminary language training from those who have other problems. Through this system, the schools come close to providing an initial language immersion course that can later be completed with other types of procedures and policies.

Among the less integrative adaptations, those found in schools CP2, IES3 stand out. In these schools, compensatory education is applied without distinguishing between linguistic and non-linguistic competence (that is, between second language acquisition and curricular gaps), while it increases the number of hours these students spend in separate groups.

To sum up, we see on the one hand that efforts have been made towards integrative adaptations of the proposals developed by the government. Regrettably, a series of circumstances concurs to increase the effect of segregation of this compensatory education. Circumstances such as mixed classrooms, high student/teacher ratios, the loss of motivation of the staff, who are distressed and disappointed by educational reforms and the lack of appropriately trained human resources, impel other adaptations that increase the negative effect of compensatory education. The survival of an ideology of social equality based in linguistic assimilation works in the same direction. In this context it becomes easier, indeed often the only solution, to separate out any pupils with linguistic difficulties, or who have come from schools with different curricula, traditions, and customs.

What we have seen up to now shows that we are in a transitional stage, but also that the majority of educational models chosen by schools to deal with linguistic diversity are also predominantly assimilationist. We have also seen that there is a wide variety of configurations depending on the way the state, regional and local dimensions interact, and also on the interaction between the existence or absence of social policies and the will and need to respond to specific situations experienced on a daily basis. It is also evident that many efforts are made but that they are unfortunately not always coordinated. Nor are they articulated around principles and policies, which means that effort is often wasted.

6. Ideological Dilemmas: Some Concluding Thoughts

In the government discourse, and in teachers' discourse, as is usually the case in times of change, there are internal contradictions that in turn generate and convey confusion or enhance certain specific applications. Obviously, these mixed discourses are linked to significant social changes that are taking place, such as gradual changes in gender relations, the increasingly unbearable gap in the distribution of wealth between the North and the South, and the increase in migration. What is most interesting is that these 'double discourses', as I have called them, circulate even in academic debate, and the same is true of professionals in performing their educational function. Here, they reveal ideological dilemmas that do not seem easily resolvable. The problematic nature of these debates is attested in the fact that they are constructed as oppositional, as a choice between two mutually exclusive terms (opting for equality or for respecting diversity). Because this research on these dilemmas is still in progress, in this section I will explore only a few key elements.

The first dilemma raised is how to tackle inequality in education. On this issue, it is common to find that questions such as how to understand and acknowledge culture, or how to achieve equality through the redistribution of material and symbolic resources, are conceived as if they were independent or even antagonic struggles (Fraser 2000). As Bourdieu suggests (1982), in a discourse purporting to pursue equality, the rules of play are actually based on the majority standards and language, with which it is often difficult to compete.[11] It is surprising to note just how deeply rooted is the notion that in order to achieve equality, there must be assimilation. The basic assumption is that only people who are identical can be equal.

This trend is undoubtedly reinforced in Spain, since Spanish nationalism

---

[11] This idea is developed in Alcalá's research (2002).

is ethnic;[12] shared historical and cultural aspects (i.e. language, traditions, myths, and the original community), are stressed as the basis for belonging to the group and of group identity (as opposed to 'civic' nationalism which is based on citizenship and emphasises belonging to a political unity).[13] Ethnic nationalism emphasises the distinction between the group and the others, setting out rigid and impermeable boundaries as well as exclusive criteria for belonging. This is why it becomes complicated to have two different national identities at once, or to integrate others into the national group. Rather, integration requires that people manifest the proper criteria for belonging, that is, language, traditions, loyalty, etc. It is precisely this which leads us to believe that in other historical regions and nationalities the situation is not necessarily the same as it is in the Madrid region (Grad, 2001).

As Billig notes (1991: 22), "speakers are located within the general flow of history, and historical changes in the argumentative context alter the meaning of an expressed opinion". Hence, in the present context, forced assimilation, in multicultural schools, in democratic societies, can no longer be understood as a liberating political action. Furthermore, this dilemma is particularly evident in a new socio-cultural context where people claim the right to be different, and multiculturality is perceived as wealth, the heritage of individuals and their communities. It is not surprising in this context to find government promoting educational methods and procedures such as compensatory education which tend to standardise and homogenise everything that is different whilst postponing indefinitely such problems as the promotion of several languages or including intercultural content throughtout the different subjets in the curriculum.

The second dilemma is related to teaching and maintaining languages: it is perceived as impossible to integrate cultural components and different languages in the same subject. An essentialist, homogenous, and simplistic understanding of identity and culture prevails, meaning that the incorporation of new cultural traits (for, instance, a second language) seems to be considered as not compatible with the maintenance of previous cultural traits (or languages). As May indicates (this volume), the arguments

---

[12] Previous studies have shown historical (Riquer 1996), anthropological (Stallaert 1998), socio-psychological (Grad 1999), evidence of 'ethnic' codes of discourse in Spanish nationalism.

[13] The distinction between the two ideal types of nationalism, ethnic and civic, has become classical in political science. Because these are prototypical categories established for analytical description, they are never found in a pure state, but rather tend to be combined (see Grad 2001).

associated with this understanding present the maintenance of the home language as linked to preserving one's original identity, while acquiring the language and culture of the host community is considered useful, and associated with greater integration, social progress and success. Nevertheless, experience shows that both are useful; both facilitate integration and are mutually compatible. On the other hand, losing one's first language and not fully acquiring a second language seem to lead inevitably to marginalisation. However, as students in the multilingual schools of Madrid demonstrate, multiple identities and multiple linguistic competences are now the order of the day. If this multiplicity were fostered, it would enable their integration, and even insertion in the labour market, as we have seen.

The third dilemma resolves around the question of whether language and educational policies should give priority to individual rights or to those of groups. It is perceived as incompatible to attend to both the social and the individual dimensions. It follows from this perception that education should ensure the free choice of individuals, rather than contributing to the imposition or perpetuation of a specific language.

Of course, this is also an ideological stance, generally legitimated by the argument of 'freedom of choice', the individual's inalienable right, which May also examines critically (this volume). Often, I have found that data related to these 'choices' (for instance, the number of students that are not competent in their home language) are discussed at length, and numbers are even inflated. These linguistic choices are also interpreted as evidence of social affiliation with the majority. Proponents of this argument ignore the possibility that rejecting one's own minority language, or perceiving it as a source of marginalisation, are not 'free' choices but effects of internalising dominant values under social pressure. In Spain this is an argument frequently used in neoconservative discourse (also among linguists; I call it neoconservative because it is referred to as progressive), which appears not only in relation to immigrants' languages, but also frequently in relation to the regional languages of Spain's bilingual Autonomous Regions.

Undoubtedly, these ideological positions are sustained by obvious scales of value and of prestige, which sanction as better or more positive the language of the majority group (Spanish), while immigrants' minority languages are not seen as social capital (they are considered not useful, or even primitive). Otherwise, immigrants students' refusal to use their home language would be regretted.

What we have seen up to now is that Spanish (and in particular, in the Madrid Autonomous Region) policy on linguistic diversity is fundamentally unclear, and a debate must urgently be fostered in order to tackle the dilemmas it creates. Overcoming these dilemmas means that, firstly, new discourses, policies and practices have to be produced, integrating both terms of these oppositions, instead of inducing the mere suppression of one of them. In order to do this, various concepts, including 'equality', 'nation', 'citizenship', language 'proficiency', and so forth, must be re-examined and re-defined.

Such redefinitions could help to understand and to deal with this new situation and the populations it brings. It is frequently forgotten that these students not only are, but should be able to go on being people who speak more than one language, are familiar with more than one culture, and construct their identity by bringing together the culture, history, tastes and customs not only of the country in which they are being educated, but also of their parents' countries. They cannot be said to be exclusively the product of one or the other, nor even the sum of both. Their personal history is unique. It is this uniqueness that links the cultural baggage one has when one arrives or when one's family arrives, with the baggage to be acquired. This study shows that the adoption of certain educational models (the assimilation and the compensatory models) entails not balance between diverse languages and cultures, but dominance, and assimilation. For this reason it is very important to introduce other models, like Home Language Teaching Programmes and intercultural models, into Madrid's schools.

References

Alcalá, Esther (2002) '¿Cómo normalizar y respetar las diferencias?', Comunicación presentada en el XXIII Seminari Llengües i Educació (ICE UB), Barcelona. ['How to 'Normalize' and Respect Differences?', paper presented to the XXIII Seminar on Languages and Education, Barcelona].

Bernstein, Basil (1975) *Class, Codes and Control: Towards a Theory of Educational Transmission*, London: Routledge and Kegan Paul.

Berry, John W (1990) 'Psychology of Acculturation', in J. Berman (ed) *Nebraska Symposium on Motivation, 1989, Cross-cultural Perspectives*, Lincoln: University of Nebraska Press, 201-234.

------ and L. David Samd (1997) 'Acculturation and Adaptation', in: John W. Berry, Marshall H. Segall and Cigdem Kagitcibasi (eds) *Handbook of Cross-Cultural Psychology* (2nd edition), Boston: Allyn and Bacon, 291-326.

Billig, Michael, (1991) *Ideology and Opinions: Studies in Rhetorical Psychology*, London: Sage.

------, Susan Condar, Derek Edwards, Mike Gane and Dai Middleton (1988) *Ideological Dilemmas: A Social Psychology of Everyday Thinking*, London: Sage.

Blommaert, Jan and Jef Verschueren (1998) *Debating Diversity*, London: Routledge.

Bourdieu, Pierre (1982) *Ce que parler veut dire. L'économie des échanges linguistiques* [Language and Symbolic Power], París: Fayard.

------ (1998) *Capital cultural, escuela y espacio social* [Cultural Capital, Schools, and Social Space], México: Siglo XXI.

------ and Jean-Claude Passeron (1977) *Reproduction in Education, Society and Culture*, London: Sage.

Broeder, Peter and Laura Mijares (2003) *Plurilingüismo en Madrid. Las lenguas de los alumnos de origen inmigrante* [Multilingualism in Madrid: The Status of Immigrant Languages at Home and at School], Madrid: CIDE.

Chouliaraki, Lilie and Norman Fairclough (1999) *Discourse in Late Modernity: Rethinking Critical Discourse Analysis*, Edinburgh: Edinburgh University Press.

Cummins, Jim (1997) *Negotiating Identities: Education for Empowerment*, Trentham Books Ltd.

------ (2000) *Language, Power, and Pedagogy: Bilingual Children in the Crossfire*, Clevedon: Multilingual Matters.

Fairclough, Norman (1992) *Discourse and Social Change*, Oxford: Polity Press.

------ and Ruth Wodak (1997) 'Critical Discourse Analysis', in Teun A. van Dijk (ed) *Discourse as Social Interaction*, London: Sage, 258-284.

Franzé Mudanó, Adela and Laura Mijares Molina (eds) (1999) *Lengua y Cultura de Origen: Niños Marroquíes en la Escuela Española* [Home Language and Culture: Moroccan Children in Spanish Schools], TEIM. Madrid: Ediciones de Oriente y del Mediterráneo.

Fraser, N. (2000) '¿De la redistribución al reconocimiento? Dilemas de la justicia en la era "postsocialista" [From Redistribution to Recognition? Dilemmas of Justice in the New "Postsocialist" Era], *New Left Review* (January), Spanish edition, Madrid:Akal, 126-155.

Grad, Héctor M. (1999) *Valores personales, identidad nacional y conducta de voto nacionalista: Un análisis transcultural* [Personal Values, National Identity and Nationalist Voting Behavior: A Cross-cultural Analysis]. Unpublished PhD Dissertation, Dept. of Social Psychology, Faculty of Psychology, Universidad Complutense de Madrid.

------ (2001) 'Universalist and Particularist Value Orientations in "Civic" and "Ethnic" Nationalist Cultures: Implications for Acculturation Strategies', poster presented at the 5th Regional Congress 2001 of the International Association for Cross-Cultural Psychology, Winchester (UK).

------ and Luisa Martín Rojo (2002) '"Civic" and "Ethnic" Nationalist Discourses in Spanish Parliamentary Debates', *Journal of Language and Politics* 1(2), special issue on Parliamentary Discourse, 225-265.

Gumperz, John (1981) 'Conversational Inferences and Classroom Learning', in Judith L. Green and Cynthia Wallat (eds) *Ethnography and Language in Educational Settings*, Norwood, N.J.: Ablex Publishing Corporation, 3-23.

Heller, Monica (1999) *Linguistic Minorities and Modernity: A Sociolinguistic Ethnography,* London: Longman.

------ (2002) *Crosswords: Language, Education, and Ethnicity in French Ontario*, The Hague: Walter de Gruyter.

------ and Marilyn Martin-Jones (2001) 'Introduction', in Monica Heller and Marilyn Martin-Jones (eds) *Voices of Authority. Education and Linguistic Difference*, London: Ablex Publishing, 1-28.

Jodelet, Denise (1986) 'La representación social: fenómenos, concepto y teoría' [Social representation: phenomena, concept and theory], in Moscovici, Serge (ed) (1986) *Psicología Social, II. Pensamiento y vida social. Psicología social y problemas sociales* [Thought and social life. Social psychology and social problems], Barcelona-Buenos Aires-México: Piados, 469-494.

Kroch, Anthony and William Labov (1972) 'Linguistic Society of America: Resolution in Response to Arthur Jensen (1969)', *Linguistic Society of American Bulletin* (March), Washington: Linguistic Society of America, 17-18.

Labov, William (1969) 'The logic of Nonstandard English', *Georgetown Monographs on Language and Linguistics* 22: 1-22 and 26-31.

Lambert, Wallace E. and Donald M. Taylor (1986) 'Assimilation versus Multiculturalism: The View of Urban America', *Sociological Forum* 3: 72-78.

Martín Rojo, Luisa (1997) 'Jargon', in: Jef Verschueren, Jan Ola Östman, Jan Blommaert and Chris Bulcaen (eds) *Handbook of Pragmatics.* Amsterdam: John Benjamins, 2-19.

------ (2000) 'Enfrentamiento y consenso en los debates parlamentarios sobre la política de inmigración en España' [Conflict and Consensus in Parliamentary Debates on Migration Policies in Spain], *Oralia*, vol.1, nº 5, 113-148.

------ (2001) 'New Developments in Discourse Analysis: Discourse as Social Practice', *Folia Lingüística* XXXV/ 1-2: 41-78.

------, Ester Alcalá, Aitana Garì, Laura Mijares and Angeles Rodríguez (2003) *¿Asimilar o integrar? Dilemas de las políticas educativas ante los procesos migratorios*, Madrid: CIDE (Ministerio de Educación y Cultura), vol. 24.

May, Stephen (2001) *Language and Minority Rrights*, Harlow, GB: Pearson Education.

------ (2003) 'Misconceiving Minority Language Rights: Implications for Liberal Political Theory', in Will Kymlicka and Alan Patten (eds) *Language Rights and Political Theory*, Oxford University Press, 123-152.

McAndrew, Marie (2001) *Immigration et diversité à l'école: Le débat québécois dans une perspective comparative*, Montreal: Les Presses de L'Université de Montréal.

Molina, Monica and Luís Maruny (in press) 'Hacia un diseño de objetivos en la enseñanza de lengua a escolares inmigrantes, a partir de datos sobre adquisición' [Designing Goals in the Linguistic Training of Migrants, Taking into Account Acquisition Data], Vigo: Estudios de Sociolingüística.

Montreuil, Anni and Richard Y. Bourhis (2001) 'Majority Acculturation Orientations toward "Valued" and "Devalued" Immigrants', *Journal of Cross-cultural Psychology* 32 6): 698-719.

Moscovici, Serge (1961) *La psychanalyse, son image et son public* [Psychoanalysis, Its Image, and Its Public], Paris: PUF.

------ (1994) 'Social Representations and Pragmatic Communication', *Social Science Information* 33(2): 163-177.

Rampton, Ben (1995) *Crossing: Language and Ethnicity among Adolescents*, London/New York: Longman.

Riquer, Borja (1996) *El nacionalismo español contemporáneo. Interpretaciones históricas y debates políticos* [Contemporary Spanish Nationalism. Historical Interpretations and Political Debates], Madrid: Centro de Estudios Constitucionales (Cuadernos y debates, serie minor, nº7).

Skutnabb-Kangas, Tove (2000) *Linguistic Genocide in Education. Or worldwide Diversity and Human Rights*, Mahwah, NJ: Lawrence Erlbaum Associates.

Stallaert, Christiane (1998) *Etnogénesis y Etnicidad en España: Una aproximación histórica-antropológica al casticismo*, [Etnogenesis and Ethnicity in Spain], Madrid: Proyecto A Ediciones.

Todorov, Tzvetan (1989) *Nous et les autres: la réflexion française sur la diversité humaine*, Paris: Seuil.

Tusón, Amparo (2002) 'Iguais perante a lingua, desiguais no uso' [Equal before the Language, Unequal in Its Use], in Carlos Lomas (ed) *O valor das palabras*, Lisboa: Asa Editores, 73-89.

------ and Virginia Unamuno (1999) '¿De qué estamos hablando? El malentendido en el discurso escolar' [What Are We Talking about? Misunderstanding in the Discourse of School], *Discurso y Sociedad* 1(1): 19-34.

van Dijk, Teun (1987) *Communicating Racism*, Newbury Park, CA: Sage.

------ (ed) (1997) *Discourse as Social Interaction*, London: Sage.

van Leeuwen, Theo (1996) 'The Representation of Social Actors', in Carmen Caldas-Coulthard and Malcolm Coulthard (eds) *Texts and Practices. Readings in Critical Discourse Analysis*, London: Routledge, 32-71.

Wetherell, Margaret and Jonathon Potter (1988) 'Discourse Analysis and the Identification of Interpretative Repertoires', in Charles Antaki (ed) *Analysing Everyday Explanation*, London: Sage.

------ (1992) *Mapping the Language of Racism: Discourse and the Legitimation of Exploitation*, London: Harvester Wheatsheaf.

13. Language Rights and Wrongs
A Commentary

ALEXANDRA JAFFE

One of the strengths of the chapters collected in this volume is that collectively, they address not only the issue of language rights, but also, discourses about language rights, and how these discourses work to further or obstruct particular social actors' claims in the linguistic marketplace. In one way or another, all of them reveal the way that discourses about language rights are essentializing ones. They essentialize languages, identities, and the link between languages and identities. Put another way, discourses about language rights do not capture the complexity of the linguistic practices, experiences and forms of identification of their 'target' populations ('speakers of language X'). Even the formulation 'speakers of language X' oversimplifies the processes involved in language shift, language maintenance and language revitalization in multilingual contexts, for in such contexts, there are complex answers to questions such as, "What does it mean to 'speak language X?'" or "Who counts as a speaker?" or "How are criteria of linguistic 'ownership' linked to criteria of social or cultural ownership?"

Many of these chapters make the important point that these discourses about language rights – and their ideological underpinnings – are constitutive of the practices of both champions of language rights and opponents of language rights; of both insiders and outsiders; of linguists and non-linguists. That is to say, all participants in the discursive field of language rights are implicated in the process of essentialization.

In the following comments, I want to take up four main perspectives or themes that cross-cut this volume and that relate to the experiential, political and discursive dimensions of language rights:

1. A process-oriented approach to linguistic and cultural identities that views them as relational, situational, multiple and potentially ambiguous/fraught with ambivalence as opposed to fixed and bounded. The central object of study, for all of these authors, is thus communicative practice in social context, not 'language' or 'languages' as formal and abstract systems.
2. The difficulty of engaging in a 'radical resistance' for those seeking rights and resources within dominant structures of power: the politically compelling nature of dominant discourses that essentialize language, identity and the relationship between them. Related to this,

the difficulties and tensions inherent in the development of an academic discourse about language rights that might empower people and groups whose language practices and repertoires are objects of passive or active discrimination.

3. A close attention to, and respect/legitimation for the experiences of speakers and to the widely divergent kinds of identity claims and stances they take with respect to language and identity in the context of their experiences of and through dominant discourses.
4. Relative to point #1, above, the implications of the contingent relationship between linguistic variables and processes of linguistic identification for what it means to 'save' or 'lose' a language.
5. As a consequence of all of the above issues, a formulation of 'rights' that takes into account the multiple political, cultural and economic contexts in which language affects individual and group access to symbolic and economic capital. This perspective acknowledges the pragmatic role of 'language rights' defined within a traditional ideological linguistic paradigm but crucially refocuses attention on control over communicative practices and economies.

Below, I take up all of these issues, roughly, though not rigidly, in order.

One of the common perspectives uniting the contributions to this volume is a process-oriented approach that focuses on *acts of identification* rather than essentialized linguistic or cultural identities. These acts of identification are often multiple and situational, and they confound traditional views of identities as single, fixed and local. May writes about multiple identities as "the order of the day"; Blommaert evokes identities that move across space and are not essentially localized. Laakso and Östman point out that what being a Solfian means can change from one generation to another, and emphasize that Solfians position themselves within, and on the margins of multiple fields of identity. Freeland shows us the multiple linguistic and cultural references – Creole, Black, Costeño – to which Nicaraguans may align themselves or differentiate themselves, each with different implications for identity and social power. She also illustrates the way that Creoles can simultaneously identify with and distance themselves from dominant languages and ideologies, reinforcing Laakso and Östman's point about the crucial role of ambivalence in the processes of identification. Darnell describes a continuum of individual and collective modes of identification with particular, named Aboriginal cultures, showing that 'being Aboriginal' in Canada has a variety of meanings and forms of expression. Those forms of expression include, but are not limited to speaking Aboriginal languages, as shown by Darnell and Valentine's research project on the English spoken by Aboriginal peoples in south-western Ontario, and by Patrick's review of language practices in many Yup'ik and Inupiaq communities. This is because, as Patrick reminds us, indigenous (in her case, Inuit) and dominant (in her case White) ways of life overlap in complex ways (page 183). Heugh and Stroud document how "would-be gangsters and rebellious township youth" in South Africa have crafted a nonstandard, hybrid language, Tsotisitaal, that fuses elements of Afrikaans and Zulu. They also describe the alternative linguistic economy in Nigeria's markets documented by Ufomata (1998), where women use creative mixtures of "local, regional and pidgin languages in ways that reinforce their own carefully structured market-based social and welfare systems" (Stroud and Heugh page 199 here). All these contributions to this volume challenge the assumption that people are either/or; that they can either speak Language A or Language B; that identities are necessarily bounded and exclusive.

The complexities of the on-the-ground sociolinguistic realities described in all these chapters would seem, on the face of it, to be a powerful antidote to reductionist, essentialist and static notions of language and identity. However, collectively, these studies also illustrate my second theme, which has to do with the difficulties of escaping from dominant discourses about language and identity. The problem is that elevating the status of a processual, multiple and hybrid view of identity – what I consider an act of radical resistance to dominant language ideologies – challenges both fundamental ideological structures and concrete structures of power and access to them. Ultimately, the difficulties of a radical resistance complicate the practical and moral implications of academic work and academic discourses in the domain of language rights. This is both because discourses that 'deconstruct' dominant language ideologies can work against speakers of unrecognized or subaltern languages or language varieties as they work within dominant ideological and material structures to obtain greater recognition and resources and because all discourses about language and rights have effects related to those very same structures. I will return to this second point at the end of the section.

We see the obstacles to a radical resistance quite clearly in Martín-Rojo's chapter, where the 'integration ideology' – one that facilitates minority linguistic and cultural maintenance and promotes intergroup relations – amounts to a redefinition of community that would include the new diversity of language and culture brought by immigrants. Her study makes it clear that in Spain, this redefinition of community is not readily forthcoming. In this respect, the Spanish case is by no means an isolated one, as shown by Hélot's recent work on French educational policy with respect to languages of immigration (2003). Wright's chapter shows a similar dynamic at work at the level of the European Union, where the commitment to multilingualism recognizes 'national' languages, but not 'minority' languages, at least not among the Union's 'working languages'. In other words, structures of power – whether local, national or supranational – only recognize those linguistic differences that legitimate (reproduce) those structures of power. In Martín-Rojo's chapter, we see how this plays out in school contexts, where difference is most often discursively constructed as a form of deficit. Moreover, Martín-Rojo demonstrates that (superficially) democratic discourses that conflate equality with equivalence lead to policies of segregation-for-assimilation. Such policies ultimately insure that linguistic difference remains socially salient: not as a challenge to the dominant social order, but as a 'problem' for those who are in the minority. Ultimately, in this context and many others, this discourse is one of the resources that protects the monolingual standard language ideologies that are the cornerstone of the social and linguistic capital of 'mainstream' speakers and social actors.

Stroud and Heugh and Wright also draw our attention to the hidden inequalities of ostensibly inclusive discourses of diversity, and to how difficult it is to challenge them. In South Africa (as well as in many other national contexts), Heugh and Stroud nicely summarize the source of those inequalities, writing that "(Neo)liberal attempts to manage diversity seem not to want to question the viability of trying to accommodate difference in a framework that is explicitly constructed around explicit denial of difference in the interests of commonality" (Stroud and Heugh page 206). It is interesting, in this light, to consider the discourse of 'unity in diversity' that is found in many multilingual nations, as well as in the European Union. This is a discourse that has been brought about by new demographic, political and philosophical realities, but it is clear that it is in perpetual conflict with traditional and historically rooted models of unity through homogeneity. In the European Union, the discourse of unity in diversity represents a similar and unresolved source of tension: between national and supranational forms of identity and political control. It is in fact this conflict that generates the discourse itself – the constant reference to diversity and its positive value is like anti-smoking advertising: necessary only when it is *not* a self-evident value that acts as a ground for normative practice (that is, so long as people are still smoking). Ultimately, as Wright and Stroud/Heugh point out, this kind of discourse obscures the real politics of difference – the real advantages that accrue to speakers of the languages that have de facto dominance – acknowledging only 'safe' differences with no consequences; difference as superficial. As an aside, from this perspective, France's much-maligned position on minority languages looks preferable to Wright's description of EU discourse and practice, since France admits that within its paradigm of national belonging, linguistic difference is not safe.

All of these points help to answer to the rhetorical question posed by May, when he asks why cultural and linguistic change and adaptation should always be unidirectional, from the minority to the majority language and culture. In short, the majority does not need or have to adapt, and has a great deal to gain by maintaining social and linguistic boundaries. On the one hand, we are justified in viewing majority responses to linguistic diversity as calculated expressions of self-interest. But this is also not the entire story, because from the experiential standpoint, we have to recognize that majority experiences of the relationship between language and identity seldom allow them to empathize, as May hopes they might, with minority speakers and thereby grant legitimacy to their claims for language maintenance. That is, for majority speakers, the identity functions their language fills for them are so powerfully inscribed in the day-to-day experiences within dominant social institutions and domains of practice that they are rendered almost invisible. This invisibility makes it possible for those majority speakers to be dismissive of the identity functions of language in general. This dismissal emerges discursively in the exploitation of the contingent relationship between language and identity (that we endorse as linguists and social scientists) to trivialize minority speakers' socially, politically and historically grounded experiences of identification through language.

Alternatively, as Martín-Rojo also shows, majority, monolingual speakers can turn the discourse of language and group identity against minority speakers, and insist that it is their responsibility to adapt linguistically to a single linguistic code in the name of national unity. That is, the unexamined majority experience of identity/unity through a single code becomes the basis for a condemnation of diversity as inherently unsettling and divisive. At one level, we want to recognize these dominant discourses as forms of ideological mystification. At the same time, we want to recognize that there is a real way in which the recognition and promotion of minority languages (and any policies that make them socially or economically instrumental) do erode the majority power base. The majority understands the connection between symbolic and material resources, and having a monopoly on legitimate language is both symbolically and materially significant. This emphasizes a point made by Patrick, Darnell, Wright, Heugh/Stroud, Blommaert, and Whaley: which is that issues of language rights, and the potential for language maintenance or revitalization are never just about language, but are embedded within wider political frameworks and struggles for control over cultural and economic resources. Since language is one of those resources, unequal outcomes of that struggle guarantee linguistic inequalities that are not easily remedied by any kind of policy. This can be seen in Wright and Heugh/Stroud's description of the inequalities of practice and philosophy associated with multilingual policies. And it lurks behind Wright's advocacy of English as an official European lingua franca. Her suggestion is that 'International English' could attenuate the advantage of anglophones by forcing Mother Tongue English speakers to become bidialectal. This is an appealing idea – that the 'hidden' advantage of Mother Tongue English speakers could be defused by being exposed – but it is unclear what kinds of social, economic or political contexts would disrupt the legitimacy of high-status Mother Tongue English Speaker's dialects, or even prompt the recognition of what they speak as a 'dialect' rather than simply 'English', or 'good English'. The issue of 'good English' brings up another point, which has to do with the hope of providing more people greater access to resources through 'a language' of power like English. As we well know, valued linguistic capital is owned by powerful social players, whose very power resides in their ability to define what will count as good language, and to 'move' that target in response to potential encroachment on their exclusive territory by the masses. As Blommaert writes (2001: 135) "what counts is not the existence and distribution of languages, but the availability, accessibility and distribution of specific linguistic-communicative skills such as competence in standard and literate varieties of languages". I will return to this point in the last section, where I consider the way these chapters conceptualize linguistic rights.

In the political context of language rights, there is another issue that makes a radical resistance problematic for linguists and minority language activists alike when they engage in the real-life quest for language rights and resources to insure them. That is, given the long tentacles of dominant ideologies of language and identity, the celebration of multiplicity, hybridity and ambivalence is not a powerful discursive position. That is, the pragmatic, political contexts of seeking language rights tend to impose an essentialist discourse. You do not get money, or books, or official recognition by claiming ambiguous relationships with several identities, and shifting and contingent forms of identification with multiple linguistic codes. This is very clear in Patrick's description of Inuit language politics, and we see the same general principle illustrated in a different form in the Oroqen situation, where linguistic rights come pre-packaged with dominant categories of identity that solidify or fix forms of identity that may have been more fluid before language rights were invoked as a form of political action. So it is no surprise that, when language becomes salient with respect to identity or access to resources, people want to connect their identities to languages or codes of power, that they want to represent those codes as having a direct and unproblematic relationships with equally clear-cut identity categories. Hence, the Creole proponency of Standard English in the context of Mother-Tongue rights in educational contexts, or the impulses to write down Creole or Solf (and the processes of standardization that is implied by this codification), and the effort to standardize and differentiate SiNdebele from isiNdebele reported by Heugh and Stroud. We also glimpse this strategy in Darnell's chapter, where it is clear that while Aboriginal peoples sometimes embrace non-essentializing ideologies of language and identity, they also engage in more or less essentializing discourses when they talk about their codes as "pillar[s] of reconstituted cultural authenticity and pride" even when those languages are not widely practiced. Clearly, these kinds of practices complicate the laudable principle of putting the power of definition of what will count as language into the hands of speakers that is advocated by Heugh and Stroud, following Roberts (1997), who argues that linguists should take account of these conceptions in building their descriptions of language, thereby "integrat[ing] the investigation of fundamental linguistic processes with dialogue with the community and the professions" (Roberts 1997: 5).

As Patrick puts it, "endangered languages have thus become socially, historically, and politically constructed" (page #). This means, as she points out, that the promotion of language rights by all social actors – including the local speakers – has to be viewed as social, historical and political.

This does not mean, of course, that there is not a great deal of merit in collaborative projects that do not privilege only the researchers' points of view (described in some detail by Darnell and Valentine). But it is important to recognize the political conditions in which those dialogues take place, and therefore what the implications are of various types of discourses about language and identity on different players' access to symbolic and material resources. To start with, there is the fundamental question of who 'speakers themselves' are. Who counts as a legitimate speaker? Who gets to represent a community? Who will have the authority to define what 'counts as' legitimate? How do we define community (linguistic or otherwise)? These are always profoundly political issues, from the local to the global level. There is no neutral position on language to be had by anyone, and there is no neutral decision about whose position is to be given moral and political authority.

But it would also be a mistake to overemphasize the role of language in the articulation of identity, a point that is made in the chapters by Darnell, Whaley and Laakso and Östman, who show that we need to pay attention to both the circumstances in which language does become salient for identity and the circumstances in which it does not (see also Fishman 2002). Perhaps, in the case of Solf, nothing critical in terms of access to symbolic or material resources has yet been at stake with respect to identity and language, whereas in other contexts, histories of oppression make oppositional linguistic and cultural identities almost perpetually salient. And of course, there are other situations that fall somewhere in between these two poles of a continuum. One of the crucial consequences of this perspective, articulated in different ways by Patrick, Laakso and Ostman, Freeland, May, Darnell, Heugh/Stroud and Blommaert, is that our focus should not be on identities and languages, but rather on the social processes of identification and distinction and the variable role language plays in these processes, both as a practice and as an object of discourse. One of the strengths of this collection, in my view, is the foregrounding of people's experience in the authors' accounts. These experiences are at once multiple, complex and non-essentially (that is, contingently) linked to language **and,** at particular moments (personal, historical, social) crucially linked to language because of the privileged place of language in dominant discourses about identity. These papers, together, acknowledge the way the experiences of language domination and dominant linguistic discourses affect the experience of language and identity at the personal level. That is, even though language is theoretically a situational, contingent index of identity, it is not experienced that way all of the time. People's essentializations of the language-identity link are ideational, but they are also experientially real. As May writes, a 'contingent marker' can still be significant and constitutive of identity in historical/political context. It is also the case that dominant discourses form part of the habitus within which individuals can experience the self. One cannot, perhaps, experience identity completely outside this habitus or Discourse (in Gee's sense of the word).

If we take this experiential dimension together with the processual emphasis on identification and with the focus on multiple identities found in this collection, we are forced to problematize some of the features of our own discourse about language rights: namely, the oppositions between majority and minority, between local and global, between instrumental and cultural forms of identification. Sometimes, for example, multiple identities, whether linguistic or cultural, are not experienced as oppositional. In other cases, important identity work for members of a linguistic or cultural minority can be done through the medium of the dominant language. The language of love for Solfian teens may be English; Gangsta English or Tsotsitaal may be the 'authentic' vehicle for youth culture in an African township; a Nicaraguan Creole person may comfort and cuddle a child in standard Spanish or English; mothering may take place outside a mother's 'Mother Tongue'. Practices on the ground in Africa that exploit the potential of linguistic continua and 'transborder' languages, as Heugh and Stroud point out, challenge the widespread notion that linguistic diversity necessarily amounts to social divisions (Djité 1993: 150).

And, sometimes to our own dismay, speakers of threatened languages may not always endorse campaigns to save or promote those languages, focusing instead on the social mobility offered by powerful codes (as in Wright's and Blommaert's examples). Or, their support for modernization and standardization may be tempered by the conflicting desire to preserve a local or indigenous communicative economy organized around very different cultural principles (as in the Nunavik case). As sociolinguists, we need to acknowledge the legitimacy of these experiences and practices.

To conclude, let me suggest that an adequate discourse on language rights needs to move beyond a conceptualization of language as a bounded, autonomous code. For we know, in sociolinguistics, that the social processes of distinction, or affiliation, or identification, can hinge on any linguistic variable, no matter how small. We see this at work in Solf, where younger generations feel that they have a distinct identity and talk about it in linguistic terms ('speaking Solf') even though that distinctiveness, from a quantitative, outside perspective is becoming less and less linguistically visible. Conversely, if we look at the situation on Sabah, we see that people can view themselves as having both a Kadazudusun unified language and identity within which exists a Rungus language and identity (ideas reflected in evaluations of 'intelligibility').

This general approach would lead us to a position of associating rights, as Freeland advocates, with language practices rather than with languages, without specifying the necessary nature or content of those practices. This would perhaps usefully extend the discourse on language rights to include mixed codes and non-standard varieties of dominant languages, and could lead linguist activists to focus their energies on exposing the standardization process as a 'site of struggle', as Heugh and Stroud recommend. This is consistent with Wright's perspective on the use of and access to English in the EU: both seek to foreground how language is implicated in political processes of domination, with the aim of stopping those processes from remaining invisible. This perspective would also help to buttress the individual rights to fair access to both symbolic and material capital associated with language that are often sacrificed in the discourses of diversity within national and supranational contexts. These rights, as Darnell's chapter persuasively illustrates, would include the prerogative to choose between a wide range of personal and collective responses to language shift and cultural reproduction, as well as the right to choose situationally (and therefore, 'inconsistently'). Finally, with regard to both individual and collective rights, this kind of approach would focus academic attention where it belongs (and where it is focused in this volume): on issues of control over communicative economies and the kinds of capital that count within them, and not just over 'languages'.

References

Blommaert, Jan (2001) 'The Asmara Declaration as a Sociolinguistic Problem: Notes in Scholarship and Linguistic Rights', *Journal of Sociolinguistics* 5(2): 131-142.

Djité, Paulin (1993) 'Language and Development in Africa', *International Journal of the Sociology of Language* 100/101: 149-166.

Fishman, Joshua (2002) 'Commentary: What a Difference 40 Years Make!', *Journal of Linguistic Anthropology* 12(2): 144-149.

Gee, James Paul (1996) *Social Linguistics and Literacies*, London: Taylor and Francis

Hélot, Christine (2003) 'The Language Policy and Ideology of Bilingual Education in France', Paper presented at the 4th International Symposium on Bilingualism, Tempe AZ, April 30-May 3.

Roberts, Celia (1997) 'There Is Nothing So Practical as Some Good Theories', *International Journal of Applied Linguistics* 7(1): 66-78.

Ufomata, Ttitilayo (1998) *Voices from the Marketplace: Short Stories*, Ibadan: Kraft Books Limited, University of Ibadan.

14. Analysis and Stance Regarding Language and Social Justice

MONICA HELLER

In this brief commentary, I want to consider some questions that this collection raises. This is not a consideration of specific papers, but rather a pondering of some fundamental issues which, in my view, bear continued work and reflection. These issues flow from what I understand to be this volume's underlying question: what happens when sociolinguistic analysis of linguistic variation, or of ties between language and identity, meet legal discourses of rights in the framework of a shared concern for social justice? My concern here is to put the sociolinguist at the centre of my reflection: how can we position ourselves regarding the struggles for social justice which are at the heart of language rights debates? How do we decide what is the right thing to do?

It seems fair, and probably rather obvious, to say that we are having this conversation because no one thinks it is all right for people to suffer discrimination because of the language they speak. At the same time, addressing that problem seems to have led us onto terrain in which elements of the dominant discourse contradict some of what we believe, and which in any case turns out to be more complicated than a simple question of 'language' or of 'rights'. Let me take up a few dimensions of these concerns.

The first has to do with the relationship between discourses of rights and sociolinguistic discourses of language. The problem of linguistic discrimination is one that takes its very shape from the way language is bound up in the construction of the State. The equation of language with nation, and nation with monolingualism (and with the development of standard languages) lays the groundwork for the construction of the very idea of a bounded 'language', and for the construction of hierarchies of legitimacy which marginalize and stigmatize non-national 'languages' or linguistic varieties (which do of course indeed get constructed as 'dialects', 'patois', 'jargon', 'gibberish' and so on, that is, not as 'languages' at all). Resistance to this process can take many forms, but the dominant form of resistance that we have witnessed in the past forty or so years has been to attack linguistic discrimination in its own terms. That is, rather than rejecting the principles that make such social injustice possible (the notion of 'language', the language-nation equation, and so on), groups have rejected the categorization of some languages and nations as more legitimate than others. Linguistic minority movements tend to argue not that languages and nations should not be equated, but rather that some nations have been given an unfair deal, and that they should have their own language-nation-State nexus. A great deal of dialectological and sociolinguistic work has been involved in these debates, taking for granted the possibility of establishing expert discourses which can disambiguate boundaries and identify groups. Such sociolinguistic discourses do fit well with the primary means nation-States have for adjudicating social justice problems, namely, to accept the fundamental existence of groups as the basis of collective rights.

This book, however, challenges those assumptions, pointing out that sociolinguistics has also established the ideological nature of the linguistic categories we, and everyone else, work(s) with, as well as of the relationship posited between language and other social categories. A critical sociolinguistic perspective requires us to ask where these ideologies come from, and whose interests they serve, as well as what the relationship is to the linguistics of the case. What we find usually is that what counts as language boundaries is less than clear. People attend to certain phenomena which become ideologically salient, but can ignore others which serve their interests less well. So it becomes harder and harder to take a sociolinguistic 'expert discourse' stance which permits unambiguous identification of the relevant units over which language rights legislation can obtain.

Second, linguistic minority movements which remain within the dominant paradigm of language and nation tend to reproduce the marginalizing effects from which they suffer and against which they struggle. Because linguistic boundaries are not clear, because languages and nations do not come in tightly tied unified bundles, the work of constructing linguistic minority identity is just as hard as is the work of constructing nation-state identity (well, perhaps harder, since there tend to be fewer resources available; let us say hard in similar ways). It entails the same kind of struggles over the discursive space of identity construction, with the same kinds of differences of opinion (and interest) in defining things one way or another, and with the same kinds of necessary marginalization of some views in favour of others. A discourse of linguistic rights has difficulty in coping with this kind of recursivity, unless somehow for once everyone can be made to act in uniform ways (in which case we would not have had a language rights problem in the first place).

Third, even if it has been possible to some extent over the last 200 years or so to at least pretend that languages and nations are more or less unified fields, it is increasingly difficult to sweep the deviations under the rug, and there is less and less interest in doing so. The globalized new economy has made mobility, complexity, hybridity and multiplicity more and more interesting and harder and harder to avoid, making it less and less obvious what languages and groups a discourse of language rights would be about. Not that the problem has gone away; but the grounds have shifted.

Finally, struggles over language actually are not centrally about language at all. Language becomes a terrain for struggles over power involving social groups whose categorization is somehow part of the fundamental principles of social organization of the people in question. A language rights discourse cannot address this displacement, since it places language at the centre of its understanding of group identity, and for similar reasons, sociolinguistics also fails to examine this phenomenon closely. Yet it seems clear that in the case of modernist democratic State-focussed linguistic minority struggles, the terrain of language seems to make sense as a proxy insofar as democratic states are supposed to be inclusive and language can be held up as something one can learn (while remaining sufficiently ambiguous to be able to in fact function as a masked criterion for the construction of essentialized ethnic boundaries). Many of the post-1960s linguistic minority movements have also been developed and led by intellectuals and members of the bourgeoisie (much like the nationalist movements of the nineteenth century), who have had an interest in masking class differences in the interest of national solidarity and the furthering of their own class interests through nationalism. There are, then, historically-situated explanations for how it comes to pass that we worry about language at all, but ones which require a certain decentring of language to be able to discover. It may seem paradoxical to suggest that sociolinguistics questions the centrality of its object in order to best address some of its major questions, but to do so would, I believe, allow us to better grasp the nature of how language is constructed and how it functions in the context of relations of difference and inequality.

Throughout this discussion, I have been advocating distancing ourselves from taking on the role of language experts, and from an uncritical acceptance of the categories of language and collective identity which inform the struggles that concern us. At the same time, I do not want to argue that we have nothing to say, or that the matter does not concern us.

Rather, I want to argue that the matter of stance needs crucially to be linked to the nature of our analysis. What we can best contribute is an analysis which helps reveal why people care about language at all, and why they care about it the ways they do, both with respect to what they understand language(s) to be, and with respect to the values they attach to it or them. We can contribute to explanations of how language gets bound up in processes of construction of social difference and social inequality; and to descriptions of how, exactly, it functions in those processes, as well as of the consequences those processes have and for whom.

Those descriptions and explanations are likely to serve some people's interests better than others, and we need to be prepared for our work to be taken up by others accordingly. And while we can resist being constructed as objective, neutral 'experts', two facts remain: first, that if it serves people's interests to construct us that way, they will, no matter what we say; and second, we have, by the very fact of arrogating to ourselves the right to say something on the matter, entered a discursive space as active participants, a role which carries both rights and obligations, first among them the obligation to be part of the conversation. We need to be especially aware that the discourse of rights in a legal framework does carry with it an expectation that a sociolinguist is available to be constructed as an expert. What I want to argue here is that we can take the position that we have something important and special to say, something that others with different approaches to the question might not see, and that in some ways we would even want to qualify as 'expert', at least in the sense of being based on systematic and long-term enquiry. That is, knowledge can be 'expert' without being objective or neutral in the positivist sense.

At the same time, other participants in the conversation might take up the knowledge we produce in ways we are not happy with, refuse to acknowledge our input despite our conviction that it is useful, or otherwise refuse to accord legitimacy to us as speakers or hearers, or to our knowledge as knowledge. People may not want to hear how complicated it is, or how it helps these people in some ways but not in others, or is good for X but not for Y. They may find all or part of our analyses illegitimate and even dangerous or threatening, or simply ridiculous and misguided; or no matter what we say, they may not want to hear it from *us*. Even under the best of circumstances, when we are welcomed generally as participants in a conversation about something we care about as deeply as language and social justice, there are unlikely to be obvious, straightforward stances for us to take, but we have to take them anyway, even if it is in the form of a refusal to take a stance. But we need to be clear about the relationship between our analysis and our stance, which needs to include being free to decide to set aside complexity in the interests of strategic simplification, or else, on the contrary, to argue for a complex understanding when everything pushes for a simple one. It also needs to include speaking or being silent, trying (or not) to engage in multiple conversations (in academia, in the legal system, in communities, in government, and so on), that is, generally, understanding ourselves as socially- and historically-situated social actors, just like everyone else.

List of Contributors

Jan Blommaert is Professor of African Linguistics and Sociolinguistics at Ghent University, Belgium. His research interests include linguistic ideologies especially in multilingual environments, linguistic inequality, discourse theory and narrative. Major publications include *Language Ideological Debates* (edited, 1999), *State Ideology and Language in Tanzania* (1999) and *Debating Diversity* (with Jef Verschueren, 1998).

Regna Darnell is Professor of Anthropology and Director of First Nations Studies at the University of Western Ontario. Research areas are First Nations (especially Plains Cree, Ojibwe, Mohawk, Slavey) language and culture, First Nations English discourse, cross-cultural mis-communication, and history of anthropology. Major works include: *Native North American Interaction Patterns* (1988, ed. with Michael Foster), *Edward Sapir: Linguist, Anthropologist, Humanist* (1990), *And Along Came Boas* (1998), *Theorizing Americanist Anthropology* (1999, ed. with Lisa Valentine), *Invisible Genealogies: A History of Americanist Anthropology* (2001). She served as Chair of the American Anthropological Association Centennial Commission for 2002 and is a Fellow of the Royal Society of Canada.

Jane Freeland is a Visiting Research Fellow in the School of Humanities at Southampton University, UK. Her main area of research has been the implementation of linguistic and other minority rights in the multilingual, interethnic region of Nicaragua's Caribbean Coast, during and after the Sandinista revolution. She has contributed to intercultural-bilingual teacher training in Nicaragua at the University of the Caribbean Coast Regions of Nicaragua (URACCAN), with units on Sociolinguistics and on Language Planning. She is currently involved in the preparation of the book on language in a series of books to support the training of teachers for Nicaragua's intercultural-bilingual programmes.

Monica Heller is Professor at the Ontario Institute for Studies in Education of the University of Toronto. Her work focuses on the relationship between language practices, social structuration, ideology and political economy, in the construction of social difference and social inequality, with a focus on linguistic minorities and in particular francophone Canada. Her most recent publications include: *Éléments d'une sociolinguistique critique* (Paris, Didier, 2002) and *Voices of Authority: Education and Linguistic Difference* (co-edited with M. Martin-Jones, Westport CT, Ablex, 2001).

Kathleen Heugh is a language policy researcher based at the Project for the Study of Alternative Education in South Africa, University of Cape

Town. She co-ordinated an NGO, the National Language Project, whose purpose was to make proposals for post-apartheid language policy, from the late 1980s to early 1990s. This included the editing of a national periodical, 'The Language Projects' Review'. During the 1990s her work included language policy proposals and development in South Africa with the Departments of Constitutional Development and Arts & Culture, and also as a member of the Pan South African Language Board during its first term of office from 1996-2001. She works closely with multilingual programmes for teacher education in townships and informal settlements outside of Cape Town and currently works with trainers of language-in-education trainers for schools in the Southern African Development Community. Most recently she completed her doctoral dissertation with the Centre for Research on Bilingualism at the University of Stockholm.

Alexandra Jaffe is Associate Professor of Linguistics at California State University at Long Beach. She received her PhD from Indiana University in Linguistic Anthropology in 1990, and has taught in Rhode Island, New York and Mississippi before taking her current post. Since 1988, she has been doing research on language politics and ideology on Corsica. Her publications on Corsica include a range of topics: orthographic debates, bilingual media, public discourse about language, minority language translation and literature and bilingual education. Her 1999 book *Ideologies in Action* was published with Mouton de Gruyter and takes up the problematics of resistance to language domination. Her most recent research project on Corsica is an ethnographic study of bilingual education, conducted during 2000.

Villa Laakso is finalizing his PhD on the usefulness of the Gramscian concept of hegemony in anti-foundational approaches to linguistics at the Department of General Linguistics at the University of Helsinki. He has done fieldwork on Basque and Solv, and written a number of articles on postcard discourse, normativity, and the formation of social subjectivity. He is the co-editor, with Jan-Ola Östman, of three volumes on interdisciplinary approaches to postcards and postcarding as a socio-cultural phenomenon.

Luisa Martín Rojo is Associate Professor of Linguistics at the Universidad Autónoma de Madrid. Her work generally applies sociolinguistic and pragmatic perspectives to research on the languages of minorities in Spain. This chapter is part of a larger piece of research into the discursive dimension of social exclusion (sexism, racism), and the relationship between language policies and immigrants' integration. She is currently a member of the editorial boards of *Discourse & Society*, *Language and Politics*, and *Spanish in Context*.

Stephen May is Foundation Professor and Chair of Language and Literacy Education, and Research Professor in the Wilf Malcolm Institute of Educational Research, School of Education, University of Waikato, Hamilton, New Zealand. He is also a Senior Research Fellow in the Centre for the Study of Ethnicity and Citizenship, Sociology Department, University of Bristol, UK, where he worked for much of the 1990s. Stephen has written widely on language rights, language education, ethnicity, nationalism and multiculturalism, and has a strong interest in social theory, particularly the work of Bourdieu. His recent books include *Language and Minority Rights* (Longman, 2001), which was shortlisted for the *British Association of Applied Linguistics (BAAL)* Book Prize 2002, *Indigenous Community-based Education* (Multilingual Matters, 1999) and *Critical Multiculturalism* (Routledge Falmer, 1999). He is a founding editor of the international and interdisciplinary journal, *Ethnicities* (Sage) and is on the editorial boards of *Journal of Language, Identity and Education* (LEA) and *Language and Education* (Multilingual Matters).

Jan-Ola Östman, a native of Solf, is Professor of Scandinavian Languages, and Director of the PIC Project at the University of Helsinki. His research areas include, on the one hand, pragmatics, implicit cueing, text and discourse linguistics, with a special interest in common sense, pragmatic particles, postcard discourse, persuasion, and media discourse; and, on the other hand, issues of ideology, responsibility and intercultural communication, with a special emphasis on minorities and Otherness, and on indigenous languages and cultures of the Americas (Hualapai and Nahuatl), signed languages (Finland-Swedish Sign Language), and Finland-Swedish dialects and contact issues in the Circum-Baltic Area. He also works on grammar, and has especially contributed in the field of Construction Grammar. Östman is an elected member of the Finnish Society of Sciences and Letters, the Consultation Board and Executive Committee of the International Pragmatics Association, and the Executive Board of the International Communication Monitor. He was co-editor of the *Journal of Pragmatics*, and is presently co-editor of the *Handbook of Pragmatics*, and of the book series Constructional Approaches to Language. His publications include *You know: A Discourse-Functional Approach* (1981), and (co-edited with Frances Karttunen) *Issues of Minority Peoples* (2000).

Donna Patrick is Associate Professor in the Department of Sociology and Anthropology and in the School of Canadian Studies at Carleton University, Ottawa, Ontario. Her current research focuses on political, social, and cultural aspects of language use in Inuit communities of Northern Quebec. Recent publications have investigated issues of sociolinguistic aspects of minority language maintenance and second and third language acquisition. Her most recent publication is *Language, Politics, and Social Interaction in an Inuit Community* (2003 Berlin/New York: Mouton de Gruyter).

Veronica Petrus Atin is a Lecturer with the Centre for the Promotion of Knowledge & Language Learning at Universiti Malaysia Sabah, Malaysia. She holds a B.A. in English Language Studies (Hons.), and an M.A. in English Language Studies & Linguistics both from the National University of Malaysia Her research interest is in semantics, sociolinguistics, and discourse. Currently she is the Coordinator for Foreign Languages Program at Universiti Malaysia Sabah.

Jeannet Stephen is a Lecturer with the Centre for the Promotion of Knowledge & Language Learning at Universiti Malaysia Sabah, Malaysia. She holds a B. Ed. TESL (Hons.) from the National University of Malaysia, and an M.A. in Applied Linguistics & Bilingualism from the University of Newcastle Upon Tyne, UK. Her research interest is in language maintenance, second language acquisition, and sociolinguistics.

Christopher Stroud is Professor of Bilingual Research at Stockholm University, although currently on long term leave at the National University of Singapore, where he teaches courses in Ethnography of Communication, Language planning and policy, and Social Thought in Language. Research fields of interest span literacy, politics of language, multilingualism and education, code switching, and language maintenance and language shift. He is currently in the process of completing a volume on development and language.

Lindsay Whaley is an Associate Professor of Linguistics & Classics at Dartmouth College in Hanover, New Hampshire, where he also chairs the Program in Linguistics & Cognitive Science. He has been doing field work on several languages of northern China since 1997 and is currently working on a reference grammar of Oroqen. He is the author of *Introduction to Typology* (1997), *Endangered Languages* (1998, co-edited with Lenore Grenoble) , and is currently completing a book on language revitalization with Lenore Grenoble to be published by Cambridge University Press.

Sue Wright is a Senior Lecturer at Aston University, Birmingham, UK. From 1994-2000, she was editor of Current Issues in Language and Society, a journal dedicated to examining the social and political aspect of language issues. She has published widely in this area, including *Community and Communication: The role of Language in Nation Building and European Integration* (Multilingual Matters, 2000) and *Language Policy and Language Planning: From Nationalism to Globalisation* (Palgrave, 2003).

Index